Taking Reform Seriously

Perspectives on
Public Interest Liberalism

Taking Reform Seriously

Perspectives on
Public Interest Liberalism

Michael W. McCann

Cornell University Press

ITHACA AND LONDON

First published 1986 by Cornell Univesity Press.

International Standard Book Number 0-8014-1952-2
Library of Congress Catalog Card Number 86-47647
Printed in the United States of America
Librarians: Library of Congress cataloging information
appears on the last page of the book.

The paper in this book is acid-free and meets the guidelines for
performance and durability of the Committee on Production
Guidelines for Book Longevity of the Council on Library Resources.

For my mother and
in memory of my father

Contents

Preface

The themes of this book developed from reflections about the disintegration of liberal progressive political influence and organization which began during the 1970s in America. The breakdown of the New Deal consensus supporting continued expansion of the social welfare state, the fragmentation and exhaustion of both Old and New Left, and the triumph of Republican conservatism all created cause for sober speculation about the failures and future of progressive politics in America. It seemed to me at the start, and still does now, that much scholarly analysis was being directed toward the increasing popular success of conservatives and the decline of the Democratic party, but that much less work addressed the fate of the many independent liberal and progressive groups that have continued to struggle in national politics since the 1960s. Liberal public interest advocates were one such category of relevant actors. Of special interest to me have been the ways in which they have represented a curious and complex fusion of many of the most important trends and influences at work in modern American liberal politics. Indeed, much of my analysis focuses on the tenuous synthesis of inherited Progressive and New Deal era liberal reform values and the more recent New Left criticism of those traditions from which public interest liberals have crafted their general political project. I attempt to present this story in a spirit respectful of the reformers' noble aims and achievements but also frank about their limitations and deficiencies. As such, my goal is to say something about the great difficulties of initiating progressive change within the dominant structures of the American empire as it sputters toward the twenty-first century.

9

Preface

I could not have attempted a project so broad in its designs and long in its development without the help of many people. Foremost among these were two primary dissertation advisers at the University of California, Berkeley: Michael Rogin and Robert Kagan. They contributed two very different and invaluable intellectual perspectives to critical commentary on my work, yet they were united in their unceasing support and warm encouragement at every point; their examples of high scholarship, intellectual commitment, and friendship demonstrated for me what great teaching is all about. In addition, I am grateful to three other teachers: Hanna Pitkin, who provided enormous inspiration and guidance in the art of political theorizing; William Muir, who offered copious encouragement when it counted; and David Vogel, who shared his vast knowledge and insights about public interest politics with me in several discussions related to my work.

My list of debts includes many others. First, a host of former graduate school colleagues contributed indirectly but most significantly through both intellectual exchange and friendship to the formative stages of the project. In particular, I acknowledge the influence of Cyrus E. Zirakzadeh, Donald Downs, George Shulman, Michael MacDonald, Patricia Boling, and everyone in the Berkeley chapter of Caucus for a New Political Science. The commentary of several colleagues at the University of Washington during the later stages of the manuscript development likewise was valuable in helping me to render my arguments more coherent to myself first, and then to others. Stuart Scheingold, Daniel Lev, Lance Bennett, and Ruth Horowitz scrutinized and commented on the entire manuscript; John Keeler, Nancy Hartsock, Christine Di Stefano, Margaret Levi, and Paul Peretz provided useful criticism and advice on specific parts. A number of scholars less personally familiar to me also deserve special thanks. Andrew McFarland graciously granted me access to early drafts of his book on Common Cause. Aaron Wildavsky, Theodore Lowi, and several anonymous others likewise provided formal reviews of great use to me in crafting the final work.

Special gratitude is extended to the dozens of public interest activists in Washington, D.C., who shared with me personal experiences and organizational information during the summer of 1980. I hope that they and their colleagues accept the critical commentary advanced by this work in the spirit of serious respect and support for their efforts that I intend. Nelson Polsby also deserves thanks for arranging a grant from the Center for National Policy Studies at the

Institute for Governmental Studies at the University of California, Berkeley, which made much of this field research possible.

Many people contributed to the technical preparation of the manuscript. Berkeley Parks and Cheryl Mehaffey patiently and ably typed various sections of the final work. I owe abundant gratitude to all of those at Cornell University Press who helped to make the publication process a relatively short and painless experience. Walter H. Lippincott, Jr., in particular deserves thanks for his prompt and enthusiastic response to the submitted manuscript. Marilyn M. Sale did an admirable job of coordinating the various stages of transforming the work into a book. Most important, she provided me with a superb editor: John Thomas contributed countless improvements in the style, format, and, above all, accuracy of the manuscript; all authors should be so lucky to have an editor like him.

Finally, Donna Sarvis McCann has provided a source of inspiration and support for this project from beginning to end. She lovingly endured my fits of frustration, helped me to clarify my thinking, and took on extra duties in our shared lives so that I might have more time to write. But I thank her above all for always helping me to keep in focus those things that matter most both within and, more important, beyond the concerns of this manuscript.

Michael W. McCann

Seattle, Washington

Acronyms

ACE	Army Corps of Engineers
ACLU	American Civil Liberties Union
AEC	Atomic Energy Commission
CAB	Civil Aeronautics Board
CARG	Corporate Accountability Research Group
CED	Campaign for Economic Democracy
CEQ	Council on Environmental Quality
CETA	Comprehensive Employment Training Act
CFA	Consumer Federation of America
CLASP	Center for Law and Social Policy
COIN	Consumers Organized against Inflation in the Necessities
CORE	Congress of Racial Equality
CPSC	Consumer Product Safety Commission
CU	Consumers Union
DOE	Department of Energy
DOI	Department of Interior
DOT	Department of Transportation
DSOC	Democratic Socialist Organizing Committee
EA	Environmental Action
EDF	Environmental Defense Fund
EFFE	Environmentalists for Full Employment
EIS	Environmental Impact Statement
EPA	Environmental Protection Agency
EPEA	Exploratory Project for Economic Alternatives
ERISA	Employees Retirement Income Security Act
FAA	Federal Aviation Administration
FCC	Federal Communications Commission
FDA	Food and Drug Administration
FECA	Federal Election Campaign Act
FOE	Friends of the Earth
FOIA	Freedom of Information Act
FTC	Federal Trade Commission

13

HEW	Health, Education, and Welfare (Department of)
HRG	Health Research Group
ICC	Interstate Commerce Commission
INSPIRE	Institute for Public Interest Representation
IPS	Institute for Policy Studies
IRS	Internal Revenue Service
LCV	League of Conservation Voters
LWV	League of Women Voters
MAP	Media Access Project
NAACP	National Association for the Advancement of Colored People
NAM	National Association of Manufacturers
NEPA	National Environmental Policy Act
NHTSA	National Highway Traffic Safety Administration
NIRA	National Industrial Recovery Act
NORC	National Opinion Research Center
NOW	National Organization for Women
NRC	Nuclear Regulatory Commission
NRDC	Natural Resources Defense Council
NWF	National Wildlife Federation
NWRO	National Welfare Rights Organization
OCAW	Oil, Chemical and Atomic Workers Union
OMB	Office of Management and Budget
OSHA	Occupational Safety and Health Administration
PAC	Political Action Committee
PCR	Project on Corporate Responsibility
PIRG	Public Interest Research Group
RARG	Regulatory Analysis Review Group
RUCAG	Residential Utility Consumer Action Group
SCRAP	Students Challenging Regulatory Agency Proceedings
SDS	Students for a Democratic Society
SEC	Securities and Exchange Commission
UAW	United Auto Workers
USDA	United States Department of Agriculture
VISTA	Volunteers in Service to America
ZPG	Zero Population Growth

Introduction

Contrary to much popular opinion, the flames of liberal political protest did not burn out in the 1960s. Nor did the fiery passions of dissent consume all of the young, leaving behind only the ashes of cynicism, apathy, and opportunism. Indeed, during the 1970s manifold new groups of liberal middle-class activists made their voices heard on the stage of American politics. At the national level alone, over one hundred citizen organizations representing more than six million dues-paying members formed to press for change in the political process. Nearly an equal number of legal advocacy firms developed to supplement these citizen groups through both independent and coalitional action in various arenas of public life. Taking their cues from older liberal reform movements and the political experiences of the previous decade, the new advocates held out the promise of providing a novel program for the revitalization of American liberal democratic politics. The agents of this reform impulse labeled themselves "public interest activists."

By most standards, the impact of these new groups has been impressive. Their legislative achievements surpassed those of the Progressive Era in quantity and significance. Hundreds of court victories gave life to these and already existing laws that might have been ignored otherwise by governors and governed alike. With the victory of President Carter in 1976, the reformers' achievements seemed to be secure and their future promising. Carter not only pledged policy decisions favorable to the demands of the new groups; he also appointed over eighty former public interest activists to positions in his administration. It thus is no wonder that the movement's most prominent spokesperson, Ralph Nader, once proclaimed

15

enthusiastically that he expected to achieve "nothing less than a qualitative reform of the industrial revolution."[1]

The reformers' ambitious crusade fell on hard times during the latter part of the decade, however. Legislative victories dwindled to a few, congressional assaults upon administrative allies increased, and once sympathetic federal judges closed the door of access to movement lawyers. On top of these setbacks, the hopes placed in the Carter administration proved largely unfounded. Most of the public interest appointees were not given positions of power, while the counselors who did wield influence in the Oval Office reneged on campaign promises. As time wore on, executive initiatives ranging from regulatory reform to energy policy increasingly snubbed the urgings of liberal activists whom the president had previously courted. "In short," summarized a 1979 ACLU report, "the Carter administration has been a disappointment when measured against the expectations it aroused."[2] Finally, with the election of Ronald Reagan and other conservative Republicans in 1980, stalemate gave way to retrenchment among the beleaguered reform troops as the new decade dawned.

Such wounds have been significant, to be sure. But an autopsy of public interest reformers certainly would be premature. Although the ascendant public agenda has recently shifted to the right, commitments to staple public interest concerns about the quality of life have not been abolished. "Even the worst that could happen is not as bad as the worst that could have happened 10 years ago," acknowledges Sierra Club's Brock Evans. Moreover, bolstered by renewed conviction and expanding membership in reaction to Reagan, the groups themselves have shown considerable staying power in the 1980s. As Public Citizen litigation expert Alan Morrison has put it, "we are established. We have been here, we are here, and we are likely to continue."[3]

The purpose of this work is to analyze the promises and limits of this enduring public interest liberalism within the context of contemporary American politics. Specifically, my focus is on the essential understandings and aspirations—the elements of what I call their "political vision"—that have animated these new advocates. The book includes discussion of their achievements in the courts, legislatures, regulatory agencies, and corporate boardrooms, but the center of attention is the reformers' ideas about what they are trying to do in the larger scheme of things. The remainder of this introduction outlines the character and substance of this analysis.

Introduction

The Subject Defined

The first task is to define in greater detail the scope of my subject. In short, who is to be included within the category of public interest activist? Most generally, I am in agreement with the definition offered by political scientist Jeffrey Berry. In his words, "a public interest group is one that seeks a collective good, the achievement of which does not selectively and materially benefit the membership of activists of the organization."[4] Of course, all public actions toward nonexclusive collective goods can be understood to initiate complex ripples of change that affect individuals in quite diverse, inconsistent, and unequal ways. For example, the creation of tougher air pollution standards benefits everyone generally, but it surely affects asthmatics, joggers, and corporate shareholders differently. However, the assumption is that the benefits of collective goods are not intended to substantially favor those who belong to the groups advocating their creation. As one scholar puts it, "those who do not purchase or pay for any of the public or collective good cannot be excluded or kept from sharing in the consumption of that good."[5]

The critical point at stake here is that the goals of public interest groups are fundamentally unlike the self-interested, exclusive, and privately enjoyed benefits sought by most economic interest groups (business, farm, labor groups) and extolled in prevailing models of liberal pluralist politics. Indeed, most public interest actions have been designed to win recognition for those shared material and social needs often ignored in the narrow calculations of the political and economic elite establishment. At the same time, however, this categorization of public interest groups according to the collective goods they seek also excludes many other progressive reform organizations—for racial and ethnic minorities, women, homosexuals, prisoners, children, the elderly, the handicapped, and the poor. This is a difficult distinction to sustain because most of the reformers with whom I am concerned actively support the rights of these groups and share with many of them hopes of forging an eventual political coalition for progressive change. Nevertheless, such special interest groups as NAACP, NOW, and NWRO must be excluded formally from my analysis for the same reasons as are corporate- and labor-sponsored lobbies. My subject thus includes only groups promoting what the Council for Public Interest Law calls "general-population" and "cause-defined" issues exclusive of minority-specific political interests.[6]

In particular, middle-class public interest liberals have emphasized four general categories of collective goods: (1) *environmental protection* as advocated by groups such as Environmental Defense Fund, Friends of the Earth, Sierra Club, Environmental Action, and Natural Resources Defense Council;[7] (2) *workplace health and safety* concerns such as those advanced by the Health Research Group, Health Policy Advisory Center, and Environmental Policy Center; (3) *consumer interests* in health, safety, quality, and fair exchange of goods such as those promoted by Ralph Nader's Public Citizen, Center for Auto Safety, Consumers Union, and Consumer Federation of America; and (4) *democratic reform of government processes* such as that initiated by Common Cause, the League of Women Voters, Nader's Congress Watch, and the American Civil Liberties Union. Given the particular understanding of the modern corporate state entertained by the new activists, the last category also includes various other influential groups concerned with direct reform of tax policy (Tax Reform Research Group), mass media (Media Access Project), and the "private government" of big business (Project on Corporate Responsibility). Finally, a variety of research centers (Center for the Study of Responsive Law), multiissue public interest law firms (Center for Law and Social Policy), and coordinating organizations (Alliance for Justice) are extended recognition as well.

The specific advocates with which this study is concerned can be distinguished by several other salient characteristics as well. First, I am interested only in those activists who fit easily the contemporary definition of political "liberal." This categorization can be misleading, of course. While one study finds that over 80 percent of public interest activists identify themselves as liberals, their ambitions for change vary from relatively moderate (Common Cause) to quite radical (Environmentalists for Full Employment), and group memberships often include substantial numbers of partisan Republicans.[8] Nevertheless, the label of "liberal" is still useful; it connotes the progressive and reformist character of the movement; it identifies the activists as pro-worker and anticorporate yet still accepts capitalistic economic foundations; and, above all, it distinguishes the movement from both corporate and social reform forces on the Right and socialist advocates on the Left in modern America.[9]

Another important limitation to the subject of this book is the association of collective and public goods with primarily national issues and concerns. While many policy actions of the activists are specific to one geographic area or corporate enterprise, the emphasis here is on group endeavors that have national implications and involve the advocates directly in the workings of the federal regulatory state. Thus the groups considered are restricted to those with nationally based organizations, most of which have at least one of their offices in Washington, D.C. This criterion both confirms our prevailing tendency today to equate "public" with "national" and permits generalizations that can be more easily validated than those that also include the myriad independent local citizen groups throughout the nation.[10]

A final defining characteristic of the groups discussed in the work is their relative economic independence from the state. In traditional terms, we can say that while the objectives of the activists are public in nature, the sources and resources that promote these goods are primarily private, nonpartisan, and voluntaristic as well as nonprofit. It is true that many of the groups have received government aid in the forms of research grants, attorneys' fees, reduced costs of access, tax exemptions, and other indirect subsidies. Such matters of changing reform-group financial dependency on the state provide an important topic of inquiry in the following pages. But, overall, the focus of this book is primarily on those organizations that receive less than 25 percent of their total funds from government sources.[11]

A Common Cause

The new activism initiated by these groups has not gone unnoticed by academic social scientists. Several books and scores of articles in law reviews and social science journals have emerged to analyze various dimensions of public interest advocacy. Most of these studies thus far have proceeded along two different but related paths. One approach, undertaken primarily by political scientists, attempts to generalize about the organizational incentives and structures that characterize public interest activism.[12] The analysis is largely behavioral; its models are the pluralist orientations to interest-group action which dominate the academic discipline. The other prevailing form of study is more technical, specific, and case oriented. Its authors are generally public policy analysts concerned with evaluation of particular public interest policies and programs or lawyers who focus on the legal significance of discrete legal decisions and rights claims initiated by the advocates. The important contributions of such studies derive from the detailed analyses they provide concerning the diverse contexts, strategies, and achievements of public interest reform action.[13]

While drawing upon the valuable insights of these two approaches, the basic perspective of this book is different.[14] Most important, the emphasis here is on treating the broad range of diverse public interest groups and activists collectively as the self-proclaimed vanguard of a larger social reform movement.[15] In this view, public interest groups constitute the formal organizations of leadership, resource mobilization, and interest articulation for a broad constituency within the nation.[16] Admittedly, the exact boundaries of this movement are quite difficult to demarcate. No authoritative founder arose to initiate the reformers into a united quest; no formal social compact ever developed to bind them in mutual action toward commonly formulated goals. The apparent evolution of their programs, organizations, and tactics was multifarious and uneven rather than uniform and linear. Nevertheless, there are good reasons to support the argument that the new reformers can be treated as the core of a coherent, self-conscious movement. The simplest of these reasons is that public interest activists themselves express a group consciousness, one that has deepened since the early 1970s. As the press, academy, and general public have expressed increasing recognition of a collective "them," so have the reformers come to speak of a "we" that extends beyond individual groups.[17] Indeed, although eliciting somewhat varied responses when pressed for definition, most environmental, consumer, and other advocates mentioned in previous pages have accepted openly, and even proudly, the label of "public interest" activists. Common Cause founder John Gardner writes that "we're part of a public interest movement that arose in the late 1960s.... Public interest law, Ralph Nader, the environmentalist movement, these are the parts of it."[18] A Consumers Union research article in *The Big Business Reader* likewise confirms that "the movement was a loose coalition of organizations, interested in such things as consumer affairs, environmental affairs, and political reform."[19]

Another important indication of such collective group consciousness has been demonstrated by efforts of reform spokespersons to publish to, for, and about their colleagues. Simon Lazarus's *The Genteel Populists* and various works by Ralph Nader, Mark Green, David Cohen, John Gardner, Charles Halpern, and others represent such endeavors. Moreover, the emergence of diverse clearinghouse organizations such as the Council for Public Interest Law and coalitional projects such as Earth Day and Big Business Day have signaled a similar propensity to stand collectively even when divided on some separate issues. What is most significant, however, is that a common framework of ideas and values has developed to unite public interest activists in what participant and observer Simon Lazarus calls "a

20

crusade for a vision of the whole society." It is true that their activities remain mostly independent and uncoordinated. Different explorers have investigated different territories and proposed different routes of travel. Yet my hypothesis is that the map by which they travel is fundamentally the same. In short, it is their *cause* which is most common to them.

This should not be surprising, for many scholars have agreed that "it is the more ideological... motivations of individuals that make it possible for most public interest groups to exist."[20] My only departure from this assessment is a preference for employing the concept of "political vision" rather than "ideology." The reason for this derives from the common pejorative use of "ideology" to imply conceptual dogmatism, irrationalism, or naivete.[21] By contrast, the term "political vision" is more respectful of the reformers' stated intentions. First, its emphasis on the "political" aspects of the new reform project is important. The activists self-consciously contrast themselves with both earlier liberal reformers and most other contemporary participants in government by their own uniquely democratic political approach to effecting social change. They emphasize that the interests they promote are inherently public and collective in nature. Likewise, the very practices, structures, and forms of public life themselves constitute an important object of their reform aspirations. In short, their vision professes to take very seriously democratic politics as both an end and a means of liberal reform. The particular concept of "vision" likewise is uniquely appropriate. As Sheldon Wolin has argued, the term "vision" evokes two different but complementary senses.[22] On one hand, the word implies "seeing," "perceiving," or "observing." The emphasis here is on the interpretation and rendering of events. A political vision in this sense refers to the activists' understandings and critical interpretations of existing political facts—policies, power relations, and so forth—by which they define existing maladies and opportunities for redress. On the other hand, "vision" also implies the propensity toward imagination, idealism, and aspiration. The focus of this sense is on the goals, values, and images that inspire action for change toward a better world. It implies conceptual understanding of both strategies to achieve particular ends and the nature of those ends themselves.

The idea of "political vision" thus resembles what often is called the "belief system" of the public actors specified here. It constitutes a bond among the groups to the degree that it provides a collective lens through which the world of the imaginable is refracted into common meanings and commitments guiding the choices made by its constituents. Such a conception should not be understood as applying merely to what political activists say rather than to what they do, to their rationalizations rather than to their reasons. My analysis instead begins from the premise that what the reformers say is a dynamic, animating element of their reality; what they say is both cause and constituent of what they are doing. This approach follows the logic urged by scholar Charles W. Anderson. Politics is "more than a state action or activity," he argues. "It is a contrivance reflecting human purposiveness."

> Seen in this light, a policy cannot be satisfactorily "explained" simply as a product of certain socioeconomic conditions, or a given configuration of political pressures, or as the outcome of a particular process, all of which are dominant motifs in contemporary policy study. It is also necessary to know what people *thought* of prevailing socioeconomic conditions, what claims and grievances interested parties brought forward, and how they debated and assessed these problems.... To study the logic of public policy making one must look at the language of political discourse—the way public actions are argued, explained, and justified. Doing this entails the significant assumption that what policymakers think and say makes a difference.[23]

At the same time, the principles and ideas at stake here should be understood to transcend the specific terms of individual policy positions. My argument is not intended to obscure the fact that the particular public interest-initiated programs, laws, and actions have been diverse, inconsistent, and often conflicting in character. The guiding assumption is that the political vision from which they spring provides only a general set of cues rather than a dogma of intractable mandates. It limits definition of the desirable without determining which particular course of action is best. Yet the distinction between fundamental ideas and discrete positions on issues should not be overemphasized. Some issues, such as regulatory reform, environmental health, and opposition to nuclear energy, have attained considerable symbolic significance among most liberal activists and illuminate well the general substance of their basic value orientation.

A Note on Sources

The claim that liberal public interest group activists share a common vision is complicated somewhat by the difficulty of locating its expression. No great thinker has emerged as spokesperson for the movement. No classic text rests upon the shelves of the activists for quick reference and sure inspiration. In short, my project poses the paradox of addressing a philosophy without a philosopher. Consequently, the primary sources from which I draw patterns of public interest thought are many and diverse. The most important of these include articles, speeches, and books by leaders of the groups; conference proceedings and project reports such as *Balancing the Scales of Justice* by the Council for Public Interest Law; official pamphlets and annual reports of the individual groups; and formal interviews and statements published in the journalistic or academic press. Direct contact and personal interviews with dozens of public activists during the past several years has shaped and confirmed my understanding as well.[24] However, I have chosen to quote mostly from materials intended by the groups for a general audience to emphasize the formal, public character of their claims.

I attempt here to be representative of the diversity of voices within the movement. But, at the same time, I must acknowledge that the distribution of authors is quite unequal; some sources are utilized far more extensively than others. The justification for this, quite simply, is in the unique merits that the favored possess. Publications by the Council for Public Interest Law and collections of essays such as *The Big Business Reader* and *The Environmental Handbook* offer a distinctly general, reflective, and sophisticated level of discourse about public interest commitments which transcends the distinctions among individual groups in a way most useful to my own approach. The abundant use of statements by Ralph Nader and Mark Green of Public Citizen, by John Gardner and David Cohen of Common Cause, by environmentalists Joseph Sax, David Brower, and Hazel Henderson, and by establishment allies Simon Lazarus and Michael Pertschuk are defensible on similar grounds. These activists constitute something like the founders of the movement. Also, they tend to speak the most often, the loudest, and the clearest; their words have been most influential among and beyond the movement participants. Indeed, the role of "entrepreneurs" like Nader and Gardner in providing examples of leadership, the mirrors in which other actors dress themselves, cannot be overemphasized in addressing the movement as a whole.

Introduction

The Argument Summarized

Having cleared most of the underbrush of conceptual definition, we can now stake out the specific design and argument of the analysis to follow. The study is divided into two general parts. Part One is devoted to outlining a comprehensive interpretation of the new political reform vision. In my emphasis on the liberal activists' own understanding of their actions as well as on their specific historical context, the discussion here closely resembles what Clifford Geertz has called "thick description."[25] This interpretive analysis begins in Chapter 1 with a descriptive overview of the reformers' critique of contemporary American politics and their campaign for reform which developed in response during the 1970s. Specifically, I argue that the reform advocates' general "public-rights" strategy has aimed to combat widespread corporate abuse of power by opening up new channels of access to direct citizen action within and through the modern regulatory state.

In Chapter 2, I examine in some detail the philosophical foundations and historical significance of this new politics. I acknowledge that these new activists have much in common with earlier middle-class liberal reformers in America such as the Populists, Progressives, and New Deal radicals. To this reform tradition the new activists owe much of their anticorporate skepticism, "populistic" rhetoric, and faith in government as an agent of increased social welfare and justice. Yet I argue further that the experiences of the 1960s have rendered public interest liberalism a novel response to distinctly contemporary historical conditions. For one thing, a notable fidelity to countercultural quality-of-life social values and ecological ethics has led the middle-class activists to question the logic of commitments to maximizing economic growth that were so important to earlier generations of American liberals. Second, the New Left commitments to participatory democracy and direct action for restoring power to the people greatly influenced the recent reform leaders' conceptions of politics. When translated into legal advocacy for new public rights, the result has been a campaign for the transformation of the regulatory state into a labyrinth of increasingly judicialized forums that are neither strictly pluralist nor corporatist in form. These two orientations are not entirely unprecedented within the American tradition; but I contend that this fusion of values into a single vision of reform action constitutes a uniquely modern challenge to conventional liberal public priorities.

In Part Two of this book I subject the new political reform vision to critical analysis. This scrutiny is critical in several senses. For one, I entered into this task with a conviction that the systemic deficiencies to which public interest advocates have responded are critical in their significance. I must admit some sympathy with many of their professed goals and admiration for their noble achievements in the formidable task of promoting liberal democracy and social justice. At the same time, however, the analysis is also critical in that significant problems are revealed concerning the reformers' specific interpretation of existing political affairs and proposals for change. I attempt to illuminate not only the sources of the apparent recent decline in the reformers' influence, but more fundamentally the limits and paradoxes of the entire vision that has guided their proclaimed successes as well. In other words, the focus is on tensions *within* the reformers' conceptual and normative orientation rather than merely on the inevitable distance *between* their aspirations and achievements.

These critical perspectives are developed in three chapters. While independent in substantive focus, all three are united by the theme of my chosen title, *Taking Reform Seriously*. Simply put, it is demonstrated that the new reformers have taken seriously some important issues mostly ignored by earlier liberals, but that they still remain uncommitted about some of the most fundamental challenges of democratic politics within modern society. Specifically, in Chapter 3, I argue that the activists' novel social demand for limits to growth has provided an important social criticism of corporate capitalism while remaining largely silent about serious domestic economic problems of primary concern to most American citizens. In Chapter 4, I contend that the reformers' animus against hierarchical bureaucratic institutions likewise has been laudable, but that their own professional elite-dominated organization and liberal voluntaristic idealism have inevitably undercut the movement's contributions to creating more democratic forms of action within modern society. Finally, in Chapter 5, I demonstrate that the activists' interest-group tactics for creating "civic balance" have expanded formal institutional representation within government without developing either sufficient organizational cohesion or moral authority to significantly challenge the substantive priorities of the modern corporate state. Shunning programmatic concern for such basic exigencies of economic policy and majoritarian political organization, therefore, the public interest reform agenda has remained a mostly peripheral force in American public life.

A second set of themes developed in these chapters is suggested by my title's implicit parallel to Ronald Dworkin's classic study, *Taking*

Rights Seriously.[26] In short, I argue throughout that the activists' characteristic legal-rights approach to expanding democracy has significantly narrowed their conception of political action itself. Their innovative legalistic strategy has both reflected and encouraged their lack of concern for addressing structural economic maladies (Chapter 3), for developing organizational linkage with citizens at the grass-roots level (Chapter 4), and for building new partisan bonds with other organized participants in national politics (Chapter 5). All in all, the reformers' emphasis on achieving legal change within the state seems to have eclipsed commitments necessary to effect fundamental social change in a variety of ways.[27]

The structure of this book is cast in the mold of traditional political analysis and draws upon a wide range of sources, including classical political theory, contemporary social science models, and quantitative empirical data. My project aims not to provide a case study illustrating the validity of any particular theory, but to utilize a variety of theoretical approaches to illuminate the complex character of a particular political movement. Moreover, while critical in substance and suggestive about alternative political reform options, the primary goal of the analysis is neither to condemn the past of public interest liberalism nor to chart a sure course to a better future. Indeed, my discussion stresses the powerful constraints of inherited American ideology, social structure, and state organization which continue to discourage alternative strategies of action by the reformers. All in all, my emphasis is on illuminating the complex character and historical significance of the movement's professed commitment to initiating a "revolution... in our values, outlook, and economic organization."[28] If my efforts provide only some greater clarity in understanding the dilemmas confronting attempts to promote progressive change in contemporary America, then my task has not been undertaken in vain.

PART ONE

Public Interest Liberalism:

Aspirations and Achievements

The Origins of the Movement

Public interest liberalism was conceived in America amid the passionate promises and protests of the 1960s. Against a background of escalating economic prosperity, rising education levels, a liberal social consensus, and the explosion of popular mass media technology, the most important movement leaders began their purposive quests for public attention. In that decade, eventual movement patriarch Ralph Nader launched his much-publicized assault upon big business by attacking General Motors in *Unsafe at Any Speed*. Common Cause founder John Gardner served in the same years as secretary of health, education, and welfare and chairman of the Urban Coalition. The first Consumer Assembly was convened in 1966 to initiate a national coalition of citizen groups which would soon become the Consumer Federation of America. The League of Women Voters proclaimed a new profound political commitment to working for greater racial and economic equality. Finally, and perhaps most important, the major catalysts to the environmental movement emerged during the decade as well. Barry Commoner was well into his fight against nuclear arms and for an ecological science. The publication of Rachel Carson's *Silent Spring* and Paul Ehrlich's *The Population Bomb* shook the public conscience about the environmental dangers of human carelessness. And successful efforts by the Sierra Club and others to protect California redwoods, the Washington Cascades, and the Grand Canyon all contributed further to the growing sense that effective political action to save our natural environment was possible.

However, the evolving convictions that these disparate endeavors could be fused into a larger collective movement for wholesale social reform also depended on other more disruptive events during the decade. In general, at least three precedents of political action and

29

aspiration during the 1960s shaped the perceptions of the liberal reformers: the civil rights movement, the welfare rights movement, and the antiwar movement. The impact of these events seems to confirm political scientist David Truman's "disturbance theory" concerning the origins of collective political action. Truman argues that organized action on the part of some discontented groups can stimulate a wave of competitive mobilization among other groups similarly frustrated by existing social relations.[1] But at least equally important, these earlier forms of activism also expressed a unique political style and content that proved to be influential for the subsequent public interest movement as well. Several themes deserve mention in this regard.

First was the common critical awareness of pervasive moral and institutional failure in American public life targeted by these different movements. The civil rights movement politicized the anger of blacks about the crippling injustices of racism. The welfare rights movement nurtured discontent about the structural sources of economic poverty and unemployment. The antiwar movement protested dramatically about the moral poverty and corruption of the military-industrial complex. Together, such allegations of social injustice became mutually reinforcing, even contagious, in undermining public faith in American public institutions. Tom Hayden's famous words in the "Port Huron Statement" expressed the feeling of a growing number of young and dispossessed in the land: "The American political system is not the democratic model of which its glorifiers speak," he said. "It actually frustrates democracy by confusing the individual citizen, paralyzing policy discussion, and consolidating the irresponsible power of military and business interests."[2] While many citizens were shocked by both the ends and means of the New Left, pollsters during the decade discerned a parallel rise in political cynicism, alienation, and distrust in government throughout the general public as well.[3]

Furthermore, each of these major movements identified big-business corporations specifically as the primary agents of corruption in modern society. From the time of the Greensboro boycotts against the racial segregationist policies of Woolworth's in 1960, the hiring and foreign investment policies of business giants such as General Motors, Chase Manhattan Bank, Eastman Kodak, and Xerox increasingly were chosen as prime targets of civil rights protests. Congress of Racial Equality chairman Robert Curtis evoked the growing hostility to corporate enterprises by vowing that "we have to fight with the same weapons as the man with his foot on our neck."[4] Other large corporations such as Dow Chemical and Honeywell were blamed for murderous American imperialism in Southeast Asia as well as for promoting economic inequality at home. Antiwar activist Todd Gitlin thus proclaimed typically that "the dual engines of industrialization and war have created a tightly planned corporate complex that dominates the economy."[5]

The major forms of action formulated in response to these perceived evils also shared two different components of organizational strategy. On one hand, the professed preference for direct action was exhibited in frequent mass demonstrations, protests, rallies, and other dramatic events of collective expression. Sit-ins, shop-ins, phone-ins, boycotts, and marches—most peaceful, but some violent—to stimulate public support had come to define a basic tactic of black activists ever since 1955, when Rosa Parks was denied a bus seat in Montgomery. Both the welfare rights movement and student antiwar movement likewise relied heavily on such tactics of public display, media manipulation, and dramatic confrontations as essential resources of power.[6] Indeed, drawing upon Saul Alinsky's civil rights organization leadership, the New Left came to herald the ideals of participatory democracy as both the end and means of the new radical politics: "Politics has the function of bringing people out of isolation and into the community," argued Staughton Lynd, "thus being a necessary though not sufficient means of finding meaning in personal life."[7]

On the other hand, from the outset each developing social movement enlisted the aid of professional lawyers to promote its various causes through legal action. As Robert Rabin has suggested, each movement represented a consecutive wave of law reform leading to important new legislative statutes and court actions to extend and enforce their effectiveness.[8] The Civil Rights Act, the Voting Rights Act, and diverse Great Society welfare legislation were all products of such contributions. Likewise, judicial decisions for school desegregation, criminal and welfare due process, and protection of free speech for antiwar protesters provided crucial victories in the different struggles. So significant was such legal action to the new political movements that many specialized legal groups within government (VISTA, Legal Services Corporation) and society (ACLU, NAACP, NWRO) arose to provide reliable support for reform battles against the establishment. The new role of lawyers for each cause, summarized radical legal activist Michael Tigar, was "a combination of offense and defense to protect the Movement against attack and to use the rules of the courtroom game to keep its leaders out of jail and to prevail in particular confrontations which circumstances dictate must take place in the courtroom."[9]

It is clear that the attitudes and aspirations generated by these collective movements branded deeply the perspectives of most later middle-class public interest activists, shaping their understandings about the distance between American political practices and our elevated public pieties. This was a period that shook the consciences and challenged the roles of the elder statesmen in the movement such as Ralph Nader, John Gardner, Charles Halpern, and David Brower. Participation in the civil-rights campaign and student protests provided a younger generation the schools of political experience which prepared them for later reform efforts. For the most recent recruits into the reform troops, public interest activism provided a bond to a past of progressive commitments among the Armies of the Night. Collectively, the events of the 1960s constituted an important equivalent to a founding story for the movement which has united its diverse aspirations through the bonds of shared memories.[10]

Evidence of these attitudes is widespread. A 1976 Ford Foundation monograph confirmed the historical connection with an opening quote by Thurgood Marshall proclaiming that "today's public interest lawyers have built upon the earlier successes of civil rights, civil liberties, and legal aid lawyers, but have moved into new areas."[11] Phillip Moore, an early leader in Campaign GM, likewise echoed that the effort at "corporate reform today is a natural and appropriate extension of social and political movements of the sixties."[12] Moreover, Ralph Nader learned to generate support on campuses by linking his reform goals to previous student activism with rhetorical chants: "Who began the sit-in movement in civil rights? . . . Who dramatized for the nation the facts and issues regarding the revelation of environmental contamination in the cities? . . . Who helped mobilize popular opposition to Vietnam?" In another context, he had speculated that "we will see consumer demonstrations someday that will make civil rights demonstrations look small by comparison."[13] Sierra Club director Michael McCloskey initially attributed great significance to the events of the immediate past as well: "With the causes of the Sixties—civil rights, anti-poverty, and peace—activism became a less lonely vocation . . . Now, as the Seventies begin . . . a revolution truly is needed—in our values, outlook and economic organization."[14] Finally, John Gardner's founding treatise, *In Common Cause*, also described how his proposed group was to represent an update of the tactics for extending power to the people formulated by others earlier. Building upon the "feeling for citizen action [which] reappeared with extraordinary vigor... in the 1960s," he wrote, "what we are seeing are the beginnings of a powerful movement to call the great institutions of our society into account."[15]

If public interest liberalism was conceived amid the passions of the 1960s, however, it was born into its own unique identity as a moderate reform alternative to the New Left in 1970. That year witnessed the formation of Common Cause, Friends of the Earth, Natural Resources Defense Council, Environmental Action Foundation, and Center for Law and Social Policy; the official Earth Day kickoff for environmentalism; the IRS declaration that most public interest groups enjoyed tax-exempt status; and the signing of the National Environmental Protection Act, the Clean Air Act, and the Occupational Safety and Health Act. In the same year some of the most important public interest tracts, studies, and statements of purpose were published, including Garrett De Bell's *The Environmental Handbook*, Sierra Club's *Ecotactics*, Gardner's *In Common Cause*, Joseph Sax's *Defending the Environment*, Mark Green and Bruce Wasserstein's *With Justice for Some*, James Turner's *The Chemical Feast*, John Esposito's *Vanishing Air*, Charles Reich's *The Greening of America*, and Robert Lefcourt's *Law against the People*. Consequently, in addition to common aspirations and experiences there were now available new resources of shared knowledge, organizational networks, and legal mandates to support liberal cause-oriented action.

Other factors contributed to deepen this newly developed common identity of the activists in subsequent years. First, the most significant events of the 1970s—the completion of eight years of conservative Republican presidency, the Watergate scandals, the energy crisis, the increased awareness of environmental dangers—sustained and extended the critical commitments to political change initiated in the earlier decade. Moreover, a close proximity in space reinforced the bonds of temporal awareness among the reform leaders. The fact that most of the new advocates located themselves in Washington, D.C. —and, more specifically, in the once low-rent areas around Dupont Circle—facilitated the opportunity for frequent interaction.

These opportunities were promoted further by the shared background and personality traits of the activists. Surveys in the mid-1970s found that about 76 percent of the activists were male, and 66 percent were below the age of 40. The percentages of blacks and other racial or ethnic minorities is unknown, but they have remained very few, perhaps less than 1 percent. Another important fact is that 88 percent of the reformers had college degrees, and at least 65 percent had done some graduate work. As a result of such common experience in higher education during the 1960s, many young activists were no doubt exposed to the popular and provocative political works of John Galbraith, Grant McConnell, Gabriel Kolko, and Herbert Marcuse. Moreover, of those with advanced study, over one-half (35 percent of all activists) were lawyers.[16] This striking number of lawyers in the movement further encouraged mutual intercourse built upon shared vernacular and specialized understanding of the world. From these estimates, it is not surprising that a stereotypical picture of the professional activist has often been drawn: white, middle class, predominantly male, and politically liberal, "he" is the mirror of his consitutency. In Common Cause leader David Cohen's words, the new reformer was "by education and occupation ... distinctive, concentrating in the professions, technical-management groups, and the knowledge industry."[17]

While professional in status, however, from the beginning the activists also have been unique among the ranks of elites. Unlike most Washington bureaucrats with whom they dealt, they approached their tasks with unusual dedication. One scholar notes in his study that their "commitment ranged from merely strong to fanatical."[18] Many lived the lives of political monks, having replaced horsehair shirts with ties and jackets, Biblical texts with legal briefs, and dark parish cloisters with crowded low-rent offices. The wealth, leisure, and job security guaranteed most persons of their status they soberly sacrificed for their causes. One indication of this is that, in 1973, about one-half of the reform advocates earned less that $15,000 a year, and three fourths less than $20,000.[19]

The reformers' status as ultra-liberals and political pariahs within the elite circles of the capital city surely intensified their common insularity from others even further. One aspect of this insularity was expressed visibly by the unconventional lifestyles that the activists projected to reflect their antiestablisment political propensities. Rock and jazz could be heard frequently amid the ringing phones in many of their crowded offices. Their preferences for crumpled corduroy and faded demin contrasted generally with the sartorial formality of corporate lawyers and government officials. The inflated rhetoric of campus radicalism which surfaced in even the most sophisticated of their discourse likewise betrayed the distance that separated most of them from the traditional politics of other Washington actors. Even more important, the gradual mobilization of the formidable establishment oppostion intent on defeat of the new radicals impressed deeper in them a sort of negative identity as outsiders. Indeed, an ironic consequence of the exaggerated fulminations voiced by conservatives concerning the "new class" ascendance has been to encourage over time a common affiliation among the reformers difficult to sustain on other grounds.[20]

Such a public identity, forging together 1960s idealism, elite professional training, and experience in modern government, suggests the appropriateness of attribtuing to the reformers the characteristics of what Weber called a "status group."[21] This term was developed to define collectivities of persons united by self-consciously created bonds of shared social roles recognizable to both insiders and outsiders alike. The emergence of such groups, in contrast to class identities, can be understood to reflect the modern character of mass society broken down into its functional parts, each having a quasi-autonomous culture distinguishable from the general patterns of life in the larger society. And, like all status groups, the most important bonds among public interest reformers developed from the distinctive principles, programs, and struggles to which they collectively have given birth. These aspirations and achievements constitute the subject of Part One of this study.

CHAPTER 1

The Campaign for Reform

As power begets power, large corporations are able to pursue their activities beyond the law, above the law, or against the law—a state of affairs clearly incompatible with democracy.

—Ralph Nader

Ideas of how to carry out a reconstruction of the system are not lacking, and more would be forthcoming if we had the kind of political movement necessary to enact them. Without such a movement, no idea is worth trying and all are just dreams.

—David Riley

A revolution is truly needed—in our values, outlook, and economic organization.

—Michael McCloskey

A Crisis in the Republic

However different their response, public interest liberals developed their critical perspective from much the same sense of anger, discontent, and anxiety which moved their precursors in the 1960s. Everywhere, their attitude of what Andrew McFarland calls "civic skepticism" has been apparent. A League of Women Voters solicitation letter typically expresses the sentiment: "I think you'll agree that the last few years have left a lot of Americans feeling disillusioned about their government," it begins.[1] Quite commonly, the problem at hand has even been defined by the reform advocates in the dramatic terms of an impending "crisis": "As the Seventies begin, we face a crisis that affects everyone in ways some of the earlier crises never did," warned an introductory essay in the Sierra Club citizens' handbook, *Ecotactics*.[2] John Gardner admonished similarly that "unless the society can recapture a belief in its values and in the possibility of making those values live in action, its days are numbered." Elsewhere, he described our contemporary crisis of "paralysis" as a "waking nightmare." Ralph Nader has often espoused the same sober view, noting in 1970 that "during the past decade, this country has begun to show that it can destroy itself inadvertently from within."[3]

While the nature of the purported crisis has been defined in various ways, nearly all the reformers have followed earlier radicals in identifying "corporations to be the core of the problem." In short, the general antipathy to big business has constituted "the common ground which unites all of these people and movements."[4] Once the military hubris of the military-industrial complex was tamed momentarily by withdrawal from Vietnam, the industrial functions of powerful corporations logically became the focus of the reform impulse. "The intention . . . is not to praise the country's present industrial arrogance, but to put a stop to it," claimed the editor of *The Environmental Handbook*. Indeed, to those in the reform movement, nearly all of the "discontents and abuses" that plague modern life "flow from the unbridled power corporations have over the marketplace and government."[5] Recalling the earlier Congress of Racial Equality vow of battle against the corporation "with his foot on our neck," the unofficial public interest logo thus has become the Big Business Day banner picturing an imperious thumb crushing down upon the head of a helpless citizen. The broad range of understandings behind these attitudes can be summarized briefly.

Corporations in the Marketplace. Reformers have argued that the immense power of corporations in the economic marketplace alone establishes them as "the dominant institution of American society."[6] The vast corporate reach into all facets of modern life is claimed to exacerbate further the traditional insensitivity to social needs always typical of capitalistic modes of production. Most important to the new reformers has been that existing corporate profit-oriented decisions take little account of significant "externalities" such as environmental quality, occupational safety and health, consumer product safety, and long-term resource depletion. Because many important spillover effects of production are not internalized by producers, argues ecologist Jon Breslaw, "the automatic market exchange process fails" to provide for citizen welfare. The manipulations of the invisible hand are seen as simply too clumsy to protect our most important public goods. A large share of collective resources used and abused freely by private corporate producers—air, water, land, human minds and bodies—thus constitute implicit social subsidies for which no reciprocal public responsibility is exacted. "The corporate drive to reduce corporate costs and . . . enhance sales and profits is calculated to inflict as social costs on the public the contaminants of corporate activities," noted Nader in *Ecotactics.*[7]

Furthermore, the reformers have pointed out that the vast size and power of many modern firms frees them from even traditional competitive market constraints as well. In Nader's "dual economy" scheme, the problem is one of the "controlled market sub-economy." More often, the structural malady is summed up simply in the evocative charge of "monopoly."[8] After a century of successive waves of mergers to promote both vertical and horizontal corporate integration, declared one study, we have inherited an economy where two hundred manufacturers control two-thirds of all manufacturing assets and numerous sectors are dominated by a few firms. As Walter Lippmann once put it, "Competition has survived only where men have been unable to abolish it."[9] Such increasing insulation of big business from market pressures, the new liberals charge, has replaced the older democratic ideals of consumer sovereignty with modern realities of hierarchical producer sovereignty. The activists have documented in protest the baleful results: continually rising "administered" prices and profits, persistent inflationary trends and sustained unemployment, stabilized inequality of wealth, and declining incentives to promote efficiency of scale and technological innovation. In sum, two reform advocates conclude that "The evidence is that few benefits, if any, can be expected to result from conglomerate mergers. The current bumper crop of takeovers offers little prospect of socially desirable results."[10]

If corporations have amassed unprecedented power to exploit the public, the reformers have argued, they have also developed a peculiar genius for leading citizens to believe otherwise. The primary tool of this spellbinding effort is advertising. Reform critics point to the startling statistics of corporate expenditures to emphasize the significance of advertising to corporate profit making. For example, one Public Citizen study revealed that, in 1972, U.S. businesses paid 50 percent more on commercial advertising than all other noncommunist nations combined. Total mass media expenditures in 1976 were estimated at about $31 billion, or over $140 per person.[11] The proclaimed corporate justification for such massive investment is to furnish useful data that will enhance consumers' freedom to choose. "In reality," argues public interest lawyer Beverly C. Moore, Jr., "much of the economy's . . . advertising budget is devoted to creating and manipulating consumer preferences."[12] Not only does this promote fraudulent sales practices and obscure real product differences and dangers; corporate advertising further serves to turn faster the treadmill of ecologically disastrous commodity consumption by feeding citizen desires for material status and hedonistic indulgence. "The modern ad writer sells happiness, envy, fear, and excitement, and along with them some product"—all for the sake of increasing private producer profits.[13]

Finally, modern business corporations have been portrayed as no more accountable internally to the wishes of those who own them than to external market pressures of consumers. The logic behind the corporate ideal of "people's capitalism" is that corporate management should be responsible and responsive to the dictates of citizen stockholders. Yet, as Adolph Berle and Gardiner Means illustrated long ago, ownership and control have become almost entirely severed in modern national and multinational corporate giants. The reasons are several. On one hand, few shareholders even bother to exercise their privileges of influence. Most are concerned primarily with maximizing monetary returns on their investments rather than with the social or moral significance of corporate action. Furthermore, those who do become discontented with management usually choose to sell their stocks (exit) rather than to challenge (voice) the corporate directorate.[14] On the other hand, public interest critics point out that shareholder challenges are futile because management monopolizes all of the reigns of power. For example, one reform study concludes that "management so dominates the proxy machinery that corporate elections have come to resemble the Soviet Union's euphemistic 'Communist ballot'—that is, a ballot which lists only one slate of candidates."[15] Specifically, corporate organization systematically assures that management possesses near total control over money, information, expertise, personnel, and legal rules to which most concerned citizen investors can pose no reasonable challenge. In short, therefore, the reformers have decried so-called shareholder democracy as a capitalist myth masking the exercise of vast social power for the sole purpose of private profit: "Corporate responsibility and accountability . . . is a sham," declared legal activist Robert Fellmeth in 1970.[16]

The Corporate Capture of Government. Liberal activist critics have further contended that the unrestrained economic power of corporations in the marketplace is only secondary to, and dependent on, their entrenched power within modern government. John Gardner thus asserts that "the gravest danger in the concentration of economic power is the increased capacity to influence the public process."[17] The image of "capture" provides the ubiquitous metaphor invoked to describe this corporate preemption of government authority. Ralph Nader has summed up the perspective this way: "Much of what passes as governmental power is derivative of corporate power whose advocacy of sufferance defines much of the direction and deployment of government activity.... So much of government resources is allocated and so much is utilized to transfer public wealth into corporate coffers that Washington can be fairly described as a bustling bazaar of accounts receivable for industry–commerce."[18]

The reformers' ubiquitous allusions to the facts of corporate capture have not implied a simple or singular understanding of the situation, however. The concept of "capture" is more metaphorical than analytical and refers to a broad range of vaguely defined phenomena.

One general example of this pervasive corporate influence identified by the reformers is in national electoral politics. Corporations are cited as working in several ways to undercut the values of elections as tools for promoting official accountability to the public. The first concerns the vast expenditures of funds by business interests to dominate electoral campaign competition. In the liberal reform perspective, money is the root of all political evil: "The key to political power in the Special Interest State is money," claims a Common Cause monograph.[19] For example, a Media Access Project study has claimed to illustrate the decisive link "between overwhelming corporate media spending and voter behavior in referendum contests." Basing their findings on the defeat of three Colorado ballot initiatives (on nuclear safety, returnable bottles, and public utilities regulation) in 1976, they found "clear" evidence that "those who spent the most [corporations] won the elections."[20]

Of particular concern to the critics has been the corporate domination of congressional electoral politics. To Mark Green's rhetorical question *Who Runs Congress?*, nearly all of the reformers have agreed with his findings that the answer is "big business." "By lavishing contributions on candidates, well-heeled special interests have come to exercise decisive leverage over the outcome of elections," claims John Gardner.[21] Such corporate expenditures have always been great, the liberals acknowledge, but they have increased dramatically through the 1970s. Green cites that between 1976 and 1978 alone the number of corporate political action committees (PACs) rose from 450 to 821 and their total expenditures from $4.3 million to $9.8 million. These corporate investments are apparently worth the gamble. One Nader-sponsored study of corporate lobbies cites as an example that the vote by fifty-eight House members who received PAC money was fifty-five to three against a windfall profits tax on oil companies.[22] A CFA newsletter thus has summarized that "money buys votes, more money buys more votes. The romance between business and government . . . is not merely a sometimes thing; it is an ongoing if at times uneasy relationship."[23]

Campaign financing is only the most obvious dimension of corporate subversion of public electoral control over Congress identified by the reformers. Its significance largely "has been replaced by a more sophisticated skilled wooing by well-financed corporate lobbying groups."[24] Since the 1960s, lobbying expenditures have grown to unprecedented proportions. By 1972, one public interest study reveals, over eight hundred of the thousand largest American firms had established lobbyists in Washington. The oil lobby has been most powerful, including activity by 229 lobbyists in nineteen associations, the largest of which alone spends over $2 million a year. American Electric Power is said to have spent $3.6 million in 1975 to promote a single coal development project before Congress. Other business interests such as the dairy, airlines, and trucking industries routinely spend considerable sums to secure government subsidies or to maintain protection against unwanted market competition.[25]

To such individual efforts, the reformers complain, have been added massive coalitional efforts coordinated by the powerful Business Roundtable as well as computerized grass-roots mobilization programs to pressure congressional representatives from afar. With finely calculated precision, "the word goes out from a Washington trade association or lobbying consulting firm to mobilize the 'grass roots' of the business world . . . on the theory that members of Congress pay more attention to their constituents than to a Washington lobbyist."[26] Such tactics have proved especially effective in defeating both liberal publicly financed election measures and the proposed agency for consumer protection. A Consumers Union essay summarizes the situation this way: "From the top, the corporate chief executive officers use their influence; from the bottom the grassroots businessmen and women use their numbers. In the middle are the legislators—pressured from both directions."[27] This description applies only to the legally sanctioned influence of corporations, the critics add, and does not even account for the routine bribes and payoffs such as revealed in the Abscam and Tongsun Park affairs.

"Thus is the public interest bought and sold," claimed a Common Cause manifesto in 1970.[28] From the reformers' viewpoint, the established rules and practices of government only encourage such cozy corporate relations. Political parties are said to be dominated by entrenched professionals unaccountable to party members, and electoral campaign rules were nearly nonexistent until the liberal critics took action themselves during the 1970s.[29] Likewise, the activists protested early in the decade that congressional processes and practices themselves were designed to secure the power of those most responsive to corporate interests. Rules of seniority, "franking" privileges, and campaign and lobbying disclosure exemptions "get right to the heart of how the power structure maintains itself," noted Gardner.[30] All in all, the consequent public interest attitude has been that elections are generally a sham, what Jacques Ellul once called a "political illusion." Where presidents are "sold" routinely to the public and congressmen are "bought" by the highest bidders, "such periodic checks as elections [become] little more than rituals," says Nader. In short, modern "politics is the only game where the real action begins after the public has filed out of the stadium."[31]

This imperious presence of corporate influence in government is understood to go far beyond contact with elected officials. Indeed, it is within the federal regulatory agencies that corporate capture has been understood to be most common and consequential. "Government regulation...has failed to protect the public, largely because the regulatory bodies have served the private interests they were designed to regulate," claims Campaign GM activist Donald Schwartz. "Actually, government regulation, to a large degree, has strengthened the power of large corporations."[32] Nader associate Robert Fellmeth's essay on the regulatory–industrial complex is perhaps the most comprehensive exposition on the topic. In his view, the goal of industry intervention in agencies is twofold: to prevent meaningful government regulation that impedes profits; and to obtain government protection from other regulators or market competition. "The capture of these 'regulators' is a *fait accompli* for many industries, enabling free exercise of abusive and dangerous monopoly power."[33] Fellmeth astutely recognizes that the alleged manifestations of collusion between regulators and regulated are many—through informal favors and contacts, formal industrial advisory committees, routine revolving-door personnel exchange, direct lobbying, and persistent pressures in hiring decisions. Other reformers point to different causes for regulators' submission. Some recognize the simple propensity to organizational inertia which saps agency resolve.[34] Environmentalist Joseph Sax similarly blames what he calls the narrow insider perspective of bureaucrats more concerned about agency stability than results: "By taking the position of neutral arbitrator, EPA...increases its vulnerability to industry's pressure," agrees an Environmental Action essay.[35] Still others point more charitably to the simple lack of resources— money, time, personnel, information—which forces agency passivity toward industry.[36]

Such incestuous relationships between industry and government have been cited to support the public interest claim that democratic pluralism is nearly nonexistent in modern America. As John Gardner puts it, "special interest pluralism hasn't worked as some of its advocates assured us it would." The reasons are several. First, "all relevant interests aren't there to do the appropriate clashing."[37] Given the low visibility of regulatory agency activity and the great difficulty of mobilizing citizens for action, many important interests are left without a voice in the political process. "Everyone is organized but the people."[38] In particular, the reform-minded advocates have pointed to the widely acknowledged political fact that support for diffuse public interests is less mobilizable than support for narrow, specific private interests of small constituencies like businesses. Hence, adds Mark Green, "for more than half of the consumer proceedings there is no consumer representation whatsoever."[39]

Moreover, even when organized, most citizen groups have been denied the access to government agencies available to business interests: "It isn't a free market; its rigged to prevent unfettered play of competing interests," claims Gardner.[40] Even more important, citizens traditionally have possessed few legal rights to participate directly in government proceedings. David Riley observed in 1970 that no regulatory legislation "establishes or even recognizes the right of corporate constituencies...to participate in running our corporations," nor have "the courts...recognized the people's right to participate" in regulatory agency processes.[41] In particular, reformers identify several doctrines with which "justices slam the door" routinely on citizen groups: restrictive definition of public injury, rejection of class-action suits, and refusal to pay attorneys' fees in public law disputes.[42]

As a result, most reformers have seemed convinced that the entire government machinery virtually thrives on exclusiveness and, most important, on secrecy. Regulatory muckraker Robert Fellmeth claims that "the actual atmosphere of the bureaucracy is shrouded in secrecy that is buttressed by an effective enforcement mechanism."[43] The implication of such claims is that the notion of an open American government is a myth. "The big winners in the pluralistic system are the highly organized, wealthy, and motivated groups skilled in the art of insider politics."[44] As these reformers have seen it, the American experiment in liberal governmental regulation has been largely a charade. "Regulation of industry would have to be regarded as one of the least successful enterprises ever undertaken by American democracy," proclaims Simon Lazarus.[45] This hypothesis has been supported by the findings of numerous studies by Nader's Raiders, environmentalists, and other reform groups into the practices of the FDA, FTC, FCC, DOE, OSHA, ICC, SEC, CAB, EPA, and ACE. Each study has revealed to the liberal activists a "usual pattern: corporate practices with devastating social consequences, the law protecting such practices from serious public scrutiny, [and] corporate ignorance in the face of a challenge to its authority."[46]

Indeed, the reformers have protested that the rule of law itself—whether it be antitrust law, environmental regulations, freedom-of-information procedures, or OSHA standards—is ignored and subverted routinely. They point out that the great amount of discretion granted to agency officials in most regulatory matters only invites corporate capture: "under the agency's legal structure," argues ecologist Harrison Wellford, "they can delay action, decide what portions of the law to enforce or not to enforce, and even adamantly refuse to carry out programs mandated by Congress." Large corporations thus are able to pursue their activities "beyond the law, above the law, or against the law," adds Nader.[47] What is more, this subversion of law by government officials is exacerbated even further by the input of the "other government"—the Washington lawyers who represent corporate interests. Like the reformers' evaluation of the legal process itself, their verdict on lawyers typically has been that they have "become the servant[s] of the haves rather than the guardian[s] of the have nots."[48]

The general image of modern American government portrayed by the liberal critics is summed up by their favorite labels, "special interest state" and "corporate state." We have a "corporate state run by a few without the informed consent and participation of the many," attests a Nader group.[49] While such claims often tend to border on theories of "power elite" conspiracy, the reform spokespersons have usually refused to go so far. As John Gardner puts it, "The error is in the word 'few.' I've been behind the scenes, and its so crowded you can't move around." In fact, the proliferating size, complexity, and fragmentation of the modern state is at the very heart of the problems they define: "A large part of what is called Federal Government is not a coherent entity at all," complains a Common Cause manifesto, "but a collection of fragments under the virtual control of organized special interests."[50]

44

The Crisis Defined. Reformers have catalogued the costs of unrestrained corporate power over state and society in unambiguous terms. As they see it, modern corporations may not pose a threat tantamount to tanks rattling down our streets, but they still constitute a subtle tyranny of significant proportion. The result is that every day we are exposed to the dangers of a dirty environment, unhealthy workplaces, unsafe products, fraudulent trade practices, and depletion of natural resources. Everywhere can be seen the signs of deception, inefficiency, waste, and exploitation of collective goods for private profit. Nader paints a startling picture in vivid detail:

> When this waste and fraud are added to the preventable fatalities and injuries which occur because of dangerous automobiles, drugs, household products, flammable fabrics, medical malpractice, and a score of other consumer hazards, it becomes clear that a social and economic emergency prevails.
>
> When the polluting byproducts of producing goods and services—the lethal chemicals, gases and particulates—result, as they do, in massive compulsory consumption which leads to diseases such as cancer, emphysema, and other ailments, the situation becomes even more precarious. But all this, serious as it is and has been, pales before the prospect for the next generation as the risk levels of consumer and environmental technology (e.g., nuclear power plants and their wastes) threaten the very foundation of organized society.[51]

Given such claims of environmental danger and consumer abuse, it is no wonder that the reformers have spoken of a "crisis" so freely.

This crisis has been identified by the activists as penetrating deep into the very structure of American society itself: "Our ailment is not a minor annoyance, such as a head cold, but [is] more nearly comparable to a disease of the central nervous system, dangerously disabling and possibly terminal," claims Gardner.[52] Above all, the institutional practices of American public life have become profoundly undemocratic. Where corporate power remains "unaccountable," "unresponsive," "irresponsible," and "unrepresentative," popular sovereignty is denied. "The powerlessness of the people to participate effectively in the institutional decisions that affect their lives marks the end of a true democratic society," begins Sax's *Defending the Environment*.[53] Moreover, power has been removed not only from the constraints of popular will, but also from the guidance of shared moral principles essential to a just polity: "We are seeing the breakdown of established patterns without the emergence of new ones," laments the Common Cause statement of purpose. "The consequences in loss of shared principles and purpose... are apparent to all."[54] In sum, the public interest movement during the 1970s began from the assumption that the very legitimacy of established power within modern society was in serious question.

A Strategy for Change: Mobilizing Citizen Resources

Organizing for Action: A Professional Approach. The liberal reformers' unique understandings about the modern American crisis provided both motive and method for their efforts to challenge corporate abuse of consumers, the environment, and liberal democracy. "Without such a movement, no idea is worth trying and all are just dreams," speculated David Riley in 1970. The discontented middle-class activists understood that such a citizens' movement was possible only through the development of durable public interest organizations. If questioning values was the first step, pondered Riley, then organizing for power was the second task at hand.[55] "A program without organization is a hoax," agreed John Gardner. Ralph Nader expressed a similar sentiment as well: "our goal is to use... new organizations to secure significant reforms of economic and political institutions more quickly.... Organizations are necessary to bring about large-scale change."[56]

These public interest organizations were new in several senses. First, of course, was the relative youth of most public interest groups as a force in American politics. Over half of the citizen groups were founded after 1968, including such influential organizations as Nader's Public Citizen, Common Cause, Consumer Federation of America, Friends of the Earth, Environmental Action, and the Exploratory Project for Economic Alternatives. One study reveals that the number of public interest law firms increased from forty-five in 1969 to more than ninety in 1975.[57] To be sure, some important movement organizations—the League of Women Voters, Consumers Union, Sierra Club, The Wilderness Society, and American Civil Liberties Union—were founded much earlier. However, it is also indisputable that most of these groups have grown in size and engaged themselves politically far more since the late 1960s than ever before. For the first time, many long-established groups advocated meeting "power with power." Hence, while mature in years of existence, they came to exhibit the political vigor, vitality, and commitment of regenerated youth in the movement.

A good example of this change is illustrated by the history of the almost century-old Sierra Club. Although active under David Brower's leadership during the early 1960s in important preservationist campaigns to save California redwoods and Grand Canyon National Park, the organization suffered a deep split in 1969 over whether a more radical ecological politics should be promoted. The newly emerging contingent argued for a departure along these lines: "The traditional conservation groups are afraid to be openly political. . . . Their official purpose is educational. . . . We are free to take sides and to channel the growing concern about the environment into a unified political force."[58] The result of the struggle was not only an increase in subsequent Sierra Club commitment to a broader political agenda, but also the founding of the even more politically active Friends of the Earth by Brower. Similar observations of changes in other established organizations have led one scholar to summarize that "what is new is the amount of influence that [older] public interest groups have acquired in a relatively short time."[59]

The activist leaders' very concern about the need for novel, innovative, dynamic institutional forms to wage the reform battle itself has constituted a distinctive dimension in the new politics. It is crucial that political associations are specifically "organized for action," proclaimed the Common Cause manifesto, for "activity in members is directly related to forms of organization."[60] This has required, on one hand, that the reform movement avoid the tendencies to bureaucratic rigidity and elitism that characterize most existing political structures. Environmental Action says of its citizens' lobby, for example, that "we wanted to experiment with a more 'humane' office structure— no bosses, no secretaries, democratic hiring and firing, and shared decision making. We're proud of our non-hierarchical structure." To activate effectively a polity that is "long established, complacent, and routine ridden" requires, after all, a new kind of creative political organization.[61] "If we want to develop a majority coalition," agrees Citizen Action League leader Mike Miller, "what we need are independent, mass based, multi-issue organizations, democratically controlled by their members, taking action on the issues of their time."[62] This largely explains the characteristic aversion of the new reformers to existing political parties as a resource for change. Increasingly dissatisfied with the tendencies to centrist inertia displayed by the two major party organizations, they came to believe that "public interest groups offer a more effective means of influencing public policy" for most citizens in the land.[63]

On the other hand, the leading activists insisted that the excessive spontaneity and passion generated by political movements in the 1960s must be avoided as well. "Much of this activity was diffuse, erratic, and poorly organized," complained many of the new advocates. The student politics of the earlier decade simply had too little staying power, was easily coopted, relied too heavily on guerrilla tactics of dramatic display, and too often degenerated into unnecessary disorder and violence. "It is odd that many groups that profess an interest in action are not in fact organized for action," instructed the influential Gardner.[64] In contrast, public interest organizations were designed to combine passion and professionalism, creativity and discipline, coordination and commitment into a powerful new force for change. "Protests can lay the groundwork," noted Sierra Club director Michael McCloskey, "but in a mass society changes are made only when controlling institutions are forced to make them through the political process." What is needed, summarized David Riley, are new "counter-organizations" with enough power to "stand up to other massive organizations that dominate modern life, those of government, business, and labor."[65]

The actual groups that developed from such designs can be divided into two types of organization: membership and staff groups.[66] A *membership group* is one that has a large group of supporters in the general public who participate by contributing funds and electing a board of directors. The League of Women Voters (140,000 members), Sierra Club (153,000 members), and Common Cause (over 200,000) members all fit this model. One study estimates that only 12 percent (ten groups) have developed such large constituencies of over 100,000 members, however, while 27 percent have fewer than 25,000 members.[67] A unique variation of this model includes groups like Public Citizen which have dues-paying memberships but no elected board. *Staff groups*, by contrast, have no general public membership at all. Constituting perhaps about one-third of all liberal public interest groups, the bulk of these staff-oriented organizations are public interest law firms that both aid other citizen groups in legal matters and act independently for those interests that lack organized constituencies.

Consciousness Raising. One of the most important functions of public interest organizations from the beginning has been public education and "consciousness raising" about the disturbing facts of public life. "All fundamental change depends upon the proper use of facts," states a Big Business Day bulletin. "Facts are the iron frame around which the edifice of reform must be constructed."[68] Indeed, the reformers have seemed almost obsessed with the commitment to exposure, revelation, and disclosure of all the shadowy dimensions of public life. "Exposure of how the system actually works is a prerequisite to building the political power to change it," they affirm. As illustrated in earlier pages, this impulse has initiated a perpetual campaign to document the facts concerning nearly every sector of the public realm—regulatory agency performance, corporate investment and production effects, voting records of elected politicians, campaign finance disclosure, legal counsel, and judicial behavior. "The public interest lobby wants to tell the whole story—what's at stake, who stands to gain or lose, who's making what deals," says Gardner.[69]

This labor to expose new facts has been intended to achieve at least two important goals. For one, revelation of facts can spark new interpretation of events by the citizenry, which in turn expands the range of public debate and deliberation about the proper course of collective action. Most activists have emphasized the view that "self government works best when the public has access to a variety of viewpoints." Invoking the legacy of earlier reform movements in America, Donald Schwartz argued for Campaign GM that "the mere engaging in open debate is at least a partial victory . . . ; it was one of the main objects of the campaign." In other words, the effective communication of political knowledge to citizens has been a worthy end in itself for the new reformers. "An informed electorate has been essential to the working of democracy," proclaims a Media Access Project report.[70]

At the same time, however, activists have also attempted to use such educational efforts to mobilize public opinion and support on behalf of the liberal public interest position in various debates. Because "ignorance is a . . . pervasive barrier to change," it follows that "effective communication is the most powerful single weapon of the public interest lobby."[71] Success in this regard depends, first, on the ability to convince people of their exploited, powerless situation. "The issue must be dramatized. If the public is apathetic, it must be aroused," instructs Gardner. Building upon the experiences of the antiwar movement, many of the new activists have assumed that "an American electorate that learns about the relative strength of corporate . . . power will become very aroused."[72] Moreover, the reformers have also been aware of the need for aggressive communication of new affirmative values and programs to alter public perceptions of desirable goals and aspirations. Wary of the fact that "it's so much easier to say what the revolution is against," the liberal activists have labored to "articulate clearly what the revolution is for in terms that can be understood by everyone." Another *Ecotactics* essay has been bolder in its prescriptions. "To maneuver forces against the enemy," it proclaims, "the tactician first indoctrinates the troops."[73]

Such endeavors to educate the public have constituted an important source of power and influence in the reform strategy. As E. E. Schattschneider once put it, public education about political issues expands the scope of conflict to balance concentrated private power with the weight of collective public opinion. "He who defines the battlefield can win the battle," argues League of Conservation Voters leader Marion Edey. David Cohen of Common Cause likewise has heralded "the ability of public opinion to correct the abuses of power."[74] Indeed, public interest activists have tended to rely on the power of publicity to influence elected officials in much the same way as many others use campaign contributions.[75] Nader's highly visible war against General Motors, EDF's battle against pesticide use, and the ongoing campaign to fight nuclear power have provided but a few manifestations of the effective use of publicity as an important reform strategy.

If the goals of public education have been generally uniform for most groups, however, their chosen forms of communication have been quite diverse. One reason for this is that the reformers routinely address several different publics—the entire formal group membership, the activists among group members, the nonmember public, and government officials.[76] Probably the most important and broadly directed efforts have been the various muckraking exposés churned out by many groups. The goal of such book- and article-length features is not merely to present the facts, of course, but also to create a sense of political drama and cause for alarm. "The hallmark of these studies is overkill," observes advocate-scholar Jeffrey Berry in an issue of *Citizen Participation*. Part empirical investigation and part moral allegory, these works seek "to give people in government and business unholy hell for their transgressions," adds another activist.[77] Examples of such enterprises range from official voting record publications (Environmental Action's "Dirty Dozen," CFA's consumer ratings, etc.) to ambitious "research-and-destroy" studies of administrative agencies, Congress, corporate giants, and any other perceived enemy.

National magazines like *The Nation* or *The New Republic* and major book publishers have provided the favorite battlegrounds upon which most reformers have waged their war of words. The potential of such resources was illustrated by the impact of an Amory Lovins (FOE) essay on energy in 1976 which attracted the largest number of requests for reprints in *Foreign Affairs* history.[78] In addition, regular cooperation with influential syndicated national journalists such as Jack Anderson, Drew Pearson, Morton Mintz, and even Herblock has proved a useful resource for humbling public wrongdoers through public censure. Finally, many organizations such as Friends of the Earth and Sierra Club publish their own magazines and books to inform the public regularly about their specified enemies and moral campaigns.

Other strategies for public consciousness raising have been more personality- or event-oriented. These include public speeches, interviews, and good-will appearances by noted reform leaders to win visibility for the movement's causes. In particular, the use of press conferences and participation on public panels like "Meet the Press" has been effective in this regard. Ralph Nader, David Brower, and Barry Commoner have been the most successful in utilizing this tactic, although recruitment of outside celebrities like Jane Fonda, Robert Redford, and various popular music stars has proved quite helpful in winning public recognition. More dramatically, the activists have also occasionally engaged in well-planned 1960s-inspired peaceful protests, boycotts, sit-ins, and teach-ins to generate public awareness about their campaigns. Earth Day, Sun Day, Big Business Day, the multidimensional COIN rallies, and regular anti-nuclear power demonstrations are common examples of such enterprises.

What all of these publicity-generating stagecraft activities have shared is a strong dependence on the popular mass media of modern television and newspapers to communicate their message. As one public interest magazine put it, "All . . . groups understand the importance of the media in contemporary politics. Without extensive media coverage, many citizen group lobbying campaigns would be stillborn."[79] It thus is not surprising that both *Ecotactics* and *The Environmental Handbook* devote separate essays to use of the media for political advocacy. In sum, capturing the public forum, projecting the image, dramatizing the issue, "preempting the rhetorical high ground"—these have been the key goals in what Simon Lazarus calls the public interest "pageant of reform."[80]

Generating Citizen Participation. The intent of the new reform organizations has not been confined to merely educating and elevat-

51

ing citizen awareness. More important, the groups have attempted to generate widespread voluntary citizen action on behalf of the reform cause. After all, a democratic political movement requires some form of mass participation. It is clear that "only a return to large scale citizen involvement at all levels can turn us from our destructive path," argued *The Environmental Handbook* authors in 1970.[81] Consequently, the new group structures have also become the primary sources of both leadership and member allegiance necessary to spur collective citizen action. "Without a strong grass roots movement," three public interest lawyers speculated, "the leadership at the top will be merely shouting, or whistling, in the dark."[82]

Like their radical New Left precursors in the 1960s, public interest activists have professed to take participatory democracy quite seriously as a basic commitment of the movement. "We strive for a reawakening of the democratic impulse—the promise that people can shape the decisions which affect their lives," proclaims a Public Citizen Report.[83] Collective citizen action is heralded as the essential democratic means to achievement of a more responsive, representative, and responsible government. In the reformers' common purview, only with the weight of a united public constituency behind them can the movement hope to balance the scales of justice and redirect public power for the common good. "Power to the people does not mean a few spokesmen leading around a disinterested flock of 200 million consumers," exhorted one public interest law firm study in the early years of the movement.[84]

Beyond such instrumental goals, activists have argued that citizen political action is an important human endeavor of great value in itself. Ecologist Hazel Henderson thus muses, "I have learned that it is almost impossible to be a thinking, fully functioning human being in a complex society without doing politics—not necessarily the old politics of geography, but issue politics, public-interest-group politics."[85] Freely recalling inspiring phrases from Pericles and Cicero, Jefferson and Tocqueville, the reformers hold out the promise that new forms of genuine direct democracy can be rebuilt within modern American government. "We want a society in which . . . participation is real and consequential—all this to the end that the individual may recover his capacity to act, to act for himself and in behalf of his community, with confidence and good spirit."[86]

The tasks these goals have required of the reform advocates are several. First, they have understood the need for organizations to combat the tendencies to citizen privatism, passivity, and feelings of powerlessness with exhortations to faith in latent resources of citizen efficacy. "A major task has been to persuade . . . citizens that they can and should act politically," announces Gardner. Nader similarly has outlined the need to "help show the way to overcome the early inhibitions against getting started on an unknown terrain."[87] To recall Schattschneider's popular imagery, the reform leaders have been committed to transforming citizens from their passive roles as fans in the stands into active players on the actual field of national politics. The reformers have recognized that such exhortations are not enough, however. In addition, public interest organizers have labored to instruct the public in the appropriate tactics and strategies of effective action. Through myriad magazines, newsletters, and specialized "how-to" manuals (such as *Ecotactics, The Environmental Handbook,* and *A Public Citizen's Action Manual*), the reform leaders "propose workable alternatives to our present patterns of living" and "gather together projects which can serve as models for constructive action."[88]

Finally, the role of influential individuals as personal leaders capable of inspiring and exemplifying reform action has been crucial to the success of the movement. "People still are in the habit of learning more by example than by exhortation," recognized the *Ecotactics* editor.[89] In particular, Ralph Nader, David Brower, Hazel Henderson, and John Gardner have provided popular models for citizen emulation. As ecologist Harrison Wellford once said of Nader, "His pursuit of the public interest is a game everyone can play." Indeed, numerous articles testify that this is what the reformers have meant in their claims to promote "initiatory democracy." As public citizens, we all should attend meeetings, express ourselves on public issues, defend our interests, write our congressional representatives, and generally take on the establishment—just as Nader and the other reform activists and leaders have done. "Given what a few citizens have done," Nader himself has noted, "it is a source of optimism to ask what many, many more like them could do in the future."[90]

In short, Gardner summarizes the reform enterprise in this way. "The people are the soil. The movements are the seeds."[91] In this sense, reform leaders can claim to have done a fair job of political gardening. Collectively, the groups attracted membership commitments from over six million citizens during the 1970s. More important, thousands of full- and part-time activists have been mobilized for action in letter writing, telephone calling, speech making, pamphlet distribution, demonstrations, teach-ins, and various forms of direct lobbying.

Mobilizing Resources: The Professional Edge. Public interest organizers have been well aware that their leadership responsibilities
extend yet further. Specifically, professional activists must mobilize,
coordinate, and transform the various interests of citizens into resources for effective action. "If citizen action is to be successful,"
instructs the Common Cause manual, "it requires careful preparation, effective organization, and stamina."[92] A few of these tasks are
worth mentioning.

1. One crucial challenge, of course, is *raising money*. The range of
mobilized financial resources has varied widely among the different
groups and over different spans of time. As one yardstick, Jeffrey
Berry found in 1973 that one-fourth of the groups worked with less
than $100,000 a year, while one-fifth of the polled groups possessed
over a $1,000,000 in their annual budgets. Whatever the amounts,
however, for most groups "money is always a problem."[93] Funds come
from two primary voluntary sources. First, private contributors,
through both large donations and regular membership fees ($15–30),
have constituted an indispensable source of group funding for most
mass membership groups. Indeed, the explosion of direct mass-
mailing solicitation technology in the early 1970s was one of the most
important factors encouraging the growth of the new groups. During
the course of the decade, specialized firms such as Craver, Matthews,
and Smith developed as centralized coordinators responsible solely for
tapping general public resources in this way for many public interest
organizations. Such voluntary sources are the most costly to obtain—
absorbing often up to a third of what is raised—but the moderately
high rate of membership renewals (over 70 percent for many groups)
makes them among the most reliable of funding alternatives.[94]

Many organizations have also relied on private foundations for
support. Perhaps at least one-third of all groups—and most public
interest law firms—received at least half of their funding from
foundation sources during the 1970s. In particular, public interest law
firms such as the Citizens Communications Center and the Center for
Law and Social Policy developed through almost total dependence on
foundation support. The Ford Foundation has been by far the biggest
contributor, but others such as the Carnegie, Rockefeller, and Stern
foundations have been important as well. Most of such foundation
funds have been intended as seed money to bring the new groups into
existence, however, and hence they are granted for only limited
periods of time. Indeed, the termination of grants by the Ford
Foundation spelled near doom for many liberal law reform groups

during the late 1970s. While adding flexibility to the reform potential, therefore, dependence on foundations and other institutional patrons has also imposed a measure of ideological constraint and general uncertainty to the financial outlook of the movement.[95]

It is of great consequence in this regard that both private individual and foundation contributions are subject to very significant IRS guidelines. Most important is that the crucial tax-exempt status of public interest groups (under Section 501 (c) (3) of the Internal Revenue Code) depends on their restraint from "substantial" congressional lobbying activities. Because such guidelines traditionally have been quite vague, the IRS has been able periodically to undercut the financial base of some groups, such as the Sierra Club and the Center for Corporate Responsibility. Public interest organizations have fought back, however, through a variety of lawsuits in specific cases as well as through support for legislation such as a 1976 tax reform bill that specified an exemption status allowing up to 20 percent of organizational budget expenditures for lobbying purposes. Moreover, some groups have circumvented the IRS rules somewhat by establishing special affiliate foundations to receive contributions reserved exclusively for judicial and administrative advocacy permitted by the tax guidelines. Jeffrey Berry found in the early 1970s that nearly two-thirds of all polled organizations enjoyed 501 (c) (3) status or possessed such bifurcated affiliate structures.[96]

To these primary sources have been regularly added other minimal private resources from book and magazine sales, speeches, and articles in national journals. In fact, Consumers Union receives nearly all of its revenue from its publication of the popular *Consumer Reports*. Another of the most interesting models for mobilizing direct voluntary citizen funding in the future is Nader's plan for developing what he calls Residential Utility Consumer Action Groups (RUGAGs). Rooted in typical skepticism about corporate monopolies and the agencies designed to regulate them, the plan requires that "consumer checkoff" forms be included with all utility statements to solicit citizen contributions. This money would be collected by the utility and given to a full-time staff of experts and board of directors elected by contributors. In this "piggyback" concept, citizen money would be directed to fund ongoing research, direct corporate counsel, and representation before agencies, courts, and legislatures on behalf of consumers. What they would seek to fund, says Nader, "is a multiplicity of specialized electorates, each with full-time advocates and analysts, which will focus their collective power in an organized way on institutions that affect them."[97] Such a plan would not be limited to utilities alone; it could be adapted easily to consumer clienteles of the U.S. Postal Service and automobile, insurance, and airline industries. The most successful implementation of the idea so far has been in the Wisconsin Citizen Utility Board and the student-funded PIRGs on college campuses throughout the country.

2. A second major well-used resource in the movement's success is professional *knowledge*. It is undeniable that, from the outset, the high degree of involvement by young professionals and technical specialists has enhanced the effectiveness of public interest groups. The reformers have seen no conflict between this fact and the commitment that "citizen effort is everybody's business and that everybody can engage in such effort."[98] Rather, they simply profess the realistic understanding that successful combat with the establishment requires mobilization of considerable information, knowledge, and skill in technical matters not available to most citizens. "You must amass the technical skills appropriate to the issue," argues an *Environmental Handbook* essay. "The vital issues are complex and technical. They demand the interdisciplinary expertise of... people with special skills."[99] The reform leaders have also realized that highly educated young professionals constitute one of the most stable sources of constituent support for the reform cause within the general public. Nader thus has described the public interest organizational commitment as "providing an outlet for the enthusiasm and idealism of our professional school graduates, who might otherwise be channeled into mainstream professional concerns against their wishes." Gardner similarly affirms that Common Cause appeals to the "percentage... who see their profession as part of the larger social enterprise and who know that their special interest and the public interest are not wholly separable."[100]

It is not surprising, then, that the full-time staffs of most public interest groups have been loaded with experts of all kinds—biologists, zoologists, economists, health technicians, doctors, and a variety of academic specialists. In fact, groups such as the Center for Science in the Public Interest are composed solely of technical specialists who provide permanent resources of research and counsel to other advocacy groups: "A lot of citizen groups need scientific help. We wanted to serve as an example to scientists," they proclaim.[101] The widespread recruitment of lawyers into the reform cause has probably been the most important innovation by most reform organizations. Ralph Nader is only the most visible exponent and example of the profound presence by lawyers in the larger movement. As such, he exemplifies the conviction of most reformers that, in the often quoted words of

56

Justice Brandeis, "lawyers have a social obligation as an economic, intellectual, and managerial elite . . . to act as more than the adjuncts of great corporations."[102]

3. Finally, "another elementary rule for the citizen groups is to form alliances with other citizen organizations."[103] *Alliances* have been understood as essential to consolidate scarce resources, to share experience, to multiply influence, and to generate a broader foundation of public allegiance to their reform cause. Over three-fourths of the groups polled in the 1970s felt that coalitions with other public interest-type organizations were "important" or "very important." "Everyone has to cooperate," they have affirmed repeatedly.[104] While the most desirable coalitional activity celebrated by the reform groups typically has been voluntary and ad hoc, some efforts at sustained coordination by diverse leadership organizations such as the Council for Public Interest Law and Barry Commoner's Citizens' Party have met with some success as well. Big Business Day, the struggle for a federal consumer advocacy agency, the fight for new campaign finance laws, and countless environmental legislative battles are but a few of the enterprises that have united a broad range of groups in such cooperative action.

Mobilizing Government Authority:
The Doctrine of Public Rights

From the beginning, liberal public interest advocates have understood that the mobilization of citizen resources is only one-half of the democratic task at hand. The processes of consciousness raising and generating citizen participation alone "cannot alter the features of democratic government which make it an unreliable curb on special interest," argued Simon Lazarus in his classic statement on public interest perspectives.[105] In addition, the vast power of the federal government must be tapped, mobilized, and consolidated for the reform cause. The new liberals' distinctive strategy to effect this goal has centered on a legal campaign for the promotion of what are often called "public rights" throughout the modern political process.

This doctrine of public rights proposes no comprehensive program or legislative grand design in the traditional sense. Rather, it has constituted at once a general moral orientation and an instrumental strategy for the advancement of a variety of collective goods often ignored or abused in our purportedly profit-obsessed political economy. In the words of one activist, public-rights advocacy is defined simply as "legal representation involving an important right belonging to a significant segment of the public." Such advocacy has been rooted in the assumption that "public rights—must begin to be viewed in a fashion similar to private rights—to be seen as capable of direct evaluation on their merits within the framework of the common-law system."[106] While precedents in the "public trust" doctrines of ancient Roman law and English common law have often been invoked to legitimate such rights, the particular substantive claims by advocates have remained quite diverse. Ecologist Paul Ehrlich has listed fifteen different "inalienable rights," for example, to which can be added a host of other consumer, civil-rights, and democratic-process claims voiced by fellow activists.[107] The most commonly promulgated rights to collective goods concern the preservation of wilderness areas, wildlife, and open spaces; the conservation of natural resources for future generations; the safety and quality of air, water, food, workplaces, and commodity goods; the opportunity for subsidized citizen participation at all levels of government; and, generally, full disclosure of information about the exercise of public and private power. Overall, the basic logic behind claims for such rights has been that "the health of the environment in which man functions is crucial to his well-being in the here and now and for the quality of life in the future."[108]

The efforts to win state recognition for such public-rights claims have been as diverse as the efforts to articulate their content. Nevertheless, the tangible manifestations of the reformers' intent and impact everywhere are apparent. The battle for state support of public rights generally has been waged on two fronts—through various procedural reforms to render political and economic institutions more responsive to public-rights advocates, and through publicly funded subsidies to finance such advocacy. Significant examples of each endeavor are reviewed in the next two sections.

Procedural Reform: Strengthening Citizen Access. A fundamental assumption of the public-rights doctrine has been that substantive change in government policy requires an increase in the responsiveness of existing political processes to social need. The most important strategic goal of most liberal activists thus has been to win legal rights of direct access to government decision-making authority for a variety of new interests. "If the citizen is to regain command of his political institutions, he must begin at the beginning," instructs John Gardner. "And the beginning is 'access'—the citizen's access to his political and governmental institutions." Nader similarly calls access the "great democratizer." "Rights of access ... should be viewed as fundamental in our scale of values as citizens of this country as is the view that we extend to some of the procedural safeguards in the United States Constitution."[109]

This pursuit of access to power generally refers to several related phenomena. One is the institutionalization of rights requiring government to disclose important information and to open decision processes to public view. "To tear away the veil of secrecy," proclaims the Common Cause manifesto, "we must have 'freedom of information' and 'open meetings' statutes in every state of the Union and in the federal government."[110] Such provisions for the citizens' right to know have been designed to enable continuous scrutiny by unofficial public interest watchdogs and to help stir public debate concerning the workings of government. The other key aspect of access has involved expanding rights to direct citizen action within the more visible government process itself. If participation is an important value, after all, then opening up government to new participants is essential. "The opportunity for citizen participation ... at all levels of government is unlimited and must be exploited," encourages one *Ecotactics* essay.[111] It has been hoped that, through direct intervention in state arenas, citizens and their representatives will check abuses that undermine existing laws, initiate new statutory programs, and alter the overall design of federal government policy administration. In sum, what public interest liberals have wanted are the same procedural rights to state access for public interest advocates as have been enjoyed traditionally by large economic producer interests.[112] Nearly every modern political institution now bears the imprint of such expanded rights to public disclosure and citizen participation.

1. One of the very first arenas of reform action, for example, was the candidate-selection processes of national *presidential party organizations*. Convinced that established "party leaders resisted the influence of new blood and ideas," some early activists encouraged numerous reforms to render "parties ... responsive to their own rank and file members."[113] In particular, many public interest advocates supported the McGovern-Fraser committee proposals for increasing the numbers of direct primary elections and changing selection process rules—for expanded notice requirements, non-exclusionary policies, proportional representation, and minority quotas, and against proxy voting and the unit rule—to open the Democratic party to new sources of citizen input. The result was that the total number of

citizen participants in national candidate-selection processes nearly tripled (eleven to thirty-three million per year) during the decade after 1968.[114] In addition, a coalition of public interest groups headed by Common Cause and Nader's Congress Watch successfully pressured for passage of the Federal Election Campaign Act of 1972 to begin "cleaning up the public [election] process." By placing limits on both candidate expenditures and private contributions, by closing legal loopholes, and by creating an official body to enforce the laws, it was hoped that the responsiveness of politicians to the people could be enhanced at the cost of declining special interest corporate influence. During subsequent years, Common Cause in particular has made further campaign reforms a primary continuous commitment. Its leaders initiated and supported several additional revisions to strengthen the election campaign act, as well as filing over a dozen court cases to assure fair interpretation and effective implementation of the statutory guidelines.[115]

2. This same commitment to opening government processes to the direct participation of citizens was extended to the chambers of *Congress*. Public interest reformers for several decades have successfully employed various conventional forms of lobbying tactics—testimony at public hearings, direct mail campaigns, personal contacts, information, exchange, media pressure—to cultivate support for their substantive goals, of course.[116] These tactics have contributed to the successful passage of numerous pieces of federal legislation: the Water Pollution Control Act (1962), the Clean Air Act (1963), the Motor Vehicle Air Pollution Act (1965), the Water Quality Act (1965), the National Traffic and Motor Vehicle Safety Act (1966), the Fair Packaging and Labeling Act (1966), the National Emissions Standards Act (1967), the Deceptive Sales Act (1968), the Coal Mine Health and Safety Act (1969), the National Environmental Policy Act (1970), the Occupational Safety and Health Act (1970), the Consumer Product Safety Act (1972), the Resources Conservation and Recovery Act (1976), the Surface Mining Control and Reclamation Act (1977), the Alaska National Interest Lands Conservation Act (1980), and a host of amendments to many of these and other acts. Yet, many activists felt that further advances were impeded by established procedural rules and practices that insulated congressional officials from public accountability. Spearheaded by the Common Cause OUTS (Open Up the System) program and a general Committee for Congressional Reform, diverse groups thus provided massive pressure leading to more internal reforms of Congress in the mid-1970s than in all the years since 1946. Believing that legislative bodies should

conduct their affairs openly, the reformers lobbied hard for new "government-in-the-sunshine" rights to publication of official voting records, to increased public hearings, to review of committee deliberation records, to lobbying and campaign finance disclosure, and to open congressional party caucuses. Successful pressures to reorganize committee seniority systems aimed to broaden congressional accountability to citizens and colleagues alike. Passage of the Ethics in Government Act (1978) likewise was urged to increase the moral responsibility and responsiveness of representatives to the popular will. Finally, "sunset" legislation was supported to establish periodic review and evaluation of programs often sponsored or subverted by special interests at the expense of public interests. "On balance," argued consumer advocate Peter Schuck, such "ongoing devolution of power in Congress . . . has worked to the benefit of the public interest groups."[117]

3. Perhaps even more important and innovative have been the channels of access opened by public interest advocates in *federal regulatory agencies*. Most activists have believed that the best solution to the problem of unresponsiveness in agencies "is to broaden citizen involvement and participation in administrative decision-making." As the Council for Public Interest Law has summarized, the reformers "have tried to make their case at the administrative level by participating in agency proceedings" to the fullest possible extent.[118] Indeed, for nearly every regulatory agency in the federal government there exists at least one regularly participating public interest watchdog group. The EPA, DOI, and NRC are petitioned routinely by environmentalists, the FTC and SEC by consumer groups, OSHA by Public Citizen and the Health Research Group, the CAB by the Airlines Consumer Action Project, and the FCC by Media Access Project and Citizens Communication Center.

The indispensible rights for such citizen access within agencies were derived from a series of landmark judicial victories in 1966. By expanding the affirmative rights laid out in the older Administrative Procedure Act of 1946, these decisions ordered agencies to admit "those who by their activities and conduct have exhibited a special interest" in agency policy concerns to a broad range of rule-making and adjudicatory proceedings. Such rights, the court held, are essential to assure representative, responsive, and responsible agency action in the public interest.[119] Various other legislative statutes have expanded such access rights in federal agencies further. One critical piece of legislation was the Freedom of Information Act. Initially passed in 1966, this act mandated all federal agencies to respect the rights of citizens to review most federal regulations, policies, research, and internal communications. Convinced that "information . . . is the currency of power" within the government, public interest activists have repeatedly exploited such rights to aid their ongoing battles for influence on agency policy administration throughout the 1970s. Moreover, a coalition of reform groups pushed successfully for amendment legislation in 1974 to further "strengthen the procedural aspects," to reduce exemptions, and to effect "more efficient, prompt, and full disclosure of information" legislated by the original act.[120]

Many specific legislative grants of authority to regulatory agencies have similarly recognized the rights of citizen groups to participation. For example, the National Environmental Policy Act mandated that all federal actions must be preceded by disclosure of environmental impact statements and formal public participation programs for environmental group input into relevant agency decision processes. The result has been to "provide a means by which environmentalists can force administrative decisions affecting the environment into the open for public scrutiny" and collective action. Whether to halt, to delay, or to bargain for alternative regulation of corporate behavior, such rights provisions have proved indispensable tools of leverage for many groups. As environmental scholar Paul Culhane concludes, "The creation of legitimate access to agency decision making is the single most important consequence of NEPA."[121] In addition, other public interest–inspired legislation during the 1970s, such as the Clean Air Act amendments, Water Pollution Control Act, FTC Improvements Act, and Occupational Safety and Health Act, included similar provisions of rights to citizen participation in agency rule making and enforcement proceedings. By the end of 1978, as many as 150 federal grant programs included participation requirements largely as a result of the reformers' influence. Finally, in response to pressure from various public interest groups on agency heads and President Carter, several agencies, such as the FDA and the CPSC, voluntarily institutionalized procedural access rights even further along parallel lines in nearly all aspects of decision making.[122]

Yet another quite different form of access to agencies has been created by the piecemeal recognition of citizen rights to formal representatives or "in-house allies" within the federal regulatory establishment. The goal of such formal public interest representation has been to provide a supplement and complement to, rather than a substitute for, the direct participation by outside citizen groups. In other words, what the activists have sought is to institutionalize a sort of "reverse capture" policy for the public interest constituency much like that long enjoyed by private corporate interests. The most common manifestations of this demand have included formal omsbudsmen in local and state offices, experimental "people's counsels" on state utility boards, and public counsels participating in federal administrative proceedings on behalf of consumers within the Postal Rate Commission, CAB, NHTSA, FDA, and ICC.[123] While the relative power accorded to the new appointees has often been disappointing to the activists, they nevertheless enjoyed considerable in-house administrative support throughout the 1970s. Indeed, President Carter appointed more than sixty activists to high-level administrative posts, including David Hawkins (NRDC) at EPA, Carol Tucker Foreman (CFA) at USDA, Joseph Onek (CLASP) as deputy counsel to the president, Joan Claybrook (Congress Watch) as the head of NHTSA, Gus Speth (NRDC) at CEQ, and Michael Pertschuk, who completed as chairman a decade-long revitalization of the FTC into what has often been labeled the "largest public interest firm" in Washington.[124]

The most ambitious endeavor in this direction has been the highly popular proposal to create a federal agency for consumer advocacy. Although narrowly defeated several times in Congress by massive business-backed lobbying campaigns, such an agency was a very high priority for a large public interest coalition that included Public Citizen, Consumer Federation of America, Consumers Union, Sierra Club, and the Friends of the Earth. The intent of the proposed agency, explains consumer advocate Peter Schuck, was "to assure an effective voice for consumers in the regulatory process."[125] Like other formal institutional allies, the agency would not have acted directly as a watchdog on big business or as a litigant in suits against agencies. Rather, its primary function would have been to act as participating adviser and representative in agency proceedings throughout the federal regulatory establishment. The public interest justification for such grants of authoritative counsel is simple. As Nader puts it, "A number of government agencies ... have represented the business side inside government. This would be the first agency inside government to advance the consumer view."[126]

4. Perhaps the most novel point of access successfully opened by the new reformers has been in the *federal court system*. Indeed, environmentalists such as Joseph Sax have gone so far as to say "that access to the courts ... is the most effective means for citizens to participate directly in environmental decisions and may be the only way to assure that democratic processes are brought to bear on environmental problems."[127] Most important, the ability to mobilize judicial review of agency actions has provided an influential, if indi-

rect, source of leverage to challenge, check, and alter government regulatory policy with respect to corporate power. Successful judicial strategies have been employed to dramatize publicly important issue conflicts and dangers, to expand legal interpretation of significant regulatory statutes, and, of course, to force agencies to adhere to the guidelines of statutes and citizen demands alike. "The problem today is making sure the laws we have helped enact are properly enforced, rather than getting new laws on the books," says William Butler of EDF.[128]

One lever that has pried open court doors to public interest claims is the liberalized interpretation of "standing"—those rules governing who may bring suit—won by the activists. While some congressional acts mandate relatively liberal terms of judicial review to "aggrieved" and "interested" citizens in agencies such as the ICC and FCC, such codified provisions did not exist for most agencies prior to the late 1960s. For these, federal courts generally have determined standing for review of agency action by a test of "legal wrongs." Traditionally, this meant that standing was to be granted to any "person suffering wrong because of agency action." The legal coup executed by the reformers was to win broad interpretation of such "legal wrongs" criteria to include "injuries in fact" and claims within certain "zones of interest" beyond clear statutory or common-law rights.[129] Specifically, from the late 1960s federal courts began to recognize various collective environmental, consumer, aesthetic, and recreational interests as valid legal claims for review. For example, *Sierra Club v. Morton* (1972) stated: "Aesthetic and environmental well-being, like economic well-being, are important ingredients of the quality of life in our society, and the fact that particular environmental interests are shared by many rather than a few does not make them less deserving of legal protection through the judicial process."[130]

Such liberal judicial interpretations of standing as well as of statutory rights to direct participation have enabled the reformers to initiate litigation challenging agency action on the vague provisions of the NEPA, FOIA, OSHA, Clean Air Act, Water Pollution Control Act, and other statutory programs to a degree never before paralleled. It is not surprising that a key section of the as yet unsuccessfully advocated corporate democracy bill would give legislative sanction to such rights of judicial review in all regulatory actions that affect public interests.[131] To these court actions have been added numerous legal challenges to official presumptions of "sovereign immunity," public antitrust suits, private regulatory enforcement (*qui tam*) actions, and a host of other conventional private lawsuits directly against corporations. The most significant among the latter, of course, have been class-action suits against corporate producers to recover damages for pollution, poisoning, and product dangers under common-law liability, nuisance, trespass, and negligence doctrines. In sum, it is no wonder that two movement leaders have proclaimed that "the primary weapon of the public interest practice thus far has been litigation."[132]

5. If expanded indirect access through the courts has constituted the most successful public interest innovation, the radical attempt to open access channels directly within *corporations* themselves proba-bly has achieved the least results. Beginning with the early efforts of Campaign GM to enhance shareholders' democracy through advocacy of sophisticated federal chartering proposals, public interest activists have worked to open, penetrate, and transform the internal practices of large corporate decision-making processes. Nader in particular has long argued for the reform goal of institutionalizing "new rights and remedies [that] can be accorded affected citizens by making the large corporate structure more anticipatory, self-correcting, and sensitive to public needs."[133] The consistent design of such participatory-rights proposals has been summarized in the corporate democracy bill through provisions for citizen rights to mandatory corporate informa-tion disclosure, increased shareholder and independent public constit-uent representation on boards of directors, and constitutional rights protecting privacy, autonomy, and free speech for "whistle-blowing" employees. The underlying logic of each reform proposal is that "if we are to have a democratic society, concentrated economic power has to come under control" by all affected citizens.[134]

Although these collective approaches to direct corporate control have been mostly unsuccessful, liberal activists have utilized the state somewhat effectively to expand individual citizen rights to fair partic-ipation and information disclosure in the economic marketplace. These new rights have been manifested in changing contract and tort case law as well as in formal legislation such as the Fair Packaging and Labeling Act (1966), the Consumer Credit Protection Act (1968), the Deceptive Sales Act (1968), the Consumer Product Warranties Act (1972), and various other laws regulating the inherent fairness of commodity exchange. The underlying faith behind these procedural rights again affirms that "for self-regulating models [of the market] to work justly, the legal system must maintain the structural and the informational conditions."[135]

The Subsidization of Reform. Most reform advocates have been well aware that securing equal legal access to public decision processes still is not enough. The fact is that financial resources expended by large corporate interests in the political process easily dwarf the meager voluntary citizen and foundation contributions that fund the reformers' advocacy efforts. Consequently, reform spokesperson Simon Lazarus argues, institutionalized "methods have to be found to finance legal representation for heretofore neglected public interests before agencies and courts." In other words, the right to state access must be supplemented by rights to funds for advocates similar to affirmative action grants for racial, ethnic, and women's interest claims. And, "in the absence of such affirmative action, the legal victories achieved in the courts may be a hollow prize."[136] The legitimating logic of such public interest demands once more is simple, consistent, and compelling. The reformers have claimed to be asking only for the same government support traditionally extended to big business in the form of price subsidies and tax write-offs.

Of course, many of the government-sanctioned rights discussed so far can be understood to provide substantial public subsidies in themselves. Mandatory information disclosure, appointments to administrative positions, and institutionalization of official in-house representatives all constitute important state financial expenditures for the reform cause. Likewise, the generally liberal tax-exemption privileges discussed earlier as well as greatly reduced postal rates for mass mailing since 1977 have provided indirect government support for many public interest organizations. Indeed, Public Citizen litigator Alan Morrison has speculated that "perhaps the single most important factor in our ability to seek creative solutions to problems is the recently enacted changes in tax laws."[137]

Another crucial indirect form of government financial aid alluded to earlier is the liberal grants of class-action awards by federal courts. A perennial problem for public interest advocates has derived from the disporportion between the great costs of individual legal action and actual monetary returns to compensate for a corporate-imposed injury. However, "class action turns the economics of litigation upside down" by overcoming "the high costs of bringing people with similar interests into communication with each other." The logic of class action, reform lawyer Beverly Moore explains, is that it "allows the individual to sue as a representative of all similarly situated persons and to recover in their behalf the aggregate damages to the entire class."[138] This "absolutely crucial weapon" of diffuse citizen groups was undercut somewhat by several court decisions in the early 1970s that raised minimum individual injury claims and imposed upon citizens the notification costs concerning pending suits. However, public interest exponents have pushed continuously in recent years for various forms of "comprehensive" legislation to rectify these crippling legal guidelines.

Three other forms of governmental direct assistance to the public interest cause also deserve acknowledgment. One involves persistent pressure by the middle-class activists for direct grants and loans from the state such as those provided for the Legal Services Corporation to help the poor. While little success has been achieved in this regard, Congress Watch and the Cooperative League of the USA did manage to win enactment of the National Consumer Cooperative Bank Act to provide $300 million in seed money loans for consumer cooperative development in housing, food, and health care.[139] A second claim of subsidy rights has been won through awards of attorneys' fees in public court cases. Against the older "American rule" denying compensation for successful "private attorneys general" action, federal courts began to rule in the late 1960s that successful plaintiffs were to be awarded litigation fees where such action "furthers the interests of a significant class . . . of persons by effectuating strong congressional policy."[140] The Supreme Court's *Alyeska* decision in 1975 temporarily undercut such provisions by limiting court awards to those policy areas specified by (over fifty) congressional statutes. But public interest and other reform activists responded again with sustained lobbying pressure to expand such entitlements by legislative statute. "Establishing the authority of courts to award attorneys' fees is of the greatest importance for the institutionalization of public interest law in this country," defiantly proclaimed the Council for Public Interest Law. This commitment contributed to the successful enactment of dozens of piecemeal statutory provisions as well to as to support for more comprehensive bills in 1976 and 1980 which sought to enlarge funding rights in many important areas of public interest legal advocacy.[141]

Such court-awarded fees do not extend to costs of direct participation in regulatory agencies, however. Hence a final public interest commitment has developed from the belief "that administrative agencies should underwrite the costs of citizen participation in their proceedings to assure that citizen groups with limited resources can be heard on matters that affect them."[142] This has led to several achievements. Indirect, facilitative subsidies have been won through waivers of transcript and copying fees, through routinized notice of agency actions, and through removal of other costly procedural barriers in agency operation. Moreover, in the late 1970s activists won congressional legislation specifying direct payment of attorney and expert fees—up to $1,000,000 a year by the FTC—for rule-making participation in several agencies. A 1976 decision by the comptroller general likewise freed all agencies to fund "useful" group participation on a voluntary basis, although affirmative responses have been inconsistent and limited to relatively few government offices. Activists also pushed hard for a 1975 public participation in government proceedings bill and various other legislation during the Carter administration to legalize direct agency subsidies for attorneys' fees and other participation costs.[143] As two reformers have concluded, the basic assumption behind the new democratic rights campaign has been that "before non-industry interests can be properly represented before the regulatory agencies, public interest advocates must be adequately financed."[144]

Balancing the Scales of Justice

The consistent logic of this new participatory public-rights ethic has been cast most often in terms of "balancing" and "equalizing" political power in America. "Balancing the Scales of Justice" is thus the title adopted for the financial report of the Council for Public Interest Law. Common Cause and others have embraced Andrew McFarland's concept of "civic balance" as their unofficial rallying cry: "There is a need for citizens to organize into groups and participate in the political process in order to balance the power of the special interests," McFarland argues. Environmentalists similarly seek "much more equal balance of power," insists Conservation Foundation president William Reilly. And Nader's aspiration "to build countervailing forces on behalf of the citizen" expresses the same goal in only slightly different language.[145]

Three primary democratic values inform and justify the commitments behind this orientation of civic balance. The first has been the hope of reappropriating power to the people. "We are committed to helping citizens gain control over decisions affecting their lives by creating new channels of action that will increase the impact of all citizens in those decisions... at all levels of political and economic decision making," proclaims the Environmental Action statement of purpose. For citizens both as discrete individuals and as members of the larger public community, public interest politics has been exalted as a hope for the reassertion of political freedom in modern society. Their "greatest contribution," heralds the Council for Public Interest

Law, "is demonstrating that ordinary citizens can influence and sometimes prevail against powerful political and economic institutions."[146]

Second, as citizens win more autonomous power in public life, so it has been hoped that elite officials will become more responsive, responsible, and accountable to the people as well. "The more leverage citizens have, the more responsive and responsible their officials and fellow citizens will be," predicts ecology lawyer Joseph Sax. David Cohen of Common Cause has agreed: "The goal...is to enhance the representation of 'public interests' and to decrease the influence of 'special interests.'"[147] At the very least, the reformers have contended that a ruling elite that is checked on all fronts by an active citizenry will be less capable of excess, abuse, and tyranny in the exercise of public power. Nader ally Donald Schwartz thus muses that "political experience teaches us that the restraint of power through...republican government best serves the collective interest."[148]

The tangible benefits of this restored civic balance have been demonstrated in the myriad substantive achievements generated by the reformers throughout the 1970s. The list of statutes and social regulations initiated, expanded, and enforced by public interest liberals alone is most impressive. As a result, prominent public and private authorities alike have been mobilized to prevent or remedy a host of serious dangers to society—air and water pollution, toxic-waste poisioning, the risks of nuclear radiation, wilderness loss or abuse, depletion of natural resources, unsafe consumer goods, and unhealthful workplaces. All in all, "something is struggling to be born," the reform advocates once anticipated optimistically. In other words, the third and ultimate goal of the liberal activists has been that these commitments to a reordered social agenda and a more participatory politics might initiate a rebirth, a renewal, and a revitalization of legitimate public authority in the nation. They have "share[d] a belief that the decision-making processes of government are most effective and legitimate when all viewpoints are permitted the opportunity for full airing and critical scrutiny."[149]

Public interest advocates have insisted that such democratic commitments are no luxury or wistful indulgence in idealism; rather, these prescriptions pose a sober imperative to our society at a critical juncture of its history. "Our nation is in the greatest possible danger—danger of losing its vitality and confidence and coherence as a society. Citizen action can play a significant role in averting that danger," John Gardner has exorted. As the reformers have seen it, the imperatives of basic survival and moral right together animate the new reform cause. "Legitimacy, responsibility, and accountability are essential to any power system," liberal lawyer David Riley summarized in 1970, "if it is to endure."[150]

CHAPTER 2

The New Liberal Philosophy

The kind of movement we need is not a new idea. The progressive thinker Herbert Croly suggested it when he spoke of the need for individuals who make up the public to join together in a counter-organization with enough strength to stand up to the other organizations that dominate modern life, those of government, business, and labor. . . . Our past attempts . . . contain basic concepts on which to build a program of reconstruction.

—David Riley

The current generation of populists resembles their turn-of-the-century forebears more nearly than they resemble the New Dealers. The new populism is ambivalent about government. . . . Because the Progressives and the new populists distrust government, they both designed measures to permit private citizens to intervene directly in governmental affairs and to put a halt to official wrongdoing.

—Simon Lazarus

We have seen that the liberal public interest agenda for change has been enormously broad and far-reaching in scope. The sheer breadth of policy issues, arenas, and tactics embraced by the reformers is almost mind-boggling. What has provided the common thread binding these diverse elements of activity, I contend, is the animating liberal political vision shared by most reform advocates. This vision has included much that is familiar within the American political tradition, to be sure, but it has contributed some genuinely innovative ideas to contemporary political discourse as well. My aim in this chapter is to employ a largely historical perspective to delineate in some detail the most distinctive and important dimensions of the new public interest reform philosophy.

71

The Liberal Tradition in America

From the beginning, public interest liberals have been undeniably alarmist in spirit and critical in substance about contemporary American politics. Nevertheless, it is still true that the intellectual mantle with which the recent reformers have dressed themselves has been cut unmistakably from the fabric of ideas that has clothed the American body politic for centuries. As one commentator puts it, "The political perspective that informs the public interest movement is not at all peculiar to the last decade; it is deeply rooted in the American political tradition."[1] Surely the most respected chroniclers of our national history, such as Louis Hartz, Richard Hofstadter, or Daniel Boorstin, would find little challenge in adding to their respective accounts a chapter about the new reform-minded activists.

This should be of little surprise. The leaders of the modern movement themselves seem quite self-conscious about establishing their continuity with the grand legacy of the American political experiment. They have realized that one of the greatest assets of the movement has been its capacity to voice its critical dissent and to frame political alternatives in terms familiar to most Americans. While relative outsiders to the elite establishment, the activists have always kept one foot firmly planted in the mainstream of traditional American ideals. Hence they have commonly invoked the ideas and actions of past heroes like Paine, Jefferson, Madison, Lincoln, and the Roosevelts to justify their own novel projects. As with all earlier American reform efforts, their rhetoric is redolent with the desire to revitalize old causes, to regenerate new faith in inherited ideals, and to return to the "original ideas" of our nation's founders. For example, the authors of *Taming the Giant Corporation* begin their argument by drawing a historical analogy between the fight of American revolutionaries two centuries ago against "the tyrannical potential of unlimited governmental power" and the present efforts of liberal reformers to check the abuses of mammoth corporations set on undermining democracy. "If the Constitutional Convention were convened in 1976 instead of 1787," the authors continue, "can we imagine that this time the Founding Fathers would fail to mention the business corporation?"[2] Similarly, Donald K. Ross's *Public Citizen's Action Manual* opens with Nader discussing the virtues of early American town meetings where "regular participation in government ... was an obligation of every citizen."[3] His intent, clearly, is to emphasize that we epigones have failed to live up to the duties incumbent upon a truly democratic people. A 1975 Common Cause brochure restates these ideas in typically melodramatic terms: "Our nation's founding did not leave a completed task.... they left us a beginning. It is an obligation to define and dislodge the modern obstacles to the fulfillment of our founding principles."[4]

The principles of this inheritance recycled by the new reformers are few and familiar. They define the essence of what Louis Hartz has called the "liberal tradition" in America.[5] At the very core of this tradition is a characteristic uneasiness concerning the inherent conflict between private autonomy and public authority. Around this central tension revolve the most constant of our other political propensities: the pessimistic assumptions about human nature driven by selfish interest satisfaction; the romance with social voluntarism, both through the initiatives of independent individuals and "natural" civic associations; the commitment to equality of economic opportunity and equality before the law; the formulation of public claims in the language of subjective interests and objective rights; the emphasis on formal procedures rather than substantive standards of justice; and the faith in mechanistic, external, impersonal forms of public control such as marketplace competition, countervailing powers, and legal rules to regulate social interaction.

The Liberal Reform Tradition. We have already noted that the modern activists' aspirations further bind them to the American liberal tradition in a narrower, if more commonplace, sense as well. "Liberalism" in this sense has been severed from its original seventeenth-century social and philosophical moorings and employed as a descriptive term signifying something like "progressive reform." This understanding of the term connotes a sense of dynamism, innovation, and experimentation. It implies a measured optimism at odds with the rigid closures and reactions of conservative thought. Two contemporary scholars of American ideologies distinguish this reformist meaning of liberalism as the belief that "politics can be purposeful—it can be the means toward societal solution of shared problems and of qualitatively different and more important ends" than those acknowledged by its philosophical parent.[6] In this sense, the label establishes an affinity of public interest activists specifically with earlier generations of political, legal, and social reformers in America. Indeed, the motives, goals, and strategies of the new activists have often been located within the liberal reform tradition that developed during the previous Populist, Progressive, and New Deal eras. Such a perspective has been adopted in Simon Lazarus's early book *The Genteel*

73

Populists, as well as in several prominent scholarly analyses. Activist David Riley acknowledges the connection clearly:

> [There] has been a recurring pattern in the American past, and it's the emerging pattern today. The strength of the environmental movement and the radical movement generally, the prominence and power of Ralph Nader and Saul Alinsky's campaign against corporations—these are some of the indications that today we may stand on the verge of another resurgence of the . . . instinct that held sway over the Jacksonian era, the Populist and Progressive movements, and the New Deal.[7]

Several prominent characteristics in particular can be identified as constitutive of this ongoing liberal reform tradition in America.

1. The first crucial theme, of course, has been the pervasive suspicion of corporate power.[8] Both old and new reformers have consistently located the source of our civilization's discontents in what Thomas Jefferson called "the aristocracy of our monied corporations which dare . . . to challenge our government to a trial of strength and bid defiance to the laws of our country."[9] The specific terms of understanding those evils inherent in corporate power have varied surprisingly little during the last two centuries. For one thing, corporate hegemony has been diagnosed consistently in instrumentalist rather than class terms. Corporations are usually portrayed as relatively independent, discrete entities fiercely competing for narrow economic interests of profit and market control. John Gardner's colorful comment about national politics is typical: "It's like Times Square on New Year's Eve. Not just your special interests and my special interests but the maritime interests and . . . the bankers . . . the textile manufacturers and so on and on and on."[10] Consequently, reform battles generally have been waged against particular capitalists rather than against the structural foundations of capitalism itself.[11] "Failure to hold individuals accountable allows them to substitute corporate irresponsiblity for individual conscience," contends one environmentalist.[12] For the Progressives, the culprits were G. W. Plunkitt, J. P. Morgan, and Standard Oil; for modern activists, the culprits have been Richard Nixon, James Roche, and, still, Standard Oil. This is well illustrated by the recent emphasis on criminal sanctions and class-action suits as enduring tools of the campaign to limit corporate exploitation. Public interest scholar and activist Jeffrey Berry thus argues that "individuals . . . and not organizations, must be held accountable for their actions."[13]

2. The instrumentalist and individualistic understanding of political power has been parallelled by an almost obsessively moralistic posture among most liberal reformers. In this sense, social problems have been defined not so much as reflections of flaws in inherited cultural traditions and values, but rather primarily as the result of abuses and aberrations by self-interested individuals which depart from those fundamentally sound ideals. The pervasive emphasis upon "corruption" as the disease that plagues an otherwise healthy body politic is the most salient manifestation of this change. "Some of us are simpleminded enough to believe that when public policy is bent... that is corruption, embroider it as you will," admits John Gardner. "Corruption in American politics is nothing new. But today... it is easier for corruption to flourish and spread like a cancer."[14] For both old and new reformers, the message has been the same: "The better classes—the businessmen—are the sources of corruption" which must be opposed and reformed.[15]

This moralistic propensity has often led new and old reformers alike into rather simplistic definitions of the situations at hand. Simon Lazarus notes that traditional liberal reform dogma characterizes social conflicts as clear contests of "the relatively few, extremely powerful 'special' interests against the will and interests of 'the people,' the majority, the masses, or some similar concept."[16] Such a Manichaean vision often takes on conspiratorial, even paranoid, overtones. Indeed the "myth of conspiracy" that Lazarus identifies as guiding modern reformers recalls vividly the Populist and Progressive visions described by Richard Hofstadter and others.[17] Contemporary examples of this perceived battle between exploiters and exploited, vampires and virgins, are plentiful. Corporations have been pictured in the Big Business Day logo as a huge black thumb crushing citizens like fleas, in environmentalist rhetoric as "gigantic monsters tearing away" at the land and sky, and by consumer activists as "mechanical Leviathans" squeezing life from the nation.[18] "The people," by contrast, are described typically as inherently virtuous and innocent. It is as if only the rich and powerful seek profits, and the masses would treat all fairly, promote safety, and clean the air if they had their way. Political struggle thus is charactierized by the activists as a campaign of Davids against Goliaths, of the Lone Ranger against outlaws, and of the little guy against City Hall. One ecology advocate portrays the situation in this way: "We believe there is this giant conspiracy, see. That the heads of Con Ed and Union Oil and the mayor, and for all we know, Spiro Agnew, get together periodically Costra Nostra style in some mountain retreat to figure out how to murder the world. That's *them.* And I am poor little *me.* Victim of environmental larceny."[19] Another consumer advocate has summed up this propensity in more self-conscious terms: "As with any grade B Western, there should be a clearly identifiable villian, as well as a hero wearing a white hat."[20]

Such a morally self-righteous posture has been manifested most notably in the persistent reliance of liberal reformers on muckraking journalistic tactics. If moral weakness has been identified as a pervasive root of evil, then moralistic strictures and admonitions have constituted valuable weapons in the reform battle. Leaders of both old and new movements have agreed that "before there could be action, there must be information and exhortation." As Josiah Royce put it long ago, "This then is the generic reform—the education of public opinion and of the popular conscience."[21] The very style and tone assumed by those in the muckraking tradition boasts of a relentless realism, a passion for getting the inside story, and a drive to get to the bottom of things characteristic of their precursors. The trademark of such a mentality has been the pervasive suspicion about the illusory nature of all appearance and the inherent chasm between rhetoric and reality.[22] Echoing his precursors, Nader thus exhorts us to "stop this terrible emphasis on symbols. Don't fight over symbols, but over reality."[23] It is not surprising that Nader himself acknowledges his debt to Progressive Era muckraker Lincoln Steffans as the model for his early efforts. The very parallels of famous muckraking works in the Progressive and contemporary eras are quite remarkable: David Phillips's *Treason in the Senate* (1906) and Mark Green's *Who Runs Congress?*(1972); Ira Tarbell's *The History of Standard Oil* (1902) and James Phelan and Robert Pozen's *The Company State: Report on Dupont in Delaware* (1973); Samuel Adams's *The Great American Fraud* (1905) and Joseph Page and Mary Win-O'Brien's *Bitter Wages: Report on Disease and Injury on the Job* (1973). Similarly, it takes little imagination to see in contemporary journals such as *The Nation, Mother Jones, Harper's,* and *New Republic* formats for public exposure much like *McClure's, Collier's,* and *Hampton's* in an earlier age.

3. These moralistic tendencies have been joined by a profound commitment to pragmatic, result-oriented instrumental action. This curious pairing of propensities is not as contradictory as it may seem. Because most citizens have been united by commitments to a Lockean liberal consensus, the invocation of moralistic motivations has often constituted a powerful strategic weapon of, rather than an alternative to, pragmatic political action in America.[24] This unique fusion of moralistic intentionality and instrumental, result-oriented thinking

found its most profound expression in the doctrine of philosophical pragmatism that emerged to inform the explosion of Progressive reform early in this century. Ever skeptical of what William James called "a priori reason, fixed principles, and closed systems," liberal reform advocates in that era self-consciously began to measure their moral ideals above all by their ability to pass through "the gate of purposive action."[25] "If ideas . . . are instrumental to an active organization of the given environment, to a removal of some specific trouble and perplexity . . . they are reliable, sound, valid, good, true," insisted John Dewey. "If they fail to clear up confusion . . . they are false."[26]

Contemporary public interest liberals have to a large degree continued this legacy. They are not moralists who disdain practical politics, as some critics have suggested; they see themselves as giving effective voice to practical social goals left unrealized by romantic radicals in the 1960s. "Nice sentiments are not enough," ecologist Joseph Sax argues; rather, committed reformers must focus their energies on the "dreary task of dealing with the . . . problems that must be met and resolved in a thousand individual cases."[27] John Gardner has urged the same counsel: "Purity of motive is no substitute for well-conceived, well-executed, sustained action," he repeats often.[28] Indeed, many public interest advocates have often seemed obsessed with demonstrating the realism and tough-mindedness of their campaigns. Their handbooks and treatises exhorting citizen action thus are carefully tempered by a concern for tactical navigation between the rocky shores of ideological extremes. Careful to avoid loaded terms such as "capitalism" and "socialism," they have expressed disdain for the "childhood affirmations," "false illusions," and "empty moralism" of those on the far Right and Left alike. Emphasizing instead the subtle "art of the possible," they stick to "winnable" issues like flies to a carcass. As a Public Citizen worker has observed, "In the Nader movement, the issue comes first." "The concrete nature of the goal is crucial," echoes Gardner.[29] Suspicious of academia, of think tanks, and even of theorizing itself, most activists remain wary of any intellectual activity that might "lessen the sense of urgency and delude people into thinking they are acting."[30] Much like their Progressive and New Deal precursors, therefore, they have frequently likened their efforts to doctors curing the diseases of the body politic or mechanics tinkering with a broken governmental machine: "Making government work better is just as practical as a problem in repairing and redesigning any other machinery," proposes one group newsletter.[31] All that is needed, urges another, is a "vision in their heads," "a monkey wrench in their hands," and a "simple operating philosophy: with rare exception, we do nothing but fight specific battles."[32]

4. This peculiar mix of pragmatic strategy and moralistic intention points to yet another striking similarity between old and new reformers: that of their overwhelmingly middle-class professional social status. On one hand, the credentials of both old and recent reform activists as lawyers, labor lobbyists, and government officials has provided them the experience and credibility necessary for successful action against the establishment. As Robert Rabin has observed, long experience and specialized training has enabled many public interest lawyers in particular "to develop sufficient expertise in highly complex regulatory areas... to litigate [and lobby] on equal terms with the most highly accomplished private law firms."[33] On the other hand, the reformers' social status has largely conditioned the character of their perceptions about desirable change. Historian Richard Pells's assessment of Progressive and New Deal reformers, that "seeking to represent the 'public' as a whole... they spoke only for the bourgeoise," is largely true also for the recent liberal activists, as is illustrated in the following pages of this volume.[34] The tendencies to emphasize issues of individual moral responsibility, to define social ills as matters of ethical corruption, and to preach the gospel of good citizenship all reflect the middle-class, professional origins common to old and new reformers alike. Even many of the basic issues around which the recent groups have rallied—safety and quality of consumer goods, workplace health and safety, conservation of natural resources, tax reform—recall those voiced in earlier periods.

At the same time, the sense of disillusionment, rebelliousness, and acerbically critical temperment exhibited by each generation of reformers has reflected a common self-perception as outsiders and pariahs to the existing elite establishment. Robert Wiebe's interpretation of Progressives as a new vanguard of the emerging middle class seeking to transform society around new values in particular invites interesting parallels with the modern public interest phenomenon.[35] Indeed, much of the heated debate about the recent evolution of a new class of professional liberal elites recalls unmistakably the analysis of the "status revolution" through which scholars have interpreted earlier Progressive reform motivations.[36]

5. Modern public interest activists have also carried on the central reform faith of the Populist, Progressive, and New Deal eras that the best antidote for big business is big government. As Theodore Roosevelt explained, in order to deal with the great corporations "on terms of equality," it "becomes necessary for... ordinary individuals to com-

bine . . . to act in their collective capactity through the biggest of all combinations called government."[37] Of course, such reliance on government for control of corporate power has always fallen short of the demand for public ownership of productive forces. Nader typically extols the "modesty" of the movement's efforts to alter the balance of power by noting that "there is little by way of demanding basic ownership changes," much as had Louis Brandeis or Thurman Arnold before him.[38] Consequently, not only is the rhetoric about antitrust and restoration of market competition as common among today's liberals as among those of earlier generations, but the underlying acceptance of regulation against big business as the most effective means of control for the public welfare is still an enduring reality. As Pells argued of earlier reformers, so are their modern counterparts "ambivalent in their analysis and contradictory in their legislation, . . . constantly hovering between the desire to break up the monopolies and restore laissez faire on the one hand, and the need to make corporate capitalism function more effectively on the other."[39]

6. Modern public interest liberals have also harbored a profound ambivalence about expanded state authority, much as did their reformist ancestors. Specifically, they have stipulated that more government is desirable only if it is rendered more popularly accountable for its actions; in short, the best remedy for the corrupted state of democracy has been understood to be more democracy within the state. As Lazarus has noted, "Both themes—'big government' and 'direct democracy'—are opposite sides of the same ideological coin." Both commitments seek to "enhance the capacity of the public, through the mechanisms of democratic government, to control the special interests that dominate the nation's economic and social structure."[40] And again, in many of the same policy areas—electoral reform and party organization, public disclosure requirements, reform of legal codes, statutes, and professional ethics, extension of civil rights—we can hear today distinct echoes of earlier efforts by liberal reformers to ensure popular control over public life.

The Reform Tradition Reconsidered. To identify the modern public interest activists as merely new spokespersons for old ideas can be superficial and misleading, however, for the history of liberal reform activism in America is not nearly as uniform as is often assumed. For example, many scholars—most notably, Christopher Lasch, R. Jeffrey Lustig, Michael Rogin, Bruce Palmer, and Lawrence Goodwyn— have shown that the origins, character, and aspirations of Populist radicals were quite distinct from, even opposed to, the efforts of later

Progressive and New Deal liberals.[41] Populism was gounded in the experiences of farmers in the 1870s and 1880s suffering from steady price erosion, inabilities to control land, declining political clout, and other uncertainties amid a rapidly changing economic environment. Building upon the older Greenback tradition, the Populist movement aimed to build a cross-sectional, multiracial coalition of urban workers and rural farmers who sought to explore the democratic possibilities of locally constituted, politically determined cooperative institutions. In general, Populists were more interested in escaping from, rather than participating in, the emerging culture of corporate liberalism.

By contrast, the Progressive Era signaled political aspirations of quite a different sort. While borrowing much of the Populist rhetoric celebrating "the people," individual self-reliance, and moral community, Progressivism as a model for social change meant different things to different people; it constituted a far more complex labyrinth of voices, interests, and perspectives than its more insular Populist counterpart. But beneath all of this complexity thrived a generally identifiable aspiration for unity, integration, stability, efficiency, and social control—collectively, what Robert Wiebe has called "the search for order."[42] Unlike Populist designs, however, the terms of this restructuring were thoroughly middle-class, urban, cosmopolitan, and, above all, pro-corporate. Whether through humanitarian, legal, technocratic, or religious forms of expression, the Progressive impulse was formulated and developed in cooperation with those who enjoyed a dominant position in the land—"the more sophisticated leaders of America's largest corporations and financial institutions."[43] And although undeniably more progressive in its redistributive impact, New Deal reform politics largely continued along the same lines.[44] Such "twentieth-century American reform," Goodwyn argues, "has in a great many ways proven to be tangential to matters the Populists considered the essence of politics."[45]

As assumptions about a unitary liberal reform tradition have tended to obscure such critical differences among earlier movements, so can they tend to discount the most unique elements of contemporary public interest liberalism as well.[46] The fact is that the most recent activists have introduced both a new key and unique instrumental arrangements into the continuing chorus of American liberal reform. We should not be misled by familiar bars in their rhetorical melody. However similar in various ways to earlier generations of middle-class liberals, the new activists have constructed a genuinely novel response to the dilemmas and deficiencies of contemporary corporate capitalism. Indeed, while not uniform in their understandings, the new reformers often have expressed a self-consciousness about the innovative departures initiated by the movement which distinguishes it from past efforts. Activist Simon Lazarus's catchy title *The Genteel Populists* may be somewhat misleading about the American reform tradition, for example, but his book-length critique of earlier reform efforts itself is a classic expression of public interest originality. Activist David Riley similarly sums up the dissatisfaction with previous liberal reform in this way:

> We have never really had the kind of sustained consumer movement to force a restructuring of the whole system. The Populist movement was too shallow. . . . The Progressive movement . . . resulted in correcting only the worse abuses, while leaving the general system of unaccountable corporate power intact. The New Deal . . . goal was economic recovery, not a restructuring that would provide public corporate accountability.[47]

The sources of this criticism are not difficult to understand. As noted earlier, the widespread exposure to academic criticisms of earlier reform efforts as well as to the new radicalism of the 1960s convinced many of the modern reform leaders of the need for a more sophisticated approach to overcome the failures of the past.[48] In fact, perhaps the most salient factor distinguishing the modern activists from most of the previous reformers has been their self-conscious commitment to just such an ambitious mode of practical "political" action. And it is this posture as innovators as well as imitators within the American reform tradition that we must explore further to illuminate the significance of public interest liberalism.

The New Philosophy of Public Ethics

Redefining the Public Space. The first important dimension of liberal public interest innovation concerns its ethical challenge to the status quo. Although similar to earlier reformers in their curious mix of moralistic and pragmatic tendencies, the recent activists have staked out new ethical ground in several senses.[49] To begin with, the new reform campaign has been committed to expanding dramatically both the scope and character of legitimate debate about potential state policy action within modern public life. As a result, myriad choices concerning a wide range of social concerns—in matters of environmental protection, energy conservation, worker health, product safety, commodity exchange—have been shifted successfully from

81

private to political forums of deliberation and hence relocated from within the lax authority of market mechanisms and common law to that of federal government regulation. "If we are to solve these problems, if we are to ever regain command over the situation, we must look first to our political and governmental institutions, for politics and government are the chief instruments through which we can achieve our shared purposes."[50] Such government regulation is not unprecedented, of course. Pollution controls were established at the individual state level as far back as the 1880s, and federal workplace and environmental regulations were initiated early in this century. But the sheer diversity and quantity of such social demands for increased federal government action articulated by the new activists has constituted a challenge to corporate prerogative almost unparalleled in American history. As Nader defines it, "The principle call is almost primeval in nature. It is a call for corporations to stop stealing, stop deceiving, stop corrupting politicians with money, stop monopolizing, stop poisoning the earth, air, and water, stop tyrannizing people of conscience within the company, and start respecting long-range survival needs and rights of present and future generations."[51]

This politicization of new issues has contributed to nothing less than a fundamental redefinition of the legal boundaries between politics and markets, state and society, and public and private life in modern America. It is imperative, argues Mark Green, that "the older notions about the clear distinction between the public sector and private sector should give way to a new conceptualization."[52] On one hand, we have seen that the reformers have attempted to elevate new public rights of citizens "to put them on a plane with traditional private property rights" of economic producers.[53] On the other hand, the activists have advocated a fundamental transformation in the legal status of corporate producers as well. They have recognized that corporations are not small businesses grown up nor merely special interest lobbying groups. While privately owned and independently managed, the modern corporation is collective in essence and public in function. The fact is that the historical emergence of the corporation as the center of economic production has generated new forms of institutional dependency for citizens which touch nearly every dimension of contemporary life. "For most Americans," activists assert, "there is no escape from the corporate embrace." Through both statutory mandate and direct citizen action, therefore, the movement has aimed at "giving public control, or at least substantial influence, at every point where the corporation has contact with the public."[54] In short, the reformers have insisted that contemporary corporate policies, processes, and executives be increasingly scrutinized according to public criteria that have long been reserved primarily for official government action.

Such efforts signal the political implementation of ideas long espoused by progressive students of American political economy. The belief that corporations should be treated by law as private governments and discrete political systems rather than as private property has been widely endorsed at least since Adolph Berle and Gardiner Means first recognized the formal separation of ownership and control of economic power over a half-century ago. The list of respected exponents of the position, including Robert Gordon, James March, Richard Eells, Peter Bachrach, Arthur S. Miller, and Abram Chayes, is long and diverse. Robert Dahl's arguments have been particularly influential to the modern reform advocates. "Whatever may be the optimal way of governing the great corporation, surely it is a delusion to consider it a private enterprise," he argues in a movement publication. "Why should people who own shares be given privileges of citizenship . . . denied to other people who also make vital contributions to the firm?"[55]

These efforts to politicize new issues and values point more toward a qualitative than a quantitative transformation in government authority over society. The activists do believe that "a democratic government must eventually attempt to impose some form of public authority over private power."[56] To this end, public interest reformers have supported the creation of more new federal agencies (twenty-nine) since the mid-1960s than emerged from the New Deal heyday (sixteen) between 1930 and 1945. However, the new liberals are not uncritically pro-government. Rather, they are "selective statists" who seek to reorder the substantive priorities of government action away from certain goals and toward other new ones. Theodore Lowi has labeled their redefinition of the New Deal political agenda a sort of "neo-laissez faire idealism": "It anticipates the substantial deflation of government in general with a strengthening of certain aspects of government in particular." As Gus Speth of NRDC puts it, "A clear distinction must be made between efforts to reform regulation and those to deform it."[57]

The new balance sought by the activists derives from a concerted shift in the kinds of state control from old "economic" to new "social" forms of federal regulatory policy.[58] Older types of regulation, mostly created during the Progressive and New Deal eras, were intended primarily to stabilize and rationalize competition among private producers to offset the dislocating effects of the market. They aimed not to limit the capacities for corporate production, but to eliminate irrational competitive practices and coordinate previously undirected economic development. This kind of regulation was typified by the mandates of agencies like the Interstate Commerce Commission, Civil Aeronautics Board, and Federal Communications Commission. Such economic regulation characteristically was focused narrowly on specific sectors of related industries, delegated through broad mandates of discretionary executive authority, and restricted primarily to the limited ends of governing prices, market control, and professional entry. While these laws often emanated from initiatives by industries seeking to protect themselves, their formal rationale was to preserve market competition against the destructive tendencies of big-business monopolies.[59]

It is this type of regulation encouraged by older liberal reformers which has been the object of much of the modern reform wrath. Whether a result of corporate capture, corruption, or inertia among agency officials, such regulation is accused of undermining rather than encouraging effective market performance. "Defects of design and process often result in regulatory policies which often frustrate, rather than promote, economic competition," write Green and Nader.[60] Thus, argue the reformers, if the problem is overregulation based on "irrational economics," the most effective remedy is to implement selective deregulation. Hence the significant if unevenly successful efforts of liberal reformers to reduce widespread state interference that allegedly promotes only higher profits and poorer performance in the trucking, dairy, sugar, maritime, airline, and other concentrated industries.

The modern reformers have advocated that deregulation should be attempted with a scalpel, however, not a scythe or an ax. "It should not be applied to non-economic regulation which aims to complement, rather than replace, a market system incompetent or uninterested in fulfilling certain needs."[61] In the place of the old "corporate welfare state," new forms of protective "social" welfare regulation have been extended for the benefit of all. This new regulation is typically embodied in the mandates of agencies like the Occupational Safety and Health Administration, the Environmental Protection Agency, the National Highway Traffic Safety Administration, and the Consumer Product Safety Commission. It is distinctive in that it concerns primarily functional interests of the entire society rather than any specific business sectors and hence is binding across a broad range of industrial and commercial settings. Furthermore, whereas older legislative statutes usually were highly discretionary in the legal authority delegated to executive officials, new statutes such as the Clean Air Act tend to be extremely detailed, complex, and means-specific.[62]

These relatively new forms of social regulation and legal accountability have constituted fundamental qualitative departures from the inherently capitalist terms of older liberal regulation in other ways as well. First, the older types of regulation greatly respected the fundamental capitalist principle of private control over productive processes. Most earlier laws applied to corporate enterprises only at the.level of market exchange, beyond the actual productive activity itself. Hence, legislation seeking to prevent monopoly, to maintain food quality, and to protect worker health all focused on issues of output, entry, or prices rather than directly on how production was controlled and managed. To be sure, much of the recent public interest pressure for antitrust action, fair-trade legislation, and productliability claims has only extended this type of regulation to new areas and with new intensity. Yet much of modern regulation by OSHA, EPA, and FDA also applies directly to the actual production process itself—to labor practices, machine designs, work environment, technological standards—in ways that surpass older consumer- and laborsponsored regulation. In other words, the movement has extended public authority yet further over managerial prerogatives within the most sacred realm of capitalist autonomy. The workplace itself has become contested terrain of public significance.[63]

Another advance from earlier regulation is a change of sorts in the basic character of authoritative social control by the liberal state over modern capital. Capitalism, Marx argued, progresses through the transformation of labor and other human relations into commodities. This commodification process transforms the need-related "use values" of goods, services, and other human dependencies into alien, "exchange values," primarily transacted through the formal medium of money. In this way, for example, labor becomes a commodity in that workers sell and capitalists buy their labor power. This contractual relationship thus enables employers to entice workers to accept extreme health risks in exchange for higher wages, or to make significant profits from shoddy merchandise sold at low cost to poor consumers. Of course, earlier regulations established restrictions on the sale of consumer goods (health standards, safety warnings) and labor power (maximum hours, minimum wages) to provide services and benefits ignored in so-called voluntary market exchanges.[64] Yet this regulation for the most part only altered the terms of market choices between trade-offs of risk and return; it aimed primarily to structure more rationally, rather than to replace, market exchanges of goods, services, and labor. For example, price supports sought to maintain quality by discouraging intense competition in food and dairy industries. Even the workers compensation and social security systems were based on market principles: people were to be paid, after the fact, for a life of work, for injury, or even for death.[65]

Many public interest legal reforms continue this same logic, as demonstrated by efforts to expand class-action awards for injuries from corporate negligence, to raise oil prices to encourage conservation, to win subsidies for sewage treatment plants, to use tax incentives to reward investment in antipollution equipment, and to impose monetary fines upon corporate lawbreakers. Yet, in addition, by replacing market control with legally authoritative standards in new areas of social concern, much new regulation has also effectively "decommodified" important domains of public policy implementation. In other words, certain basic commitments—to clean air, secure incomes, healthful workplaces, safe products, and controllable energy resources—have become increasingly codified as legal mandates of specified action binding upon corporate managers and unalterable by contractual bargains with employees, by deals with consumers, or even by monetary payment in fines to government and compensation for damages to citizens. The logic of such regulation has been to undercut the ability of capitalist producers to lure the public with unsafe or unfair options through the promise of high wages or lower prices. Examples include federal air and water pollution cleanup targets, OSHA standards of "maximum feasible protection," mandatory installation of automobile seatbelts and other safety equipment, FDA "no-risk" bans on saccharin and many drugs, restrictions on residential housing in wilderness areas, and far-reaching civil tort remedies mandating injunctive and nonmonetary punitive actions. All in all, these new legal guidelines have constituted a novel and controversial approach to implementation of public standards largely independent of the market mechanism.[66]

A New Public Ethics. These new forms of social regulation have been guided by basic ethical principles that challenge the very foundations of the liberal corporate order in a yet more general sense. It is important to recognize that traditional forms of regulation intitiated since the Progressive Era were motivated by the desire "to create a modern economy that would deliver the enormous growth and other benefits made possible by large-scale, technologically progressive, corporate capitalism," argues Paul Weaver.[67] In short, economic expansion and capital accumulation were considered the highest priority of the effort to increase the public welfare. By contrast, perhaps the most radical dimension of the modern public interest program has been its fundamental questioning of just this cardinal principle. Following the lead of countercultural thinkers such as Paul Goodman, Theodore Roszak, and Herbert Marcuse as well as doomsday ecologists such as Paul Ehrlich and Barry Commoner, the new activists have often insisted that our long-accepted commitment to economic growth undermines rather than promotes the welfare of most citizens in society. "Growth for the sake of growth is the ideology of the cancer cell," ecologist Edward Abbey has mused.[68] This explains the meaning of David Riley's seemingly radical complaint that earlier "progressives in power always thought in terms of a capitalist framework." The new reformers have not contested their liberal precursors' acceptance of capitalism per se, of course. Rather, they have sought only to thwart the rapacious impulses to ceaseless material growth in production and consumption promoted by large corporations which subvert the virtues and exacerbate the vices of an inherently humane capitalist system. Riley thus contends typically that the "performance of our economy can no longer be measured by its wealth, but must be measured by its effects on men, politics, and values."[69]

Such a shift from expansionist economic to protective social priorities is built upon four fairly specific arguments variously cited in criticism of the growth ethic.

1. *The ecological imperative.* Probably of greatest importance to the reformers is that "there is serious doubt about whether we can maintain [growth] ecologically."[70] On one hand, maximizing productive capacity necessarily requires immediate threats to human health and welfare from air and water pollution, industrial waste, nuclear radiation, and workplace risks. While corporations reap the benefits of growth, Nader argues, "society inevitably pays the bill in impaired health, damaged property, and aesthetic despoliation."[71] On the other hand, rapid economic expansion hurries the long-term depletion of natural resources. A general awareness about the fragility of our interdependence with nature has convinced many reformers that the assumptions behind unlimited growth are not only unrealistic, but suicidal as well. Paul Ehrlich espouses a common reform sentiment in his claim that "Western society is in the process of completing the rape and murder of the planet for economic gain."[72] In sum, material growth is understood to pose a serious threat for the security of life in both present and future generations.

2. *Inevitability.* As we approach what Andrew Hacker called the "end of the American era," some activists have accepted slow growth as an inevitable fact. Arguing that the contemporary declines in productivity "are not temporary aberrations in a basically sound economy," Barry Commoner notes that "a fundamental change may be taking place in the American economy, ushering in a time of slower growth, lower investment, and the need of more people to work."[73] The explanation behind such a position has varied from increasing world market competition to decreasing domestic consumer demand to the previously mentioned fact of resource depletion. Whatever the stipulated cause, the basic challenge the liberals pose concerns not how to produce more, but how to use best what we have already.

3. *The rejection of materialism.* Some reformers have seen such a decline in economic growth as an opportunity for enhanced freedom and welfare rather than as a setback. Their reasoning has been that the acceptance of limits on affluence would deter the rampant American obsession with material self-indulgence, hedonism, and cupidity now impeding our concern for genuine self-development. "One of the weaknesses of our age is an apparent inability to distinguish between our needs and greeds," they have suggested.[74] Consumption must be balanced with conservation, civilized wants must be adjusted to nature's "necessity," and desires for quantity must be tempered by emphasis on quality. While this emphasis on alternative forms of self-development according to our "inner needs" varies from quasi-religious and individual to political and collective endeavors, the rejection of increased material abundance in the name of human freedom and welfare has been pervasive among the new advocates.

4. *Injustice and empire.* Activists have often identified the impulse to boundless economic growth with American propensities for exploitation of others. At home, the demand for growth only justifies high unemployment, low wages, and inflation—in short, austerity measures for the nonaffluent—to accumulate capital for reinvestment.[75] The emphasis on growth thus avoids rather than solves the problem of unequal distribution. "If the present unequal distribution of [wealth] continues apace, the country is likely to be in shambles from internal strife." The consequences of American economic expansion for the world are even more appalling. That the United States consumes over one-half of the world's consumable resources is wholly unjustifiable in itself. But "if the American economy is to continue expanding...then such an imbalance will have to continue, even increase." Such blatant imperialism, the reformers protest, must be halted. "People over profits" thus is their motto.[76]

All in all, argues one spokesperson, a central theme of the public interest challenge has been that our "gains in material well-being are being bought at considerable social and political cost." We therefore must learn to adapt ourselves to our historical "givens" and responsibilities, reform activists insist. We must "design the economic system to fit mother nature."[77] To cite Kenneth Boulding's popular terms, we must effect the shift from a "cowboy" economy to a "spaceman" economy. Whereas the former is committed to expansion as an end in itself, in the latter "the essential measure of the success of the economy is not production and consumption at all, but the nature, extent, quality, and complexity of the total capital stock, including in this the state of the human bodies and minds included in the system." Whether in terms of controlled growth, no growth, or a steady-state economy, the reformers have argued that the foundations of American public policy must be rooted in new social principles of human need and natural scarcity.[78]

This ethical challenge departs from that of earlier Progressive and New Deal–era reformers in yet another important way. As we have seen, public interest liberals have reaffirmed the older reform concern that corruption among the powerful few undercuts the maintenance of civic virtue among all citizens within society generally. "Unless there's really an exemplary performance by the people who've got the power, and the privilege and status, you can't expect a similar restraint on the part of people who have less," argues Nader, echoing Jane Addams, Lincoln Steffens, and other earlier reformers.[79] But whereas the primary concern of the latter was to instill middle-class "values, manners, and morals" of hard work and accumulation in poor immigrant workers, the new reform activists have challenged key aspects of those middle-class values themselves which now legitimate our indulgent, privatistic consumer society. Indeed, the primary thrust of the reformers' survivalist ethic and back-to-nature slogans has been to urge affluent Americans to restrain their boundless wants for wealth and to resist those well-organized corporate forces that encourage them. Consequently, contemporary public interest liberals have proven themselves "socialists of the heart" at odds with the traditional American "emphasis on the success ethic, on materialism, [and] on commercialism" to a degree unparalleled by earlier reformers.[80] In fact, it is not difficult to understand the new social regulatory ethic as an implicit effort to overcome in large part the fundamental division within capitalist culture identified by Marx. In his seminal work "On the Jewish Question," Marx wrote; "Where the political state has attained to its full development, man leads, not only in thought, but in reality, in life, a double existence. . . . He lives in the political community, where he regards himself as a communal being, and in civil society, where he acts simply as a private individual, treats men as means . . . and becomes the plaything of alien powers."[81] Through the attempted expansion of formal public authority over private power, and of principles esteeming quality over quantity, the new activists have encouraged the ascendance of universal concerns for common social needs to a degree rarely advocated in concrete terms within the American political tradition.

The New Philosophy of Political Forms

The ethical challenge raised by the new reformers has extended to the very institutional processes in which public policy is formulated. Specifically, public interest liberals have labored to expose not only the political character of the modern corporation, but also the invidious corporate character of the modern state. "The corporate state is an immensely powerful machine," argues Charles Reich, "indifferent to any human values . . . [and] subject to neither democratic controls, constitutional limits, nor legal representation."[82] In other words, the second significantly novel dimension of the recent reform movement has been it extension of long-standing liberal criticism about the undemocratic structure of big business to criticism of big government on much the same grounds.[83] This is what Andrew McFarland implies by labeling public interest advocates "civic skeptics." More like their contemporary right-wing opponents than traditional liberal statists, they have identified the existing governmental organization as at least as much a problem as a solution. They "no longer believe that government, as it is constituted at the present, can accomplish great social reforms."[84]

Of course, we have seen that such an ambivalence about big government is itself hardly new to the liberal reform tradition. Walter Lippmann recognized long ago that "the real problem with collectivism is that difficulty of combining popular control with administrative power."[85] The Progressives thus attempted to democratize government through reliance on primaries, initiatives, referenda, and other electoral reforms along with the creation of a "neutral" administrative apparatus of experts to increase the accountability and responsiveness of government. Yet it is just such goals of extending electoral control directly over legislators, and indirectly over administrative elites, which have drawn the most skepticism from the modern liberals.

"The ballot isn't enough," insists Gardner. The problem, explains Joseph Sax, is that "none of these [earlier reforms] gets to the heart of the matter—a fundamental realignment of power."[86] First, electoral accountability is an insufficient tool for controlling the complex apparatus of the administrative state. "To take office is not to take power," David Riley claims, "particularly in a capitalist society where so much power lies beyond the reach of the electorate."[87] Moreover, electoral institutions provide little opportunity for genuine democratic participation and control of government decision making. The various schemes to increase control of elected elites over bureaucrats still "continue to consider the citizen as an outsider, but not an active initiator with the authority to tip the balance of power."[88]

The public interest approach to democratizing state power, by contrast, has differed in two ways. First, activists have largely shifted their reform energies away from the traditional emphasis on electoral activity and party building to a more direct focus on the policy-making process itself within the legislative and administrative arenas of the modern state. "It is futile to rail against unpleasant outcomes if one will not take the effort to master the details of the policy process which yielded the outcome," professes one ecologist.[89] Eschewing the older liberal desire to keep public administration above politics, public interest activists have thus deemed the ability to lobby, to bargain, and to roll logs with the best of the Washington power brokers as the key hope for their success. Second, they have attempted at the same time to change the very character of those policy-making processes. In particular, the recent reform movement "to extend control over big business is tempered by a deep citizen distrust of [those] overly bureaucratic institutions" in which older liberals once invested their hopes for effective political management.[90] This skeptical attitude toward bureaucratic policy processes has been the central thrust of Lazarus's critique of the New Deal "grand-design" mentality, of Nader's vitriolic exposés of government agencies and corporate hierarchies, of Fellmeth's strictures against the regulatory-industrial complex, of Sax's hostility to "bureaucratic middlemen," and of Gardner's rejection of the need for "more bureaus, more departments, more officials, and more regulations" as the answer to social problems. It likewise is the central meaning of Mark Green's awkward claim that "the system is a corporate socialism hiding behind the myth of competitive enterprise."[91] Such a collapsing of distinctions between corporate liberalism and state socialism may be rather dubious, but the implicit antibureaucratic, antimanagerial bias it reveals nevertheless is clear.

While only marginally populist in character, public interest activists thus have offered a radical critique of what might be called the inherited "ideology of form" governing modern liberal state organization.[92] A primary concern of the self-consciously "post-Roosevelt-Johnson" liberals has been to address the widespread "dissatisfaction with the functioning of the institutions of the national government," acknowledges Common Cause leader David Cohen.[93] If the fundamental goal of earlier reformers was to extend the control of public over private bureaucracies, that of the recent advocates has been to reform the hierarchical, closed, elitist character of both bureaucracies so as to revitalize participatory democracy within and between them. Ecologist Hazel Henderson notes that "the same demand for greater participation in the decisions that affect their lives" goes hand in hand with "disaffection with large bureaucracies of both business and government."[94] It is not enough that "new committees, task forces, and commissions proliferate" to implement the new social programs desired by the liberal radicals. This would "seem little more than a revival of old institutional mistakes with new names." What is needed is an alteration of the very organization as well as the functions of existing government and corporate decision-making authority. "It is not sufficient to rely upon external forces and standards to humanize corporate decisions," Nader has proclaimed. "The internal governance of institutions must be addressed."[95]

Such a concern about the forms of modern public and quasi-public institutional organization explains in large part the procedural emphasis that characterizes the plethora of reforms discussed in Chapter 1. The primary long-term goal of the new activists "is to help remove the fixes, deals, and other collusive arrangements that rig the political market."[96] Of course many of these procedural reforms have been essentially instrumental in design. Their purpose has been to facilitate opportunities for the effective exercise of power by the liberal advocates over policy concerns such as consumer, energy, tax, environmental, and subsidy issues. As Phillip Moore explains, an axiom of effective politics is that "you have to deal with the way . . . decisions are made. . . . You have to deal with the power base itself."[97] This is the thrust of David Vogel's insightful argument about the similarity of public interest group tactics to those of their business rivals. What the new reformers have wanted, he argues, "are the same opportunities to influence public policy that business has historically monopolized."[98] In these terms, the pragmatic commitments of the new activists thus appear hardly reformist at all; they simply represent a new addition to the mainstream of American interest-group politics.

Yet such instrumental policy orientations should not obscure the more radically reformist challenges posed by the activists concerning the very organizational structures that constitute the truly democratic polity. The new liberals have aspired, not merely to join a preestablished process on conventional terms, but to transform at once both the substantive and procedural character of the entire political system through public-rights advocacy. Charles Halpern and John Cunningham, two influential public interest lawyers, have put it this way:

> It is important to evaluate the new practice within its broad context to understand that ultimately it is not simply concerned with environmental or consumer causes, but with something much deeper. Its concern is with the fundamental structural reform . . . of the way public bureaucracies dispose of public policy questions. The process of reforming corporate and bureaucratic power begins slowly with manageable issues, but its ultimate aim is far reaching.[99]

And it is this self-conscious struggle to render those administrative institutions that are now public in *function*—the state, corporations, labor unions, parties—more public in *form*—open, accountable, representative—that most distinguishes the new liberal activists as a force within the prevailing political establishment. As Sax argues, the reformers stress that we "must never lose sight of the fact that it is how we are governed that is an issue." The ultimate object of environmental cases is "not simply to obtain a legal precedent isolated from the real world," but rather "to activate the democratic process."[100] In short, the new ethic of public-rights participation has constituted a fundamental democratic challenge to the prevailing ethic of bureaucratic management traditionally associated with liberal reform in America during this century. "The real question emerging from the breakdown of the New Deal seems to be how to guarantee more self-government, while eliminating remote bureaucracy, and how bureaucracies which are necessary can be kept accountable rather than insulated from the public."[101]

A brief examination of the essential values that inform this challenge to existing political forms will illuminate further the unique vision that has inspired the modern public interest movement.

The Reevaluation of Efficiency. We can begin by examining the logic of the public interest reorientation toward the value of efficiency that long has dominated public administration in America. The ideal

93

of efficiency has provided perhaps the most important single goal guiding the aspirations of liberal reformers throughout this century. It has signaled a sort of magical catchword, what George Simmel called a "germinal idea," that has captured and inspired the imagination of the modern age. In all areas, it has defined the ubiquitous standard of choice and action. As Herbert Croly once put it, efficiency is the key to the realization of "the promise of American life." It was this "gospel of efficiency," as Samuel Hays labeled it, that guided and legitimated all of the major organizational transformations from agrarian to advanced industrial America—corporatization, bureaucratization, rationalization—initiated by earlier reformers.[102]

Contrary to popular caricatures as backward-looking Luddites or starry-eyed primitivists, most public interest activists have also been interested in promoting more efficient forms of economic production and political decision making. Like earlier conservationists, modern environmentalists in particular have complained that "both our renewable and nonrenewable resources are not being used optimally" by the unbound Prometheus of modern corporate production. Modern activists also resemble earlier Progressive reformers in their desire to eliminate waste, to purge corruption, to cut prices, and to assure that the public "gets what it pays for" from the public and private sectors. "Having created so many subsequent transfer and regulatory programs," notes Mark Green, liberals must act "to rediscover a lost art—the efficient management of government."[103] In this sense, then, the value of efficiency itself has not been challenged; rather, it is only the conventional Weberian assumptions about rational bureaucratic and scientific means which have drawn criticism.[104] For example, arguments about the need for "alternative" technologies of a more democratic nature reflect a direct assault upon our inherited "bigger-is-better" orientation toward increasing productive efficiency. "Modern technology does not require large corporations in order to be used efficiently in production," argue two reformers. Likewise, contends another group, corporate Leviathans "seldom yield significant efficiency" but instead "have damaged the economy, contributed to inflation, and led to wasteful government spending."[105] Most industries could be democratized "with respect to control structure," they argue, and thus be "more widely distributed across the country without loss of efficiency."[106]

More important, however, public interest reformers have protested that the prevailing logic of managerial and technical efficiency itself tends to encourage a "hidden agenda" of undesirable social ends. Liberal activists have been quick to note that organizational efficiency is always relative to other independently defined ends: "It is never a question of efficiency for efficiency's sake," they emphasize. Such confusion of ends and means by those who celebrate efficiency is castigated as an "antiseptic rationality" blind to its own deficiencies and limits.[107] The ethic of efficiency, like technology, is not autonomous; rather, it "develops within a context of economic and social institutions."[108] On one hand, the reformers have often implied that the common invocation of bureaucratic efficiency serves only to justify the exclusion of vital social interests and values from the corporate-dominated political process. For example, liberals took issue with the Trilateral Commission report a few years ago which argued that an "excess of democracy" has created a crisis in Western nations by undermining the capacities for efficiently administered government. "Order is the way to achieve efficiency, which is the condition of a well-functioning society," its authors claimed. "Due process is not the cardinal element of this belief."[109] John Gardner well summarizes the opposing position adopted by most public interest advocates: "Government and politics will never be genuinely efficient," he proclaims; "But when they are no longer responsive, when they are no longer held accountable, then we all suffer."[110]

On the other hand, the reformers have suggested that prevailing bureaucratic and technocratic conceptions of "efficiency" tend to perpetuate the socially destructive myth of unlimited economic growth against which they have rebelled. Drawing upon John Kenneth Galbraith's argument in *The New Industrial State*, activists often express the sentiment that "large-scale organization, technology, and the success ethic" all thrive on a similar impulse.[111] While efficient production is justified as necessary to improve the living standards of all, the reformers insist, it is primarily elites who benefit from expanded opportunities for power, advancement, and status within bureaucratic structures. One study identifies the parallel incentives to "status, prestige, income, and wealth of the rulers" in both private and public governing institutions: "In both cases, society is asked to pay for the psychic and material benefits rulers gain from empire."[112] All in all, ecologist Hazel Henderson has agreed, "efficiency is assumed to be the goal of increases in 'productivity,' but it cannot be easily assumed that the inevitable costs and dislocations incurred will burden us all fairly."[113]

The general perspective of public interest reformers has not just been that bureaucratic institutions are often inefficient, therefore, but also that they operate from a logic of power relations fraught with dangers and high social costs. Public interest liberalism "start[s] from the premise that present-day reality is increasingly a product of a structure of economic and political power that consolidates and sustains itself through the systematic destruction of man and his physical world."[114] Consequently, the reformers' counsel is that the ideal of efficiency must be reevaluated and redefined in relation to other values of freedom, community, safety, health, and natural beauty, which mere concerns for aggrandizing power ignore. This is the significance of the shift from the older conservationist to the newer preservationist ethic by environmentalists. Whereas the goal of the former placed national efficiency above all else, the latter has defined our greatest challenge as "protecting the national heritage."[115] And if inequality and reckless exploitation are inherent in bureaucratic forms of interaction, then reform of one requires reform of the other. The public interest strategies for substantive policy change and structural reform thus converge. This is captured perfectly in the symbolically powerful campaign against nuclear power production. As activist David Dellinger has put it, most reformers "see the antinuclear effort as part of a larger struggle to change society. Our aim is to make the society more democratic."[116]

The Devolution of Power. Another related and important goal for the new liberals has been to decentralize the concentrated power of existing hierarchical corporate and government institutions. Of course, this would require a major reversal of those historical trends that Tocqueville rightly predicted long ago.[117] Beginning in the late nineteenth century, increased concentration, coordination, and rationalization of social power gradually centralized the institutional framework of American national life. The efforts of most earlier liberal reformers only added to these trends. For example, many historians have suggested that the fundamental Progressive Era reforms of the electoral system through increased primaries and initiatives constituted an attempt to replace local party structures with large, national, centrally coordinated mass party systems. As Hofstadter puts it, "The trends toward management, toward bureaucracy, toward bigness everywhere had gone so far that the efforts of reform had to be consistent."[118] And so it has been with subsequent developments of liberal reform politics—the New Deal, Fair Deal, New Frontier, and Great Society. Each new plan only increased concentration of power in fewer public and private hands, far from the effective control of the people. Institutional structures "were designed to translate central decisions into peripheral action," notes Samuel Hays, "rather than to translate peripheral impulses into central action."[119]

Public interest activists have seemed fully aware of the undemocratic implications of these developments. Like Tocqueville, they understand the threat to human freedom and welfare posed by the "subtle despotism" of centralized bureaucratic rule. The activists seem to agree that distance in politics makes neither individual hearts grow fonder nor wills grow stronger. Their proposals for decentralization have pushed in two different but related directions. For one thing, they have argued that "size is a problem in itself."[120] The flaw in earlier liberal politics is that reformers provided "no general assualt upon bigness" in either corporate or state organization. Therefore, the public interest mandate has been "to develop... alternatives which move us away from a future dominated by the values of giant corporate and bureaucratic institutions."[121] From this perspective of the new reform mentality, therefore, "small is beautiful," or at least bigger is not necessarily better. Hence we can detect in the new program widespread efforts to effect a wholesale devolution of political power to a more comprehensible human scale. As Donald Schwartz has put it, the reformers "ultimately want to relocate... power more within individual hands since they believe that shifting the power to government hands is no shift at all."[122] It is this sentiment that has inspired the Tocquevillian affinity for local government action, community mobilization, and participation in voluntary citizen groups to return power to the people. It likewise has provided the rationale for the various consumer cooperatives, RUCAG experiments, and PIRGs sponsored by the movement, which neither "create taxes nor... create another giant organization." Each of them, Nader boasts, "is a mode of building a civic institution."[123]

The same criticism of bigness has informed much of the public interest economic vision. Unlike their liberal Progressive and New Deal precursors, however, the public interest activists have launched their assaults upon large-scale corporate production for purposes other than maximization of market efficiency. They have tended to agree with Justice Hand that "great industrial consolidations are undesirable regardless of their economic results."[124] Their commitments to democracy, welfare, and community power have justified the desirability of corporate devolution as well: "Environmental recovery means the recovery of community control, communities organizing to achieve their right to a rich and varied self-sufficiency," claims one advocate. Most reformers thus fundamentally oppose the inherited faith that corporate "bigness is goodness, oligopoly is inevitable, and competition is anachronistic."[125] Instead, they have invested their hopes in the emergence of a viable new "countereconomy" characterized by the progressive fragmentation of capital ownership, the revitalization of market competition, and the diversification of productive enterprise. Lobbies for selective industry deregulation and subsidy elimination, traditional antitrust lawsuits, and numerous local consumer, farming, and solar energy cooperative experiments have all aimed to initiate changes toward such a new "people's capitalism."

By contrast, a second problem posed by centralization has been less one of size and scale of power itself than of the accountability of concentrated decision-making authority. Thus the goal has often been less to dissolve centralized bureaucratic networks than to decentralize and democratize control over and within large-scale institutions. In government, specifically, this has meant an emphasis on expanding access to, rather than dismantling, concentrated state authority. Indeed, the biggest problem with the New Deal was its implementation of "reform from the top brain trust down, not from a popular consumer movement up." For the new activists, hierarchical administration of state policies cannot best promote the public interest; rather, what is needed is "an increased diffusion of power... inside the structure of government through greater public scrutiny of its workings and leadership."[126]

One important illustration of this posture has been the novel suspicion exhibited by activists about the inadequacies of centralized executive authority as the locus of reform leadership in the state. John Gardner argues that "neither the President nor any elected official... can accomplish what needs to be done." Reflecting the pervasive disillusionment with the shattering of New Deal ideals by the Johnson and Nixon administrations, the new reformers have adamantly resisted the common temptation to invest any leadership at all with high hopes. "We'd all be better off if we quit looking for a savior," they admonish.[127] Likewise, public interest support for fragmenting authority in the Department of Energy and the Nuclear Regulatory Commission, for widespread agency infiltration by official consumer advocates and ombudsmen, for various efforts to limit the coordinating power of the executive Office of Management and Budget, and for fundamental commitments to expand participation throughout government all reflect the efforts to decentralize decision-making authority within the existing modern bureaucratic state structure while at the same time insulating it from corporate influence.

Finally, this same goal of decentralizing control over large-scale organizations has been implicit in many of the activists' proposed economic reforms as well. It has informed the essence of the federal chartering provisions of the proposed corporate democracy bill, the various experiments in "shareholder democracy," the participatory worker rights secured by OSHA, and the use of consumer boycotts and demonstrations to protest exploitive corporate practices. All of these actions have aimed to "strengthen the position of the citizen who will act directly . . . against corporate abuses" within the prevailing structure of corporate capitalism.[128]

Expropriating the Experts. A third component of the reformers' participatory ethic has been manifested in their inherent distrust of the professional ranks of bureaucratic elites in whom earlier generations placed their greatest hopes for social improvement. It is no exaggeration to claim that American government in this century has largely "belonged to the manager, the technician, the bureaucrat, the expert."[129] As Robert Wiebe has argued, Progressive reform largely grew out of the impulse toward professionalization of both government managers and the private ranks of doctors, lawyers, scientists, and businessmen. These new managers sought to substitute one system of decision making, that inherent in the spirit of modern technology and science, for another, that inherent in the give-and-take among particularistic groups competing within the larger system. Scientific rationality, technical expertise, and incremental pragmatism thus were exalted as the highest virtues that the new technocrats could offer to improve public life. "Scientific government . . . would bring opportunity, progress, order, and community," many hoped.[130] Moreover, the new managerial class provided a distinctly impersonal, neutral, and independent stature for government administration which transcended the corruption and irrationality of the older "interest" politics. "If any praise be due to Wisconsin laws, it is probably because of the appointive commission, the nonpartisan spirit, the expert, and the civil service law," wrote Charles McCarthy in 1912. And this same faith in the growing technostructure composed of the "best and the brightest" constituted a stable cornerstone of American liberal hopes in this century through the Great Society programs of the 1960s.[131]

The undeniably high percentage of professional specialists that dominate the modern public interest movement, including lawyers, scientists, doctors, policy analysts, and the like, may seem at first only to have continued this tradition. But although unabashedly proud of their own expertise and faith in technological advances, public interest liberals nevertheless have been highly critical of the managerial authority traditionally delegated to supposedly neutral technocrats. Indeed, it is against the very ideal of government by scientists, experts, and bureaucrats understood to be above politics that the new reformers have pitted themselves. "Politics is too important to be left to experts," warned E. F. Schumacher, and "if politics cannot be left to the experts, neither can economics and technology."[132] While hardly opposed to technology, public interest liberals have been profoundly critical of rule by technocrats. Several arguments are proposed by the reformers in support of this perspective.

First, the activists have contended that no one, however expert, has a monopoly on claims to possess the information, insight, and skill necessary to good policy formulation. Indeed, the opposite side of expertise is often a tendency to myopia and narrow-mindedness, a tendency no doubt familiar to the highly trained and often specialized liberal advocates themselves. "No matter how qualified the policy maker and staff may be," concludes one reform group, "the range of their experience, expertise, and innovative capacities are necessarily limited"[133] More important, the reformers have held that the traditional faith in the impersonal rule of independent experts obscures the fact that all policy decisions turn on choices among competing values. In short, despite claims of scientific impartiality, all policy decisions are ethical in nature. "Though there are plenty of technical and managerial problems to solve, the big problems of our economy are social and political," they insist.[134] Reform activists thus often seem to reflect a quite specific understanding about the conflict between political and technical forms of knowledge. If the older liberals were more children of Saint-Simon and Frederick Taylor, the new liberals have revealed more of an affinity with Thomas Paine's captious "common sense" approach to political speculation. "The toughest questions cannot be resolved by technological expertise," protests one Friends of the Earth pamphlet. Too often, therefore, the result of bureaucratic rule in public policy is "to reserve for the judgement of experts decisions where their expertise is of very little relevance."[135]

To be sure, such arguments often have merely served the desires of public interest elites to introduce their own information, values, and perspectives into the process of technocratic management. In short, if bad policy is the result of bureaucratic myopia, then all that is needed is enlistment of more experts with varied knowledge and values (including the reformers themselves, of course). Yet more often the reformers have contended that democratic participation and accountability are independent values against which technical expertise must be balanced in policy making. In other words, the reform claims extend beyond challenges to the wisdom of prevailing experts to issues of their political legitimacy. As Joseph Onek asserts, "Decisions without public participation are undemocratic, and, in the long run, unacceptable, no matter how 'wise' the decision." Hence the EPEA interpretation of Louis Harris polls reflecting public dissatisfaction today: "The mandate is for participation, not discretion," they concluded in the 1970s, "no matter how benevolent or expert."[136]

These arguments have sometimes led to criticism about the very fact of citizen dependence on elite-staffed regulatory agencies. Joseph Sax has exclaimed in a fit of democratic enthusiasm that "the citizen does not need a bureaucratic middleman. . . . He is perfectly capable of fighting his own battles."[137] More commonly, though, the general tendency of the reformers has been to challenge only the insularity of technocrats and bureaucrats which earlier reformers thought essential to the rule of a truly "publicly interested" state. Since "independence of agencies was always an empty ritual," the new liberals usually have attempted to increase rather than limit the vulnerability of the state to the pressures and demands of groups within society.[138] While aiming to expand the *indirect* accountability of bureaucratic elites through electoral control of officials, much as did earlier reformers, the new liberals have also sought more *direct* forms of accountability by administrative experts. "Above all, each [group] takes a new view of how the government and business should work," two public interest leaders recognize. "Each rejects the theory that a governmental agency can, by itself, adequately understand or represent the public interest in its dealings with the public in its regulation of industry."[139] Against the older ideal of bureaucratic elite *autonomy*, therefore, we can perceive the significance of the new reform goals extolling citizen *access*. "The myth of the expert," argues one ecologist, "is a priceless asset to the public or private operator who wants to manipulate the environment." Only through maximizing openness to scrutiny, pressure, and initiative from citizen groups, the activists have contended, can the technocratic establishment of elite policy makers be bound to their duties to society at large.[140]

The Code of Conflict. Public interest activists have offered a further challenge to the very values of cooperation, conformity, and consensus on which modern elite bureaucratic politics thrives. The fact is that the older liberal reform tradition inherited from the Progressives reflected in many ways an obsession with the dangers of disorder. "The earlier homogeneity of American society has been impaired," worried Herbert Croly long ago, "and no authoritative and edifying, but conscious social ideal has yet taken its place."[141] For most previous liberal progressive leaders, conflict itself, rather than injustice or inequality, was the greatest evil in need of redress. In the marketplace, wrote Rev. Washington Gladden, "competition is the creature of warfare, and warfare the source of immorality which brutalizes all."[142] In politics, the assault upon the local machines and regional parties reflected the same distaste with diversity, disunity, and disagreement. Everywhere the demands for unity, integration, even Christian brotherhood—all captured in Edward Bellamy's illustration of "the principle of fraternal cooperation . . . the only true science of wealth production"—could be heard and witnessed in practice. This language extolling "community" expressed little hope of return to the spontaneous relations of rural utopia, of course. Rather, harmony could be imposed from above by an independent administrative state.[143] All of the diverse endeavors of the age were woven into attempts to provide the social engineering necessary to a well-coordinated, smoothly functioning machine oiled by a pervasive moral consensus. A "frictionless bureaucracy" and the "ethereal communion between leaders and citizens"—such have become the underpinnings of the American governmental process guided by "professional," pragmatic elites which are still widely celebrated.[144]

In contrast, modern public interest activists have aimed to regenerate conflict, competition, and confrontation throughout public life. The new reformers simply have had little respect for the prevailing rational "liberal consensus" exalted by social scientists. In the eyes of the outsiders, the call for cooperation too often justifies cooptation, "flexibility" is a code word for selling out, and favor-trading invokes memories of Faust's pact with the devil. Indeed, such heralded consensual norms define the essence of modern political corruption. "It is all very civilized. And low keyed. And polite," comments John Gardner.[145] Likewise, the inherited middle-class ethos praising citizen integration and adjustment into the bureaucratic order smacks of passivity and powerless resignation before an exploitive status quo. Hence Nader has proclaimed himself an active enemy of all that "continues to close minds, stifles the dissent which made us strong, and deters the participation of Americans who challenge in order to correct, and who question in order to answer." Only that political activity is legitimate and democratic, therefore, which permits "all viewpoints" and promotes the "clash of many voices."[146] Environmentalist Odom Fanning has gone so far as to proclaim that "adversaryism" is one of the "four imperatives of citizen action."[147] Of course, practical-minded reformers know that the adoption of a statesmanlike posture can be a timely asset in the battle for influence. Likewise, most activists have preferred negotiated settlements or mediated dispute resolutions where such more consensual decisions can be reached. Yet they have believed that a genuinely civic posture must never be allowed to nurture complacency or temper conviction. "We must critique our country" always, admonishes Gardner, precisely to show our "care about it."[148]

These confrontational ideals can be witnessed in all of the public interest efforts toward procedural reform. "The need," Sax argues, "is for institutions that know how to expose and resolve, unsentimentally, the elemental issues in a dispute." Through their efforts at public education and defense of free-speech rights, the activists have affirmed their fundamental belief in the "political marketplace of ideas."[149] The professed faith of most reformers in the need for "fostering genuine free enterprise and putting the people back into people's capitalism" likewise has extolled the conflict and competition encouraged by small-scale market exchange. In their attempts to expand citizen participation within, and competition between, government agencies, Congress, and the parties, we can perceive the similar belief that "a free market of competing interests . . . [is] a worthy goal to aim at."[150] Likewise, the primary justification for the "shareholder democracy" program was precisely to "reduce the 'harmony' of executive management." Public interest reformers argued instead for the institutionalization of a "healthy friction between operating executives and the board [of directors] to assure that the wisest possible use is made of corporate resources."[151] Perhaps not since the arguments by the Federalists long ago has such a defense of the virtues of systemized conflict, diversity, and competition been so fully promulgated in America.

As their conservative detractors have asserted repeatedly, the very style of the activists exudes this ideal of conflict and confrontation. Gardner has professed that "we have every right to raise hell when we see injustice done, or the public interest destroyed, or the public process corrupted."[152] The activists have consciously sought not only to lend the sophistication of professionals to the street politics of the 1960s, but likewise to introduce some of the passion, intensity, and spontaneity of outsiders in the street to an otherwise overly routinized political process—hence the significance of the guerrilla tactics, the dramatic pageant of reform, and the novel lifestyles of the activists which clash with the more reserved manner of the Washington establishment. As Lazarus has noted, this also explains in part the close relations of the reformers and the press. The reformers understand that the press tends to view public affairs as a species of athletic contest, he suggests: "Conflict is what [the press] are looking for and what they like to write about."[153]

Perhaps more than anyone else, Ralph Nader has symbolized the confrontational politics that the movement seeks to infuse within prevailing corporate and government hierarchies. Lonely, circumspect, angry, and tenaciously dedicated to his cause, Nader has thrived on his "outsider" role as perennial challenger to the status quo. Indeed, one biographer quotes Nader as admitting that he "welcomes the adversity because it produces harder thinking and harder drive to get to the objective." Although always self-consciously conventional in appearance, Nader's essential message has been "simply a plea not to adjust" to the values, practices, and wants that most Americans have accepted as normal.[154] No one, not even former colleagues like Joan Claybrook or old allies like Edmund Muskie, are safe from harsh judgment according to Nader's high standards. He is an equal-opportunity critic. "Don't ever assume you are immune from criticism because of... friendship," Nader once admonished. "If you compromise our principles, you'll be attacked as my worst enemy."[155]

Radical Pluralism. All in all, these basic elements in the public interest vision of democratic state reform add up to the goal of, in David Vogel's words, "promoting pluralism."[156] This is the general label that Lazarus has loosely posed as an alternative to "populism." It has been canonized by ecologist Hazel Henderson as "pluralistic futurism" and Gar Alperovitz as "radical pluralism," and it is recognized unequivocally by John Gardner: "The primary goal of Common Cause," he argues, is to transform the administrative processs into "what the theorists of pluralism so often said it was: a free market of competing political interests."[157]

It is important to note, however, that this vision of radical pluralism differs significantly from the pluralist model embraced by many academic political scientists.[158] First, the liberal activists have been critical of the traditional assumption that political demands are most rational when they are narrowly self-interested and that the general interest or common good will emerge out of the conflict of special interests alone.[159] Without representation for collective interests such as health, safety, and resource conservation as well as direct debate over social values, the reformers have argued, public policy making will be neither democratic nor effective. "We need the special interest groups," they admit, "but we also need a strong voice for the public interest."[160]

Second, the new activists have gone well beyond the academic

104

model in emphasizing the importance of pluralistic competition for influence within as well as among functional social organizations.[161] The problem with hierarchical bureaucratic institutions, the reformers have insisted, is that they contribute to "anonymity, loss of identity, dehumanization, suppression of individuality, [and] a sense of powerlessness" among those who are bound to them. In other words, most large-scale organizations inherently develop the "tendency to squeeze out pluralism."[162] Hence we can understand the reformers' efforts to expand public participation within government not only through new citizen groups, but directly within all existing organized power structures—labor unions, corporations, parties—as well. "We are committed to . . . creating new channels for action that will increase the impact of all citizens . . . at all levels of political and economic decision making," claims one environmental organization.[163]

Third, the radical pluralist model has been clearly committed to revitalizing the role of the regulatory state as an autonomous broker and impartial arbiter within the political process. If corporate clientelism and capture undercut the independent authority of the existing state, one reason has been the insularity, inertia, and irresponsibility inherent in the bureaucratic organization of the state itself.[164] By expanding citizen access to state officials, therefore, it has been hoped that the state will assume a more autonomous leadership role as it increases its responsiveness to a broader range of social interests. The role of the state would not be as just one of many contending parties in the political process, as older pluralist theories often presume, but to "mediate among the competing interests, work out compromises, and shape national policy on the basis of agreements that may satisfy no group entirely, but take into account the concerns of all."[165]

And finally, the reformers have expressed the sentiment that this more fully realized pluralistic state structure might actually counter the fragmenting, alienating, and individuating propensities of existing bureaucratic organization. With the state freed from the hold of special interests and bound to respect new public interests, the possibilities might exist for nurturing new citizen public commitment, solidarity, and what the New Left used to call "community." "We want a society in which a sense of community is still alive and sense of identity is possible," the new liberals proclaimed in the 1970s.[166] These desires for a more manageable scale of endeavor, for a more human face, and for a more accessible and meaningful public life have constituted the radical fringes of hope derived from an earlier decade with which the new professional advocates have embroidered their reform program.

105

The Judicialization of Politics

The various efforts to implement radical new principles within the structure of the national political process have been diverse and far-reaching. Yet, the most important and novel dimension of the reform project has been the movement's unflagging faith in the legal process as the primary resource and model for social change. Public interest activists have understood well the admonition offered by C. Wright Mills several decades ago that "we live in a society that is democratic in legal forms and formal expectations. We ought not to minimize the enormous value and considerable opportunity these circumstances make available."[167] As earlier pages have illustrated, the activists harbor no illusions about widespread uses of "law against the people" by corporate and state officials. Nevertheless, they have expressed a deep belief in the legal structure as both a valuable end and a means of progressive politics. In the words of one influential scholarly spokesman, the reformers have believed that "the formalist legal tradition [can] be transformed from a shield against hostile power to a sword, an instrument for direct attack on inequality, domination, and alienation."[168]

Such an affinity for legalistic politics is hardly novel in America. Tocqueville was most astute in his observation that "There is hardly a political question in the United States which does not sooner or later turn into a judicial one." Ever since Thomas Paine brandished his rhetorical sword to slay the legitimacy of monarchy and proclaimed that "in America law is king," many of our fundamental conflicts have been settled around the bar of legal justice.[169] Moreover, both Progressive and New Deal reform politics drew heavily upon leadership by lawyers and the new demystifying doctrines of legal realism and sociological jurisprudence.[170] Yet, again, the temptation to find in the recent reform efforts only resonances of the familiar can obscure the creative contributions of the new politics. The new activists have not been so timid as simply to adapt their reform activities to accepted legal modes. Merely correcting the transgressions against particular laws by powerful elites is not enough in their eyes. Rather, public interest activism has been "based on a critique of the traditional model of law and professional organization itself, a critique formulated in terms of the ideals of the tradition itself."[171] The new reformers thus depart from their liberal precursors not just in their attempts to democratize the managerial corporate state, but likewise in their parallel attempt to establish radical new legal practices and institutional

106

forums for the "democratization of the rule of law." This general commitment is manifested in several related transformations.

Politicizing the Judiciary. Perhaps no phenomenon better illustrates the novel departure of modern public interest activists from previous liberal reformers than their pervasive reliance on the federal judiciary as the most important source of access to political power.[172] This strategy is novel because the courts traditionally have provided one of the greatest obstacles to progressive expansion of state control over corporate power throughout American history. The legacies of nineteenth-century commerce clause, contract clause, and substantive due-process constitutional doctrines along with common-law tort principles provide powerful testament to the once near-sacred legal status of private enterprise against government regulation.[173] Likewise, as public interest activists often point out, the legal profession itself has effectively promoted conservative, pro-corporate government policies throughout most of our national history. In the words of one advocate, "the lawyer class has been anathema to our agrarian and debtor classes, to the Jacksonian, populist, muckraking, and other movements seeking large reforms."[174] It thus is no wonder that earlier progressive reformers believed that "the courts should rarely question either the wisdom or the motives of legislators and administrators and should frame legal doctrine . . . so as to insulate decisions of such bodies from most outside challenges."[175]

However, the political revolution initiated by the New Deal which consolidated the state as manager of the economy was accompanied by a "constitutional revolution" that has been well demonstrated in court decisions since 1937.[176] Most important of these is the withdrawal of federal courts, with the Supreme Court in the lead, from their intensely active roles in protecting corporate autonomy. Once the fundamental principle of the new welfare-managerial state was accepted, the "presumption of constitutionality" was adopted readily by the courts as they ceded economic authority to the legislative and executive branches.[177] Judicial withdrawal from economic judgments did not signal a retreat into passivity, however. Rather, the federal courts slowly adopted a new constitutional role as primary defenders for the civil liberties and political rights of powerless groups within and against the powerful new state process. The Supreme Court clearly outlined this new role in the famous footnote 4 of the *Carolene Products* decision, which reinterpreted the Fourteenth Amendment to permit "more searching judicial scrutiny" in three areas: where (1) specific provisions of the Constitution were involved, (2) the government

107

restricted normal political processes, and (3) statutes were directed at insular and discrete minorities.[178]

The significance of this implied transformation in the political role and substantive orientations of judicial officials was prodigious. Guided by a receptive Supreme Court, the federal judiciary increasingly heard and responded to the claims of those long-standing "minorities . . . systematically shortchanged by the [presumably majoritarian] political branches."[179] In particular, judicial officials extended to civil-rights, welfare, and antiwar groups an invitation specifying, "where lobbying fails . . . continue opposition by litigation."[180] And while the courts have proved limited in their direct contributions to the improvement of the American underclass, the role judicial victories played in granting dignity and nurturing political action among many long-powerless groups cannot be ignored.

It is not surprising, therefore, that a political strategy seeking to exploit both private and public law resources of the new liberal judiciary was also seized upon by subsequent reformers claiming to promote long-neglected public interests.[181] In the new reformers' eyes, these latter concerns had been as much excluded from the political process as were the "particular" interests of minorities. Moreover, the middle-class liberals argued adamantly that "it is entirely consistent with democratic principles for courts to play an active role in checking bureaucratic and corporate abuse."[182] The ironies of such developments again are striking. This innovative judicial strategy not only distinguishes public interest activists from previous liberal reformers, but in doing so it embraces the very tactics utilized by big business against earlier progressives prior to the New Deal.[183] Just as corporate interests once exploited conservative judicial activism to *invalidate* unwanted regulatory and antitrust policies, so have the modern radicals utilized liberal judicial activism to *expand* and *enforce* legal authority over corporate interests. Because "the weakness of modern United States legislation . . . leaves much of the decisive framing of issues and the resolution of meaning to the courts," two supporters point out, the judiciary has provided an effective instrument to fortify public control over economic power.[184] In particular, liberal judicial interpretations of NEPA statutes played a crucial role in elevating environmentalism from obscurity to one of the most important domestic policy concerns in the early 1970s.[185]

The implications of this developing role of the courts for liberal policy making—frequently labeled the new "judicial populism"—have been significant. For one thing, although the relative percentages of federal cases remain small, the number of total court cases involving public interest–oriented policy issues has risen measureably. For example, about 10 percent of all environmental impact statements in the 1970s were contested in court.[186] Between 1969 and 1973 alone, some 373 public lawsuits were filed to promote compliance with the newly enacted NEPA statutes.[187] Another study speculates that in recent years the Freedom of Information Act has generated more lawsuits than any other statute in American history.[188] And while less clearly illustrative, a recent government report shows not only significant increases in the total number of cases filed in the district and federal courts, but an increase of over 20 percent in the proportion of publicly oriented (the U. S. as a party) lawsuits. Many of these were initiated by private businesses against regulatory agencies, it is true. For example, it has been estimated that 22 percent of all OSHA citations for noncompliance ended up before administrative law judges in the late 1970s.[189] But the fact is that public interest action to increase state regulation has played a key role in provoking even these instances of judicialized politics. Such developments have contributed to an ever-growing burden on already overcrowded federal dockets, of course. But if there is a problem of too many cases for the present system to handle, the activists respond, "the answer in a democracy cannot be in the denial of access to the courts. If we need more judges, we should have more judges."[190]

Liberal judicial activism has also increased the power of the courts relative to that of other branches within the state. This has resulted not just from the exercise of court authority over new areas of state activity, but also from the judicial assumption of authority delegated to legislative and executive bodies concerning job and product safety, corporate liability, release of official information, and election finance policy. As Donald Schwartz of Campaign GM predicted in the early 1970s, "one result of arming and arousing public interest lawyers as enforcers of the public interest would be to judicialize many of the conflicts . . . that are presently dealt with in other ways." James Ridgeway, one-time public interest ally turned critic, puts the point more dramatically: "The effects of this attack by lawyers is profound: the court becomes the legislature."[191] The significance of such expanded judicial influence extends well beyond the actual cases decided by judges. Indeed, at least as important has been the reformers' reliance on simple threats of judicial action to gain regulatory compliance, to deter undesirable economic development, and to encourage negotiated compromises on policy disputes. As Joseph Onek of CLASP has recounted, "In the early days we had to sue because no one would listen to us. . . . Once we succeeded in some cases, the threat to sue

109

automatically gives us more weight" in battles with corporate and government opponents alike.[192]

Numerous legal scholars have observed in recent years that this extensive engagement of contemporary federal courts in public law litigation has altered the very character of the courts themselves. In other words, the judicialization of politics has created a judiciary more politicized in form and practice. One change induced by increased intervention involves the widespread propensity of judges to rule more directly on specific substantive as well as procedural issues in the determination of legal rights and remedies.[193] Likewise, several distinctive transformations in the structure of relationships among judicial participants are also noteworthy. These include a more aggressive role of judges in fact-finding and policy resolution; an increased reliance on empirical social science research and public policy analysis to implement principled policy determination; the growing proclivity of judges to mandate injunctive remedies in place of traditional monetary damage remedies; the frequent transformation of bipolar into multipolar party representation; the replacement of jury trials by more informal judicially supervised bargaining settlements among claimants; and the use of creative mechanisms such as "special master" appointees to develop and supervise policy formulation in conjunction with other government branches. All in all, as Abram Chayes summarizes, "these developments are interrelated as members of recognizable, if changing, systems and . . . taken together they display a new model of judicial action and the judicial role, both of which depart sharply from received conceptions" about court forms.[194]

This reform-oriented judicial activism in which courts have played a more prominent and less interstitial role in promoting the public interest has generated considerable criticism, especially from conservative quarters. Scholars such as Alexander Bickel, Nathan Glazer, and Donald Horowitz have accused the activist lawyers of a sort of political vampirism that feeds judicial authority on the lifeblood withdrawn from the more "democratic" and capable agents in the legislative and executive branches.[195] While there is some truth to this, such has not been the professed goal of the reformers themselves. In their view, the utilization of the courts is conceived primarily in terms of revivifying a moribund government of separate powers that check, balance, and motivate one another for the public good. As Joseph Sax puts it, "the role of the courts is not to make public policy, but to help assure that public policy is made by the appropriate entity, rationally, and in accord with the aspirations of the democratic process." Hence the increasing exercise of judicial authority initiated by citizen litigation has not really been intended to replace the role of the legislature. Rather, the goal has been to promote and protect the authority of the legislature, to make it more responsive to its constituents, and to thrust upon it the obligation to affirm openly its true intent. In short, "the court serves as a catalyst, not a usurper, of the legislative process."[196] Likewise, the role of the court is not to replace the regulatory agencies, but instead to engage in "continuous review and reevaluation" of their performance as agents of Congress. Public interest activists have employed courts only to interpret congressional mandates and to "reprimand public and private bureaucracies for brazenly defying the statutory commands to respect the public interest."[197] Judicial action has been necessary not to diminish executive responsibility, but rather to encourage it.

The Judicialization of Administration. The creative use of the courts is but one facet of the liberal reformers' legal enterprise. What is even more novel and radical has been their effort to transform the entire political process itself into a labyrinth of increasingly judicialized legal institutions. The most significant manifestation of these efforts has been in the administrative apparatus of the national executive state. The result has added up to what Richard Stewart calls the "reformation of American administrative law."[198]

The outlines of this transformation are quite clear. During the past century, a model of administrative law developed to secure the legitimacy of increasing state intervention into American social and private life. Rooted in the conviction that discretionary policy was anathema, the traditional model placed a premium on the administration of formal positive rules by independent bureaucrats accountable to judicial and legislative overseers. This Weberian "transmission belt" model, Stewart points out, was effective in legitimating limited state action. The problem, however, was that it "did not touch the affirmative side" of government, "which has to do with the representation of individuals and interests" in the development of official policies on their behalf. As a result, Congress since the New Deal has tended to eschew such legalistic "command-and-control" statutes, preferring instead to delegate broad grants of discretionary authority to the growing corps of technocratic experts supposedly capable of making impartial, publicly interested, scientifically reasoned policy judgments. In short, many liberals believed that "expertise could plausibly be advocated as a solution to the problem of discretion if the agency's goals could be realized through the knowledge that comes from specialized experiences."[199]

111

Yet we have seen that such technocratic "solutions" have only ignored and exacerbated the problem in the reformers' eyes.[200] "Bureau administrators, trying to evaluate the morality of acts in the total system, are singularly liable to corruption, producing a government by men, not laws," argues ecologist Garrett Hardin.[201] The resulting dilemmas of the traditional legal model are thus essentially triangular; general rules are too vague to facilitate effective policy, legal discretion is too easily subverted by corporate pressures, and the rule of independent experts denies legal restraint and politically sensitive resolutions of policy conflicts.

The reformers' participatory public-rights strategy to remedy these evils constitutes a quite different model of administrative law altogether. Simply put, their adversarial forms of legal advocacy have aimed to encourage the judicialization of administration itself within the modern state.[202] Indeed, the reformers' efforts to create a "surrogate political process" for "consideration of all interests" within state agencies largely parallels as well as derives from the expanded exercise of judicial review. For liberalized rights of review to be meaningful, after all, those with standing must also have participated in the agency process of decision making and had an opportunity to contribute to the record.[203] In other words, the grants of formal rights to citizen participation directly within the agencies has been a logical corollary to the granting of rights to judicial review. Likewise, as agencies have learned to anticipate frequent review of discretionary policy making under pressure from public interest activists, so they have learned to adapt their processes to judicial standards so as to preserve autonomy over substantive decisions. When augmented by selective OSHA, NEPA, and Clean Air Act legislative provisions mandating rights to direct intervention, the nature of the subtle transformation effected by the new activists is clear. In public interest lawyer Beverly Moore's words, now "the administrative process, like the judicial process, is an adversary process."[204]

Perhaps no institutional reform measure better illustrates the distinctiveness of the new reformers' legal orientation than their creative use of the Administrative Procedure Act.[205] New Deal liberals generally decried this 1946 act, which mandated judicial review over, and minimal formal adjudicatory procedures within, federal agencies, as a tool created by conservatives to undercut effective government regulation. By contrast, later public interest liberals eagerly seized upon these same legal provisions as effective resources to advance their policy claims against recalcitrant government and corporate executives. Far from being a threat to liberal reform, the procedural requirements of the act were criticized by the new activists for not going far enough in judicializing administrative processes of rule making and enforcement. The most important of its flaws included the inadequacies of purely voluntary terms of compliance, the generous exemptions granted to administrators on many issues, the lack of government financial aid necessary to facilitate citizen use of their rights, and the overall vagueness of many important provisions mandating administrative action.[206] In response, the multitude of new public rights won by the reformers through legislative and judicial lobbying to rectify these deficiencies—including rights of citizens to expanded judicial review, to direct intervention, to information access, and to government subsidies—has been aimed to institutionalize more fully quasi-judicial, trial-type hearings in administrative and regulatory bodies throughout government. These legal procedures "have moved beyond protection of the rights aggrieved by administrative action." They have institutionalized further due-process rights to "participation in problem solving and protection of more general public interests against agencies accused of indifference to the public interest."[207]

Examples of this judicial design for political decision making in state regulatory bodies predictably have been most evident in "social" agencies such as the FDA, OSHA, EPA, FTC, and CPSC.[208] Such structural propensities can also be witnessed in those governmental institutions created or designed by the activists themselves. Most important have been the many state-level "people's counsels," the New Jersey Division of Public Interest Advocacy, and the proposed national office for consumer advocacy. The last in particular, although narrowly defeated in Congress, is noteworthy. Reflecting the inherent distrust of the managerial "grand-design" mentality behind earlier agency mandates, the primary goals of this agency were to initiate lawsuits for judicial review of agency policies and to expand participation of consumers by "seeking to improve the way rules, regulations, and decisions are made" throughout government. Two respected students of public interest politics have confirmed the uniquely judicial model on which the new institution was to be constructed: "It substitutes the legal clash of adversary interests for the decrees of administrative regulation," they conclude.[209]

The Judicial Model of Democracy. Such judicially oriented reforms in existing state administrative and regulatory processes illustrate only the most dramatic examples of the unique organizational changes promoted by public interest advocates. The political pressures they have created to formalize legal access to policy-making procedures within bureaucratic corporate boardrooms and workplaces, within party nominating caucuses, and within congressional hearings likewise reflect the quasi-judicialistic propensities at the heart of the new political vision. The logic of such reforms is clear. As David Riley puts it, "governing power, wherever located, should be subject to the fundamental constitutional limitations of due process of law."[210] In other words, judicial institutions have constituted the very models of participatory democracy in action toward which transformation of modern governmental forms must be directed. They have defined for the new activists something like what the agora was for the Greeks, the tribunal was for the Romans, and the town meeting was for colonial New England citizen politics.[211]

The obvious reason for this attraction to judicial forms, of course, has been that they are nonbureaucratic in design. In the words of two Washington analysts, "judicial populism" provides one solution to the problem of "how to beat bureaucracies without increasing them."[212] Rather than signaling an alternative to "politics," as many critics have claimed, judicialized forms of interaction have provided the activists with the very instruments for democratizing the recalcitrant, unresponsive, and irresponsible leviathan of modern government. "Since in reality it is the political system's only point of access to the individual citizen," argues public interest lawyer John Denvir, the judicial form "in many ways has a greater claim to a democratic base than either its legislative or administrative governmental counterparts." Unlike the impenetrable, distant, dark cloisters of bureaucracies, Joseph Sax maintains, "the courtroom is an eminently suitable forum for the voicing of citizen concerns."[213]

That the recent reformers have conceptualized their structural designs for democratizing the state in terms of the same institutions with which they have been most familiar and successful in the past should not be surprising. We should only expect that those who invoke the courts against the regulatory agencies and other government institutions will extol the qualities of the judicial process as the ends and means of good government itself.[214] This is not to say that all activists openly extol the virtues of a judicialized state with equal reverence. Quite naturally, the most ardent spokespersons for judicial ideals in the movement are lawyers.[215] Yet a brief examination of the reasoning behind these ideals illustrates their homology with the basic values informing the overall reform vision of a democratic state.

114

1. The first and most significant dimension of the court model is the ideal of the *adversary process*. Public interest advocates have been both adamant and articulate in defending their goals for the enlargement of the adversary process through the judicialization of political institutions. "To strengthen the adversary system" throughout government, proclaim two spokesmen, has been "one of the most important goals of public interest advocacy." Indeed, we have seen that this commitment constitutes something like the founding principle of the movement. Two other founders of the new activism have put the idea in unequivocal terms. The "underlying commitment" of public interest lawyers and advocates, they argue, "is not to specific platforms, whether liberal or conservative; it is, rather, to the adversary process system itself."[216] In the legal adversary process, we can find all of the most fundamental structural propensities that guide the reform effort to democratize the modern state.

For one thing, judicial adversary forms provide unique opportunities to expanded citizen participation. Courts are democratic because they rely directly on the initiative and voluntary efforts of citizens for their mobilization into action. In sociologist Donald Black's terms, judicial institutions are "reactive" rather than "proactive."[217] Courts not only encourage citizen action; they depend on it to be effective political agents. Joseph Sax thus argues that "litigation is . . . a means of access for ordinary citizens to the process of governmental decision-making" which allows a "repudiation of our traditonal reliance upon professional bureaucrats."[218] Ralph Nader adds that most of the rights created and utilized by the reform efforts "are enforceable by individual citizens themselves." He asks further: "Which laws can be enforced by the government and which are primarily enforced by citizens? How can we extend the latter? . . . These laws don't rely so exclusively on who happens to be appointed to what agency or department of government, and they also permit diversity of initiative throughout the country."[219] Whether it be workers blowing the whistle on corporate abuse or consumers protesting loan fraud, adversarial judicial forums have offered a unique model of accessible political institutions worthy of imitation elsewhere.

The inherent judicial reliance on citizen initiative and resources also provides an institutional foundation for the decentralization of public authority desired by the activists. This involves more than admiration for the existing decentralized state structure of the federal court system. Whereas the earlier Progressives had sought to shift the locus of insitutional authority from the judicial and legislative branches to the central executive branches of government, the modern attempt to shift authority back to judicialized institutions has intended to facilitate the return of power more directly to the people. Judicial adversary processes uniquely "permit broad, decentralized access for advocates throughout the country," argues Nader.[220] Likewise, the "reactive" nature of the court model ensures that the multiple enclaves of state access preserve a measure of autonomous citizen power over the public agenda. Unlike the hierarchical statist model of entrenched elite rule, the judicial model guarantees the independence of citizen groups contending for influence within the adversary process. In this sense, the class-action suit by voluntary citizen groups against corporations symbolizes the classic model of potential democratic reappropriation of power from bureaucratic functionaries.[221] All in all, notes Abram Chayes, the new public law model "does not work through a rigid, multilayered hierarchy of numerous officials, but through a smallish, representative task force, assembled ad hoc, and easily dismantled when the problem is finally solved."[222]

Another purported virtue of the judicial adversary process is its inherent fairness in balancing the interests of contending participants. Jeffrey Berry notes that because "there is great faith in the fairness of the law," most advocates "accord much greater legitimacy to the federal court system than to the administrative agencies."[223] One reason is that judicial forms require fewer monetary and human resources for effective citizen participation. Consequently, relatively underfinanced, unorganized, and decentralized groups can compete on more equal terms in court forums than by lobbying against powerful, established corporate interests elsewhere in government. "There must be an adversary process . . . with someone representing the counter-corporate side," insists Robert Fellmeth.[224] For example, scholar Richard Liroff has noted that environmentalists, like other minority groups, chose the tactic of mobilizing judicial authority for their cause during the early 1970s precisely because of their paucity of financial resources. Of course wealth and organization are not irrelevant to success in the court processes. Indeed, it often takes considerable time and money to win lawsuits in modern public law-oriented judicial institutions. But with the aid of attorneys' fees awards and altruistic legal activists, the reformers believe that "the amount of money needed to influence social decisions through the litigation process is, in general, slight compared to what it takes to have a systematic effect on the legislative branches."[225] In sum, no other institutional form has been understood to afford equality of both access and influence to citizens as completely as do judicial forums.

A further element ensuring judicial fairness is the procedural formality of adversary processes. "Formal, regulated participation... results in more openness and less imbalance," argues one public interest research group. "The more informal the participation, the more likely public participation becomes contorted into an opportunity for the government to hear from those it chooses, rather than for the public to express its views when it chooses."[226] Most important of these formal elements, of course, is the legislation of "public rights" to citizen participation and substantive entitlement. Formal rights consolidate citizen access as assured and predictable amid the welter of ever-changing and often adverse political environments. Consequently, whereas citizens have the status of mere supplicants before traditional administrative institutions, Sax argues, the citizen who participates within judicial institutions has "quite a different status." Simply put, "he stands as a claimant of rights to which he is entitled."[227] Indeed, that public interest liberals have placed the commitment to the institutionalization of "public rights" at the very center their agenda both exemplifies and encourages their commitment to the judicial model of democratic politics.

Finally, while accessible to all and committed to formal representation of plural interests, the judicial model also legitimates the role of legal specialists in lending a dimension of professionalism to political conflict. Recalling Tocqueville's characterization of lawyers as the functional equivalents of aristocratic leaders in democracies, one activist asserts the faith that "the lawyer is still... the indispensable middleman in our social progress."[228] Legal experts fulfill this gatekeeping role in two ways. First, they contribute their specialized knowledge and skills to render citizens' claims comprehensible and amenable to state officials. An activist group pamphlet proudly quotes District Judge Charles Riley: "Everytime I see somebody... like the NRDC come into my court, I say 'Thank God' because I know I am going to have competent counsel." Likewise, lawyers provide the important role of leadership necessary to educate and coordinate citizen aspirations. They "help citizen groups formulate and clarify their objectives... and suggest appropriate techniques by which to work for those objectives."[229] From conceptualizing interests to developing a principled claim, the task of the lawyer in the judicial model of politics has thus been deemed invaluable.

2. A second general dimension of the "court" model of politics appealing to the new activists has been the *authority of the judge* who presides over the adversary process. Indeed, as opposed to the conventional technocrat or bureaucrat, the judge embodies the arche-

117

typal posture of the virtuous state official for the new reformers. Judges, above all else, are praised as independent, neutral, and impartial in ways that bureaucrats cannot be. "Their 'independence' is the first resource the federal courts can use to aid public and majority interests systematically neglected by the elective branches," argues Simon Lazarus.[230] This is so because judges are not preoccupied with appointment insecurities and generally serve longer terms (fourteen years on average) than bureaucrats; hence they are free to be more sensitive to the enduring political and moral forces in society at large than to the volatile swings of public opinion or special interest pressure.[231]

Joseph Sax has noted that their "professional frame of reference" further insulates judges from vulnerability to only narrow interest concerns typical of most bureaucrats. Judges are committed to what Lon Fuller called "the inner morality of the law," which esteems fairness, disinterestedness, and procedural regularity.[232] With sure hand and detached mind, they are trained to balance the scales of justice as a navigator reads a compass. Abram Chayes proposes that the judge is "governed by a professional ideal of reflective and dispassionate analysis of the problems before him and is likely to have had some experience in putting his ideal into practice."[233] Indeed, some activists have gone so far as to argue that the very mystique and authority commanded by judicial leaders tends to discourage efforts on the part of special interests to seek favor and pressure for special influence.[234]

Consistent with the reformers' antipathy to narrowly technocratic policy experts, therefore, the generalist posture of court authorities has been considered a unique virtue. The facts that most political issues are not of a kind where technical competence is central, that judges must deal with a broad range of public questions, and that they are not subject to a vast number of shifting, short-term political pressures all enhance the stature of the judicial official as a model agent of state authority. Equally open to all perspectives, the judicial official is "an impartial arbiter who shares neither the agency's 'insider perspective' nor its vulnerability to political pressure" of powerful established interests.[235] Removed from the day-to-day log-rolling of legislators and capture which corrupts supposedly "autonomous bureaucrats," the judge is a virtual outsider to the concerns of those who participate in the process. The judicial authority thus is the great American hero of abstract, impersonal, disembodied justice— with a white hat, a dark mask, no name, and no corrupting links to anyone.

3. Finally, the *judicially determined decision* represents to the new activists a valuable model of enlightened and fair policy making. Judicial opinions, it is argued, are uniquely individualized. They deal only with discrete and definable aspects of public problems on a discretionary case-by-case basis. As judges cannot avoid problems brought to them and must resolve issues through specific decisions, "the judicial process ... demands that controversies be reduced to rather concrete and specific issues rather than allowed to float around in the generality that so often accompanies public dispute."[236] Such an individualized approach to problems likewise places a premium on the collection of facts, the full airing of different viewpoints, and a flexible resolution. Indeed, the adaptability of judicial decision-making processes in responding to diverse, complex problems and in balancing myriad participating interests through incremental adjustment has been most important to the reformers. The "public law model," one sympathetic scholar contends, permits "ad hoc applications" of broad national policy and solutions that "can be tailored to the needs of the particular situation and flexibly administered or modified as experience develops" from cases. Consequently, such virtues of adaptability, responsiveness, and long-range perspective render the judicial model most conducive to rationally planned and coordinated public policy. It is "ironic and amusing," argues one environmental activist, that "all the goals so much lauded by planners" can be realized best in the forum to which "experts have hardly ever turned, the judiciary."[237]

In the reformers' perspective, this inherent flexibility and discretion of judicialized authorities renders decisions less rather than more arbitrary. After all, judges, like navigators, are aided by both map and crew in their calculations. The reformers have emphasized especially that judicial-type decisions are rooted in traditional moral and legal wisdom. In arguing the virtues of judicial "generality," John Denvir notes that "the court should rest its decisions on principles that it is willing to apply in other situations rather than approach each case on an ad hoc basis" totally.[238] Each decision must be defended not only by the benefits it will bring, but likewise on its continuity with established legal rules, rights, values, and guidelines. Hence we can see the homology between judicial forms and the uniquely legalistic social-reform posture toward much public policy promoted by the new activists. "The defense of the public interest," asserts Lazarus, "demands that law be applied to situations where ... unbridled discretion was formerly the rule" for bureaucrats.[239] This means as well that the interpretation and application of law must be conceived in terms of the fundamental moral principles of our political tradition—equality, freedom, and other principles of right relative to particular institutional contexts.[240] It is this concern for principled decision making by which the reformers explain both their past success and future hopes through a more judicialized politics.

Together, these assumptions about greater responsiveness to the law and citizens alike in decision making have been summed up well in ecologist Hazel Henderson's argument for the superior logic of judicial over economic public decision-making institutions. Because economic processes attempt to reduce all calculations to quantifiable monetary terms, she explains, they tend to avoid "efforts to study the many targets of constantly changing human values and preferences." By contrast, she contends further that "a sister discipline, law and the judicial process, does embody an often highly satisfactory system" for "dynamic" reconciliation of our inherited wisdom and changing citizen needs. "Through the continuous building up and reinterpreting of legal precedents, changing consumer values and precedents become codified in law and custom."[241] In short, judicial decisions emphasize the logic of competing ethical rights rather than that of efficiency, expediency, and economic gain. Two other public interest law representatives make a similar point: "The absence of any visible scientific benefit-cost yardstick seems to argue the appropriateness of the judicial forum. Courts are accustomed to weighing the equities and reviewing the decisions to determine whether they have been properly reached."[242]

Similarly, the judicial decision has been esteemed not only for its fidelity to law and moral principle, but likewise for the imperative that judges explain and defend their decisions to the entire public. The New Deal faith in the objectivity of bureaucratic experts "made it unnecessary for them even to explain their decisions by giving rational argument in their behalf," writes Lazarus. As a result "they were above the law." In contrast, the essence of the judicial decision is its careful attention to rational discourse and legal reasoning to justify particular policy choices. "Not the least important aspect," note Harrison and Jaffe, "is that as it takes place in the open, it can contribute to public understanding."[243] Courts are to a large extent educational bodies, some activists suggest, and judges the teachers who elevate, elucidate, and extend the knowledge of public life throughout the government and society.[244] More important, judicial decisions transform words into action only through the rightness of reasoning which legitimates them in the eyes of the public. Judicial decrees, in Alexander Hamilton's famous declaration, have "neither Force nor Will, but merely judgement."[245] Because judicial decisions rely on consent and voluntary compliance for their effectiveness, they are both less dangerous and more democratic than decisions of other, low-visibility bureaucratic institutions. In short, "the court's authority rests upon the public view of the court as responsive to its felt social needs";[246] hence the parallel hope of modern reformers that the progressive judicialization of government will contribute to the legitimation of public authority throughout the land.

All in all, this new model of public interest–inspired politics, judicial in form and regulatory in function, points toward the values of "responsive law" described by some contemporary academics.[247] Consistent with the recent reform aspirations, sociologists have defended this analogous vision in terms of providing the appropriate legal forms for the development of new "post-bureaucratic" public institutions. In contrast to both "repressive" and "autonomous" forms of law, it is argued, the judicialized "responsive-law" paradigm has been structured around the principles of increased participation by diverse citizen interests; emphasis on rights of mandatory institutional access and publicity; flexible, discretionary decision making; fidelity to purpose and principle over legal rules; responsiveness and competence in individualized, incremental policy development; and balancing of concerns for procedural with substantive justice. As two noted scholars summarize, "to be responsive, the system should be open to challenge at many points, should encourage participation, and should expect new social interests to make themselves known in troublesome ways."[248] A better summary of the new public interest vision of the judicialized democratic state could not be formulated.

PART TWO

Public Interest Liberalism:

Challenges and Limitations

The Fate of the Movement

That liberal public interest groups were very successful in most regards during the early 1970s is indisputable. They stimulated the enactment of over thirty pieces of significant new legislation, won scores of court victories, and altered the basic patterns of regulatory decision making and enforcement across a broad range of programmatic concerns. Building upon the progressive gains of the previous decade, the new middle-class activists "had considerable success in opening up political processes, in forcing greater accountability, [and] in achieving...new rights to information and participation in decisions."[1] By the time of Jimmy Carter's ascendance to the presidency, the liberal consumer–environmental public interest network in Washington commanded great attention, respect, and sometimes even fear from the establishment. The new president himself reflected this influence in his vow to make government "a forum for the people and the protection of the people themselves" by promoting appointments "that would be acceptable to Ralph Nader."[2]

Opinion polls similarly confirmed the impact of the new reformers within American public life. In 1971, a Harris poll revealed that over 69 percent of Americans believed that public interest muckrakers and advocates were a "good" force in our political system.[3] Likewise, the most vocal proponents of the new public interest creed—Barry Commoner, David Brower, Ralph Nader—ranked consistently high in popularity polls in the early 1970s. Indeed, Nader placed high among the top ten most-admired Americans for years and sparked popular demands to seek presidential candidacy in 1972.[4] Americans in the early 1970s were highly supportive of the reformers' environmental, consumer, and democratic goals in particular. A *Public Opinion Quarterly* review of numerous studies concluded that "by 1970, conservation had crept into the volunteered list of the most important national problems facing the nation today."[5] A 1970 Gallup poll revealed pollution to be the second most pressing problem according to the public; a whopping 86 percent of the public was at least significantly "concerned."[6] Roper polls throughout the 1970s also confirmed that never less than two-thirds of all citizens believed that existing environmental protection laws and regulations had either "struck the right balance" or "not gone far enough."[7]

Increased government regulation of business in general was likewise supported in 1976 by over two-thirds of Americans, although fewer felt that regulation did a "good job," because it too often had "done more to help corporations than to protect the consumer." Attitudes about regulation in the abstract grew more hostile as the decade wore on, but support for particular consumer-oriented regulations remained consistently high. One study by two conservative scholars in 1979 revealed this about public attitudes toward government regulations: "For over four decades, Americans have been ambivalent in their attitudes toward regulation. A majority has always said they opposed greater regulations, but over the years—as more and more regulation has been enacted—a majority has also voiced approval of existing regulations and indicated that it did not want to roll back the tide."[8]

This general support for the reformers' policy goals was joined by support for their democratic participatory values as well. An EPEA report cited a 1972 Harris poll concluding that "the mandate is for participation... and the message, obviously not heard yet by the leaders surveyed, is that people want to be included and informed, not managed and ignored."[9] This public demand was especially liberal, progressive, and antibusiness in orientation. Another study of participation patterns in the 1970s concluded that "one has to go back to the 1930s in American political history to find comparable stimulation for Left-orientations."[10] What is more, the new advocates collectively succeeded in mobilizing formal commitments of time, money, and energy from nearly six million of these sympathetic citizens. "The basic strength of the movement has been evident," concluded an EPEA study in the middle of the decade. Claiming to benefit from more voluntary contributors than did both major political parties combined, activists often boasted that only a handful of presidential contenders could hope to match the results of reform group solicitation of funds.[11] All in all, therefore, by 1973 the new activists could identify good reasons for pride about their past and optimism about their future. "The fact is that the program advocated by the public interest movement in the early 1970s was passed," concluded Simon Lazarus. "They were wildly successful."[12]

Such "wild" success among the reform troops was tamed significantly in the latter years of the 1970s, however. On almost every front, new gains were slowed or halted, and old victories once taken for granted were placed in jeopardy. To appropriate the imagery of one *National Journal* article in 1980, the movement's maturity into middle age found the liberal activists wary of its declining strength and fearful for its health in the future. "The burst of youthful energy that translated many of its goals into public policy has given way to a struggle to stem erosion in both the movement's vitality and the achievements of the 1970s," concluded the article.[13] A brief review of a few indicators illustrates the point.

The reformers' power within Congress quite obviously withered dramatically. Defeats of efforts to create a new agency for consumer advocacy, to expand regulatory procedural reform, and to legislate the corporate democracy bill signaled the triumph of the new conservative attitudes developing on Capitol Hill. Lacking clear electoral clout, Ralph Nader's habitual appearances in committee hearings also became less intimidating to foes and less welcome to allies among elected officials. At the same time, acknowledges EDF leader William Butler, a revitalized business lobbying establishment set upon the task of "undoing in Congress what we have done in the courts," such as in the trans-Alaskan and Tellico Dam disputes.[14] Even more important, the federal courts themselves proved to be no longer reliable allies for liberal social causes. After years of generally favorable decisions, justices again began to "slam the door" in landmark cases, limiting grants of attorneys' fees, benefits of class-actions suits, and standing for review to environmental advocates. As Washington legal activist Mitchell Rogovin dourly lamented, a "slow but steady decline in public interest law" effectiveness gradually sapped the potency of the movement.[15]

Increasingly rebuffed in Congress and the courts, the activists' influence within executive regulatory agencies also appeared to suffer. Not only were rights to agency access and information disclosure less respected, but liberal allies within the FTC, OSHA, and EPA came under increasing attack from multiple sectors of public power. Moreover, the once-heralded presidency of Jimmy Carter proved a bitter disappointment. Carter failed to deliver on promises for numerous consumer, environmental, and procedural reforms and directly defied movement positions on issues of energy management and regulatory review policies. Most public interest appointees likewise proved powerless to make a difference in the administration or too timid to even try, thus leaving them open to shrill charges of selling out from former allies. Indeed, the entire Carter epoch has often been maligned by reformers as a basic cause of their own decline in political fortune. "Four more anesthetizing years of Carter could not have inspired a program of creative liberalism," Mark Green bitterly complained in early 1982.[16]

The fate of the movement in regard to the general citizenry was little more assuring. While the breadth of popularity expressed in polls for most public interest social issues remained uniformly high, the measured intensity of support fell in relation to other concerns for the economy, crime, and declining military strength.[17] Likewise, no significant victories in shaping the platforms in either national party were registered after the disillusioning defeat of George McGovern's presidential bid, thus undercutting the potential of clearly defined electoral impact. Indeed, the unofficial liberal public interest party, Barry Commoner's Citizens' Party, won less than 1 percent of the total electoral vote in 1980. In retrospect,the reformers' characteristic aversion to sustained partisan electoral activity throughout the 1970s probably reflected as much as contributed to their early failures to influence voting patterns in the public. As Mark Green remarked in 1972, "We have been counting all along on a massive citizen-action response. . . . If this is all McGovern can get from the people, when and where is that citizen-action response going to come from?"[18]

The grass roots of the citizen groups themselves showed signs of undernourishment as the decade progressed as well. Not only did few new liberal mass membership groups emerge to augment the movement, but some established groups showed significant drops in numbers of contributors from their peak in the early 1970s. For example, Common Cause membership fell by over one-fifth (60,000 lost) and Wilderness Society losses totaled nearly one-fourth (16,000 lost) during the last few years of the decade.[19] Indeed, it has become commonplace among analysts to identify the apogee of popular participation on behalf of environmental politics as early as 1971. A parallel decline in the reserves of full-time reform advocates and leaders was manifest as the currents of public values shifted in direction. Public interest law organizer Charles Halpern had already noted in 1976 that "the law student activism and idealism of 1970 that helped start the movement is scarce now. . . . This is a time of emotional depression, and many people don't think these programs are worthwhile."[20]

Furthermore, losses of private individual financial contributions and government support were paralleled by rapid evaporation of private foundation funding. In particular, severe cutbacks or termination in projected Ford Foundation grants made the always insecure financial basis of the voluntary organizations even more precarious. "People think we're here forever," warned Center for Law and Social Policy codirector James E. Barnes, "but we do not have such a secure foothold. The main problem is money." Hard pressed to compete among themselves for scarce financial resources and waning citizen support, the overall outlook in the late 1970s was appropriately summed up by a Citizens Communication Center leader as "dismal."[21] And this decline in resources came at the same time as regulatory goals became more complex, organized opposition more powerful, and hence policy battles more protracted and costly.

Finally, the ascendance of Ronald Reagan and other conservative Republicans to high national office in 1980 both symbolized and quickened the plunge into hard times for liberal social advocates. On one hand, Reagan's victory signaled the collapse of citizen support for the liberal policy foundation upon which public interest politics was built. Winning with the votes of only about 27 percent of the total electorate, Reagan was handed a mandate proclaiming public disillusionment and sealed with apathy about the value of increased social welfare action by the government. On the other hand, the new president rode a new wave of enthusiasm generated by a powerful, if small and fragile, conservative coalition of "the people" across the land. This included, above all, the efforts of organized corporate and small-business interests committed to reestablishing the priority of private-producer welfare in American politics. These revitalized business organizations converged with long-standing culturally conservative grass-roots and fundamentalist religious groups seeking to redefine the social agenda along more traditional lines as well. In fact, at the national level, the single biggest rise of citizen activism since the late 1970s has been initiated by the Moral Majority and other New Right groups bent on defeat of liberals throughout government.[22]

With these twin allies of united conservative support and liberals in disarray, the Reagan "New Beginning" agenda forced public interest activists into a desperate, if not unsuccessful, effort to minimize their potential losses of legal authority and public power. The president's platform to "get the government off the backs of Americans" constituted a direct attack upon the goals of most reformers. His appointment of blatantly pro-corporate officials to positions of administrative power undercut the role of agencies like the EPA, FTC, FDA, and Department of Interior as effective allies of the activists. In particular, the autocratic James Watt revealed himself a dedicated and powerful opponent of environmentalists. Specific policies to increase offshore oil drilling, to expand wilderness exploration for minerals, to gut the Freedom of Information Act, to ban government-mandated consumer information distribution, to cut off department funding of support for citizen participation, and generally to restore autonomy to big business all represented significant assaults upon hard-won gains of the liberal public interest movement.[23]

These setbacks have by no means signaled a total defeat of the liberal reform forces, of course. Widely shared public commitments to environmental welfare, consumer health and safety, and some semblance of open government have clearly constrained the conservative assault. Administrative implementation of many policies and programs has been relaxed, but basic legislative statutes, regulatory guidelines, and judicial precedents still bind official government actors. Indeed, the reform troops have continued to be surprisingly effective in stopping new corporate development in wilderness areas, in maintaining strict air pollution laws, in combating nuclear power, in pressuring action from agencies such as the EPA and FTC, in enforcing antitrust policies, and in forcing dismissals of much-loathed officials such as James Watt and Anne Gorsuch from high administrative positions. Furthermore, many group memberships actually exploded in size again—over 20 percent increases at Common Cause, and 30 percent at the Sierra Club, the Wilderness Society, and the NRDC—in reaction to the alleged Reagan revolution.[24] In fact, some populist intellectuals and organizers even optimistically cite evidence that a resurgence of liberal public interest–oriented citizen action is incubating throughout the land in the 1980s.[25]

In general, former FTC chairman Michael Pertschuk may be correct in suggesting that the defensive retreat of public interest activists constitutes less a fall from power than a pause in development. Disconnected from their carefully constructed networks of access to government, activists have utilized the respite to renew their strength, to redefine their goals, and to reformulate their strategies for "winning back America." "Those out-of-power have the freedom and energy to describe the weakness of the ruling party and to prescribe the program for future policy-makers," reflected Mark Green in 1982. "If progressives can learn from 1980 as their predecessors did from

1946, 1952, and 1972, their past generation [of reformers] won't be the last."[26]

Such renewed hopes for a revitalized public interest politics in the future confirm the need for critical assessment of the liberal political vision that evolved during the movement's first two decades of action. This is my goal in Part Two.

CHAPTER 3

The Political Economy
of Social Reform

We hear a great deal about the class consciousness of labor; my own
observation is that in America today consumers' consciousness is growing very much faster....

—Walter Lippman

We have never really had the kind of sustained public consumer movement necessary to force a restructuring of the whole system.... Without
such a movement, no idea is worth trying and all are just dreams.

—David Riley

One of the most problematic aspects of public interest liberalism
involves the particular conception of citizen welfare—the social issues
addressed, policies proposed, and ideals advanced—at the core of the
new reform agenda. Specifically, the reformers' "new consumer"
ethical challenge to the established corporate terms of capitalist
economic growth has both reflected and nurtured a deeper insensitivity about the exigencies of economic life generally. This is not to agree
with conservative critics that public interest–oriented social regulatory
policies were largely responsible for the deterioration of American
economic health that began in the early 1970s. Indeed, I argue in the
following pages that the negative impact of such regulation has been
minimal relative to both the benefits it has produced and the other
larger forces influencing our material welfare. Rather, my point is
that it has been the reformers' general silence about, and apparent
indifference toward, those larger macroeconomic problems that has
most taken them out of the mainstream of American political leadership. However socially progressive their aims, the critical fact is that

132

the new liberalism has stopped short of addressing the most salient concerns and needs of most citizens in the public at large.

The "New Consumer" Politics

The Citizen as Consumer. Analysis of the specific substantive orientation implied by the "new consumer" social identity provides both starting point and continuing theme for development of the basic arguments in this chapter.[1] For those groups that specifically identify themselves as "consumer advocates," the appeal to citizens as consumers seems apparent enough.[2] The consumer perspective refers to the voluntary actions of individuals purchasing material goods and services in the marketplace as well as to involuntary "consumption of environmental pollution and compulsory exposure to occupational safety and health hazards."[3] In other words, consumerism has become a catchword for concern about nearly any dimension of life in which people are recipients and objects of social production, whether beneficial or harmful. It thus directs attention to the unsafe water that we drink, the dangerous chemicals that we eat in our food, the unclean air that we breathe, the defective products that we buy, the unfair advertising to which we are exposed, and so on.[4]

The underlying assumption that "we are what we consume" captures the orientations of radical ecologists as much as those of more narrowly defined consumer activists. Barry Commoner, for example, locates the "common root" of all of our problems in that "something is wrong with the way this nation uses its human and natural resources."[5] In short, we carelessly despoil and destroy rather than enhance, renew, and respect them. Likewise, the central theme of one of the most influential environmental studies, the Club of Rome's *Mankind at the Turning Point*, is that American patterns of consumption are the central cause of resource depletion as well as of waste, pollution, and disease that threaten the world.[6] Given this perspective on the "consumption" problem, then, the appropriate response by concerned citizens follows directly. As the editor of *The Environmental Handbook* puts it, "the limits can, and must, be set by the consumer. It is the consumer, ultimately, who must decide for himself what appliances he needs and which he can forego. The producers of power . . . will cease to produce that which will not sell."[7] The landmark decision in *Environmental Defense Fund v. Hardin* followed a similar logic in affirming the political status of environmental advocates: "Consumers of regulated products and services have standing to protect the public

133

interest... Furthermore, the consumers' interest... in environmental protection may properly be represented by a membership association with an organizational interest in the problem," it was proclaimed.[8]

Indeed, the entire rhetorical thrust of the new liberal reformism opposing the "people" and the "interests" vividly connotes the inherent conflict between the powerless mass of citizens in their roles as consumers and the concentrated power of corporate producers. This is expressed perfectly in Barry Commoner's campaign slogan, "people over profits." The consumer perspective likewise captures the assumed relationship between citizen and government, as is explained at length in Edmond Cahn's influential essay "Law in the Consumer Perspective." Cahn argues that the inherited "imperial or official" view of law has been "that of the processors" and government elites. "The new point of view, which we may call the consumer perspective, is that of consumers of law and government." In a free society, he contends, no influence is more cogent and active than the citizen-consumers' needs, demands, and complaints.[9] Jean and Edgar Cahn, two highly influential public interest lawyers, have expressed the same perspective on the consumer orientation of the new politics. They argue that "the lawyer's role as public champion of the citizen as consumer... [of] government policies and services—irrespective of whether they involve pollution or poverty"—is the crucial task of public interest legal reform.[10] Simon Lazarus confirms that point as well in his own analysis of the new movement. "The 'public,'" he says of the public interest vernacular, "usually means 'consumers.'"[11]

The most influential representative of this propensity to identify the public interest with the consumer interest surely has been Ralph Nader.[12] Hazel Henderson has also encouraged such a consumer posture toward comprehensive reform action in explicit terms. She not only identifies environmentalists, women's rights groups, public interest lawyers, social workers, scientists, and engineers as allies with "militant consumers"; she further summarizes and categorizes the collective crusade by all of these activists under the banner of a "post-industrial consumers' movement."[13] John Gardner similarly equates the social goal of enabling the individual to be a better citizen with that of becoming a "better consumer." "Consumerism," he has observed, defined the core of the "middle-class phenomenon" that brought forth "in the 1970s... a powerful movement to call the great institutions of our society into account."[14] David Riley has voiced the same sentiment in even more ambitious terms. The developing "environmental movement and the radical movement generally" headed by "Ralph Nader and Saul Alinsky's campaign against corporations" share the same "common ground" of a new "consumer" movement, he argues. "We have never really had the kind of sustained public consumer movement necessary to force a restructuring of the whole system. . . . Without such a movement, no idea is worth trying and all are just dreams."[15] In an obvious reference to an older form of radicalism, the new battle chant of citizen insurgents has become, to quote the words of three public interest lawyers, "Consumers of the World Unite."[16]

Consumerism Old and New. We have seen that the new consumer struggle with corporate capitalism resembles in many ways the early consumer movements that arose during the Progressive Era. Beginning in this early period, consumerism gained appeal as the basis of political reform efforts to win a measure of collective power for citizens within the rapidly centralizing economic system. "The chief offense of the trust," insisted Walter Weyl, "becomes its capacity to injure the consumer." Early liberal reformers argued that the esteemed ideal of "consumer sovereignty" was eroded by monopolistic price fixing, and that the opportunities for advancement were undermined by the unstable job market. "The high cost of living is arranged by private understanding," proclaimed Woodrow Wilson.[17] Many liberal elites saw in this perspective the roots out of which might grow significant progressive change in coming years. Walter Lippmann's *Drift and Mastery* in particular led the praise. "We hear a great deal about the class consciousness of labor; my own observation is that in America today consumers' consciousness is growing very much faster."[18] As historian Richard Hofstadter has argued, consumerism provided an important means of bringing "the diffuse malaise of the public into focus." The special appeal of "consumer consciousness," he suggested, was that "it was the lowest common denominator among classes of people who had little else to unite them on concrete issues."[19] Like images of the "common man" and the "plain people," the "consumer" captured the socially conditioned discontents and aspirations of citizens specific to the modern historical period. "Not everyone is a steel worker, after all," Nader loves to say, "but everyone is a consumer."[20]

Traditionally, this consumer politics was limited to concerns for more, better, and cheaper goods. Its most pressing preoccupations were with lower prices, more efficient means of production and distribution, and more effective control over corporate provision of commodities in response to ever-expanding and more sophisticated consumer wants. In other words, traditional consumer politics sanctioned and served citizen desires for private wealth as the greatest promise

135

of modern society. This rationale eventually spread from the early middle-class reformers to structure the New Deal contract between capital and organized labor. "What are the goals of your organization?" labor leader Samuel Gompers was asked. "More," he answered, acknowledging the basic logic of aspiration which characterized worker demands for decades through the 1960s.[21]

By contrast, however, public interest leaders frankly acknowledge that the "vantage point... of today's consumer spokesmen... is hardly representative of the mainstream of the consumer movement" in previous generations. The basic orientation of recent public interest liberals has recognized "a need for a new type of 'consumer demand.'"[22] Reflecting their reservations about economic growth, they have shrouded the traditional obsession with increased commodity consumption in much suspicion and disrepute. As outlined earlier, prevailing American consumptive habits are said to have required the wasteful use of scarce material resources, widespread damage to the ecosystem, and bellicose and exploitive action in the world to defend our indulgent interests. Likewise, the new movement has constituted something of an assault upon the entire set of moral, psychological, and social assumptions behind the conventional worship of material abundance—what Christopher Lasch calls the "cult of consumption."[23] Many of the activists, in David Riley's words, "raise questions about the unhealthy passivism that our emphasis on consumption encourages and the undue sense of power and potency which comes from material acquisitiveness."[24] Conspicuously obsessive consumption has become the new opiate of the people, they suggest. "On this view, there is nothing desirable in consumption. The less consumption we can maintain a given state with, the better off we are," proclaims influential environmentalist-economist Kenneth Boulding.[25]

A defining substantive commitment of the new activists thus has been to advocate a new public paradigm of moral values for the mass of consumers to complement the steady-state economic restraint they urge upon managerial elites at the helm of productive power. While overall growth must be controlled and income redistribution effected from the top to the bottom, those in the middle must do with what they have already, or even less. The "new consumer demand [is] not for products as much as for life styles," argues Henderson. We must shift our priorities from excessive material wants to "meta-needs" such as political participation, social justice, health, self-development, and harmony with nature. Therefore, for example, "to the new 'post-industrial' consumers the automobile is no longer prized as enhancing social status, sexual prowess, or even individual mobility."

136

Rather, the car is but a mode of transportation "forced upon them" by a "monolithic system of vested interests and client group dependencies" at enormous social cost.[26] Hence, the new consumer interest in quality over quantity, and in self-development over status, must counter impulses to "keep up with Joneses" that fuel the American drive for more possessions. When we kick the "Jonesism habit," Henderson suggests, "competition may be channeled into enhancement of phsyical fitness and well-being, and aggressiveness may reemerge as striving for knowledge and higher levels of consciousness."[27]

Once again, no one better symbolizes the movement's uniquely antagonistic posture toward commodity fetishism than Ralph Nader. Nader relentlessly attacks decadence, hedonism, and privatistic indulgences with almost religious sobriety in his speeches to students. "Those who believe deeply in humane ecology must act in accordance with their beliefs," he has admonished. "They must so order their consumption and disposal habits that they can, in good conscience, preach what they actively practice"[28]—and so, as leader, he does himself. Nader owns no automobile, dresses in conspicuous drabness, works long hours for little pay, and esteems his public commitments above all else. He is a virtual political puritan. The lessons he teaches—indeed, preaches—are the virtues of hard work, lowered expectations, patience, and sacrifice. "The drive for a firmly rooted initiatory democracy," he stresses, "rests on conviction, work, intellect, values, and a willingness to sacrifice normal indulgences for the opportunity to come to grip as never before with the requisites of a just society."[29] As a symbol as well as a moral exponent, Nader politicizes the lifestyle of "voluntary simplicity" to which he and most activists adhere and hold as example of virtuous citizenship to others throughout the land.

The Economic Costs of Social Regulation: Evaluating Conservative Criticism

The new, rather unorthodox reorientation toward collective consumer values predictably has provoked the wrath of leaders and pundits across the political spectrum. By far the most vitriolic attacks have been launched by conservative muckrakers, establishment economists, business leaders, and Republican officeholders in Washington. Their common complaint has emphasized the extensive damage to economic welfare, both collective and individual, wrought by the new liberal reformers' social policies and regulatory schemes. In this section I review and evaluate these arguments briefly. I argue that some important truths are contained in such challenges, but that they alone do not explain convincingly the failure of the public interest vision to achieve greater and more sustained influence within contemporary American politics.

The Growth Debate. Perhaps the broadest and most common attack by critics aims right at the heart of the public interest animus against economic growth itself. Many opponents of public interest liberalism have persistently criticized this value orientation as inherently myopic, destructive, even totalitarian. Direct assaults upon the "new politics" in particular have constituted a central tenet of widespread demands for reindustrialization policies by advocates of both a new corporate "social contract" and supply-side economics.[30] Popular statements of this "growthist" position include Harold Barnett's *Society and Growth,* Wilfred Beckerman's *Two Cheers for the Affluent Society,* and George Gilder's *Wealth and Poverty.*[31] The guiding assumption of this perspective, in neoconservative Irving Kristol's approving words, is that "the idea of progress in the modern era has always signified that the quality of life would inevitably be improved by national enrichment." Echoing the expansionist biases upon which America long has been built, Daniel Bell has made the point even more bluntly: "Without a commitment to economic growth," he queries, "what is the raison d'être of capitalism?"[32]

Most of these critics have not contested the general significance of those social ills identified by the reformers or the need for some social regulation in general. Rather, the primary argument has centered on the need to balance the goals of social reformers by a renewed collective commitment to greater productive growth and market efficiency. Furthermore, it is widely assumed by most critics that the American people see things in just the same way. The general will, in other words, mandates a high-growth policy: "No politician can stay in power in a democracy without economic growth, because the majority of the people want it," claims Keith Pavitt.[33] In this view, most Americans desire above all more individual material wealth and private consumer buying power in the marketplace. To defy the New Deal logic of promising ever greater affluence for all is thus said to be as politically naive as it is dangerous.

Such critical perspectives point to some serious problems in the public interest reform agenda, to be sure. However, they are misleading in two quite important points of fact. First, it should be reiterated that the liberal advocates' positions on economic growth are not

138

uniform in either their guiding logic or their intensity of commitment. Some, mostly radical environmentalists, have made growth a high-priority issue for debate. For example, one Friends of the Earth advocate has summarized their politics this way: "If one has to boil it down to one issue, I guess that issue is Growth. Growth of population, of technology, of economy, of waste, of products, of per capita consumption, of power, of things generally. They're all so interrelated."[34] However, other groups such as Common Cause, Consumer Federation of America, Nader organizations, and many environmental groups have taken more subtle and restrained positions on the growth issue. Indeed, the fact is that both public interest liberals and their growthist critics have usually been quite unclear and contradictory about just what they mean by economic "growth." While most of the reformers have agreed that the rate and character of past profit-led growth is undesirable, little consensus about the appropriate levels and kinds of future productive activity has developed in any significant detail. Some do argue for no growth, but most activists advocate instead positions of low growth or selectively controlled growth. "Business-men should stop characterizing us as no growth people. That's wrong," says EDF head Arlie Schardt.[35] Generally, the argument of most reformers has aimed only to elevate the primacy of those concerns for health, safety, nature, security, and democracy which normally have been sacrificed to the overriding goals of maximizing corporate profits or the gross national product. In other words, the thrust of the new movement has been less to halt economic expansion than to shift the balance of our aggregate wants and investments toward other less tangible and more qualitatively defined collective goals.[36]

Conservative critics are also misleading in their assessment of reigning American public values with regard to these issues. A vast array of evidence from public opinion polls suggests that the antimaterialistic quality-of-life orientations to controlled growth advocated by new consumer activists has had considerable impact upon the attitudes of most Americans, or at least did so during the 1970s. We have already seen that large majorities of Americans supported the reformers' specific attempts to expand environmental and consumer regulation, to democratize government, and to render corporate power more accountable to the public. Much of the available data on public perspectives regarding the relation between such social goods and economic abundance is equally supportive. For example, a 1975 Harris poll concluded dramatically that a roughly three-to-one majority of Americans endorsed the statement that "the trouble with most leaders is that they don't understand that people want better quality of almost everything they have rather than [greater] quantity." In addition, the survey found that 70 percent of all citizens felt that American consumption levels were too high, and even more were willing to change their lifestyles to less consumption-oriented patterns.[37] A 1977 Harris survey confirmed further, by a whopping four-to-one margin, that the public favored a transformation in American collective commitments to a society with "more emphasis upon learning how to live with basic needs . . . than in reaching a higher standard of living."[38] Likewise, a review of dozens of public surveys from the early 1970s by Hazel Erskine revealed that Americans rated increased affluence as a rather low priority. She summarized the patterns as suggesting "first and foremost . . . [that] Americans' chief aims in life turn out to be anything but materialistic. Most wish for peace of mind, family, contentment, and secondarily, health." In fact, "rarely is wealth per se given any priority among people's hopes for their lives."[39]

The most direct evidence about public opinion on the relation between economic growth and social change has been provided by a 1974 Wisconsin state survey by Frederick Buttel and William Flinn.[40] These authors used survey results to illustrate specifically that public opinion provides no clear mandate in support of the growthist position. Their survey revealed not only that support for public interest–type policies was pervasive, but that most people seemed unconcerned about possible conflicts of ecological values and economic growth. While the authors did find that awareness of goal conflict was more salient among middle-income citizens, they concluded that "working-class people do not find economic growth and environmental quality grossly as incompatible" as growthist policy analysts have assumed. The authors' conclusion, therefore, was that the decline of environmental and liberal social politics in the 1970s did "not stem from an American public dominated by pro-expansion, anti-environmental" attitudes.[41] National polls in later years present similar results. A 1977 Harris poll found that, by an almost two-to-one margin, Americans viewed cleaning up pollution as a social good that should not be compromised by concerns for increasing aggregate economic growth. Two separate polls in 1981 revealed that this margin on parallel questions had actually widened to between three- and four-to-one for social regulation. As long-time polling expert Robert C. Mitchell concluded in a review of recent studies, "when tradeoffs between environmental protection and . . . growth . . . are posed, pluralities almost always choose the pro-environmental position . . . on the order of two or three to one."[42]

Many supporters of the new consumerism have interpreted the cumulative thrust of these surveys to indicate that a large majority of citizens in middle America have become increasingly more concerned about the dislocations wrought by continued capitalistic economic growth than with its promises of ever more material benefits. As Fred Hirsch, E. J. Mishan, Volkmar Lauber, and many others have argued, a new consciousness has developed within advanced industrial nations about the social costs imposed by the productive processes created to attain rapid economic growth.[43] Scholar Ronald Inglehart has developed a theoretical model charting the entire evolution of human need fulfillment in modern societies to explain this recent "silent revolution" in "post-bourgeois values" within most Western industrial nations. While complete transition to Charles Reich's "Consciousness III" has hardly occurred, his evidence suggests that at least the "insatiable wants" of humans identified by economists may not be so clearly material or possessive in nature as has often been assumed. Or, to cite another pollster, what seems clear is that "the meaning of 'more' has changed" for Americans to include collective social goods as well as private material wealth.[44] If this is so, the new faith in activating large numbers of citizens to seek a better life through fundamental changes in the character and priorities of traditional material consumption and production may have been less naive than corporate growthist critics contend.

Productivity and Regulatory Costs. Behind the prevailing establishment challenge to the reformers' position on economic growth lies a more subtle and telling claim. The basic issue is that social regulation ultimately is economic regulation as well. After all, smokestack scrubbers, safety devices, air and water filters, drug testing, chemical bans, quality controllers—none of these are cheap. Indeed, the economic burdens of promoting safety, health, and environmental protection are significant. For example, air- and water-pollution regulation is claimed to have imposed $27 billion in new costs on industry in 1978 alone, and up to 5 percent of total capital spending in the mid-1970s generally. OSHA compliance cost another estimated $48 billion in the decade after 1970.[45] Economist-turned-presidential-adviser Murray Weidenbaum speculated in 1979 that the total costs of federal regulation amounted to over $100 billion a year. Focusing his analysis on liberal public interest–oriented policies, he thus concluded that "the rising tide of regulation has become a major barrier to productive economic activity." Like many other critics, Weidenbaum protested that the new social regulatory programs had radically undercut needed investment in basic goods and services, discouraged product innovation, and even forced the shutdown of numerous productive plants for little overall gain in social welfare. In some industries, compliance with pollution-control and workplace-safety regulations accounted for nearly one-third of total capital investment in the mid-1970s.[46] Such drains on productive capacity have not only halted economic growth, it has been widely argued, but have jeopardized existing levels of national prosperity as well.[47]

Furthermore, numerous studies have provided evidence that a pervasive insensitivity to such economic costs has been built into the structure of many new regulations and reform-inspired policies. For example, new social regulations mandating "maximum-feasible-protection" standards, "no-risk" bans on certain products, strict production compliance deadlines, and "clean-up-or-shut-down" alternatives may effectively reduce corporate freedom to abuse workers and consumers, but they do so by divorcing regulatory control from consideration of compliance costs almost altogether. The result has often been an imposition of high performance standards of the best available control technology without an assessment of the link between actual risks and economic burdens relative to other possible solutions or competing social goods. As former FDA commissioner Donald Kennedy has said of public interest–inspired standards, "Our statute does not allow us to weigh the adverse health conditions against dollars."[48]

Environmentalist insistence on rigorous use of environmental impact statements typifies the problem as well. As several studies have indicated, the obsession with minimizing disruptive impacts from development encouraged by the statements tends to divorce policy from reasonable assessments of the actual burdens and benefits of the impact at stake—economic, social, and ecological.[49] Similarly, the rigidly defined means-oriented standards often mandated by public interest-inspired legislation have been charged with impeding discretionary agency determinations of cost-effective remedies, as illustrated by the grossly expensive and ineffective Clean Air Act.[50] Overall, such arguments castigating the reformers' aversion to conventional efficiency issues as more a vice than a virtue have proved to be highly influential over time. Persistent business pressure supporting greater cost–benefit scrutiny of social regulation gave rise to a series of executive reforms, from President Ford's call for "economic impact statements" to Carter's Regulatory Analysis Review Group management to Reagan's more inhibiting policy of OMB oversight to achieve "regulatory relief" for economic producers.

Liberal policy analysts have demonstrated that most of these claims are greatly exaggerated in scope and significance, however. They cite contrary studies, such as one by economist William Tabb which contends that cost estimates by conservatives tend to be grossly inflated, fail to measure the real benefits of social regulation, and obscure the fact that the greatest regulatory costs are imposed by financial subsidies for private business interests. Moreover, a Nader-group study by Mark Green and Norman Waitzman has provided evidence that five agencies adding costs of $31 billion in 1978 also produced an estimated $36 billion in benefits.[51] In particular, reformers have insisted that critics of social regulation ignore the vast savings of public and private costs provided by anticipatory safety, health, and quality controls. After all, they argue, it is much cheaper to prevent toxic waste and water pollution than to clean them up once their damage has been done. Drawing upon statistics from a 1979 Council on Environmental Quality report, environmental economists Richard Kazis and Richard Grossman estimate a net gain of at least $44.8 billion in anticipatory benefits from air-pollution controls alone.[52]

It is clear, too, that economic benefits have been prime considerations of various public interest struggles over energy, environmental, bottle bill, and safety and health policies. Indeed, some social regulations have actually increased productive innovation toward more efficient oil refining techniques, waste disposal, and energy use. "EDF's opposition to destructive or wasteful projects and policies is always combined with efforts to propose more economical, less harmful alternatives," adds one group director.[53] What is more, we should recall, a central tenet of the recent reform faith all along has been that the protection of human life, nature, and other social goods simply cannot be translated adequately into terms of economic cost or conventional measures of productivity such as the gross national product. As public policy analyst Steven Kelman has argued in a series of influential books and articles, the liberal activists are right to fight cost–benefit analysis itself because of its tendency to devalue social goods, to distort public decision with the private logic of the marketplace, and to undercut the strategic influence of reformers within government.[54]

Supporting arguments from many economists have further challenged critics of regulation on more traditional economic grounds. For one thing, many analysts point out that America is much less regulated than most other advanced industrial nations with prospering economies.[55] Moreover, one study has shown that the growth of

American government spending relative to the gross national product actually was less during the 1970s than in the boom era of the previous decade, and that historically there is no clear pattern of relation between regulation and productivity. Indeed, the highly respected Data Resources Inc. has estimated that total environmental regulation since 1970 has lowered American productivity by no more than 0.1 percent.[56] Finally, some experts have concluded that the capital shortage cited by corporate managers during the 1970s actually had little foundation in fact. The problem is not that scarce capital has been consumed by excessive government spending or industry compliance with federal social regulations, many argue, but that corporate managers have chosen to divert their revenues from domestic production to more speculative acquisition, foreign investment markets, or private consumption. Given this existing slack in the efficiency of resource utilization, therefore, increased social welfare and economic prosperity are simply not locked into the antagonistic zero-sum relationship often assumed by conservatives. Cuts in social regulation may enhance corporate profits, but they will not ensure gains in productivity, new jobs, or general economic improvement, as was well illustrated in the automotive industry during the early 1980s.[57]

Such arguments are not intended to deny or to excuse the reformers' occasional displays of insensitivity about the need for efficient, cost-effective regulatory policies. But they do qualify greatly the significance of conservative polemics by placing them within the overall context of waste, irrationality, and injustice built into the American political economy. The fact is that, however irresponsible their designs for implementation, public interest social regulations have placed only minimal burdens on the nation's overall productive capacity, and then mostly for quite positive gains in collective welfare. What is probably even more important is that opinion polls once again tend to confirm that large portions of the American public agree in this assessment. This is reflected not only in that most regulatory controls on product safety and quality (83 percent), pollution levels (82 percent), and public corruption (75 percent) have continued to enjoy immense public support, but that large pluralities of citizens also affirm that the costs to productivity are worth it for recent gains in worker health, consumer safety, and environmental protection. Indeed, a 1983 Harris poll revealed that, although most citizens still remain skeptical about big government in general, a full 80 percent of the public agree that "the consumer movement has done a great deal or some good" on balance to improve citizens' lives. As Everett Carl

Ladd concluded from his survey of polls in 1982, Americans have shown repeatedly that they do not find existing social regulatory policies and a healthy economy to be as intrinsically incompatible as many conservative policy analysts suggest.[58]

The New Consumerism and Inequality. The regulatory designs of public interest activists have also been charged as illiberal on yet more specific grounds. The significant point is that the economic efficiency of new social regulations is politically less important than the distribution of economic burdens imposed by collective-goods advocacy. We can begin to understand the problem by addressing the simplistic premises upon which much of the reformers' appeal rests. The very logic of the consumer posture assumes a structural conflict between the public interests and the special interests, between people and profits. It pits an autonomous public of exploited consumers on one side against the nefarious concentrated power of capitalistic producers on the other. These characterizations have been invested with great significance and locked into an unyielding ethical structure that defines the shared terms of reform activist understanding and choice. The corresponding logic of creating a "civic balance" is clear. As the people have long paid the social costs of private corporate profit, so must private profits now be reappropriated to pay for increasing social welfare.[59]

The struggle for social justice has thus been conceived primarily as a matter of wealth redistribution effected through developing political power in support of consumer demands. As the reformers see it, social regulation redirects corporate profits back to the people in the form of social goods such as safe workplaces, antipollution measures, higher product quality, preserved open spaces, better consumer information, and elimination of fraudulent advertising. "The role of the legal system should be to force the 'internalization' of all external diseconomies," the activists insist.[60] Hence, the cornucopia of corporate wealth will finance the transformation to a more socially conscious consumer society. "American industry . . . could easily absorb all costs imposed by regulation out of its profit structure without significantly affecting the economy," concluded one consumer advocate in the early 1970s.[61]

The problem is that this vision is misleading about the actual implications of cost internalization in a market economy.[62] Such a simplistic view of the conflict between consumers and producers obscures the complex interdependencies of social organization painfully apparent to most working people. To be sure, all citizens are consum-

145

ers who suffer health and safety hazards, imposed by corporate producers, at home, at work, and on the road; who pay high prices for corporate inefficiency and profit hoarding; and who are deceived all too often by corporate and state officials. Yet most people are also directly dependent on private economic producers for jobs, wages, goods, and services deemed necessary to private welfare in modern mass culture. In other words, individual citizen prosperity is inherently tied to the discretionary desires of privately owned capital. Contrary to the logic proposed by the reformers, therefore, "internalization" of the costs for redressing social "externalities" rarely undercuts the profits of corporate firms or wealthy stockholders. The liberal activists are right that private corporate welfare does not translate automatically into public welfare, but they ignore the ease with which private corporations routinely redirect increased market costs to consumers in the form of higher prices, lower wages, threats of job loss, and economic austerity measures.[63] Consequently, increased state regulation of private enterprise often works to exacerbate rather than to reduce the existing inequalities in citizen wealth throughout the nation. Redistribution of resources toward new collective goods in the absence of economic growth not only threatens to undercut overall production capacity, but also tends to benefit affluent consumers at the expense of middle- and lower-income citizens. "Their idealism and the needs of relatively deprived groups must clash," observes Simon Lazarus of the reform activists.[64]

Critics have pointed to numerous manifestations of these class biases which have stirred public opposition to new reform policies. Most important are the tensions with organized labor unions. For example, organized labor opposed efforts of a public interest coalition to prevent government bailouts for Lockheed Aircraft in the early 1970s. While the reformers viewed the issue as a typical military–industrial complex subsidization of private profits, workers saw the possibility to guarantee existing, or increased, jobs and wages.[65] Furthermore, as Nadel and Vogel have documented, organized labor supported tariffs to protect domestic products against public interest free-market goals throughout the 1970s. In the conflict between certain losses of jobs in specific industries and uncertain benefits of greater product competition, the workers predictably chose jobs.[66] Likewise, in the absence of developed alternatives from which to choose, labor has been mostly reticent about the nuclear energy issue out of concern for affordable fuel prices and new sources of employment. Indeed, the AFL-CIO joined business opposition against the 1976 Proposition 15 (an antinuclear initiative) in California as well as against various public interest energy and wilderness development policies.[67] Critics have similarly pointed to the thousands of jobs lost by the reformers' opposition to the SST, advocacy of OSHA vinyl chloride regulations against B. F. Goodrich in 1974, and battle for pollution control at the Union Carbide Ohio metals plant in 1971.[68]

Reform efforts to upgrade corporate services for workers have likewise been thwarted by the cost thresholds that private capital is not willing to cross. A good example is the Nader-inspired Employee Retirement Income Security Act. Designed with large-scale productive units in mind, the act's complex provisions were so costly that an estimated 10,000 small firms altogether dropped existing pension plans for 350,000 workers. And this is but one case in which regulations framed to control large corporations have ended up undercutting the viability of small producers, who provide 55 percent of jobs in the private sector, most to lower-income workers.[69] Moreover, higher taxes required by increased state regulation have cut deeply into middle- and lower-class family budgets. Although the relative costs of regulatory practice and welfare are still quite small, their proportion of total gross national product and government expenditure continued to increase during the 1970s. The New Deal logic that turned workers against the poor has thus tended to turn workers against the new reformers as well.[70] State-mandated programs are not funded from corporate profits or publicly sanctioned disinvestments from other less desirable enterprises, but largely from rising taxes along with higher prices paid primarily by working people. As a result, the recent attempt of critics to brand liberal social reformers as welfare parasites has touched a wound felt by many American wage earners. In each of these cases, the preferences of employees for selective benefits in immediate material security over long-term collective goods has strengthened the position of capital against the social reformers. The alleged zero-sum logic of existing relations has forced workers on such occasions into the economic "growth-as-usual" camp.[71]

The same conflicts and paradoxes have been claimed to be even more apparent with regard to the American underclass. First, higher prices and lower wages inflicted by regulated producers hurt the poor disproportionately. In fact, many social regulations mandating higher product quality, "open dating information," and specific packaging policies have not only raised prices generally, but have driven some "poor people's goods" off the market altogether.[72] Likewise, attempts to save the environment from exploitive development are often blamed for greater costs of those basic necessities that absorb the bulk of most poor people's incomes. Opposition to nuclear plants, demands for relocation of energy industries, and protection of wilderness areas against suburban development, critics argue, have all imposed higher costs in energy and housing as well as discouraged job creation.[73] Finally, it is worth recognizing that tax revenues spent on wildlife preservation and accident prevention draw money away from potential expenditures for education, welfare, housing, job training, and other social programs for the poor.[74]

The class biases of the new politics allegedly extend further yet. "New consumer" programs not only impose the economic costs of social change in unequal ways, but they create benefits that are enjoyed unequally as well. While reformers claim to speak for public interests shared by all Americans, their agenda is said to reflect the bias of upper-income, middle-class wants and opportunities. It may be logically consistent to argue, as does one reform ally, that "those with the greatest privilege should be asked to make the greatest sacrifices," that most people must "pare down their material expectations to what they really need," and that "this does not imply that the poor should be content with less."[75] However, the reformers have remained quite vague about the actual terms that should distinguish the entitlements of lower- or middle-class wants, and that should distinguish who is to give and who is to receive. Likewise, despite the activists' efforts to define general continuities of interest with the disadvantaged, the vast amounts of resources expended by public interest groups are said to benefit primarily their middle-income, educated, white constituency.[76] Scholar Hugh Stretton's evaluation of environmental politics is typical: "Through all of the massive efforts, clean air was probably the only commodity that got more equal distribution. There were no solutions to the ghetto problems. Poor Americans did not get fairer shares of urban services or living space."[77]

Critics on both the Right and the Left have thus pointed out that the reformers' purported principles of concern for equality have been subordinated to the espoused wants of affluent middle-class consumers, who get the most attention. Instead of cultivating needed "communities of cooperation" for a new liberal alliance, it often is charged that the new consumerism has only added a new dimension to the conflict over distribution of private wealth which long has impeded formation of class consciousness in America.[78] As Walter Rosenbaum predicted several years ago, the reformers' "feeble appeal to the disadvantaged not only deprives the movement of additional manpower, political weight, and social appeal but creates a potentially dangerous cleavage that . . . could become a socially polarized struggle pit-

148

ting the more affluent's demands... against the less advantaged's desire for social advancement."[79] From this view, the advocates of the new consumerism offer neither results nor hopes much different from those advocates of the old consumerism. In perennial critic William Tucker's words, "Their values and positions are those of a nation's aristocracy."[80] The new politics of public rights does not overcome the dilemma of structural inequalities; it only wishes them away under the mystical label of a unified "consumer interest."

These charges of elitism leveled against public interest liberals by their detractors clearly build upon some elements of truth. However valid, though, such sweeping claims and anecdotal evidence once again must be measured in terms of competing facts and the larger context of the American political economy. Most important, while many of the burdens and benefits of "new consumer" goods are distributed unequally, they have neither created nor exacerbated the existing structural inequalities of citizen wealth in any significant way. Overall, most activists have been more responsible than their rhetoric implies. In particular, examples of actual job losses caused by the new social programs have been relatively few and isolated. Many of the threats of unemployment have been based more on exaggerated corporate ploys to protect their own autonomy, to expand profits, and to discipline workers with "job blackmail" than on a balanced interpretation of the relevant evidence. One EPA study, for example, estimated that no more than 33,000 jobs were lost because of new social regulations in the entire decade after 1971. While these figures would hardly console those workers directly affected, they also do not account for the large percentage of jobs lost in antiquated plants already destined for closing or for the thousands of jobs created by private investments shifted elsewhere. Indeed, new enterprises stimulated by social regulation and new consumer demands far more than offset the numbers of old jobs that have been terminated. For example, a Data Resources, Inc. study has estimated that new pollution-control programs alone will be responsible for creation of over half a million new jobs between 1971 and 1987.[81]

Likewise, conservative rhetoric about the costs of regulation have often been more inflated than actual rises in prices. The Council on Wage and Price Stability in 1979 estimated that government regulation added only 0.75 percent a year to prices—or about 6 percent of the total inflationary jump in that year. Another independent study concluded that environmental regulation added only about 0.3 percent to the consumer price index over the decade ending in 1980. "In contrast with fiscal and monetary policy," Reagan adviser James E.

Miller III admitted, "regulation has a very small effect on the rate of inflation."[82] All in all, the economic burdens of social regulation suffered by middle- and lower-income Americans simply are quite minimal, especially when contrasted to the pervasive losses of most citizens suffered at the hands of powerful corporate developers, callous employers, exploitive merchandisers, and hostile landlords against whom the middle-class reformers have battled. Even more important, while it is true that the primary advocates and beneficiaries of many public interest policies are mostly middle class, it should not be forgotten that workers and the poor have suffered most from the problems of air pollution, poor health, workplace dangers, urban blight, and consumer fraud which only recently have disturbed the lives of the affluent.

Opinion polls once more tend to reflect considerable public support for liberal regulatory policies in these regards. For example, Robert Mitchell's 1979 analysis of numerous opinion surveys revealed that environmental safety and health issues have developed into strong and enduring commitments of the whole American public. Not only did large pluralities (over 80 percent) consistently oppose relaxing regulatory legislation such as the Clean Air Act, he noted, but such support was found to be distributed quite evenly among citizens across all categories of income, education, race, occupation, and party identification. Turning this overwhelming evidence for such attitudes upon unsupported attacks by William Tucker and others, Mitchell thus concluded that most public interest groups "continue to represent a substantial and remarkably broad-based constituency of the American people."[83] More recent studies, such as a 1981 Harris poll, have led to the same basic conclusions. Even more impressive than the overwhelming general support for health and safety regulation, Harris claimed, was "the fact that not a single major segment of the public wants environmental laws made less strict." Indeed, his study revealed that blacks and the poor are among the *least* likely to think that social regulation has gone too far or costs too much.[84] On the basis of this and other polls, even veteran research expert Everett Carl Ladd has admitted that his own earlier claims about class biases in support for public interest liberals were wrong. While movement members and financial supporters are mostly middle-income whites, Ladd points out, many public interest endeavors provide material benefits strongly desired by all segments of modern society.[85]

It is also worth noting the many occasions for cooperation between the organized leadership of significant class groups and public interest activists during the last decade. Most important has been the

150

frequent coalition action with organized labor. The key fact is that many unions during the late 1960s began to shift the balance of their collective goals from divisive economic demands for higher wages to social demands for consumer and environmental protection, workplace safety, and government reform.[86] While tensions with the AFL-CIO and some building trades have arisen periodically, public interest group actions have often been supported by the United Auto Workers, the United Mine Workers, the United Food and Commercial Workers, and the United Steelworkers of America. Such labor unions have variously supported public interest advocacy for truth-in-lending and truth-in-packaging laws, an agency for consumer advocacy, Campaign GM, the Freedom of Information Act, rigorous OSHA enforcement, the 1976 Toxic Substances Control Act, Clean Air Act amendments, energy conservation, and tax reform policies. In return, many public interest groups have formally supported labor efforts, such as the 1973 Oil, Chemical and Atomic Workers strike against Shell Oil Company, the 1980 Mississippi farm workers strikes, and the 1981 Solidarity Day protests against the Reagan administration. Despite occasional conflicts on particular fronts, therefore, such frequent alliances have nurtured a mostly congenial relationship overall between the liberal reformers and organized workers. In the words of AFL-CIO president Lane Kirkland, "we in labor . . . have been pleased to work with the environmental movement . . . and we have appreciated environmental support during our struggle"[87]

Cooperative interaction between middle-class activists and representatives of the American underclass has been quite common as well. Indeed, the broad crossover of legal action, coalition support, policy research, and foundation funding among representatives of environmental, consumer, civil liberties, poverty, racial, and women's groups has rendered some grounds for common identity almost inevitable. For example, lawyers for the ACLU, Common Cause, and many other public interest groups routinely handle cases and issues involving low- as well as middle-income persons. Voluntary cooperation of many middle-class groups with the California Rural Legal Assistance programs, the Washington Urban League, the 1973 Conservation League conference on social justice, the 1974 San Francisco Planning and Conservation League, the National Welfare Rights Organization, the Washington Environment League, the National Conference on Alternative State and Local Public Policy, and many other efforts all reveal significant points of contact and mutual support among a wide variety of liberal social groups since the early 1970s.[88]

In sum, therefore, it is true that public interest activists have often shown insensitivity to the redistributional impact of their actions and have contributed little to remedying the problems of economic injustice within America; this fact surely undercuts the reformers' preferred image as a radical egalitarians. But conservative rhetoric notwithstanding, there simply is little evidence that Americans should or do blame middle-class public interest liberals for adding further to inequality among citizens in capitalist America.

Social Reform without Economic Reform

Economic Decline and the Decline of Reform. My central contention thus far has been that the actual *economic* impact of liberal public interest social policies has not significantly undercut the reformers' influence in modern American politics. Contrary to conservative claims, social regulation has not contributed significantly to unemployment, inflation, unproductivity, or unequal wealth distribution. A more plausible explanation of the growing deregulatory fervor within government since the mid-1970s must focus on the *political* success of corporate campaigns to exploit public fears about allegedly necessary market trade-offs and citizen ambivalence about "big government" abstractly defined. Conservatives did eventually dominate the rhetorical battle, but not by directly assailing public interest–oriented social regulatory policies, which the American public has continued to support by large margins.[89]

This is not to say that the reformers share no responsibility for their declining public influence. Indeed, what has rendered the reform politics so vulnerable is precisely that it has not been perceived to affect traditional productive performance much at all. In other words, one of the most important barriers to the success of public interest liberalism has been its apparent indifference toward the deterioration of the entire modern American economic system. Reform leaders may not have had their noses in the air, as conservatives suggest, but they also did not have their ears to the ground in anticipation of a changing social reality.

Until the early years of the 1970s, the American economy continued to appear strong and resilient under the guidance of New Deal Keynesian fiscal and monetary policies administered by the state. Energy was cheap, unemployment was perceived as a problem primarily plaguing minorities, and inflation had just begun its steady climb upward. In other words, relative economic security and aggregate prosperity, rather than any abstract faith in growth, rendered qualitative change an attractive and plausible goal to many citizens within middle America. Like youthful Fausts, the liberal activists were thus freed for creative action toward new social reform goals by a clandestine pact with the devil of corporate capitalism against which they rebelled.[90]

Yet just as significant public interest developed in the values around which the reformers struggled to rally support, the economy quickened its decline and decay, which continued into the early 1980s.[91] Inflation rose from an annual rate of 2 percent in 1965 to increasing levels fluctuating between 5 and 12 percent during the 1970s, with the greatest jumps in costs of staple goods such as food, energy, housing, and health care. While the real standard of living for most citizens continued to rise during the decade, the rate of increase slowed markedly after 1973 as the personal costs to maintain familiar levels of affluence escalated. The growth in two-earner families, in working time for individuals, and in rates of personal mortgage debts all confirmed the growing difficulty of merely "keeping up." Indeed, although real incomes of multiearner families rose during the decade, the incomes of families with only one earner fell about 7 percent behind the cost of living from 1969 to 1978. A 1980 *Business Week* study summarized the losses in individual terms: "Adjusting income...to reflect the sweat that goes into providing that income per worker shows that discretionary income per worker over the past six years declined by 16 percent." Moreover, official unemployment levels wavered between 6 and 12 percent overall and were over 40 percent in the inner cities when we add to the official estimates the undercounted, underemployed, and those who simply had given up looking for work.[92] In short, a virtual no-growth economy did evolve, but with all of the costly implications about which conservative critics had warned and few of the advantages promised by liberal reform advocates.

The sources of the economic decline were many and complex. Lingering inflationary pressures imposed by massive military expenditures in Vietnam without adequate taxation measures, the dramatic rise in OPEC oil prices and the energy crisis in general, and increasing competition from Japan and Western Europe all contributed in important ways to the American economic malaise. Nevertheless, the structural obstacles impeding more successful response to these problems derived from the same source as problems concerning transfers of social reform costs—that is, the fragmented, profit-oriented character of capital accumulation and investment by private producers. In this sense, the reformers have been right to focus their

153

attacks upon corporate self-interest, but they have seized upon only part of the problem. If anything simple can be said, the fiscal crisis of modern capitalism has been defined by too little productive investment overall and too much in socially unproductive directions—in overly capital-intensive industries, in multinational runaway shops, in increasingly costly fossil-fuel extraction, in inefficiently scaled productive processes, in high-profit consumer superfluities rather than basic necessities, and in ever-increasing corporate mergers, hostile takeovers, and other forms of speculating, to name a few commonly identified by policy analysts.[93]

The point is not that the public has blamed the reform activists for these problems, but that the latter's general reticence about the fact of economic instability rendered liberal reform concerns of only secondary significance to most Americans. Amid such a context of widespread economic stagnation and personal insecurity, it is easy to see that the new reformers' scorn for commitments to rapid growth in material prosperity quickly became anachronistic. Ironically, their pleas for voluntary simplicity added insult to injury for many. Polls continued to confirm large numbers of supporters both for the liberals' general quality-of-life values and for their attempts to regulate corporate producers, but the salience of these latter concerns dropped dramatically. It is not surprising that financial insecurity has ranked consistently as the single greatest worry of most Americans in opinion polls since the mid-1970s. "It would be necessary to go back to the 1930s and the Great Depression," pollster Daniel Yankelovich has concluded, "to find a peacetime issue that has had the country so concerned and distraught."[94] By contrast, concern about environmental risks and other public interest issues have fallen from a high of second "most important issues facing the nation" in 1972 to near the bottom of most top ten charts in subsequent years.[95]

In short, the problem with public interest liberals is that their obsession with the social costs of a modern market-based corporate economy has eclipsed their concern for its material costs to consumer welfare, which has always been the raison d'être of reform politics. Their frank refusal to acknowledge the need for more economic as well as social regulation to coordinate production and allocation of basic goods has rendered them silent about the overriding issues that dominate contemporary political debates. Failing to seize the opportunity to point the way toward policies for a dynamic, more socially responsible low-growth economic alternative, the movement's appeal plummeted in relevance only a decade after its birth.[96]

The Political Economy of Social Reform

Social Regulation without Economic Regulation. Public interest liberals have struggled to alter the calculus of American capital investment in important ways, of course. Many welcome expenditures for new collective goods and services have been achieved by new social regulations. However, these gains have been won at the expense of avoiding, even exacerbating, the fundamental dilemmas of contemporary corporate capitalism. The problem is that public interest regulatory policies have added up to little more than a patchwork quilt of diverse, uncoordinated new social demands on productive capital investment without concern for overall economic performance in providing citizens with decent, fair, and secure means of continued material welfare. Moreover, most of their policies have been largely prohibitive in aim. For example, various liberal reform efforts to halt nuclear development, to stop housing construction in scenic areas, to prohibit increased oil and coal extraction, to increase premarketing research on many goods, and to prevent marketing of certain foods and drugs altogether all aim to throttle productive action without offering alternative affirmative proposals for investment to meet basic energy, medical, transportation, housing, and other staple needs. "Stopping production [has] mattered more than distribution," notes scholar Hugh Stretton.[97] Such restrictive regulations may have stimulated development of some new technologies, of course, but they have not directly guided capital into more economically beneficial directions. Even on programs that are both environmentally and economically unsound, such as the 1982 highway–gas tax bill, opposition without a viable alternative proposal has hurt the liberal reformers' relations with labor and other potential supporters.[98]

Besides selective social regulation and political opposition against such unsafe or unwanted business enterprises, the primary strategy to alter overall social investment priorities has been the groups' educational appeal to the larger public. Through effecting a "paradigm shift" and "silent revolution" in the calculus of American consumer wants expressed in the economic as well as the political marketplace, we have seen, the reformers have hoped to initiate a radical change in the patterns of capital development undertaken by corporate and state managers. This effort to alter collective consumption preferences again has transformed and stimulated anew some viable productive enterprises, it is true. However, the implications of this tactic are fraught with paradox. First, the reformers' focus on marketplace demand has ignored the fact that much resource consumption is not by individual consumers; rather, a great deal of

155

overall consumption is by businesses themselves in discretionary productive or maintenance activities not directly dictated by consumer demands. Indeed, it is in the realms of extravagant managerial consumption habits and inefficient production processes that critics identify much of the slack of wasted capital within the existing corporate system.[99] Furthermore, even were the market perfectly responsive and consumers highly rational, such a strategy relies on impersonal, uncoordinated, highly fragmented mechanisms of private profit calculation to render authoritative public decisions.[100] In other words, such a market approach to economic change only mirrors rather than redresses the deficiencies and inequities of the reformers' social regulatory policies.

Likewise, as the activists themselves have often labored to demonstrate, private corporate capital wields considerable power over the content and character of consumer market demand itself. Prices are essentially administered by common trade agreement or amid limited competition, and new consumer wants are stimulated by sophisticated advertising for the endless array of new gadgets and conveniences promising instant happiness. The result is that the reformers' appeals to "inner needs" and collective benefits have hardly been a fair match against such pervasive Madison Avenue pandering and the long legacy extolling "possessive individualism" upon which it preys.[101] Given the structure of modern consumer society, the goal of radically altering capital investment by attacking existing consumer habits is a classic case of trying to use the tail to wag the dog.[102] It is simply futile to encourage voluntary energy conservation, ecological concern, and limited material indulgence for the masses of citizen consumers as long as many private businesses continue to profit by avoiding responsible action.

Finally, it should be acknowledged that a few efforts have been made by some groups to extend more affirmative direct control over corporate investment policies. Campaign GM was an early influential attempt to increase citizen control through reforms expanding shareholder democracy. The still-unsuccessful corporate democracy bill aimed to develop a legislative foundation for extending similar goals of citizen representation within large corporate institutions. Yet both programs have been more procedural than substantive in orientation, and neither has reflected much concern for synoptic social investment coordination.[103] It is also important to place such goals in the context of recent corporate performance. Not only has the consuming public suffered from relative economic woes during the last decade, but many corporate sectors have been plagued with significantly declining

156

profits, lowered rates of productivity, increasing resource costs, increasing world competitiveness, and hence numerous industry failures.[104] As a result, the general aim of extending greater social representation by various consumer groups within many existing corporate giants is a little like fighting for a seat in the cockpit of a plane that can no longer get off the ground.

The problem identified here is not merely one of the reformers' lack of influence within the state. Rather, the point is that their social policies have suffered from an inherent narrowness of conceptual concern. For all the breadth of relevance afforded by the new consumer-rights posture, it has stayed aloof from those traditional macroeconomic issues of income, wage, price, tax, debt, and investment management policies which concern most citizens. Eschewing identification with any comprehensive program that specifies the actions necessary to provide welfare for all in these traditional "material" terms, therefore, the new liberals have been severely limited in developing active public support for their political agenda of new values, goods, and services. Declining to contribute or support plausible solutions to the larger economic malaise, the reformers' democratic political goals likewise have remained vulnerable to attacks criticizing them as a big part of the problem. As a result, the implied social struggle between business, industry, and finance, on one hand, and consumers and workers, on the other, has fallen prey to the zero-sum logic of fiscal crisis and market trade-offs.[105] In sum, post–New Deal social liberalism has stood little chance of gaining ascendance without support from a post–New Deal economic program of coordinated state economic regulation and fiscal policy at its foundation.

This is not to say that the reformers' contributions are irrelevant to debates about how to restructure our basic productive processes and priorities. Their analyses concerning the benefits of social regulation and costs of inefficiency in the existing corporate economy have provided some important insights. But such a defensive posture has not yet provided specific responses to the question of "What is to be done?"[106] Moreover, the ecology-oriented new consumerism has nurtured a sort of deconstructionist ethic committed to building decentralized, community-based "countereconomy" institutions independent of the larger corporate culture. Experimentation in various forms of capital mobilization for urban agriculture and consumer cooperatives has been endorsed heartily by many public interest liberals. Research and development of diverse alternative technologies for soft energy, habitat-sound housing, safe farming methods, and improved health practices has also received considerable support. In the long run, all of these institutions and techniques may surely offer some potential for cultivating a more egalitarian, humane, and reasonable economic order.[107] But divorced from any larger effort to extend popular *control over* existing patterns of capital accumulation, such designs stand little chance of developing as a meaningful *alternative to* the corporatized status quo. It simply is difficult to imagine how public interest liberals can contribute to a new democratic "countereconomy" as long as they accept the division of social and economic responsibility into separate, competing hands.

These tendencies reflect some surprisingly static assumptions in the perspectives of the activists. Along with all of their gloomy prognostications about scarcity and plaintive exposés of social abuse, the reformers have exhibited a curiously naive optimism about the capacity of corporate capitalism to provide continuous levels of familiar affluence—a faith that appears little shared by either corporate captains or the larger public.[108] The activists have continued to tap the government for financial aid and to place demands on corporate producers as if the cornucopia of capital abundance were boundless. Little concerned about declining productivity, industry failure, and increasing capital flight, they have taken for granted the affluence that has characterized American life in the last generation. A capitalist economy may not be self-regulating in their eyes, but it appears to be self-generating. Once we eliminate its present abuses of nature and alter the personnel in command of wealth distribution, they claim, all we have to do is put the ship's rudder on hold in a steady state. That the wind has died and the boat may be sinking have little bothered them. Accepting their roles as captains seeking control over consumer practices, the reformers have remained reactors to the initiative of corporate capital in defining material priorities rather than as actors with economic intitiative of their own. These tendencies also explain in part the selectively espoused faith of many reformers in the free market which observers often find so puzzling. Despite their many insights into its inherent deficiencies—whether from competition or monopoly—the activists' occasional embrace of the market perhaps signals a desire to abdicate economic responsibility to the hands of others more than consistent economic principle.

Nothing could distinguish modern public interest liberalism from the promises of most earlier radical reformers more than this indifferent posture toward economic matters. The nineteenth-century agrarian Populists, for example, built their political program around the Greenback legacy of monetary reform and cooperative experiment in production and exchange. As Lawrence Goodwyn has demonstrated, the social transformation attempted by the Farmers' Alliance was motivated by a distinct vision of collective economic power independent of the larger structures of corporate control. "The discovered truth was a simple one, but its political import was radical: the Alliance cooperative stood little chance of working unless fundamental changes were made in the American monetary system."[109] In the words of one Populist paper, "The people do not want to tear down the railroads nor to pull down the factories.... They want to build up and make everything better."[110] Likewise, while more pro-corporate in substance, the New Deal programs for social change won support largely because of their capacity to generate confidence in viable new economic programs to finance desired redistributive reforms. The very terms of the New Deal stipulated that the state would subsidize and coordinate corporate capitalism as it tamed, regulated, and "humanized" it.[111] And, finally, it should not be surprising that Ronald Reagan's recent success in winning support for his conservative social agenda has been made possible largely by the appeal of his plans for economic revitalization. The costs of his programs have been great and the benefits unequally enjoyed, but he won at least temporary support from a hopeful public offered few other real alternatives.[112]

By contrast, the recent liberal middle-class reformers have thus far resembled their moralistic urban Progressive counterparts of earlier in this century. "Strong on criticism, and on proposals to strengthen their particular interests, the [Progressive] reformers were weak on ideas appropriate to the entire political economy," summarizes historian William Appleman Williams. More specificlly, "their greatest weakness was the lack of any broad conception of how the system was to be coordinated and sustained. They did not like the large corporation, but did not have anything to put in its place."[113] The new reformers have also rebelled against the social costs of a corporatized, growth-oriented, capitalist economy, but they too have offered few constructive alternatives to put in its place.

Consumerism and Work. The deficiencies of the modern liberal activists' agenda extend beyond mere silence about macroeconomic issues of collective wealth creation and distribution. This claim points to the janus-faced radicalism of the new consumer ethic. On one hand, the new advocates have developed a powerful cultural critique of the "conspicuous-consumption" practices, "more-as-better" values, and manipulative advertising techniques that have fueled the growth of modern capitalism. On the other hand, the new consumer ethos has also largely continued the silence of traditional American reform

159

politics about the class issues of control over employment and work in the production process itself. In short, the reformers have reinforced the long-established tendency within corporate America to define the political interests of most citizens in terms of their roles primarily as consumers rather than as workers, or, in Ralf Dahrendorf's enlightening terms, as economic non-authorities rather than as potential economic authorities.[114] This enduring consumer orientation has led activists to say little about the ethical concerns for promoting the economic freedom of citizens—whether individual or collective—which have always constituted the core and foundation of Western politics, including that of our inherited American liberal republican tradition. More concretely, it renders the activists' exhortations to enhanced citizen power and welfare of only limited relevance to the deeply rooted sources of abuse, injustice, and frustrated aspirations manifested in the most time-consuming activity of people's lives, their daily jobs.

The consumer posture toward redistributional policies, even if successful, fails to recognize that many people identify themselves primarily as workers. It is important to realize that the very possession of a job remains an important sign of dignity for Americans. Holding a job qualifies people for "a form of activity that has social approval or satisfies a real want of the individual to be an actor. To produce, to create, to gain respect, to acquire prestige, and incidentally to earn money"—these are the promises of secure employment.[115] For all of their concern about corporate exploitation and promises to promote security in life, few public interest activists have seriously addressed the sources of anxiety in the modern employment market. They have generally been silent about the toll of increasing competition, which turns workers against one another; the modern institutionalization of high unemployment and underemployment, which serves to keep wages down and to secure corporate control; the increasing losses of jobs attending American deindustrialization; and the indignities in status and opportunity characterizing the fastest growing sectors of employment, the service and information industries.[116] To their credit, some reformers have supported moderate employment policies such as the 1976 Humphrey–Hawkins Bill, pension plan reforms, and protection against the disruptive consequences of plant relocation. Yet most of these proposals have been initiated by others and have attracted the active support of only a small minority of liberal public interest groups.

The liberal reformers also have had little to say about the character of work itself. For all of their dislike of corporate and state bureaucracies, the liberals' recognition of inequities has rarely extended beyond the level of executive decision making to the structure of routine work activity for most citizens. It is as if the frequent protests about modern alienation voiced by middle-class reformers had little to do with the phenomena the term has evolved to signify. Even those groups most concerned to attract worker support extend little recognition to the indignities of fragmented labor division, "deskilled work," managerial monopolies, and new austerity measures imposed by managers to increase productivity at the cost of health and safety.[117] To be sure, the battles of some reformers for expanded worker rights of free speech, for worker rights to participate in the determination of workplace safety and health standards, for various labor union strikes, and for proposals for shareholder reform all constitute significant actions on behalf of workers. Likewise, many activists have supported goals of developing labor-intensive, ecologically sound forms of independent production such as household agriculture, creative crafts, and neighborhood energy generation. These efforts surely are useful beginnings. Again, however, advocacy of such actions has enlisted only a minority of the reformers and hardly constitutes a serious challenge to the power structure of the economic order. Overall, on most worker and workplace issues that have sparked the discontent of Americans, the new reformers have pretty much left leadership to the established labor hierarchies. As an interest-group strategy, this makes sense. After all, the liberal groups are limited in resources and labor can take care of itself. But for a reform movement dedicated to the transformation of social power, such narrowness of concern defines an important limit to potential success. As Allan Schnaiberg has argued, "without a political base within unorganized and organized labor, no movement can proceed to challenge and change the existing social structure."[118]

These facts raise yet larger problems for the reformers' often stated hopes to develop a broad constituency or coalition of supporters within the public. For one thing, the activists' appeals offer little to blacks and other minorities most victimized by the structure of employment in America. While it is wrong to "raise the simpleminded equation of snail darters and jobs," notes veteran civil rights leader Vernon Jordan, "that does symbolize an implicit divergence of interests between some segments of the environmental movement and the bulk of black and urban people."[119] Moreover, at a time when many women throughout the nation are struggling to increase their freedom and power as economic producers within the existing gender-based occupational caste system, the new liberal consumer appeal seems oddly antiquated. The public interest reform emphasis on social goals over traditional commodity obsessions has created some bonds to the feminist cause, and the possibilities for a synthesis of ecological and feminist values into a new radical political theory has received much attention. But the activists' relative reticence about economic issues of employment and workplace power, much less about concerns for recognition of socially productive work long denied compensation at all, has been a sure source of disaffection with many otherwise "naturally" allied progressive women's groups.[120] In short, the liberal consumer appeal largely ignores rather than builds upon recognition of fundamental racial and gender as well as class divisions within modern society. Finally, despite their professed commitments to small-scale production, some of the liberals' new consumer policies have actually tended to undercut the viability of small independent producers and merchants: the reason is that social regulations designed with corporations in mind impose devastating costs on many small firms. "While the costs of complying with the consumer laws are a nuisance to General Motors and Nabisco," explains one consumer analyst, "they are a real burden for small businesses."[121] Indeed, just as traditional economic regulation has been initiated often by big business to consolidate control over markets, so increased cartelization is now at least in part a result of more rigorous social regulation.[122] And, of course, as small businesses flounder, jobs for many workers are jeopardized.

In this light, appeals for the new consumer could be interpreted to take on a different historical significance. The new liberals' claim to promote quality over quantity could be understood to signal only a further step in the rationalization process of modern capitalism. The achieved balancing of social with economic goods only defines a new level of consumer demand to compensate citizens for the costs of present productive organization. Public interest reformers do not promise much hope for greater citizen freedom or security in those material activities that normally occupy most of our waking lives. "Instead," notes critic Robert Holsworth, they "[give] us better competition, stricter regulation, more satisfaction" to ameliorate the sacrifices in personal autonomy required by a highly organized corporate society.[123] For example, many new alternative technologies (personal computers, solar energy cells) are often celebrated as contributing to more self-sufficient lifestyles, despite the atomizing propensities and new forms of corporate dependence they may encourage. Likewise, the activists' praise for self-development (through nature hikes, jogging, yoga) tends to be every bit as leisure-oriented, self-indulgent, and commercialized as the whims of affluent Americans they criticize.[124]

Even more important are the potential implications of support by some activists for the development of new ecologically sound "information" industries. Such new consumer values not only endorse disinvestment of capital from industrial manufacture of basic goods, but also may encourage citizen resignation in response to the downward mobility and job dislocations that such transformations will require. Indeed, the recent liberal celebration of voluntary simplicity, less work, soft energy, "inner directedness," and decentralized self-sufficiency has been embraced by some corporate elites to legitimate the harsh austerity measures that a deindustrializing economy forces upon many wage-earning citizens.[125] What has appeared as a source of radical protest has actually involved a significant measure of conservative accommodation as well.

Again, this is not to deny that public interest reformers are sincere in their democratic intentions or offer important causes for alliance with working people in America. Rather, the point has been to emphasize the limits and paradoxes of a primarily consumerist vision for developing a broadly based progressive movement in modern society. Recognition of this fact does not require any particular substantive policy orientation—liberal, conservative, or radical. Indeed, the significance of addressing the hopes of citizens as producers was illustrated by Ronald Reagan in 1980. Appealing to deep fears and nostalgia for a better time, Reagan has managed to redeem the rigors of work and present hardships with dreams of heroic enterprise, entrepreneurial independence, secure jobs, and renewed dignity for all as producing citizens. Such promises somewhat obscure the actual distribution of burdens and benefits to different producer groups inherent in his overall economic program, but this fact only highlights the significance of economic appeals to Americans in their roles as producers for successful political advocacy.

Nevertheless, the majority of public interest activists have remained comfortable in their consumerist mantles. They have continued to exhibit the characteristic trait of the "new radicalism" in this century identified by Christopher Lasch: a lack of genuine experience in the mainstream of American life.[126] The irony of this is that their leadership status derives from their own unique fusion of economic and political action. Unlike most citizens, who rely on private capitalist enterprise for their basic livelihoods, most liberal activists draw a living, a source of daily income, from politics. Attacking big business is their business; reform politics is their vocation. However meager the financial returns, their occupations as professional public citizens unites both productive stature and collective identity, work and

163

politics. The benefits of such activism for the rest of us are unfortunately far less comprehensive.

New Directions and Old Constraints

The principle invoked throughout this entire analysis has been that taking political reform seriously requires taking economics seriously as well. Public interest groups have seriously challenged traditional patterns of profit-led economic growth, but their failure to offer a coherent alternative vision of democratic economic reorganization and policy-planning priorities has removed them from the mainstream of American political debate. This is not to say that public interest liberals must embrace the goals of high growth, reindustrialization, or any particular policies at all. But without a commitment to some plausible agenda for making authoritative decisions about controlling inflation, providing decent work, securing minimum income levels, maintaining reasonable credit access, and redirecting long-term expenditure of capital at home and abroad toward basic material as well as social needs, the liberal reformers' proclaimed desire for "a revolution... in our values, outlook, and economic organization" stands little chance of further advance. In fact, the lack of an independent economic policy vision has left some groups little option but to capitulate over time to corporate urgings for cooperation, partnership, and compromise in ways that significantly undercut the movement's most fundamental principled challenges to establishment politics in the modern era.[127]

This economic challenge has not been dodged by all reformers to the same degree. Ralph Nader has pressed for an economic emphasis from the beginning, and Common Cause has initiated selective measures to halt inflation by lobbying against special interest subsidies and military defense buildup as well as for oil depletion allowances, greater FTC regulation, and trucking deregulation.[128] But the primary thrust of both has been for more social regulation and less economic regulation. The so-called energy crisis of the mid-1970s likewise sparked concern about better energy investment planning among advocates of survivalist ethics and opponents of nuclear plant development. Despite the important contributions from Barry Commoner, Amory Lovins, and others concerning various "soft energy paths," however, the primary response of most groups has been to support conservation rather than to contribute directly to development of new energy resources.[129]

164

In response to increasing criticism from conservatives and to cost-benefit scrutiny of regulatory policy, some activists have increasingly shown signs of willingness to develop a more affirmative economic policy orientation in their appeal to the American public. Many public interest liberals seem to have realized that a "public-be-damned attitude toward the economy may be just as objectionable to consumers as industry attitudes toward pollution and auto safety."[130] Indeed, the level of economic discourse, analysis, and concern among the activists has heightened markedly in recent years. For example, the Wilderness Society received a Mellon Foundation grant in 1980 to create a department of resource economics, and other environmental groups such as NRDC and EDF have begun to submit cost-benefit studies justifying alternative policy proposals to their opposition as a matter of routine. The founding of new groups such as the Citizen/Labor Energy Coalition and Environmentalists for Full Employment in the late 1970s is even more promising in this regard. The latter group, in particular, has committed itself to the platform that "with well-planned transition, there need be no conflict between socially useful employment, healthy workplaces and clean, natural environments. But these transitions must include preservation of job equity, concern for job dislocation, and a wide range of effective employment and reemployment assistance guarantees."[131]

Barry Commoner's Citizens' party similarly provided interesting platforms of public interest–oriented economic policies in recent presidential elections, although few groups actually supported them. Innovative ideas about alternative technologies encouraged by journals such as *Rain, Solar Age, Co-Evolution Quarterly,* and *Appropriate Technology* have increasingly contributed to the economic orientation of many reform advocates.[132] Finally, a series of Left–Populist socio-economic manifestos published since 1980—Harrington's *Decade of Decision,* Hayden's *The American Future: New Visions beyond Old Frontiers,* Carnoy and Shearer's *Economic Democracy,* and Bowles, Gordon, and Weisskopf's *Beyond the Wasteland*—have succeeded in stimulating debate among different segments of the movement.[133]

It is clear, then, that some public interest advocates have been working toward consensus on a new economic as well as social program. Mark Green has even proclaimed, perhaps prophetically, that "the issue of the 1980s is economics."[134] Nevertheless, the formidable obstacles and disincentives to further such innovations within the movement should be recognized. Three concluding points are worth noting in this regard.

1. *The ecological ethic.* The first reason for skepticism about such future developments is that the new politics has been anchored in an ecological ethic largely indifferent to the value of productive activity itself. Despite the frequent invocations of wholeness and harmony between man and nature, environmentalist rhetoric often displays a markedly antihumanistic, antiproduction bias. Environmentalists have illustrated well the exploitive implications of the inherited American capitalist drive for technological domination of nature, to be sure. Yet, in so doing, they have tended to reify the relation of humans and their environment into a static conflict of exploiter and exploited.[135] As several scholars have illustrated, the dominant image of humans portrayed in the environmentalist worldview conforms to the traditional liberal model of self-interested, calculating wealth aggrandizers almost incapable of socially responsible action.[136]

Garrett Hardin's classic essay "The Tragedy of the Commons" exemplifies the point. For Hardin, our modern ecological plight is like that of eighteenth-century English villagers who abused common grazing pastures. Given a finite amount of land and an absence of altruism to limit human greed, the rational interests of each make any collective voluntary solution to the problems of economic organization impossible.[137] In other words, our nature as *Homo faber* commits us to the work of selfishly plundering the world about us. The specific problem of contemporary society is thus the enhanced power to destroy with which modern technological capacities have provided us. The very titles of many environmental publications— *Our Plundered Planet, America the Raped, The Chemical Feast, The Road to Ruin, Beyond Repair: The Ecology of Capitalism, The Tyranny of Survival, The Last Landscape, The Poison That Fell from the Sky*—suggest this popular equation of material production (rather than capitalism) with human exploitation. The significant implication of this view is that economic production constitutes an endeavor that primarily needs to be restrained rather than transformed, reorganized, and revitalized.

Some environmentalists frankly display their relative unconcern for matters of work and production. Ernest Callenbach's highly praised and popular novel *Ecotopia* exemplifies this perspective well. What is at stake in Ecotopia, he posits, is "nothing less than the revision of the Protestant work ethic upon which America has been built." Having rejected the degrading character of modern corporate production, Ecotopians are heralded for taking advantage of a deliberately engineered financial crisis to impose worker control, more pleasant work conditions, and more playful attitudes toward job responsibilities within economic life. This vision loses much of its luster under close scrutiny, however. First, virtually no explanation is provided concerning either how corporate financial collapse was transformed into a participatory pastoral utopia or how the new small-scale productive system actually meets the material needs of citizens. Moreover, the allegedly new productive forms seem to differ very little from the familiar insitutions of modern capitalism: "Ecotopian enterprises generally behave much like capitalist enterprises; they compete with each other, and seek to increase sales and maximize profits, although they are hampered by a variety of ecological regulations." The key transformation seems to be not a democratic reorganization of productive life so much as a dramatic reduction in the time, energy, and concern devoted by citizens to work in the new society. Indeed, the pervasive scorn for "hard work" and productivity are portrayed as a major philosophical advance: "Mankind, the Ecotopians assumed, was not meant for production as the 19th and 20th centuries had believed." Rather, humans were meant to "take their modest place in a seamless, stable web of living organisms, disturbing that web as little as possible."[138] Such a harmonious return to Mother Nature, the author reveals throughout the book, involves replacing human work with new forms of technological automation, more sophisticated but frugal social consumption activity, and plenty of time for uninhibited sexual exchange. In other words, whatever its implicit challenge to prevailing patterns of American middle-class consumer taste, the Ecotopian ideal hardly offers a serious response to the dilemmas and inequities of modern productive organization and management which sustain those practices.

These attitudes are not typical of all environmentalists, of course. An ecological ethics need not be antihumanistic or hostile to the exigencies of productive life, as E. F. Schumacher, Ivan Illich, Wendell Berry, and the growing ranks of environmental economists have demonstrated.[139] But while economic radicals on the Left have often expressed affinity with the liberal reformers' social policies, the most influential activists in public interest groups have not seemed much interested in radical economics. The preservationist ethic that guides most environmentalists has continued to encourage little political commitment to addressing the structural economic problems and injustice plaguing the nation and the world.

2. *The reform constituency.* As pointed out earlier, most liberal public interest groups rely on the support of relatively affluent middle-class professionals such as lawyers, doctors, scientists, academics, teachers, and public employees. The unsurprising logic of this fact is

that the reform movement has drawn the bulk of its support from those persons who are most economically secure and least directly dependent on private capital. However, this also means that the new politics transcends internal conflicts over economic issues by avoiding rather than resolving them. Indeed, the achieved consensus on public interest social issues actually masks some potentially significant divisions over economic policy—among conservatives, liberals, and radicals, and among Democrats, Republicans, and Independents—within the constituency of support for reform. Any attempt by the groups to develop a coherent agenda or coalition of support around specific economic policies is thus faced with the problem of exacerbating internal tensions, floundering in stalemate, and probably alienating a sizeable number of backers. Indeed, past tensions within and among groups—especially between environmental and more traditionally oriented consumer groups—on these same issues portend such an outcome.[140]

The argument suggested here, of course, is that a more economically oriented agenda and coalitional effort might enable reform groups to cultivate more widespread and active support in the long run. Yet this strategy is contingent on the viability of such a proposed economic vision, the willing compromises of potential allies, and the overall context of political and economic developments. In short, such a new approach would entail something of a gamble between present security and future uncertainty of constituent support, a gamble that established organizations are unlikely to embrace.[141] Having constructed a largely successful political campaign upon middle-class "new consumer" social foundations, most of the liberal reform groups simply have few tangible incentives to take off in a substantially new direction.

3. *The biases of judicialized politics.* Liberal public interest group reliance on judicialized forums of policy advocacy similarly discourages a comprehensive economic orientation. As Lon Fuller instructed long ago, "adjudication is an ineffective instrument for economic management and for governmental participation in the allocation of economic resources."[142] This derives not only from the fact that judicial institutions lack the authority granted to other government bodies to raise and spend revenues, but also from the basic structure of judicial action. We should remember that the greatest virtue of judicial forums for the new liberals is the opportunity they provide for input from a variety of specific issue perspectives. In such multipolar adversarial settings, each participating group is expected to argue for its own unique value orientation—corporations defend profits, labor defends jobs, environmentalists defend nature, consumers defend

168

citizen health, and so on. By the very logic of its form, therefore, the overall priority setting and issue balancing necessary to policy formulation is left almost entirely to mediating public officials rather than to contending social advocates.[143]

Moreover, by emphasizing public debate in terms of adversarial claims for competing legal rights before an independent "generalist" adjudicator, policy judgments are easily abstracted from concerns for minimizing overall costs, mobilizing resources to pay for such costs, or any collective economic policy formulation at all. Such public debate cast in terms of competing "rights" may correct for the conservative market biases of cost-benefit analysis, it is true, but it does so only by ignoring larger issues concerning productivity altogether. What is more, the very terms of our inherited constitutional discourse tend to exacerbate the problem even further. By opposing the status of social and civil rights against traditional property rights, the logic of modern judicial activism tends to obscure the important economic dimensions of the former.[144] All in all, the implication of these facts is that public interest activists have cultivated their primary resources of power and expertise around those institutions where economic issues and planning are least emphasized. Indeed, we have seen that the activists have embraced judicial institutions precisely because they provide an antidote to the narrow economic logic of corporate state managers.[145] And as long as reformers can secure a voice within government through such narrow social advocacy, there again is little incentive for them to formulate other alternatives.

CHAPTER 4

The Forms of Organized
Citizen Action

A program without organization is a hoax.

—John Gardner

For man as bourgeois, life in the state is only an appearance or fleeting exception to the normal and essential.

—Karl Marx

The only alternative to some form of despotism, benevolent or openly terroristic, is a reawakening of the democratic instinct in middle-class Americans who have no material need to revolt but who are becoming conscious of the degree to which they too are corrupted, degraded, and victimized by the very arrangements that have made possible their unprecedented prosperity.... But the institutional means by which this sterile self-contempt... can be translated into an ethical sense, a sense of injustice, a reawakened sense of the indignities and humiliations which men have permitted themselves to accept as normal, inevitable, proper, and moral—these institutions, it appears, have yet to be forged.

—Christopher Lasch

We have seen that one of the most novel dimensions of public interest liberalism has been its commitment to the goal of advancing participatory democracy in modern America. My analysis in this chapter focuses on the somewhat problematic character of this ideal and the reformers' paradoxical contributions to its further realization. In the first three sections of the discussion I establish that the reformers have managed to mobilize voluntary support from millions of card-carrying members, but also that they have actually engaged very few of these members as genuinely active participants in political life. Ironically, these two facts are inextricably related. What has often been overlooked by social scientists is that the liberal activists' success in enlisting the formal support of so many citizens has derived as much from the minimal degree of involvement required by group membership as from the mostly intangible benefits that it provides. The result is that the actual forms of interest-group organization created by public interest liberals have been built upon a structural logic inherently at odds with the task of participatory grass-roots movement building that the reform rhetoric celebrates. This argument is advanced by joining the classic insights of Tocqueville concerning the structure of democratic community with those of modern rational-choice theorists about the incentive-based illogic of collective action in modern consumer society. In the two final sections I suggest that these apparent contradictions between ideals and achievements stem not from any duplicity on the part of reform leaders, but rather from their commitments to a curious mix of unrealistic voluntarist principles and professional elite pragmatism.

Citizenship: The Problematic Ideal of Participation

Citizenship Ideals. From the beginning, public interest liberals have committed themselves to demystifying the democratic pretenses of contemporary corporate-dominated technobureaucratic politics. Although often invoking many earlier American champions of the people, the reformers' public proclamations have appeared to favor the French thinker Tocqueville as inspiration for their cause. The activists' common lament about the dangers of lost political freedom in particular recalls vividly the words penned by that philosopher over a century and a half ago: "The people's loss of the power to govern themselves has deepened as the need for such self-government has risen," echoes Nader.[1] The reform leaders seem to follow closely the pessimistic eighteenth-century thinker in emphasizing the debilitating effects of economic individualism, materialistic greed, and centralized bureaucratic administration on the potential exercise of democratic liberties in America. "I see an innumerable multitude of men ... constantly circling around in pursuit of the petty and banal pleasures with which they glut their souls" like "a flock of timid and hard-working animals," Tocqueville noted anxiously.[2] Castigating the "irresponsible, amoral, and wholly self-gratifying individuality" of many today, the reformers similarly observe that we as a people have become "less and less sure of our capacity and our initiative as citizens."[3]

171

As the new liberals have offered a parallel analysis of modern problems, so too have they put their faith in participatory politics and citizen action as the best solution. Like Tocqueville, the recent liberal advocates tend to define voluntary citizen associations as the essence of hope for American democracy. Hence, references to the French thinker and to the early American institutions he admired frequently embellish reform publications extolling citizen initiative. The opening page of Donald Ross's influential *A Public Citizen's Action Manual*, for example, begins with this hortative quote from *Democracy in America:* "As soon as the inhabitants of the United States have taken up an opinion or a feeling which they wish to promote in the world, they look around for mutual assistance; and soon as they have found each other out, they combine. From that moment they are no longer isolated men, but a power seen from afar, whose actions serve for an example, and whose language is listened to."[4]

The great value of such political participation for the reformers, as for Tocqueville, is as a means for sustaining a free, self-reliant, democratically accountable polity. "Democratic systems are based on the principle that all power comes from the people," proclaims Mark Green. Citizen participation also is understood as essential to assure greater responsiveness, representativeness, and responsibility from government and corporate elites: "A fundamental tenet of democratic government is that decisions which affect the lives of citizens should be made only with the consent of the governed," the reformers insist.[5] Beyond such instrumental goals, we have seen, the activists sometimes also suggest affinity with Tocqueville's classical view that political action is a valuable endeavor in and of itself: "By supporting the Club and participating in its activities," promises a Sierra Club pamphlet, "you will enjoy the satisfaction of knowing that you are helping to make the world a better and more livable place for yourself and future generations."[6] However, activist leaders have usually been careful to distinguish meaningful political action from other forms of superficial or coopted social interaction: "We want a society in which . . . participation is real and consequential—all this to the end that the individual may recover his capacity to act, to act for himself and in behalf of his community, with confidence and good spirit."[7]

Public interest activists have framed these claims in the timeless political language of "citizenship": "I don't think you have a new type of politics unless you have a new type of citizenship," says Nader. The first requirement of such citizenship is that all persons must be considered as equals bound in common pursuit of mutual welfare: "The ancient notion of the public trust, of which the citizen is a beneficiary, must be revived and adopted to contemporary problems," argues Joseph Sax. The second requirement is that all must be given the opportunity to be public actors as well. "What public interest law has shown . . . is that citizens can make their voices heard and help shape the public policy decisions that shape their lives."[8]

We were introduced in Chapters 1 and 2 to the activists' ideas about developing new political forms consistent with such democratic ideals. As John Gardner summarizes, it is crucial for public interest associations to be "organized for action," because "activity in members is directly related to forms of organization." Hence, the reformers have invested considerable time, energy, and money in building new organizations capable of educating citizens, inspiring action, mobilizing resources, and coordinating tasks to maximize their influence. "The difficulty has always been with the high cost of bringing those with similar interests into communication with each other," acknowledges Nader.[9] And, all in all, most of the new advocates seem proud of their efforts to create more democratic alternatives to the hierarchical, bureaucratic, quasi-corporate institutions that dominate modern life. "Public interest movements," boasts movement affiliate Michael Pertschuk, "stand as testimony to the vitality of traditions of civic virtue through association and participation in the democratic process."[10]

The Social Science Perspective. Social scientists during the last several decades have exposed some quite formidable obstacles to the realization of the reformers' participatory political ideals. Much of this work was developed in the early 1960s by various scholars who began to question some of the basic assumptions at the heart of traditional group theories of politics. The older view was rooted in the faith that political organization was a natural response to the abuses, injustices, and dislocations—often summarily labeled social "disturbances"—imposed upon citizens within modern society. David Truman's classic *The Governmental Process*, for example, suggested not only that existing groups represent well the various interests of their members, but also that any new or previously unrepresented interests can organize easily as the need to reestablish "equilibrium" develops.[11] By contrast, critics such as E. E. Schattschneider, Grant McConnell, and Theodore Lowi presented landmark studies illustrating that the group process tends to be dominated by small, cohesive, economically motivated organizations largely unresponsive to broad citizen interests and unaccountable to any meaningful public control. Schattschneider summed up the new understanding by recognizing that "interest organizations are most easily formed when they deal with small numbers of individuals who are acutely aware of their exclusive interests."[12] To such studies of groups was added the innovative work of political scientist Murray Edelman, who explored the ways in which political leaders use symbolic gestures to appease and diffuse incipient social movements.[13] While different in focus, his analysis of mass cooptation further confirmed the emerging views of many scholars who recognized the inherent organizational advantages of small, intense minority groups over more broadly based mass interests within the existing interest-group process.

But it was the incisive analysis of Mancur Olson's *The Logic of Collective Action* which most effectively cut into the heart of the pluralist assumptions about group mobilization.[14] In Olson's view, participation and sacrifice by individuals for the achievement of collective goods that also benefit nonparticipants is inherently irrational. To recall an old adage, "everyone's business is no one's business." Why should a particular farmer devote his time and energy to an agrarian reform movement that seeks the benefits of higher price supports for all farmers? In Olson's scenario, the incentives to participation are few. If the group wins its fight, the farmer will benefit regardless of his contribution. If the group loses its fight, the contributing individual will have lost twice—both his potential share of collective benefits and the resources he invested in group activity. Hence Olson derived his pessimistic maxims about the "free-rider" dilemma: the larger the group that benefits from a collective good, the less is the individual's fractional share of received benefit for organizational input, and the less is the incentive to participate for collective goods rational in its essence. Olson argued that this problem might be overcome in part by distribution of supplementary private material "selective benefits" or by sanctions compelling group membership. But, overall, his analysis provided considerable reason for skepticism about the potential success of broadly based, socially oriented, voluntaristic public interest groups in developing a sizable membership.

The impact of this explanation for the widely assumed fact of mass inertia has been enormous. What is ironic, however, is that Olson's pessimistic model was elevated to canonical scholarly status at the same historical moment that public interest and other citizen groups were mobilizing millions of dues-paying supporters—well over two million in fifteen prominent national environmental groups alone, and perhaps as many as five million overall in the peak years of the early 1970s.[15] Recognition of these facts has stimulated a variety of critical responses and studies from academic analysts. The most fundamental challenge has come from political theorists claiming that Olson's underlying assumptions about human motivation are too narrow, simple, and static. Some critics have protested that the "rational-actor" model presumes unrealistically that individuals are only selfishly motivated by personal economic gain.[16] Others have argued further that it is simply wrong to understand people as primarily autonomous calculators of rational material interests. Not only are we often misinformed and mistaken about our interests, it is pointed out, but we always understand our interests relative to the social milieu and cultural forms in which we are imbedded. In short, the rationality of human choices cannot be understood apart from the meanings, values, and expectations that evolve out of collective life.[17]

The bulk of most subsequent theorizing on the subject, however, has aimed more to revise and expand than to challenge Olson's basic assumptions about rationality. In particular, many thinkers have attempted to build upon Clark and Wilson's early efforts to emphasize the importance of intangible solidary and purposive benefits as well as material selective incentives to formal group membership. Robert Salisbury's well-known exchange theory, for example, develops the economic analogy further to understand interest-group affiliation as similar to the relation between an entrepreneur and the consumer.[18] This theory not only enlarges the categories of "benefits" at stake, but also focuses on the special role of leaders which Olson largely ignores. Salisbury posits that the success of a group depends on the efforts of "entrepreneurs" motivated by individual "profits" (prestige, salary) to develop those material, purposive, and solidary benefits sufficient to attract a public following. To this scheme Terry Moe has added yet other significant refinements emphasizing the political character of purposive incentives such as a sense of personal efficacy, ideological advancement, and information access which draw citizens to join large membership organizations.[19]

While revising many specifics of the Olson analysis, therefore, the overall thrust of these theories has sustained his focus on the vital role of organizational forms themselves as key variables of effective citizen mobilization. In short, as issue salience defines a crucial determinant of citizen allegiance to organized groups, so also are the structural relations within groups a major factor in shaping citizen perceptions of options, incentives, and purposes at stake in the issues. As Moe puts it, studies of nonmaterial motivations "have the potential for producing a more dynamic group context in which politics, political preferences, and group goals are more centrally determining factors ... linking political considerations more directly to associational size, structure, and internal processes."[20] Many studies of liberal public interest groups have provided evidence for the conceptual utility of this approach. Jeffrey Berry's empirical study in 1977 thus "concluded that purposive incentives are the most crucial type of inducement for public interest group membership."[21] Constance Ewing Cook's more recent study of three leading organizations tends to confirm Moe's more subtle analysis about the role of ideological commitment, obligations of "civic duty," and feelings of efficacy in motivating citizens to join the public interest cause. And similar conclusions have been reached in nearly every other specialized study on the subject.[22]

But although valuable in themselves, the limit of these academic theories is that they so far have emphasized accounting for the overall quantity of citizen members rather than assessing the relative quality of actual participation generated by most public interest groups. Incentives have been weighed for their capacity to attract citizen membership more than for their impact upon the character of that membership itself.[23] Moreover, references to abstract categories of "purposive," "solidary," and other nonmaterial incentives reveal little about the actual structural capacities of group relations to empower citizen participants and to enhance commitments to movement goals themselves. To this end of more detailed description and analysis concerning the dynamics of membership activity in public interest groups we now turn.

The Oligarchical Forms of Democratic Reform

Initiatory Democracy? Public interest groups have succeeded in attracting millions of dues-paying members throughout the nation since the late 1960s. But the crucial fact is that very few of those members have become genuinely active in public life. Contrary to their seemingly radical slogans, public interest liberals have thus not constructed significant new arenas for democratic experience through which the social foundations of American public life might be transformed. Indeed, the internal structures of power and initiative in most public interest groups are little more participatory than the state bureaucracies the activists openly criticize. This claim can be illustrated by a brief descriptive overview of the organizational forms and relations generated by the new politics. Particular focus on one of the most participation-oriented groups, Common Cause, will define

176

the outlines of public interest achievements from which a more detailed picture of the whole movement can be sketched.

Common Cause was founded as a "people's lobby" in 1970 by John Gardner.[24] It developed a membership of over 200,000 by 1972, peaked at 325,000 during the Watergate era, and stabilized at about 230,000 with over a 70 percent renewal rate until the Reagan era revitalization in the early 1980s. Like most public interest groups, Common Cause members are mostly white, upper-middle income, well-educated, liberal professionals interested in issues of good government. In fact, substantial numbers of Common Cause members also contribute to Nader organizations, the ACLU, the League of Women Voters, and environmental groups. They differ from members of other groups only, if at all, in that they tend to be somewhat older and more moderate in values. As a lobbying group, Common Cause emphasizes structural and procedural over substantive issues, although it has been quite active in antiwar, antimilitary, anti-Nixon, energy, environmental, and civil-rights policy advocacy. Likewise, Common Cause expends most of its efforts in legislative lobbying, political education, and litigation. Because over 95 percent of its $5–6 million annual budget is funded by members and donors, the size of the Common Cause constituency is of considerable concern to the group leaders.

As previous pages have shown, Gardner and other Common Cause activists have been among the leading exponents of democratic participatory ideals: "The participation of members is crucial. A key objective of Common Cause is to give the citizen heightened participation in his government, and to give him the moral reinforcement of knowing his own efforts are matched and strengthened by the efforts of hundreds of thousands of fellow citizens."[25] However, there is little that is novel about the structure of power and action within this "citizens'" organization. Lacking local chapters, authority has been very centralized from the beginning. The primary locus of decision-making activity is divided between a semipermanent professional staff—lawyers, lobbyists, writers—and an elected national governing board. The board is composed of sixty members elected for three years, with one-third (twenty) up for election each year. No one can sit on the board for more than two successive three-year terms. Any Common Cause member can gain nomination with a petition of twenty other member names. Likewise, a special nominating committee also chooses candidates in an attempt to promote ethnic, sexual, racial, geographic, and occupational balance within the narrow bounds of group diversity. Although inconclusive, there is evidence that the board wields at least some measure of control over the staff through both veto power and policy initiative.

Beyond formal professional staff or board activity, citizen participation through Common Cause is manifest in a number of ways, each of which enlists only a small minority of the membership. The first dimension of possible activism is in contributing to group pressure tactics upon the state to achieve certain policy goals. This includes primarily letter writing, telephone calls, and other forms of correspondence with state officials. As national issues are first in priority, most of the correspondence is unidirectional and impersonal. For the most part, these activities are administrative or executory and include little input into decisions about which issues and goals are to be pursued by the group. It has been estimated that less than one-fourth of Common Cause members have ever contributed in this manner, and that only about 4 percent are "active" or "very active" in contributing their time and energy. The limits of this form of citizen engagement were well illustrated in a breakdown of the mail alert system in 1975; when members were instructed to write congressional representatives to both promote the Ullman energy proposal and oppose the B-1 bomber proposal, few letters were sent. One analyst has speculated that sending out two letters at one time (a year) constituted an overload for most members, and that few understood clearly what issues were at stake and why the Common Cause staff took their respective stands.[26]

About 10 percent of Common Cause members are enlisted more directly and actively in political life. Since 1972, after numerous criticisms about its centralizd structure, Common Cause has established three hundred active "congressional districts," through which more personal member interaction is facilitated, within nearly every state. Likewise, coordinating structures called "program action committees" (PACs) were created in a majority of the states. However, these organizations, like the free-form lobbying activism of the general membership, have enlisted only a small minority of the membership, enjoyed little independent initiative, and engaged in mostly administrative and strategic work until the late 1970s: contacting officials in government, sparking media coverage, informing national staff of bill progress in state legislatures, coordinating membership drives. "PACs and steering committees do not discuss issues and what Common Cause's position ought to be on such issues," one observer has noted.[27] The raison d'être of this institutional arrangement, defenders have argued, is "effective action" rather than citizen participation, education, and consensus building. Indeed, when a

178

state chapter in Oregon attempted to change the national dues policies to increase local participation opportunities (especially for minorities), its efforts caused considerable reaction and conflict within the organization. The exercise of local autonomy in group agenda making, policy determination, and recruitment activities, the national staff seems to have insisted, must take a back seat in the drive for effectively coordinated national lobbying influence.[28]

Several other forms of member input into decision making about leadership and policy priorities are available, however. For one thing, all members are eligible to vote as well as to run for positions on the national board. Each candidate, once nominated by twenty other members or by the nominating board, is required to prepare for membership evaluation a one-hundred-word platform of personal values and issue commitments. In this way, votes for officials indirectly reflect member preferences for the general group political goals. However, responses from members in such elections thus far have been amazingly low—22 percent voted in 1975 and 24 percent in 1976—and actual control over the board is more symbolic than substantive due to lack of member information about the candidates.[29] Moreover, the leadership in recent years has sent referenda forms to solicit advice and support from members about group policy positions. But although the expressed disapproval of as little as 20 percent of the members can doom a proposal, the results of this experiment have also been rather unimpressive. Again, less than one fourth of the members even bother to fill out the simple polling forms to indicate their preferences. Generally, such referenda serve only to ratify those choices already formulated by the active minority within the organization.[30] The referenda results are not binding upon the governors or staff and have served most often to halt rather than to promote Common Cause action on substantive issues such as tax reforms.[31] Finally, it should be noted that members send an additional one hundred to two hundred unsolicited letters a month expressing opinions on issues and activities sponsored by the group.

Andrew McFarland, an astute and sensitive political scientist, has defended these Common Cause arrangements as inherently democratic in some important regards. Admitting its significant lack of achievement according to participatory ideals, he nevertheless praises the Common Cause organization in terms of an "exchange model" of polyarchal democratic values. While most citizen members do very little, he argues, they still have considerable control over the leadership. This is achieved not by discourse, debates, internal struggle, or elections—that is, by political action—but by the simple fact of the need for membership that limits elite leadership discretion. In other words, the most important political act of most Common Cause members is that of joining or exiting, of sending or withholding a check. Indeed, McFarland acknowledges that a large majority of members have no desire to participate. He cites a 1974 poll that found that 79 percent of Common Cause members "would [not] like to be more active in Common Cause," while only 12 percent desired more participatory experience. "All evidence indicates that the great majority of the membership like Common Cause's present avoidance of high-participation organizational structure," he concludes.[32] A 1983 study by Constance E. Cook revealed virtually the same thing. Not only did a mere 9 percent of polled members feel that they actually made decisions collectively; one-half of them either did not know how decisions were made or assumed that the staff leadership acted wholly alone. Moreover, while 10 percent of the members considered themselves "active" participants, only another 8 percent expressed any dissatisfaction with the existing organizational arrangements.[33]

McFarland's general claim about the accountability, representativeness, and effectiveness of the Common Cause organizational structure may be valid, and he is accurate in pointing out that Common Cause is no less participatory than most other interest groups in contemporary America. At best, therefore, it may be described as a benign, responsive, and formally open oligarchy. Yet such a recognition should not obscure the fact that a large gap exists between these realities of conformity to prevailing forms and the reformers' pious claims to promote a more meaningful democratic citizenship. The association is primarily a staff-led organization in which most members play no serious role in the determination of policies and values.[34] For those few beyond the Washington staff who do take part, action is primarily isolated, administrative, and infrequent. Even the most active group members typically meet only once a year to elect steering committee leaders. There is little direct debate, internal struggle, organization of conflicting groups, or sustained plurality of views expressed beyond the central offices. In fact, Common Cause leaders openly acknowledge that they do not want an organization in which careful consensus building among local discussion groups is necessary for national lobbying action.[35] Yet this admission only further justifies skepticism toward the reform leaders' lofty claims to seek a democratic reappropriation of power to the people in America.

Variations on a Theme. Compared to Common Cause, most other public interest groups offer even fewer meaningful opportunities and resources for genuine citizen involvement. "In sum, it may be said that in the majority of groups the members or constitutents have little direct influence on organizational leaders," concluded Jeffrey Berry in the most exhaustive empirical study of the reform associations to date. "In patterns similar to that of private interest groups, public interest lobbies are strongly oligarchic . . . [and] real participatory democracy is largely absent."[36] Indeed, many groups—over one-third of the total, mostly including public interest law firms or research centers—do not even have an identifiable citizen constituency. These small cadres of lawyers, scientists, researchers, and other professionals constitute mostly independent "staff groups" working for specific clients or for self-established policy goals, sometimes in coalition with other groups. In other words, these groups depart little in form from the conventional legal and technical staffs hired by the profit-seeking enterprises they challenge. As scholar Robert Rabin has recognized, "Structurally . . . the public interest law firm looks very much like its corporate commercial counterpart; it is a law office organized to manage a caseload involving the standard mix of judicial and administrative appearances as well as informal negotiation with clients and adversaries."[37] It is not surprising, then, that a 1980 Public Interest Law Center survey found that most such law firms devoted only about 5 percent of their time to community-organizing activities.[38] Such firms may be progressive in policy orientation, of course, but they hardly provide the roots for public mobilization through sustained collective action.

What is even more surprising is that most mass membership groups do not even make a pretense of concern for actual internal democracy or participatory politics. About 57 percent of membership groups in Berry's study (nearly 75 percent of all) had no structure of collective citizen policy influence at all. "In all but a few of the groups, the leaders cannot be realistically challenged," he observed.[39] The most significant examples include the Nader Public Citizen network of organizations, which exclude formal member participation altogether.[40] Another prime example is the Sierra Club, the archetype of environmental organizations. At least two independent studies have confirmed that it "maintains an oligarchy by self-perpetuating its governing officers through 'nominating committees' which are comprised of the officers or their friends."[41] Likewise, one of these studies reveals that only 8 percent of members frequently attend chapter meetings and that just slightly more than 4 percent take part in committee work. Arthur St. George thus concluded that "neither committee work, chapter meetings, nor leadership roles"—that is, the political dimensions of citizen involvement—"appear to be very important to more than a fraction of the members."[42]

Of those groups with any formal channels of access for general members, perhaps only 25 percent (less than 10 percent of all groups) have processes of citizen input even approaching the scale of the Common Cause model.[43] Again, most of these "participatory" processes involve policy-ratifying rather than policy-making opportunities, draw low rates of contribution, and require of citizens little skill, knowledge, or commitment.[44] Many groups, following Common Cause, even discourage local group or chapter participation that might impede effective, efficient national staff-led action. Leading PIRG organizer Donald Ross, for example, discourages "building from a base of existing clubs" because of the risks of "bogging down in debates on priorities, methods, goals and jealousies among clubs."[45] Consumer Federation of America does represent a coalition of over two hundred diverse groups throughout the nation, but it functions mostly as an independent lobbying staff.

Not only do most membership groups facilitate little direct citizen participation, moreover, but surveys reveal that members know astoundingly little about the organizations themselves. Constance E. Cook's study of four major groups found that only one-third of members surveyed could identify even one issue on which the organization had concentrated during the past year. Likewise, as with Common Cause members, about one-half of those polled either did not know how decisions were made in the group or assumed that the leaders took full responsibility.[46] In sum, it seems fair to conclude that the often-cited distinction between membership and staff organizations obscures the actual undemocratic, nonparticipatory qualities common to nearly all public interest groups. "There is relatively little actual grass-roots participation in the representative enterprise," Simon Lazarus has admitted.[47]

To be sure, we must be careful not to obscure real differences among the groups. Common Cause and Friends of the Earth undeniably are more decentralized and open in their distribution of responsibilities than the Sierra Club, most Nader groups, and Consumers Union. Perhaps the most exceptional and exemplary in its grass-roots participatory structure is not a new group at all, but one of the oldest—The League of Women Voters.[48] The League is thoroughly local- and state-oriented in organization, and separate groups enjoy considerable autonomy of action. Most league members meet regularly, discuss issues and policy goals at length, and engage in local as well as national political action. One study has found that 41 percent of polled members considered themselves "activists" and that 83 percent believed that policy making is a collective enterprise of interaction between members and leaders.[49] As former president Ruth Hinerfeld has claimed, "the League of Women Voters operates on the basis of consensual decision making to an extent matched by few institutions in the Western world, and has developed the process into a high art."[50] Despite an upsurge in serious issue advocacy in the 1970s, however, League activists remain primarily educational in their goals, and policy efforts remain somewhat diffuse and moderate. In addition, it is worth noting that League membership dropped significantly during the late 1970s as it stepped up its democratization efforts.[51]

It is also true that some groups have attempted to change their elitist tendencies. For example, Nader encouraged local university-based PIRGs to enlist students during the mid-1970s in radical liberal causes. However, these have remained mostly small staffs of a few students in watchdog committees that mirror, but are unrelated to, the national organization. A study by Bo Burlingham thus concluded that "ironically, what the PIRGs have *not* done is to promote widespread citizen participation in public affairs."[52] Moreover, the Nader-inspired Congress Watch program of local groups was initiated in the late 1970s. Yet, their functions likewise have been quite limited and their activity staff-dominated.[53] Among environmental groups, efforts to cultivate stronger ties with local groups have increased somewhat as well. Some groups have developed a complex organizational base of local and state chapters. The Sierra Club, for example, has spawned as many as 250 local groups and chapters, while the National Audubon Society has developed nearly 400 chapters. But these associations have developed as primarily recreational in function, and they as yet wield very little formal political power.[54]

In response to political setbacks in the 1980s, other groups have vowed to follow the lead of the League of Conservation Voters and Friends of the Earth in organizing for voter registration and electoral advocacy in some areas of the country. Yet a strong administrative, technocratic impulse within many environmental leadership circles has continued to win out over the efforts of more democratic advocates to follow through on participatory goals.[55] For the most part, efforts to develop local affiliates and grass-roots connections have been centrally directed and administrative in orientation, as are Common Cause steering committees. Local ties are created mostly to maximize the overall effectiveness of organizational power in government lobbying action rather than to enlarge the sphere of citizen action in public life. Even where decentralized organizational affiliates enjoy relative autonomy, as in the ACLU, such groups tend to be governed by small staffs of specialized elites rather than majoritarian processes of internal democratic policy making. "Failure to pay attention to administrative management will snuff out all good intention," David Cohen has summarized in explaining the organizational goals of most public interest groups.[56]

In 1970, John Gardner tempered his enthusiastic exhortations to "citizen action" ideals with practical admonition that "we must not be sentimental about what 'the people' can accomplish." Over a decade later, the goal of generating widespread citizen participation in liberal reform activity seems to have lost even more of its earlier appeal among most movement leaders. A statement by Common Cause executive Jack Conway may be typical: when asked by a journalist why the organization did not encourage local chapter activity, he responded that "the last thing our members wanted was another meeting."[57]

Membership, Participation, and Citizenship

Democratic Community versus Interest Group Forms. Before returning to the incentive-based theories discussed earlier, it is useful to analyze further the structural relations described here in terms of the democratic ideas espoused by the reformers themselves. Specifically, it should be clear that most liberal public interest organizations bear little resemblance to Tocqueville's exalted "voluntary associations," which they claim to imitate. This is not primarily because the modern groups lack formal channels of access to member participation; the important reason is that the fragile promise of democratic action praised by Tocqueville could thrive only amid a larger social landscape of institutional interaction that, as he dolefully predicted, has been long since supplanted by the forces of commerce, industrialization, and state centralization. Tocqueville specified at least three basic dimensions of those public forms essential to the nurture of active democratic citizenship.

First, political freedom can develop only from institutions and forms of action in close spatial proximity to citizens. "The strength of free peoples resides in the local community. Local institutions are to liberty what primary schools are to science; they put it within people's reach; they . . . accustom them to make use of it."[58] A politics of close proximity enables an easy integration of daily concerns and

184

history, of private and public life. It renders politics a familiar sphere of face-to-face relations among fellow citizens bound to similar circumstances. Locally instituted political forms of interaction do not just provide an alternative to large-scale politics, of course. Rather, community politics creates the foundations upon which a more rational and civilized collective life in the wider spheres of state and national concern can be built. "Public spirit in the Union is, in a sense, only a summing up of provincial patriotism. Every citizen of the United States may be said to transfer the concern inspired in him by his little republic into his love of the common motherhood."[59] By contrast, the unmediated consolidation of public power in national government far removed from the reach of ordinary citizens only encourages apathy, deference, and conformity to subtle despotism.

Second, Tocqueville insists on the importance of political forms that are temporally proximate to everyday life. On one hand, this means that political action must be built upon the established foundations of regular social interaction. While he celebrates the American propensity for voluntary association, Tocqueville suggests that this can develop only through the support of the larger "permanent associations" of traditional political, social, and religious life.[60] On the other hand, the demand for temporal proximity means that political action must be integrated into the regular and familiar routines of everyday life. It cannot be a random and infrequent exercise and still secure freedom. "Their daily duties performed or rights exercised keep municipal life constantly alive," he observes of early Americans. "What had been calculation becomes instinct. By dent of working for the good of fellow citizens, he in the end acquires a habit and taste for serving with them."[61] And it is in this way that individual self-interest is "enlightened" by the identification with, and nurturing of, social obligations to, fellow citizens.

Finally, to these dimensions of proximity Tocqueville adds one other factor essential to the generation of citizen action—that of autonomy and power. He maintains that it is crucial for citizens to be politically "sovereign in all that concerns them alone."[62] In those economic, social, and moral matters unique to each time and place, citizens must be relatively free from centralized control to determine their own fates. Such exercise of collective responsibllity is necessary to cultivate in citizens the skills of self-government, the taste for public life, and the social foundations of power against others who seek domination. "Without power and independence a town may have local subjects but it can have no local citizens." Hence we can understand the link between Tocqueville's concerns for administrative decentralization and democratic freedom which pervade all of his writings.[63]

It is easy to see that public interest organizations for the most part have not been built upon such a democratic structure of proximate forms and relations within modern life. For one thing, most reform groups have not connected their political activities to the daily lives or community milieu of most citizens. Despite their vocal exhortations about revitalizing local institutions, the primary struggle for control of public "space" by liberal reformers has been waged at levels of authority far removed from the experiences of their constituents. The activists have aimed not to create new institutions of public life accessible to all so much as to extend new interest group pressures within the organized administrative processes of those national institutions that have gradually rendered local politics in the modern era increasingly irrelevant.[64] Indeed, a defining characteristic of the new politics has been to shift political debates, legal responsibilities, and forums of decision making yet further away from decentralized structures of local and state government to the centralized regulatory jurisdiction of the federal government. The forms of political action in which the liberals engage have few roots in the local town meeting or neighborhood center; they take place mostly in the alien arenas of federal courts, administrative agencies, corporate boardrooms, or the halls of national and state legislatures quite distant from the daily worlds of "the people."[65] As one environmentalist put it in 1981, most groups have been caught up in a "Potomacentrist" view of the world: "that there is one single best solution for every environmental problem, and if that solution isn't written on the banks of the Potomac, it doesn't exist."[66] Of course, many of the structural reforms initiated by activists have rendered more responsive those who exercise legal power within the national government. However, the shift in authority, initiative, and points of access from the executive to judicial branch generally, and within the administrative apparatus to more diffused decision-making centers, has not much altered the tremendous spatial distance still existing between the formal national institutions of government and the American citizenry.

Even more important, the internal relations among members within most public interest groups reflect and sustain the great spatial distance separating citizens from each other and from the arenas of politics in modern society. Centered mostly in Washington and a few major urban areas, the organizations have provided little of the personal contact and collective interaction among members that

Tocqueville thought so necessary to a dynamic democratic citizen politics. As pointed out earlier, some groups do have decentralized structures of association such as local chapters, steering committees, and administrative networks. Yet the impersonal and remote activities undertaken in such associations hardly bridge the great gaps of unfamiliarity and distance that separate existing and potential members alike. Mary Topolsky's challenge to Common Cause applies to most of the mass-based associations: "Local members feel a lack of fellowship among themselves, and in fact don't even know who the other members are in the community" beyond perhaps a few personal friends. "How is it that one can be an active member . . . making telephone calls, writing one's congressman, reading the monthly newsletter, filling out questionnaires, voting and even running in national board elections—without ever looking another member in the eye?"[67] How, indeed?

The fact is that the primary interaction of members with each other and with the leadership are mediated almost exclusively through the impersonal channels of sophisticated technology. Carefully calculated mass mailing remains the basic means of citizen solicitation and mobilization. Newspapers, television, telephones, and computers constitute the principal—usually the only—forms of communicative interaction among leaders and members. Many influential activists even see the keys to greater citizen organization and democracy in the development of communication technology: "Gleaming in many a futurist's eye are the ultimate processes of political participation: the instant electronic referenda," observes environmentalist Hazel Henderson.[68] This movement toward alternative media may be novel in its substantive orientation, but only dubiously is it democratic in form. In sum, it is hard to imagine how the commitments to community, cooperation, and solidarity can be nurtured through such abstractly impersonal relations. The mechanical wires and circuit boards that bind modern technological society are simply inadequate to generate in citizens the sense of common identity necessary to sustained collective commitment or action.[69]

Most organized public interest activity tends to be every bit as remote in time from the lives of most citizens as it is in space. The involvement expected from citizens by the new reformers is simply not frequent, regular, or demanding enough to develop either depth or intensity of commitment in members. Seemingly more concerned with large numbers of supporters than with serious commitment to the cause, the new organizations have labored to make membership as simple, unobtrusive, and unimportant as possible. A few seconds to write out a check, a casual conversation to spread the word to others, a vote for an organizational leader or policy priority, a few minutes to read a newsletter, a few hours to read a newly published book, an annual dinner, a telephone call or letter to a public official—these are the outer limits of direct action asked from members.[70] Expectations for even this minimal degree of involvement are usually extended only to a very small percentage of the total membership. Quite obviously, such "checkbook affiliations" are hardly sufficient to challenge the learned roles and conventions of social deference encouraged by modern consumer society. To reverse a popular argument by scholar Michael Walzer, public interest activities do not take up enough evenings—or daytime life—to realign the commitments of most constituents.[71]

The point here is that public interest membership neither builds upon, transforms, nor creates anew the shared institutional structures of social life for most supporters; rather, membership activities constitute mostly occasional appendages, even intrusions, to the fragmented forms of organized interaction familiar to most of us.[72] For example, we have seen that the new reform politics remains mostly aloof from the most time-consuming act of all, that of work. While some informal ties among liberal reform leaders and labor officials have been forged, few unions or public interest group organizations have promoted substantial involvement by workers in politics.[73] Unlike both the recent peace movement and conservative moral-reform movements, liberal activists have remained aloof from established religious institutions and practices as well. Indeed, they seem to have sustained a wary, independent, and even hostile attitude toward Tocqueville's observation that religion is "the first of their political institutions" in early America to facilitate the exercise of freedom.[74] The vast majority of reform groups have also resisted building upon or attempting to revitalize the habitual identifications and institutional forms of prevailing political parties within contemporary America. Whereas Tocqueville praised mediating partisan organizations as a resource for "spread[ing] a general habit and taste for associations," the activists have found only reason for independence, pessimism, and criticism.[75] Finally, even the ritual act of voting itself within the larger political process has curiously remained only a minor concern of the reformers until the 1980s.

It should be evident that public interest membership also contributes little to the development of citizen autonomy. Activists do preach about increased self-sufficiency and collective engagement in everyday life, to be sure: "The surest cure for social irresponsibility is to give people something to be responsible about, to give them a significant role in the functioning of the community," muses John Gardner.[76] Yet such sentiments have remained mostly peripheral to the larger agenda of public interest pragmatism. Far removed from the local affairs of most citizens, professional activists have struggled to cultivate power within rather than outside the existing structures of bureaucratic administration. Indeed, the new politics has been organized largely according to the hierarchical terms of Tocqueville's feared "administrative centralization." At close range, the ad hoc, flexible, experimental staff relations about which the reformers often boast conform little to the formal organization typical of business corporations, labor unions, or public agencies. Yet, from a greater distance, the structures of most public interest groups do not bridge the immense gap between organized power and politically passive members to any significant degree. Even local chapters, we have seen, have generally been afforded little autonomy in policy initiative and action. While the new politics has increased institutional pluralism at the corporate state level, therefore, it has not contributed significantly to the social pluralism of independent self-governing citizen collectivities which it praises in theory.[77]

In fact, many new federal social regulations intended to curb corporate abuses have actually restricted the autonomy of most citizens. Unlike older forms of economic regulation, which tend to expand consumer choice and buying power by promoting market competition, newer social regulations encouraged by public interest activists tend to restrict discretionary choices and increase legal duties for producers and consumers alike.[78] As a result, such an extension of federal governmental power over daily life without parallel gains in popular citizen control over government has succeeded in offending much of the liberal constituency for whom the reformers claim to speak. For example, individual consumer discretion has been nearly eliminated with regard to the use of automobile seatbelts, motorcycle helmets, many wilderness areas, and various drugs and food substitutes such as saccharin.[79] Many educators, doctors, lawyers, social workers, and other professionals likewise have been overwhelmed in recent years with new regulatory prohibitions and paperwork. Even more significant, the extension of federal controls has also invaded the managerial autonomy of allied nonprofit institutions, such as state and local governments, private charitable foundations, and universities already under considerable economic strain.[80] In all these ways, public interest groups may have augmented the welfare of many citizens as private beneficiaries of state protection,

189

but they have provided very little power to the people as public actors and subjects within modern society.

The Unfulfilled Democratic Promise. "Everyone's organized but the people," lamented the new activists in 1970, and so it remains over a decade later.[81] However noble in intent and effective in policy impact, the inescapable fact is that the liberal reform associations simply do not re-create the classical republican forms of citizen democracy that their rhetoric frequently extols. Whereas Tocqueville's model of political association was built upon a dense network of institutional relations connecting personal volition and political life, public interest group membership has done little to bridge the abyss between these spheres institutionalized by corporate society. The possibility of forging new allegiances through what Lawrence Goodwyn calls "movement culture" and Lasch labels "alternative institutions" of government thus remains unrealized.[82] Most public interest groups do not even structurally resemble the new forms of "backyard politics" recently celebrated by Harry Boyte and others. Although sharing with the latter some common causes, a mostly similar middle-class constituency, and periodic formal alliances, few national public interest organizations have acted on the premise that the best "guarantee of independence is the subordination of other forms of activity to the priorities of grass roots organizing."[83] At best, liberal group leaders have only been able to support such activity when and where it happens.

This seems to be what recent advocates of exchange theory imply by their rationalistic arguments about the lack of organizational incentives to stimulate collective action. In particular, the impersonality of institutional relations and absence of face-to-face interaction for the vast majority of members in most groups offer few "solidary" incentives to collective commitment. A number of environmental groups have generated citizen interest by sponsoring recreational activities—camping, hiking, exhibits—for members. However, only three of the fifteen largest ecology organizations offer such outings, only a small minority of members participate in such activities, and the value of such endeavors for enhancing political efficacy is dubious. In fact, while polls reveal that recreation provides one of the greatest motivations for joining some groups, most of such member activity takes place independently of formal associational sponsorship altogether.[84] Moreover, not only have most public interest groups made few contributions to overall economic prosperity, but the selective material incentives that they offer to members are few and largely insignificant as well. Most groups provide regular newsletters and magazines—much of which provides valuable political information—as well as other private benefits to members, of course. But, again, such benefits offer few distinctive attractions in consumer society, and available studies reveal that these benefits do not play a great role in stimulating the contributions of new members.[85] Even the most appealing (*National Wildlife*) and useful (*Consumer Reports*) magazines, as well as other benefits such as book discounts, decals, and merchandise offers, contribute little at best to enhancing citizen political efficacy or obligation.

This does not mean that the choices of citizens to become or to remain members are irrational or unexplainable in these terms. Citizen support for general movement goals is undoubtedly enhanced by the perceived benefits of increased "self-esteem" and reduced personal danger from "collective bads" such as smog and resource depletion that membership provides.[86] But such rational calculations of gain themselves generally matter far less than the fact that they cost middle-class citizens almost nothing in money (from perhaps $7.50 to $25) or time (a few minutes to send a preaddressed envelope) to obtain through the direct mail process. In other words, the key motivation to public interest membership is that it provides middle-class adults a painless means to remain faithful to their liberal idealism without disturbing their conventional roles in the larger corporate society. "The most conclusive vote cast by the individual is his decision to sign or resign. . . . His joining is in effect a vote for the movement," says Gardner.[87] Beyond this initial choice, the demands placed upon members are virtually none. And where involvement is so marginal, it seems, the purported inhibitions of rational self-interest are likely to matter very little. But where the degree of actual involvement is so low, the groups also remain very limited in their ability to stimulate, to inform, and to support creative citizen mobilization around common commitments to political change. In short, the public interest group appeal for voluntary members has succeeded precisely because leaders have acquiesced to the logic of collective inaction and settled for a constituency of passive supporters rather than attempted to create more democratic forms of purposeful citizen engagement.[88]

However effective in mobilizing voluntary financial resources, therefore, the undeniable implication is that the sense of efficacy and civic duty offered by reform group membership is more symbolically gratifying than politically empowering. Public interest groups provide only "the illusion of participation" for most citizen contributors.[89] This contention is supported by the work of many social scientists. Political analyst W. Lance Bennett, for example, has argued that sustained grass-roots activity is necessary to the development of citizenship in two crucial ways. On one hand, frequent concerted action by members is important to nurture collective identity with the distinctive symbols, ideals, and programs that define the group. In this sense, regular political interaction solidifies the bonds of affective attachment and shared meaning that unite citizens in common cause. On the other hand, Bennett argues, "there is a direct link between grass-roots activism and a core democratic value: the citizen's ability to think and reason in public affairs." He specifies in particular four criteria by which to measure the impact of grass-roots action: the frequency of personal value conflict among members, the salience of outcomes from action, the degree of required individual initiative, and the opportunities to contribute to the formulation of group procedures and rules. The more intense and sustained each form of involvement is, Bennett's data suggest, the more the citizen's "cognitive complexity" is likely to be enhanced. By contrast, "some forms of participation" like voting and "hit and miss involvement in grass-roots activities" such as those engaged in by public interest group members "have little effect on cognitive development."[90] That supporters of public interest liberalism generally appear little informed about group policies and organization thus should be as unsurprising as it is lamentable.

It is Tocqueville who should have the last word, however. As long as political participation by citizens remains only a "rare and brief exercise of free will," he instructed, group membership alone "will not prevent them from losing the faculty of thinking, feeling, and acting for themselves."[91]

The Ethic of Liberal Voluntarism

Political Individualism. Most public interest reformers have appeared largely indifferent, or at best contradictory, in their attitudes toward the minimal degree of public participation generated by the movement. The reason is not simply that the activists are insincere or hypocritical about their lofty ideals, nor is it merely that they have been concerned only about the more tangible goals of financial resource mobilization. Rather, most public interest leaders appear to begin from quite different assumptions about the nature of citizen action and grass-roots political participation itself. In short, while the maximization of effectiveness in hierarchical bureaucratic arenas has defined the primary organizational imperative of most groups, their hopes for generating increased citizen participation within society have been envisioned in quite rationalistic, extraorganizational, and even antiorganizational terms. Like their New Left precursors, many public interest leaders seem to have extended their incisive animus against large-scale bureaucratic Leviathans to suspicion concerning nearly all forms of enduring social institutions and demanding political associations as undue burdens upon citizen initiative.[92] Hence, they have tended to advocate that the most productive forms of citizen participation begin *outside* formal associational structures and group membership activities. Democratic citizen action, it seems, has been understood as largely unorganized, unmediated, "voluntary" action.

"Formalism kills creativity," Hazel Henderson has summarized. Echoing a prevailing environmentalist theme, she argues that social institutions are inherently artificial, unnatural, and inhibiting to human freedom and self-development. "Entropy" and decay are the natural tendencies of formal organizations.[93] Open Space Institute founder Charles Little likewise insists that the worst thing that can happen to a citizens movement is that it "get organized . . . because from that point on organization will preclude any possibility of meaningful action." Citing a sort of Gresham's law, he concludes that "the processes of organization drive out creative action."[94] Nader has reflected a similar view in his constant fulminations against formal structures that deny individuality, demand compromise, and encourage manipulation, thus leaving participants "caged" and "restricted."[95] John Gardner perhaps works out the prevailing perspective most fully. He constantly opposes the life of individuals to the moribund qualities of institutions. "The institution is by nature prudent, rational, cool, systematic, and self-preserving. . . . Institutions are weighted with the past; the individual is on the side of vitality and the future." Elaborating a three-stage process, he outlines the inevitable pattern of ossification which turns institutional forms into an "impenetrable web" inhibiting creative action. "The tendency of all institutions [is] to decay, to rigidify, and to stifle new ideas."[96]

The activists thus emphasize that individual rather than collective action must be the foundation of a genuine political renaissance. "The one condition for the rebirth of the nation is a rebirth of individual responsibility," claims Gardner.[97] Critical of the baleful consequences inherent in the loss of liberal market individualism, the reformers have appealed to political individualism and legal "self help" as the antidote for our current maladies. One alleged virtue of judicialized institutions, it should be remembered, was that they provide "the political system's only point of access to the individual citizen" lacking the power of group identity.[98] Likewise, most of the citizen's-action (not "citizens'-action") handbooks published by the various groups direct their advice about possible projects specifically to solitary, unaligned individuals. "The responsibility for using them rests with each reader," notes author Donald Ross.[99]

The Sierra Club action manual, *Ecotactics*, provides a good example. Nearly every one of the many hortatory and heuristic essays envisions the isolated, free, willful individual as the foundation from which the new politics will grow. "Perhaps more than anything else, we shall need individual action. Each person must become ecologically responsible," argues executive director Michael McCloskey in the book's foreword. Other authors in the volume follow his lead: "There must be a search for the dissenting company engineer, the conscience-stricken house lawyer, the concerned retiree or ex-employee, the knowledgable worker and the fact-laden supplier of the industry or company under study. They are there somewhere. They must be located," admonishes Ralph Nader in one chapter. "The first level of the structure is individual action, as a private citizen during non-employed time, as an employee of a firm, or as a member" of some organization, adds Cliff Humphrey of Ecology Action. "The opportunity to assume individual responsibility is still ours, but not, perhaps, for long," stresses another essay. "By and large, the real bell ringers in this environmental emergency turn out to be individuals, not organizations," summarizes Charles Little in the concluding chapter. "Everything that gets done within a society is done by individuals."[100]

The greatest virtue of an active citizen likewise seems to be that of personal independence rather than collective solidarity. A yearning for individual independence is reflected in the emphasis on experimental lifestyles, the flaunted "outsider" posture to mainstream bureaucratic politics, and the preferences for ad hoc "call-em'-as-we-see-em" alliances rather than permanent coalitions. "No system can stay vital for long unless some of the leaders remain sufficiently independent to help it change and grow," instructs John Gardner.[101] This is of course consistent with another virtue of judicial forums—the relative independence of action they encourage from both judges and adversarial participants. "No matter how independent a politician wants to be," argues Nader, "he is still dependent upon campaign contributions just to enter the election campaign."[102] Indeed, the public interest infatuation with abstract public rights is uniquely suited as a claim for the unattached, socially undifferentiated legal person, whether acting alone or with others in the impersonal functional identity of class-action victim.[103] This propensity is expressed in the activists' independence from formal partisan identification as well. The alleged recent decline in public affections for modern parties can hardly be blamed on the reformers or their reforms, as some have argued. But it is clear that most of the liberal groups have opted to capitalize on citizen disaffection from existing parties rather than to mobilize collective allegiances around new party structures and alliances.[104]

Reform leaders thus tend to locate the sources of this esteemed ideal of citizen independence in all that is spontaneous, natural, and noninstitutionalized in citizen life. "The exhilaration of the crusade resides in the individual heart," proclaims one manifesto. "We need an education of the heart and spirit," says another. "We need an environmental conscience, a sense of social responsibility," agrees Connie Flatboe of Sierra Club.[105] Hazel Henderson similarly talks of tapping citizen "intuitions" and John Gardner of mobilizing the "inner voice" of citizen conscience as the foundations of social change.[106] In this view, membership in reform groups is but one expression of preexisting proclivities to moral action rather than a necessary source of them. As one public interest spokesperson has put it, "We have to believe that popular involvement occurs spontaneously or not at all."[107]

Generally, the reform ideal of grass-roots political action is typified by roaming "bands of outsiders," connected only randomly in response to particular issues and discrete problems as they arise. One study of environmentalists by Arthur St. George notes that some members may be relatively active in politics even while they are inactive in the organized projects of the particular groups. The most viable forms of political action, he suggests, are extemporaneous, casual, and manifested in occasional personal contacts between individual members and public officials.[108] If new forms of coordination are necessary to successful advocacy, it is assumed, they will develop piecemeal and ad hoc, crafted to the unique purposes at stake by those with the greatest interest and resources. As Simon Lazarus's work exemplifies, the activists are suspicious of sustained grand designs and specialize in pragmatic tinkerings and free-form guerrilla tactics of artfully contrived posturings by individual actors.[109] In fact, the primary forms of action advocated by the reformers—letter writing, energy conservation, consumer fastidiousness, self-education and development—are all highly individualistic in orientation. "The process [of citizenship] starts with the individual's use of his or her time and energy," proclaims Nader. Donald Schwartz likewise concludes that the reform troops want "to reduce corporate size and strengthen the position of the individual private citizen who will act directly—not through institutions—against corporate abuse."[110]

At best, the institutional forms of citizen action which the liberal activists tend to esteem and encourage are nearly formless. "There is substantial evidence that small, unstructured groups are the best setting for innovative problem solving," asserts Beverly Moore of the Public Interest Research Group. Ecology Action founder Cliff Humphrey notes similarly that "we wanted to develop a method of facilitating action without the attendant excess baggage of motions, quorums, votes, committees, and dues. It seemed to us that after a formal organizational structure was established . . . someone wanted to run it."[111] The ideal form of citizen participation, concludes Hazel Henderson in virtual agreement, is in "unorganizations." "They have no headquarters, no leaders, and no chains of command. They are free form and self-organizing, composed of hundreds of autonomous, self-actualizing individuals who share [only] a similar worldview and similar values."[112] Again, the presumed springs to such action appear to be located in personal preference and abstract purpose, largely unsupported by distinctive social practices, group sanctions, or ongoing institutionalized relations.

Political Voluntarism and Mass Society. The public interest vision of voluntary reform action is essentially plebiscitary rather than either populist or bureaucratic in its premises. To be sure, liberal activists have recognized their own crucial role as movement organizers in sparking the awareness, concern, and confidence of citizens. They have acknowledged that "no group as politically, culturally, and economically heterogeneous as the 'middle' moves of its own volition. It responds to an active ingredient within it, a leadership element, if you will."[113] Likewise, activist leaders have often formally allied with voluntary citizen associations such as local nuclear power plant opponents and consumer cooperatives, more amorphous direct action groups such as the Abalone and Clamshell Alliances, and other experiments in grass-roots backyard politics. Yet they tend to assume that "the institutions of self-government through which all elements can have their say already exist."[114] Once the doors to power are opened and officials rendered more responsive to public demands by professional reform pressure, citizens are expected to burst forth from their private lives to make their wills known. Once access to federal courts and agencies is expanded through legal action, long-exploited individuals will become assertive citizens with briefcases in hand and boldness in their step. In other words, the reformers' image of grass-roots citizen action has mirrored their own self-perception: flexible, independent, and mostly unconnected to binding networks of larger group identities and commitments. As one advocate has put it, Ralph Nader's "pursuit of the public interest is a game that everyone can play."[115]

But while undeniably sincere, such voluntaristic assumptions have tended to discount rather than confront the difficult challenge of democratic movement building. The reformers have exposed the political powerlessness of citizens as private consumers without addressing its implications for the goal of mobilizing citizens as active participants in public life. We have already seen that their conception of group membership has been framed as a consensual market contract among discrete, unattached individuals for the goal of promoting both collective and selective consumer goods.[116] Likewise, so has the communication between reform leaders and the public been dominated by the techniques of commercial advertising and media manipulation against which the activists formally rebel. One action manual thus defines the task of movement leaders as one to package "ecological ethics . . . for popular consumption" in the marketplace of public opinion. Hoping "that isolated adherents will become isolated constituents," confirm two sociologists, most of the groups "must resort to slick packaging and conventional appeals to self-interest in order to make their products more attractive."[117] The irony of this—implied by the political-science model of "entrepreneurial" exchange politics—is striking. Lacking the foundations of independent political association, the recent liberal reform campaign itself has been forced to compete as a commercialized item of social consumption for the attention of an amorphous mass audience. Most public interest organizations only "create a pretense in the media without ever involving citizens in political action," Bo Burlingham has concluded.[118] At best, the reformers' leadership role has thus amounted to little more than some loud pleas for unknown others to "heal thyselves" and a few tips about how to do so effectively.

The reformers' dilemma, then, derives from their relative inability to overcome the very organizational logic of modern mass society against which they protest. This concept of "mass society" has been invoked to portray a society characterized by increasingly nationalized politics, centralized communication media, and isolated citizens. "Thus there arises the paradox of high *aggregate* access combined with low *individual* access," argues William Kornhauser, "so that the individual who is responding as an individual feels isolated, and participates psychologically in the power of the aggregate only to the extent that he ... is capable of identifying himself with his fellows."[119] The great danger of such plebiscitary tendencies, most critics of mass society warn, is that they render citizens more vulnerable to symbolic manipulation and allegiance to abstract utopian visions far removed from the concrete realities of everyday social life. In its most dangerous form, such social atomization and extreme individualization is claimed to render the masses available for mobilization by totalitarian movements.[120]

My analysis recalls an older interpretation of the situation. In short, the reformers' ethic of individual voluntarism has implicitly embraced the very individualistic logic of market rationality so inhibiting to the politics of altruism and collective interest.[121] This voluntaristic logic may succeed in generating group membership affiliation by providing citizen feelings of enhanced purposiveness and efficacy for minimal cost in time and money, but the much greater degree of personal sacrifice, confidence, skill, and resources required for sustained individual political advocacy within modern bureaucratic arenas renders the reform appeals to "citizen action" far less realistic. Where politics remains alienated from not just paid work life but the entire network of primary social relations, appeals for direct participation on behalf of collective goods are not likely to fare well in citizen perceptions of either interest or ethics.[122] And even where small numbers of volunteers do mobilize for alliance on specific battles, public interest leadership contributes little to durable democratic institution building of significant social power or broad programmatic intent. The primary danger thus is not one of rampant irrational action by anomic citizens so much as one of an increasing political impotence to overcome the resignation and deference encouraged by the existing corporate order. As Sandor Halebsky has contended, "A population's very lack of organizational ties and involvement also makes it less likely that people will be 'found' by appeals, leaders, and movements or, if accessible, that without group support or encouragement they will as individuals become ... involved in the new ideas and movement demands."[123]

This is the same conclusion reached by social critics of liberalism from Rousseau to contemporary authors such as Marcuse and Lasch.[124] Ironically, it is also the counsel of the reformers' own political guide, Tocqueville: "Men [and women] living in democratic countries do not readily understand the importance of forms and have an instinctive contempt for them." Indeed, Tocqueville considered the formless individualism celebrated by the liberal reformers as one of the greatest obstacles to citizen politics in democratic society.[125] As he put it, "so wrong is it to confound independence with liberty. No one is less independent than a citizen of a free state." Isolated, alone, and lacking stable political ties to collective others, the independent bourgeois was portrayed by Tocqueville as helpless before the immense power of public opinion and centralized state and corporate institutions. Deprived of shared "localism of feeling" and empowering political allegiances, the American individual is "narrowly shut up in himself" amid the lonely crowd of modern society.[126]

Public interest groups may well aim to spread seeds of action in citizen soil, as John Gardner puts it; their formal support for the backyard politics of locally organized citizen action throughout the nation has been undeniable. But the fact is that their actual contributions to such grass-roots activity have been mostly indirect and insubstantial. Focusing their energies on specific high-level policy battles, the new liberals' pragmatism has shown little concern for the long-term project of aggregating citizen efforts into durable organizations of collective power. Yet a movement that develops such a weak infrastructure of institutional roots to nurture political growth out of the private yards of mass culture will be severely limited in its democratizing impact. Individual voluntarism alone, no matter how enlightened, is hardly a realistic counterpart to massive organizational structures and cultural forms centuries in the making. Without new institutions capable of linking personal and political aspirations for change into collective solidarity with others, it is simply naive to expect that individual citizens can "create real changes in the culture, the social structure, [and] the personal character from the bottom up."[127]

Voluntarism and the Law. These frustrating facts are especially relevant to the legal dimensions of direct action at the heart of the new liberalism. If collective electoral and protest action was the focus of earlier Populist, New Deal, and even civil-rights movement building, then class-action suits, test-case litigation, legislative lobbying, and administrative rule making best exemplify the participatory commitments of the new reformers. But social scientists have illustrated that the mere expansion in formal rights of access to government does not much alter the social roots of powerlessness for most citizens.[128] Sociologist Donald Black contends that legal courtrooms in particular—the celebrated public interest model of democracy—are the most intimidating, distant, and alien forums for political redress to most citizens. Because of their inherent formality, esoteric vernacular, high financial costs, and slow rates of response, legal forums usually constitute the last resort for most individuals familiar only with private life and deferential public roles. "The reluctance of citizens to mobilize the law is so widespread, indeed, that it may be appropriate to view legal inaction as the dominant pattern in empirical legal life," Black concludes dramatically.[129] Legal advocacy may be an attractive resource for power to reform-minded professional lawyers and lobbyists, but it generally is not for most citizens lacking equal resources of time, money, skill, experience, and ongoing organizational support.

A host of case studies in the areas of welfare, mental health, and civil rights for minorities and the handicapped further confirm that the successful exercise of new citizen rights by individual recipients is insufficient without the support of grass-roots associations.[130] In fact, legalistic tactics may actually tend to discourage such participatory movement building among potential citizen activists and groups. The reason is that the legal process tends to disaggregate popular struggles into discrete conflicts among limited actors over specific individual entitlements. Unlike traditional forms of partisan or coalitional movement building, legal disputes often appear as largely episodic and insular transactions unrelated to the concerns of diversely situated citizens. Legal tactics not only absorb scarce resources that could be used for popular mobilization, therefore, but such forms of pragmatic advocacy make it difficult to develop broadly based, multiissue grass-roots associations of sustained citizen allegiance. "The result is to fractionalize political action—dividing rather than uniting those who seek change," notes Stuart Scheingold.[131] Similar findings about middle-class reform politics should not be surprising. The sheer proliferation of liberal public interest law firms and advocacy groups lacking a common mobilized social constituency is testament to the fact. The bulk of liberal public interest advocacy thus "is most often carried out by a few front-line activists in Washington, in state capitals... and in courtrooms, while the public sits on the sidelines."[132]

In sum, the judicialization of government alone simply does not create the functional equivalents of the New England town meetings or the Greek *polis* that much reform rhetoric suggests.[133] The reason is that the ideal of individual voluntary legal participation is rooted in some basic illusions about the structure of modern society. Democratization of state bureaus does not alter the fact of stratified, corporatized social organization in which individuals have little autonomous role.

In this setting, agrees legal-rights expert Owen Fiss, a conception of legal democracy that "strictly honors the right of each affected individual to participate in the process seems to proclaim the importance of the individual, but actually leaves the individual without the institutional support necessary to realize his true self." What is needed is the establishment of new structures of collective power equal in power to other dominant social institutions, yet internally democratic and egalitarian in form.[134] The enormity and difficulty of such a task cannot be denied. Nevertheless, mere promulgations of hopeful idealism from liberal public interest leaders and lawyers cannot alter the facts of their limited contributions to its realization.

The Organizational Obstacles to Democracy

A Change in Strategy? Whatever their noble intentions, the new activists' participatory aspirations turn out to be rooted far deeper in the liberal professionalism more typical of Progressive and New Deal reform politics than of radical populist traditions. The activists are ambivalent professionals, to be sure. They have unmasked the democratic pretenses of the hierarchical, bureaucratic public world they have inherited. They have attempted the difficult task of rendering the vast state mechanism more representative, more responsive, and more responsible to the people in whose name it acts. Many of the reformers no doubt believe strongly in the need for "the widest participation of all segments of our society . . . in formulating alternative futures."[135] Frequent national public interest group alliance with various grass-roots environmental, consumer, civil rights, and other citizen groups is testament to this commitment. Yet public interest liberals so far have not directly contributed much to that more Sisyphean task of fundamental political movement building necessary to challenge the established corporate foundations of organized power which structure modern American society. They thus have remained trapped in what Jo Freeman calls the "classic dilemma" of social movement organizations: "the fact that the tightly organized, hierarchical structures necessary to change social institutions conflict directly with the participatory style necessary to maintain membership support and the democratic nature of the movement's goals."[136]

It is true that recent experience has given the reform activists reason to reconsider their strategy.[137] One motivation for change is their sensitivity to the problem of group legitimacy created by the apparent conflict between the rhetoric and reality of their democratic

201

participatory ideals. Lacking formal structures of collective deliberation and direct accountability to an organized social constituency, much less to the larger public, even the activists' claims to act as representatives are vulnerable to challenge. "Because interests of broad categories of individuals, such as 'consumers,' are not self-defining," sympathizer Richard Stewart points out, "we cannot say that a given litigant or organization truly speaks for 'consumers' unless there is a sure mechanism that insures this."[138] More important, public interest liberals have been branded by critics on both the Right and Left for constituting a new class of powerful individuals as elitist in organization as they are in class interests. Neoconservatives such as Irving Kristol and Norman Podhoretz, for example, have derided the reformers as paternalistic, bureaucratic, and even totalitarian managers whose greatest objective is more centralized planning and state control over society.[139] Movement patriarch Ralph Nader in particular has been attacked repeatedly for creating a huge bureaucratic network of unaccountable organizations and private wealth at the public's expense.[140]

Such scurrilous assaults obscure the fact that public interest advocates are hardly any less representative of their public constituencies than other interest groups and state officials. In fact, the reformers' direct dependence on public opinion, government allies, legal officials, and voluntary mass support probably renders them far more sensitive to public attitudes than most other contemporary political actors.[141] Nevertheless, even the activists themselves occasionally reflect discomfort about their abstract relation to ordinary citizens. Frustrated by repeated questions about her constituency, long-time Nader affiliate Joan Claybrook responded a few years ago that "I don't claim to represent anyone but myself, and maybe the contributors to Public Citizen."[142]

In addition, many liberal advocates have recognized a more instrumental incentive to taking grass-roots politics seriously. They have increasingly come to realize the structural limits of strategies that emphasize professional legal reform and manipulation of the media without ever involving citizens in political action.[143] In short, political power depends in some degree on mobilized social power. This points, first of all, to the need to develop a more stable, committed, and active foundation of membership support than the rather volatile and inert constituency upon which most groups have depended thus far. After all, an EDF report summarizes, such a "membership establishes our legal standing in court, assures us the ear of elected officials, and provides nearly half our income."[144] Many activists have come to appreciate the value of cultivating influence within electoral politics at both local and national levels as well. The achievements won by well-organized conservative groups through the polls seem to have convinced some leaders that electoral participation, while a very imperfect form of democracy, constitutes an important dimension of successful political advocacy. "Unless you are in the electoral arena, you can't enforce the gains you've won," instructs emerging leader Heather Booth. In particular, environmental groups such as the League of Conservation Voters, Friends of the Earth, Sierra Club, and the Audubon Society as well as university-based PIRGs and other Nader groups have taken a more active role in generating citizen support around electoral campaigns during recent years.[145]

In the early 1970s, Simon Lazarus predicted that before long "a proper concern for their own political welfare may convince the new populist activists to redirect their priorities ... [toward] building upon their more long-term political strengths, rather than focusing on dramatic but ephemeral triumphs on Capitol Hill."[146] In the mid-1980s, there is some reason to think that he may have been right. Many in the reform troops seem to be working to expand the participatory foundations of movement politics. As former Carter consumer adviser Esther Peterson has put it, a "new kind" of advocate now is emerging "who is active at the grass-roots level, a leader who emphasizes action in the states and communities."[147] Indeed, more than a few reform-minded elites have left their Washington offices to contribute to the increasingly celebrated progressive activism in local politics throughout the nation. Mark Green has been shouting about the need to "water the grass roots" and ecologist Marion Edey has advocated doing "some of the field work that the Democratic party stopped doing." The central goal of the 1980s, agrees Robert C. Mitchell, "is to translate the continued support into action—to mobilize these people" who feel some allegiance to public interest values.[148]

Nevertheless, there are some compelling reasons to expect that the great majority of national public interest activists and organizations will not depart significantly from past practices. In the final pages of this chapter I briefly outline some of these causes for skepticism about the likelihood of radical changes in the character of liberal interest group activity.

The Propensities of Professionals. One of the primary obstacles to a transformation in the priorities among liberal activists is the hierarchical elite structure of most existing groups. The important fact is that the very success of the movement from the beginning has depended on the far-sighted actions of entrepreneurial leaders such as Nader, Green, Cohen, Gardner, Brower, Mitchell, Edey, and a host of others. Such leaders have committed themselves to the long-term projects of resource mobilization and organizational development for which most citizens are both unmotivated and largely unqualified.[149] Beginning from such origins of elite initiative, however, most reform groups, ironically, have found themselves trapped in the same logic of organizational inertia which they have struggled to avoid. As the social theorist Robert Michels argued long ago, there exists a strong tendency for established leaders to develop over time a vested interest in maintaining their position within the organization as well as the organization's role within modern society. "It is the organization which gives birth to the domination of the elected over the electors, of the delegate over the delegators," Michels summarized. "Who says organization says oligarchy."[150] A similar conclusion has been confirmed by most scholars studying social reform groups. Various works by a host of modern social scientists have illustrated that most reform groups "once formed... operate as though organizational survival were the primary goal."[151]

But we need not invoke Michels's "iron laws" to explain this aggregation of power to the professionals in reform groups rather than power to the people.[152] As professional lawyers, scientists, and lobbyists, the full-time activists tend naturally to stick to what they do best. In the important case of lawyers, for example, the most promising options for action are narrowly legalistic. "Once the organization takes root legal tactics can continue to be useful, but lawyers may become unreliable tails unwilling to give up wagging the dog," Stuart Scheingold has observed. Given lawyers' specialized training and socialization, "they tend to find [mobilization] politics somewhat distasteful and ordinarily try to steer away from militant confrontations" or long-term commitments often required by populist movements.[153] Moreover, because reform activists are often attracted to public life at least in part by the desire for status and prestige, they tend to be drawn to more dramatic symbolic events such as test-case victories to reaffirm their noble stature before an admiring mass public.[154] At the same time, in the absence of secure financial resources and organizational roots in the public, dramatic victories in the courts and other legal arenas become especially important to stimulate, sustain, and legitimate group activity.[155] Media-oriented stagecraft and legal advocacy thus are not alternative strategies, as Lazarus suggests. Rather, they constitute the complementary tactics of modern professional policy advocates acting without a mobilized constituency. Like many other interest-group organizations representing farmers, labor, and minorities, public interest groups have become formalized mechanisms of representation long cut off from their origins in popular social struggles.[156]

These proclivities once again reflect the larger fact that most public interest activists inhabit a world somewhat removed from that of the people for whom they claim to act. As Richard Flacks's valuable study of the earlier New Left student activists reveals, so too are many older public interest professionals "the offspring of the white, upper-middle class" who were "socialized to play elite roles" but denied themselves access to power in the establishment.[157] However well intentioned and unconventional in values, their backgrounds tend to point them in directions far from the backyards in which analysts locate the soil for populist politics. In Flacks's terms, their unique personal histories and institutional status largely free them from the constraints of everyday life experienced by most Americans. They are "neither tied to the roles and routines of mundane existence nor [are they] members of the ruling class." While largely unbound to the routinized interdependencies that bind most American working people, the activists have shared among themselves the exclusive bonds of advanced education, professional skills, geographical proximity, and frequent interaction which nurture the collective confidence and shared identity about which they speak. In other words, the unique social relations that liberate them for action also separate them from the apolitical private lives of their proclaimed constituency. Consequently, they have little knowledge, experience, or motivation concerning the kind of popular politics their rhetoric often celebrates. As Flacks argues, "insofar as the movement vanguards do not share everyday commitments with the 'masses,' they are limited in their capacity to exercise leadership—at one point they are engulfed in a tide of popular upsurge, at a later point they are stranded on the beach."[158]

It thus should not be surprising that the activists remain so committed to their "tough-minded professional approach." After all, it is the full-time professionals who most embody the characteristics of the ideal citizen—independence, conscience, creativity, knowledge, and skill. Ralph Nader, for one, typically extols the institutionalization of full-time career roles for skilled advocates supported by other citizens. "We have got to look on citizenship as a professional career capable of increasing the skill levels like a quarterback on a football team, or a lawyer, or a scientist."[159] Hazel Henderson likewise suggests that our greatest promise lies in "public interest law and public interest research" and associations "run by the brightest, most creative and socially concerned scientists."[160] John Gardner argues in parallel fashion that the crucial catalyst to reform politics is action by middle-class professionals with new experiences, values, and aspirations best attuned to the unarticulated needs and problems of the nation: "Such avant-garde individuals naturally hope that the truth they see will gain wide acceptance," he says. "But they would not have seen that truth in the first place had they not been more independent-minded than their fellows... [and] contemptuous (consciously or not) of the more conformist middle range of opinion."[161]

These propensities for both technocratic professionalism and elite rule have been expressed in boldest form by a few ecological radicals such as Paul Ehrlich, William Ophuls, and Robert Heilbroner. Frustrated by the apparent failures of earlier participatory citizen strategies and driven by fears of major ecological crisis, these authors have advocated that increased state authority be delegated to a new Platonic guardian class blessed with the greatest possible knowledge, skill, and virtue: "Long-range planning in a very complex society will be reserved for wise and dedicated individuals... [if] society is to survive future challenges," admonish Ehrlich and Dennis Pirages.[162] In other words, they urge supplanting the original radical ecological concern for democratic competence of all citizens with rule by a new elite with the greatest scientific competence. "There will be no escape from the necessity of centralized administration for our industrialized world," agrees Heilbroner.[163] While we may all inhabit "Spaceship Earth" together, they imply, only a specially trained few should plot our course as the rest of us remain safely strapped in our seats. "The polity is a ship of state which must be commanded by the best pilots or it will founder," adds William Ophuls.[164]

These latter, extreme positions have attracted few adherents among the public interest ranks and run directly counter to the reformers' inherent antipathy to hierarchical bureaucratic rule. Nevertheless, they do reveal an important centrifugal force ever pulling the reformers away from the core of their publicly professed democratic commitments.

The Structure of Success. Finally, however, it is the reformers' own success at what they have attempted so far that presents the most formidable obstacle to changes in their general strategy. The fact is that there are few forms of social conflict today in America, and everywhere they are mediated by the legal apparatus of the national state. Having achieved endless small victories and numerous significant changes in federal government policy, activists have little incentive to adopt a radically new political approach. "We have learned that to succeed in this town, we must behave like every other law firm," volunteers Alan Morrison of Public Citizen.[165] Past tactics, strategies, relationships, and organizational structures have won a substantial foundation of institutional power which the activists would be foolish to sacrifice. As Jeffrey Berry colorfully pointed out in one editorial, "when you're playing poker, there's only so many chips to play. A good player doesn't play them in bad hands." Therefore, concludes Mark Green, "while the public interest movement has its ebbs and flows, it is undeniably a permanent institution in Washington."[166]

Two related dimensions of this success in particular tend to discourage the initiation of grass-roots activity. The first concerns the mobilization of financial resources. We have seen that many groups have been financially dependent on a variety of what social scientist Jack Walker calls "institutional patrons," such as private foundations, wealthy individuals, and government. His 1980 study found that about 89 percent of those citizen groups contacted receive an average of over 40 percent of total revenues from such sources. Hence, Walker speculates, in the 1980s "many of the citizen groups born during the 1960s and '70s are still in business . . . [due to] help from their patrons, even though public interest in their causes has declined."[167] The important implication is that such financial linkages not only have divided mobilization efforts between elite institutional and popularly oriented strategies, but also have encouraged a more professionalized managerial approach to the latter. Indeed, contrary to some scholarly speculations, constituency building and maintenance have continued to be important priorities for most groups, and especially so during the Reagan era. But the focus of such action has increasingly become the development of more efficient computerized means to attract citizen monetary contributions for professional advocates rather than the catalysis of independent grass-roots action. "Membership is fairly static, but the groups are generally big, healthy, and financially sound," direct mail specialist Roger M. Craver has noted approvingly.[168]

Second, the activists' "democratic" strategies of direct legal advocacy ironically have further lessened their dependence on a mobilized public constituency. Litigation, agency lobbying, and other forms of direct adversarial legal action can sometimes help to mobilize citizen support and action, as many have argued.[169] Dramatic legal victories do sometimes raise public awareness, influence citizen opinion, inspire collective confidence, and legitimate group values. Yet we have seen that such forms of direct action can also discourage and substitute for grass-roots mobilization. One reason is that the actual activity of legal advocacy—attending hearings, pressuring officials, disputing adversaries in court—tends to both intimidate and alienate most citizens.[170] More important, legal action within the modern state not only circumvents the opposition of unsympathic elected officials but also lessens the need to engage in popular education, mobilization, and coordination. "Law is the great equalizer," proclaims William F. Butler of the Environmental Defense Fund. But this is because "all it takes is one person with a good legal argument that can convince one judge, and that's it."[171] In this sense, the class-action suit—initiated by a few for the benefit of an unorganized, faceless many—is the archetypal public interest expression of pragmatic political action. As long as the reform groups can continue to attract liberal lawyers, independent elite patrons, and sizable but inert supporting constituencies, such legalistic politics for the people will provide a convenient alternative to more democratic politics by the people. Public interest liberals will continue to play many important roles in future political disputes, but mobilizing a grass-roots movement is not likely to be one of them.

CHAPTER 5

Legitimacy and the
Modern Liberal State

The outstanding fact is the decay of authority.... This does not mean...
that we are now able to command ourselves. In fact, if a man dare sum
up the spiritual condition of his time, he might say of ours that it has lost
authority, but retained the need of it.

—Walter Lippmann

As the citizen begins to see the logic of nurturing his society, he will see
other things more clearly.... He will see that chaos must be replaced by
form and pattern—but form and pattern that enrich rather than drain
life of meaning; that aimlessness must be replaced by humanly relevant
purpose; that anomie must be replaced by life-enriching principle.

—John Gardner

We live in a Hamiltonian world and dream Jeffersonian dreams.

—Wallace Mendelson

A primary goal of public interest liberals from the beginning has
been to legitimate expanded government regulatory and redistributive
authority within modern society. The liberal reformers and other
groups have succeeded in significantly enlarging the power of the
federal government, to be sure. But, ironically, this achievement has
been attended by parallel declines in public faith concerning both the
institutional effectiveness and the *overall purposive justifications* of
liberal statism. Such developments reflect a variety of complex historical factors and surely do not in themselves point toward a failure of
the liberal public interest reform project. Nevertheless, I explore in
this chapter the limits of the public interest approach for regenerat-
ing public faith in expanded liberal state authority and social regulatory
politics generally. Specifically, while affirming the general outlines of

209

their participatory democratic commitments, my analysis suggests that the reformers have encouraged some chronically disintegrative tendencies within modern government structure while failing to offer an affirmative ethical foundation for renewed hope in socially progressive causes. In earlier pages of this study I have already examined some issues relevant to these questions, of course. The goal here is to utilize the concept of "legitimacy" to integrate both previous and new arguments into a more comprehensive evaluation of public interest–oriented politics. In particular, my aim is to demonstrate the central paradox that has plagued the new activists—that their reform campaign has both exposed and exacerbated the very dilemmas of the American liberal tradition which it has sought to overcome.

The Quest for Legitimacy

The Crisis of Legitimacy. The political vision of public interest liberals was born amid the social turmoil of the 1960s and nurtured by increasing disillusionment during the next decade. From the outset, the reformers have been obsessed with the palpable erosion of government legitimacy in modern American public life. Like Faust, they have expressed the fear that "to pieces is our world now going, what's fitting loses all its might."[1] The Vietnam tragedy, Watergate and other government scandals, the energy crisis, revelations about widespread consumer and environmental dangers—these have been only the most dramatic events illustrating the liberal activists' claim. John Gardner's warning in the Common Cause manifesto expressed the typical sentiment well: "We are seeing the breaking down of established patterns without the emergence of viable new ones," he admonished in 1970. "The consequences in loss of shared principle and purpose, in social and individual breakdown, and in sheer disorder are apparent to all."[2] Whether a matter of official corruption or a deeply rooted structural malady, the activists have been well aware that the decline of faith in the modern liberal state has become a significant problem in contemporary America.

We have seen that two proverbial premises in the reformers' political gospel are most commonly invoked to explain the nature of the dilemma. The first concerns the unchallenged power wielded by big business within both the marketplace and the state. As Nader puts it, "the large American corporation has escaped from its orbit of intended restraint.... In so doing, it has gained power, but lost legitimacy."[3] The second premise voiced by the activists derives largely from the first. In short, the unaccountable structure of power in modern America—within both state and society, politics and economy—has undermined public faith in older liberal defenses of big government. As William James once put it, "we have power but no motives."[4] Our democratic philosophy is perceived as but a "list of unachieved hyperboles" and "mythology," all "more apparent than real." David Cohen's summary of the loss is typical of the reformers' concern: "Distrust and cynicism...run deep and center on the non-performance of our professed ideals—a non-performance that leads to a shattering of belief."[5] As in so many great societies before us, it is suggested, decay has set in and the moral foundations of civic trust eroded. Our ethical reserve of faith in collective public action is as polluted and infirm as our collective natural resources of air, water, and soil.

The liberal reformers have implied further that long exposure to official hypocrisy and malfeasance has undercut citizen belief that regulatory government action can ever effect positive change. If the new liberal reform elites have been moved by civic skepticism, they have feared that the masses are paralyzed by civic pessimism and apathy about the possibilities of effective government: "Citizens at every level and in every walk of life increasingly feel they are powerless before the vastness and complexity of our society, power-less before the giant institutions that stand astride over national life" in contradiction to our inherited conceptions of truth and right.[6] Even worse, some activists hint, such feelings of powerlessness in our "crisis of crises" may erupt into eventual violence and chaos. America is on the verge of dissolving into the malaise of Thucydides' factionalized Corcyra, it has seemed to many liberals in the aftermath of the 1960s. "The next decade is likely to see continued crisis of all our overloaded administrations.... Everywhere there is protest and refusal to accept the solutions handed down by some central elites," proclaimed noted environmentalist John Platt in the early 1970s.[7] As the liberals see it, the apparent shift of many citizens toward somewhat more conserva-tive values in the 1980s only further demonstrates the triumph of selfishness and cynicism over progressive liberal values supporting expanded regulatory state action and democratically structured social improvement.

The Crisis Addressed. This pessimistic scenario of declining gov-ernment legitimacy is hardly unique, of course; it parallels the claims of spokespersons on both the right and left of the liberal reformers in recent years.[8] However, the public interest strategy for restoring faith in liberal government has been novel in several regards. First, "it is clear that we must rebuild confidence and conviction concerning the aims and future of our society," pronounces John Gardner soberly. "Unless the society can recapture a belief in its values and in the possibility of making these values live in action, its days are numbered."[9] Specifically, of course, this means that the key to sparking a rebirth of public spirit is in winning citizen support for that mixture of old and new progressive policy commitments advocated by the reform movement itself.[10] Activists have also been adamant that such a recapture of lost faith in liberal ideals mandates that "the promotion of significant change" in state organization implied by these ideals is a prime goal of the reform campaign. If decay and drift define the contemporary malaise, after all, then only through "restructuring the system" of modern society can liberal values regain their eminent status. We have seen that this involves in particular the commitment to expand the participatory character of primary government institutions: "Public participation is necessary to provide legitimacy to ... [state] action."[11]

At such a level of fundamental principles, the public interest liberals' participatory commitments seem quite compatible with, and even necessary to, both the spirit and functions of legitimate public authority long recognized by democratic political theorists.[12] This is true in several very important respects. One is the reformers' belief that "the decision-making processes of government are most effective and legitimate when all viewpoints are permitted the opportunity for full airing and critical scrutiny."[13] Such a commitment recognizes the inherently dynamic and transactional character of democratic authority. As John Schaar has put it, the relationship of citizens to leaders must be "one of mutuality, identification, and co-performance. The leader finds himself in the followers, and they find themselves in the leader."[14] Indeed, political scientist Carl Friedrich has gone so far as to define authority itself in terms of the "quality of communication" among citizens within public life. Frequent public exchange not only renders leaders more accountable for their actions, but also mobilizes the diverse wisdom, expertise, and values of the entire community for collective policy making. This is what John Gardner means in his claim that an "aware citizenry ... ensures better leadership" and "good constituents produce good leaders." By enlisting open debate and critical discussion, public policy becomes a matter of collective responsibility rather than one of individual whim or narrow self-interest.[15]

Such a participatory approach has also rightly focused attention on the voluntary aspects of citizen allegiance at the heart of democratic understandings about authority. As political theorist Bertrand de Jouvenal has argued, authority is defined precisely by "the faculty of gaining another man's assent."[16] In fact, it is this very capacity to command loyalty without sacrificing individual freedom which distinguishes legitimate authority from other forms of power. "Authority ends where voluntary assent ends."[17] For assent to be truly voluntary, moreover, citizens must be informed about and involved in the ongoing construction of the polity itself. As reform movement leader David Cohen has expressed it, "consent does not mean simple acquiescence"; rather, "it is important to debate and to decide what government's different roles ought to be . . . to question institutional accountability" before consent is rendered.[18] In other words, only when citizens regularly contribute to political decision making will they truly be able to render their consent and dissent effectively.

Finally, the reformers' participatory ethic has also affirmed the ultimate source of authoritative action in the appeal to objective principles of right. "We must create political, economic, and social institutions that make possible realization of moral values—institution building with a purpose," they have insisted.[19] This is important, for the very concept of "legitimacy" has always revolved around attempts to justify action through invoking independent standards of principle or law. As Hannah Arendt argued in her classic essay on the subject, "the source of authority . . . is always this external force which transcends the political reality from which authorities derive their . . . legitimacy, and against which their power can be checked."[20] By insisting that all exercises of publicly relevant power be scrutinized according to the standards of formal law and publicly defended moral principle, modern public interest lawyers have thus contributed significantly to the quest for the democratic legitimacy they seek.

However noble and important such ideals are in general, though, the fact is that increased liberal public interest–group influence within modern politics has not in fact legitimated increased state authority. In fact, citizen trust toward institutional leadership at all levels of public and private life continued to erode during the 1970s. Both Harris and National Opinion Research Center polls concerning Americans' attitudes about the ten leading social institutions have documented the overall trend. In 1966 an average of 48 percent of the citizenry expressed "a great deal of confidence" in the people governing those institutions; in 1971 this average fell to 28 percent and leveled off at an even lower 23 percent for the rest of the decade.

213

As opinion analyst Arthur Miller has concluded, such polls reflect "a continuing disillusionment with the political authorities and institutions and their ability to manage the country's conflicts and concerns."[21] Moreover, while public interest liberals did mobilize significant support around their claims that government was the problem, it was the conservative version of this complaint and its necessary remedy that won the greatest faith over time. Indeed, nearly all indicators— partisan attachments, self-professed ideological preferences, candidate popularity—have reflected a shift of citizen loyalties in more conservative directions at least since the mid-1970s. And above all, the back-to-back elections of Ronald Reagan at once reflected and consolidated this growing disaffection of most Americans with both old liberal statist ideals and new reform proposals to render government more accountable to the public.[22]

The causes of these trends have been many and complex. They surely include the continuing effects from those very maladies focused on by public interest reformers—Vietnam, Watergate, urban violence, growing environmental dangers, consumer exploitation, and a general failure of government to make good on its promises to achieve racial and social justice. Another major cause of dissatisfaction has been the deterioration of economic health upon which, as we have seen, the reformers have had little impact. These facts alone confirm that public interest activists should not be singled out as a primary cause of declining faith in progressive liberal ideals, programs, and representatives. But public interest liberals are also not entirely blameless for the fate of themselves and liberalism in general. In the two following sections, I reevaluate the implications of both the form and content of public interest advocacy for inderstanding the problem of legitimacy in the modern liberal state.

Law, Power, and Leadership:
The Problem of Institutional Legitimacy

The Corporatist Interpretation. The first issue of relevance to the problem of legitimacy has to do with the reformers' impact upon the institutional structure of the modern state. We have seen that the reformers' primary aim has been to open up government to render it more responsive and accountable to the public it is supposed to serve. "You have to give government the authority to do the job," says Nader. "But, also, you monitor and prod and challenge the government to use that authority wisely, effectively, and justly."[23] Indeed, the three principles of responsiveness, accountability, and responsibility have attained nearly the same status in the new secular dogma of liberal legitimation as did the Christian trinity in older understandings of divine authority. But the key question for social scientists in this regard concerns the specific types and character of state participation encouraged by the reform advocates.

Here we confront a significant disagreement among scholarly interpreters. Most studies have followed, somewhat predictably, the clear cues provided by both reigning academic scholarship and the reform leaders' own self-definition in explaining the new activism by reference to the paradigm of pluralistic interest-group politics.[24] The logic of this should hardly be surprising. Simply put, the liberal activists' "direct-action" lobbying of legislative, executive, and judicial officials by professional representatives of small, well-organized constituencies has been interpreted as a classic example of the type of politics described in David Truman's *The Governmental Process* and Robert Dahl's *Who Governs?*[25] However, several more recent studies have challenged both the reformers' own understanding of themselves and the academic pluralist model in general for failing to adequately reveal the full character and impact of public interest liberalism. In particular, a diverse array of scholars including David Vogel, Michael Hayes, and Jack Walker have emphasized the parallel themes of growing reform-group dependence on the state and independence from the broader public they claim to represent.[26] Such perspectives expose not only the elitist biases of pluralist theory itself, but its inadequate recognition of the unequal social power, autonomous government initiative, and organizational incentives at the heart of interest-group "clientelism" which dominates the modern political process. More boldly yet, well-known legal scholar Joel Handler has gone so far as to suggest that the very focus of pluralism on "an unspecified number of multiple, voluntary, competitive, non-hierarchically ordered and self-determined . . . categories" may no longer be useful for understanding most contemporary organized group structures and behavior.[27] The most significant developments in modern group politics, he speculates, instead have involved a gradual transformation toward more stable integrative corporatist structures of social interest intermediation by the state. Handler, whose elaborate development of this theme is here the focus of my attention, builds his argument in particular around Philippe Schmitter's now classic definition of *societal corporatism* as "a system of interest representation in which the constituent units are organized into a limited number of singular, compulsory, non-competitive, hierarchically ordered and functionally differentiated categories, recognized or licensed (if not created) by the state and granted a deliberate representational monopoly within their respective categories in exchange for observing certain controls on their selection of leaders and articulation of demands and supports."[28]

Handler contends that the key catalyst to such a transformation within public interest sectors derives primarily from the "free-rider" dilemma (see Chapter 4) that thwarts the reformers' ability to mobilize voluntary citizen resources sufficient for organizational maintenance and success in translating legal access into desirable policy results. As a result, he concludes, many liberal public interest groups as well as other legally oriented civil-rights and welfare-rights reform groups are destined to limp along ineffectually or to wither away altogether in the near future. By contrast, the remaining groups will be able to survive only through growing reliance on exogenous financial and political resources provided primarily by the central state. Liberal social reform groups will thus become increasingly limited in number, hierarchically structured, monopolistic in functional representational capacity, and moderate in policy demands in response to promises of stable access and aid extended by state officials seeking to enhance public planning efficacy and to cultivate symbolic legitimation of political decision-making authority. In short, "all or most of Schmitter's definition of societal corporatism will be met. . . . There will be a monopoly of representation by an hierarchical group, supported by the state, and, to a large extent . . . controlled by the state."[29] If this is the case, Handler and others conclude, modern liberal reformers will have followed a path to state incorporation much like organized farm, trade union, and business groups before them. The baleful results of such a development include continued pressure not only to narrow the policy initiative of liberal public interest activists, but also to subordinate their ideals of democratic legitimation to the exigencies of the corporate state against which they initially rebelled.[30]

This provocative scenario provides a valuable supplement and corrective to the rather minimal analytic perspective offered by conventional pluralist frameworks, to be sure. It rightly emphasizes the distinctive functional character of interest-group representation, the pragmatic focus on formal regulatory policy making and legal enforcement over partisan electoral activity, the hierarchical staff-led organizational forms, the increasing infiltration of government ranks, and the subtle compromising of demands which characterized public interest liberalism as it matured during the late 1970s. The reform groups' integrative tendencies seemed to be advanced in particular by President Carter's campaign pledge to make federal government "a forum for the people... that would be acceptable to Ralph Nader."[31] That promise appeared to be honored by the appointment of over sixty public interest activists to important agency posts as well as by a growing responsiveness of other executive branch officials to liberal outsiders. In short, public interest groups managed to open revolving doors for their own representatives in government much like the ones they loudly protested for corporate interests. Moreover, the impact of such appointments and alliances was to provide the new administration with a feast of liberal populist symbolism while effectively coopting the adversarial enthusiasm of the largely inexperienced reform members in the "antiestablishment establishment." As many reform activists later confessed, important sources of policy influence were gained for the cause, but the most ambitious proposals were stifled under growing fiscal pressures at the OMB and the zeal of many new administrators compromised by demands of institutional responsibility. "I'm satisfied if the system works properly," admitted one public interest lawyer appointee with decidedly lowered expectations, "even if my views are not stamped on programs."[32] What is more, not only were the reform troops outside of government depleted of valuable talent, but large numbers of citizens declined membership renewals in the belief that the battle for good government had been won, thus ironically further deepening the reform activists' dependence on state financial support and alliance.[33] Overall, then, such developing connections between private and public actors within the social regulatory sector during the late 1970s did point in some of the directions emphasized by speculations about corporatist evolution.

Corporatism in the U.S.? Toward a More Refined Perspective. The corporatist paradigm does draw attention to some often neglected aspects of public interest evolution, but it is nevertheless misleading in several regards. First, while the model has proved useful for analyzing many Western democracies, most theorists of corporatism have agreed that it is not really appropriate for the American case.[34] In contrast to those European polities that approach the corporatist model, Americans have always been hostile to the role of the state as an active architect of political order. Consistent with liberal ideals, our system has been organized around a formal separation between supposedly neutral public authority and the plethora of private interests in society contending to influence state policy. The consequent legal constraints mandating protection for the rights of private property owners, separation of state powers, a federal administrative process, and single-member legislative districts, as well as the sheer size and heterogeneity of the American nation, have contributed to the evolution of a state that has been typically piecemeal, halting, and contradictory rather than uniform in both its assumption of formal duties and organizational structure. Indeed, the modern state apparatus in America is hardly the cohesive monolith that the model presumes; rather, it is widely divided against itself in volatile factions identifying with a broad, if hardly comprehensive, range of social interests and values. These interrelated ideological and structural constraints were well illustrated during the short life of perhaps the most corporatistic experiment in America, that of the National Recovery Administration. Not only did the Supreme Court declare as unconstitutional such broadly delegated executive regulatory authority, but this fate was actually welcomed by many members of the Roosevelt administration skeptical about the very possibility of centralized cooperative planning.[35]

At the same time, the organization of primary social interests has been far more diffuse than the corporatist model presumes. One reason is that the fragmented structure of government has imposed unique "demand constraints" undermining development of hegemonic "peak associations" among primary social groups in the United States.[36] In short, the characteristic parcelization of state authority into a mulititude of potential access points has made it relatively easy for individual organized interests to act independently in seeking to influence public policy. Moreover, the prevailing liberal ethic of voluntarism has worked to discourage potential sacrifice of group autonomy through alliances with other social groups and the state alike.[37] The result has been the continued absence of those near-monopolistic forms of interest representation within key sectors necessary to the development of stable corporatist arrangements. For example, American capital (employers) has typically remained internally divided on most discrete policy issues among financial interests, industrial manufacturers, and small business and only approaches the corporatist model of organizational unity in a few sectors, such as nuclear energy and military production. The American Medical Association once dominated the politics of the medical profession, but it has lost that monopolistic control in recent decades. Even agricultural capital, generally that sector most prone to corporatist relations with government, has become increasingly fragmented by allegiances to several separate and often hostile representational bodies.[38]

Of equal importance is that American labor unions have not developed the organizational cohesion and power of most European equivalents. The AFL-CIO is affiliated with about 75 percent of unionized labor, but it can claim to represent only about one-fifth of all American workers, it does not include many powerful unions such as the United Automobile Workers, the National Education Association, and the Teamsters, and it lacks discipline among its own affiliates. As a result, even income policy agreements—the archetype of tripartite corporatist relations—in the United States have been generally too insubstantial, voluntary, and transitory to fit the model. And perhaps most important of all, the inability of American labor to pose formidable pressure for a Social Democratic agenda through control of a major party has eliminated the very catalyst to greater state planning initiatives which has proved crucial to quasi-corporatist developments in European polities.[39]

My invocation of these facts is not intended to deny that structural bonds of interdependence, regular personnel exchange, unequal access, and hierarchical organization connect powerful social groups to the modern state; nor do I seek to discount the conservative role of the American state structure, legal forms, and policy priorities in securing capitalist social organization against democratic challenge. Rather, my point is to refute that most instrumental client relations of mutual exchange are nearly as compulsory, stable, formalized, exclusive, and pervasive as the corporatist paradigm suggests. Even the classic, if somewhat exaggerated, cases of "iron triangles" (linking legislators, public administrators, and interest groups) identified by social scientists in the 1950s fall outside such a description. While largely exclusive, cooperative, and predictable in practice, such relations between powerful social interests and relevant state officials have tended to be informal rather than formal, voluntary rather than compulsory, industry-specific rather than sectoral, legislatively as much as administratively defined, and aimed to protect private advantage more than to effect public policy planning.[40]

Such a recognition of these complex facts suggests the need for a conceptual approach that at once refines and transcends simple reliance on either pluralist or corporatist models. At the least, what is necessary is to envision these two models as opposite poles on a continuum, between which the actual group–state relations in different policy sectors can be located in distinction from one another over time. A further refinement of this approach employed by some comparative scholars is to add to such a continuum other intervening categories, such as "weakly structured pluralism," "strongly structured pluralism," "weak corporatism," and "moderate corporatism" (see

219

Diagram 1).[41] In terms of this scheme, most policy sectors in the United States would be located between the categories "strong pluralism" and "strongly structured pluralism." While such a more

Diagram 1. Interim Categories on the Pluralism-Corporatism Continuum

Strong pluralism	Weakly structured pluralism	Strongly structured pluralism	Weak corporatism	Moderate corporatism	Strong corporatism
X—————	—X—————	—X—————	—X—————	—X—————	—X

sophisticated classification scheme is no doubt useful for cross-cultural generalizations, its utility for specific case analysis is limited by the fact that the relevant factors at stake are at once many in number and independent in character. Any list of such variables is surely debatable, but it should at least include reference to the relative degrees of (1) social group organizational unity and discipline, (2) group financial and political autonomy, (3) group-state consensus, (4) formality of access to state authority, (5) exclusivity of participation by key social groups, (6) dispersion of sectoral policy authority within and without the state, (7) stability in sectoral policy resolution, and (8) state need for a social group client to facilitate and legitimate collective policy planning (see Diagram 2). The uniquely American phenomenon of "iron triangles"—discussed here as moderately corporatist in some respects but clearly not in others—illustrates the problem of even refined classification schemes in this regard. In sum, there simply is no alternative to detailed, multidimensional descriptive analyses of particular group-state relations to provide an accurate understanding of modern political complexity.

Voluntarism and the State. If invocation of the corporatist model by some scholars is misleading about relations in most American policy sectors generally, it has proved even less applicable for liberal public interest–group activity in particular. A more thorough examination of movement dynamics in terms of the factors seen in Diagram 2 illustrates this point. First, public interest groups have not developed any quasi-monopolistic mechanism of collective interest representation or "closely integrated coalition" capable of unilateral action and membership discipline of the type presumed by corporatist theories. True to their professed ideals, the liberal reform groups have remained numerous rather than singular, competitive rather than monopolistic,

220

Legitimacy and the Modern Liberal State

Diagram 2. Dynamic Elements in Sectoral Differentiation of Group-State Relations

	Strong pluralism	Strong corporatism
Group unity/discipline	very low...very high	
Group financial/political independence	fully independent.......................................highly dependent	
Group–State Consensus	generally low ....generally high	
Character of state access	formally open...formally closed	
Exclusivity of group participation	unlimited participants...........................limited participants	
Concentration of state authority	highly dispersed ....highly centralized	
Consistency of issue resolution	inconsistent...............................consistent (high planning)	
Degree of state need for client	very low...very high	

voluntary rather than compulsory in allegiance to common causes, and divided on a broad range of basic policy issues. The pervasive practice of issue specialization and independent policy action, even among environmentalists on the wide variety of air, water, toxic waste, wilderness, nuclear, and other prominent issues, has constituted an almost unwritten rule of political survival for the groups from the beginning. Consumer Federation of America does represent over two hundred state and local consumer groups, but it hardly monopolizes representation of consumer interests in federal policy making. Indeed, the deep divisions both within and between Consumer Federation of America, Consumers Union, and Nader's Public Citizen on consumer priorities, like those once created by David Brower among environmental organizations, have been well publicized. All in all, the sheer diffusion of diverse and often contradictory issues and interests represented by public interest groups casts doubt on whether the umbrella category of "consumerism" itself could ever be considered a viable sector of stable corporatist planning arrangements.[42]

Of course, various groups at different times have joined to pool resources on many legislative battles around issues such as campaign financing, congressional reform, and Clean Air Act amendments; on many judicial suits such as those concerning strip-mining regulatory enforcement and creation of energy efficiency standards for home appliances; and on large media events such as Earth Day, Big Business Day, and the like. But the activists' hearty embrace of liberal voluntarist principles and commitment to preservation of group autonomy has rendered such alliances mostly ad hoc, transient relations of convenience rather than manifestations of long-term coalitional bonds. Indeed, the Common Cause canon of political pragmatism heralding that it "has no permanent friends and no permanent enemies" generally holds for most organizations within the larger movement.[43] And even though somewhat disposed to more frequent policy alliance, environmentalists have displayed the same basic attitudes toward group diversity and autonomy. "If plurality didn't exist, we'd have to invent it," notes one ecological activist.[44] Overall, the undeniable fact is that the movement is as amorphous and undifferentiated as a jellyfish; however clearly united on values, no central nervous system or dominant organ of self-definition has yet emerged. Given its disaggregated issue-oriented legalistic strategy and independent, ad hoc, "call-'em-as-we-see-'em" posture toward potential alliances, the new liberal activism has hardly added up to a movement at all in social organizational terms.

The reform groups' relations to the state, furthermore, have been generally as tenuous and independent as those between groups. From the beginning, we have seen, the liberal activists have been both critical of bureaucratic state authority and circumspect about its cooptive powers, which defeated earlier reformers. In particular, they have been wary that "if public interest law becomes overly dependent on government subsidies, it may become vulnerable." Hence, the public interest ideal is that "each . . . group is privately funded and essentially independent of corporate, bureaucratic, or political control."[45] Handler and other scholars have rightly noted that advocates for the interests of the disadvantaged have only rarely achieved this end, however, and largely owe their existence to sponsorship by the Legal Services Corporation, Department of Justice, and other state agencies. And it is true that a minority of public interest law firms and research centers, such as the Conservation Foundation, National Consumer Law Center, and National Health Law Program, have depended on such state financial assistance.[46] But the critical fact is that most consumer, environmental, and other middle-class reform groups have succeeded in building a much more independent base of private economic funding than is often acknowledged by observers.

Even Jack Walker's influential recent study advancing his thesis about citizen group dependence on institutional patrons confirms that such groups received only 8.9 percent of their budgets on average from government in 1980.[47] His study does not isolate public interest groups per se, but his figures do closely resemble those cited by both Burton Weisbrod's 1975 study of seventy-two public interest law firms and the 1975 and 1980 Council for Public Interest Law surveys.[48] The latter reports in particular confirm that there were only neglible increases in state aid for the reformers in the late 1970s, with most groups receiving less than 10 percent of their revenues from agency participation subsidies, court-awarded legal fees, or other forms of direct government assistance.

We have already noted that the single largest source of funding for most groups has actually been the one discounted by Handler and many other scholars—that of voluntary citizen donations and membership dues. Indeed, nearly two-thirds of all public interest groups in Berry's survey—including the most influential groups addressed here—depended primarily on dues and donations from tens and hundreds of thousands of citizens to sustain the reform campaign.[49] This number actually grew in the late 1970s as some legal groups, like CLASP, for the first time solicited membership support to replace declining foundation aid. And when we add to this other sources of funds such as magazine sales (Consumers Union), university fee checkoffs (PIRGs), client services, speeches, and book sales, we can further appreciate the ability of many groups to sustain relative financial autonomy from the state. All of the relevant studies confirm that many groups were dependent to a degree on private foundations and wealthy donors during the 1970s, but Walker found that only 13 percent of overall citizen-group assets came from foundations alone. Berry's earlier, more focused study similiarly revealed that only one-fifth of the groups received half or more of their total assets from foundations, while two-thirds of them received 10 percent or less of funds in this way.[50] In any case, such dependencies on private foundations do not contribute to either more intergroup coordination or cooptive assimilation into the state.

It is worth considering in this regard the actual terms of financial dependence created by existing, if minimal, state subsidies. For one thing, the legal basis of state support—whether it be IRS exemptions, postal subsidies, attorneys' fees, or transcript deferrals—in legislative statutes and judicial rulings significantly limits the discretionary use of resources by regulatory officials to cultivate cooptive allegiances or to compel formal cooperation from independent-minded outside activists. Likewise, the fact that government financial support varies widely in source and kind only further reduces the tendency to liberal activist dependence on any particular state official or institution. For example, the 1975 *Alyeska* judicial decision significantly limited the availability of attorneys' fee awards for many groups, but this was overcome largely by shifting the lobbying campaign to Congress and the executive branch.[51] Finally, the fact that most legal entitlements providing state financial support to the activists have been framed in formally general terms implies that they potentially benefit many groups opposed to the liberal reformers as well. Hence, any legal changes intended to undercut tax-exempt status, agency subsidies, or participation support for liberal groups would apply to a host of conservative citizen groups, as well as run counter to basic democratic pretenses in ways inconvenient for foes of public interest liberalism.

For all of these reasons, then, we can see why most middle-class liberal advocacy groups have been able to remain far more autonomous from the state than their allied representatives for more disadvantaged groups with whom they are often linked. And as a result, most public interest groups, much like producer groups long active in the political process, have been able to sustain a notably independent, flexible, and adversarial reformist posture toward those state authorities they seek to influence. Indeed, although tied by clear ideological bonds to the Carter administration, public interest liberals regularly became locked into acrimonious battles with partisan appointees and civil servants alike throughout the late 1970s on fundamental issues such as regulatory reform, nuclear power, and energy policy, as well as on scores of specific regulations ranging from concerns for the dangers of cotton dust in textiles to television advertising.[52] Adopting self-styled roles as independent "bounty hunters" dedicated to bringing all wrongdoers to justice, the activists continued to rely on "private-enforcement" legal mechanisms and media exposure as much as on bureaucratic alliance. As ecologist Joseph Sax predicted in 1970, litigation has provided "a means of access for the ordinary citizen to the process of governmental decision making" which allows for "a repudiation of our traditional reliance on professional bureaucrats."[53]

In addition, there is evidence that the much-publicized claims about infiltration of government ranks by public interest liberals have probably been somewhat inflated. In 1980 less than one-half of the citizen-group members interviewed by one scholar reported that they had any staff members who were on an advisory committee or actively consulted by government, as opposed to the nearly 80 percent of all other groups that reported such in-house representation.[54] Likewise, many of the public interest appointees themselves—"radicals" and "zealots," many labeled them—simply carried their adversarial posture into government. FTC chairman Michael Pertschuk in particular showed few signs of cooptation or even cooperation as he became embroiled in conflict with everyone in sight, including former allies in Congress and the executive branch. If some other newly admitted reform insiders were coopted, their former colleagues outside government were not. Even long-time Nader allies like Joan Claybrook at NHTSA and Harrison Wellford at OMB came under fire regularly from former friends for allegedly compromising on movement commitments.[55]

All in all, such partisan appointments of public interest activists to administrative posts and developing alliances of many groups at the FTC, EPA, CPSC, OSHA, and other agencies during the 1970s may have increased the influence of the new reformers in key sectoral decision-making processes. But there is little evidence pointing to the development of those highly stable, formalized, cooperative, and compulsory relations of monopolistic interest representation within the state specified by the corporatist model.

The Disaggregating Impact of Reform on the State. As most liberal public interest groups have remained relatively autonomous *from* both one another and government officials alike, so have the reformers also collectively contributed to increased organizational autonomy and diffusion *within* government. We have seen that the effort to free government from captivity to corporations and other powerful special interests by expanding the scope of group participation at all decision-making levels has constituted a primary reform goal of the movement since its inception. Far from encouraging trends toward corporatist integration, therefore, such designs have challenged the exclusive, parasitic nature of prevailing clientele relations at the cost of actually exacerbating yet further the elusive and disaggregated character of public authority in ways typical of the conventional "interest group liberal" politics that the reformers criticize.[56]

For one thing, the reformers' campaign to expand legal "process-and-structure" rights has multiplied greatly the *number of access points* for social-group lobbying influence within the state, thus contributing to the long-developing tendencies to uncoordinated, overlapping, and inconsistent exercise of public authority. At the same time, most public interest groups not only have shunned any centralizing mechanisms in their own proposals for an agency for consumer advocacy and federal corporate chartering, they have also opposed nearly all centralized executive regulatory oversight plans proposed since the early Nixon years. For example, government energy-policy formulation at the federal level alone during the 1970s was dispersed into the jurisdiction of at least eleven different agencies, each with its own unique sense of mission, legal mandates, routine clients, and obligation to provide access to all relevant participants—and all defended by most public interest reformers against attempts by the Carter administration to establish more centralized coordination.[57] To this labyrinthine diffusion of state responsibility must be added the ever-frequent interventions of federal legislative and judicial authorities as well as the manifold actions of state and local public administrators pressured to take part in federal policy formulation and enforcement. The reform activists' pervasive reliance on the courts is particularly problematic in this regard. Although often effective in halting or delaying undesirable actions, judicial authorities are largely bound to episodic case-by-case remedies for complex social problems at odds with the long-term supervisory capacities necessary for effective means-oriented planning. As one study of environmental politics has illustrated, "the judiciary would properly refuse to adopt any . . . strategies requiring courts to assume an intimate role in on-going management" of policy administration.[58]

Liberal activists have contributed in parallel fashion to the rapidly *proliferating number of participants* at each point in the governmental process. Not only are public interest advocates themselves many in number and affiliated with over one hundred separate groups, but their expansion of generally defined formal citizen rights to state access has opened the door to a potentially infinite number of other groups, including both allies and opponents. In short, public interest liberals have been both constituent and causal component in the amazing growth—at least by several times—in social group issue advocacy in Washington since the early 1960s. The result has been to transform even the once stable, exclusive, and largely invisible "iron triangles" of corporate state relations increasingly into "elastic nets" of complex interaction and volatile alignments among ever-expanding numbers of organized social-group representatives.[59] This has no doubt rendered the state more open to the claims of diverse social interests and perspectives. But it has done so at the cost of protracting the tendencies to muddling through in a quagmire of inconsistency, contradiction, myopia, delay, and stalemate which greatly impede effective synoptic planning efforts. As Mancur Olson has argued convincingly, "coherent, rational policies cannot be expected from a series of separate ad hoc concessions to diverse interest groups."[60]

This is not to say that the minimal specifications of the academic pluralist model provide a satisfying interpretation of the new politics, of course. The model is simply too vague and general to account for the vast diversity in public interest–group relations to the state. Varying across sectors and shifting over time with changes in personal relationships, sources of financial support, and policy campaigns, the activists' roles have ranged from preferential near-client status at some agencies to routinized competition in free-form "issue networks" in other agencies to almost entirely independent judicial "bounty hunter" actions and extralegal media posturing. Moreover, pluralist accounts tend to obscure the reformist character of public interest groups acting collectively as a social movement to change government rather than merely to join it. As we noted earlier (Chapter 2), the reformers' "radical pluralism" has constituted a challenge to both the informal processes of narrow-interest negotiation and the elite liberal value consensus assumed by conventional academic pluralist theory. In short, the reformers have attempted to inject fundamental conflict over the very purposes and standards of public authority into the center of government. But this only underscores my central point: that the overall impact of public interest groups during the 1970s was to contribute to the development of a structureless, polymorphous spongelike state capable of absorbing ever-increasing social demands yet lacking a viable institutional nervous system for converting such demands into consistent programs of publicly sanctioned goals and policies. As Hugh Heclo has argued, the trend toward the "politicizing of organized life throughout the nation" has been paralleled by "a dissolving of organized politics" at all levels of government. And this fact points to a basic contradiction in public interest liberalism: the reformers have greatly enlarged the responsibilities of the state for rational policy planning while promoting the continued fragmentation of the state into a sprawling labyrinth of relatively autonomous adversarial social-group forums resistant to coordinated planning action. In neo-Marxist terms, they have further projected the social conflicts between private capital accumulation and public welfare legitimation directly into the administrative state while rejecting all radical conclusions about the institutional and programmatic means necessary for addressing them.[61]

Ironically, these tendencies toward proliferating institutional diffusion have undercut the reformers' own primary aim of enhancing political accountability as well as policy-making effectiveness. While public interest reforms have expanded the scope of conflict among elite representatives in specific policy forums, they have at the same time largely shifted political authority increasingly to those realms of government that are the least visible, accessible, and comprehensible to the general public. Consequently, more voices have been registered within various sanctuaries of state power, but fewer have been forced to confront each other in the light of public scrutiny. As Lowi has argued, "interest-group liberal solutions to the problem of power provide the system with stability by spreading a *sense* of representation... at the expense of democratic forms, and ultimately at the expense of legitimacy."[62] What is more, numerous studies have suggested that the increased diffusion of authority and interest-group access may actually encourage evasion of official administrative legal responsibility. Radical dispersion of access points and decision sites only makes it easier for state officials to avoid responsibility for overall policy implementation by diverting pressures elsewhere, shifting sites of decision making, misrepresenting positions, or seeking refuge in narrow rule interpretation.[63] To cite Lowi again, "The acountability we get is functional rather than substantive; and this involves questions of equity, balance, and equilibrium, to the exclusion of overall social policy."[64]

My argument is not intended to express agreement with the charges by neoconservatives that public interest liberals have overloaded government with too much democracy.[65] The reformers' varied efforts to break up formal hierarchies and informal corporate-dominated "iron triangles" are quite laudable. Public interest activists have provided representation for long-ignored important social values and interests and should hardly be blamed for creating the problems of administrative disarray which have been developing for decades and are deeply rooted in the very structure of modern capitalist society. Rather, my central point concerns the specifically disaggregating, piecemeal *forms* of policy advocacy and institutional restructuring that the reformers have urged upon the state. Neither essentially corporatist nor democratic in character, the response of public interest liberals to the dilemmas of our fragmented, parasitic political process has been primarily to encourage more of the same.

Legalism without Law. The reformers have not wholly discounted concern for purposive policy coordination and consistency, of course. We have seen that the new liberals have followed the advice of Lowi and other antipluralist critics in placing their faith in the rule of law to secure publicly sanctioned ends. In the liberal activists' view, law is the most effective and just resource for directing social change toward the common good. "Political experience teaches us that the restraint upon power through principles of law... best serves the collective interest," confirms reformer Donald Schwartz.[66] In particular, we have seen that the emphasis on legalistic rule formulation and enforcement at all levels has provided the reformers a convenient solution to the problems of regulatory inaction and subversion which undercut highly discretionary New Deal–type programs. As reform spokespersons Sanford Jaffe and Gordon Harrison put it, the goal of public interest advocacy is "to make the law work better, and thereby to preserve the rule of law as a cornerstone of the American social and political system."[67] Finally, the rule of law is perceived as an end in itself and essential element of the good society: "Human society must exist within the framework of law, or exist not at all," concludes ecologist James Rummonds.[68] Many liberals have even implied that a more responsive legal system is the only alternative to the "dangerous" politics of mass action. It is but one more manifestation of their dichotomous propensities in thought that, as one activist has written, "there are only two possible corrective mechanisms for social justice. One is the reformist path of law, the other is the risky business of violent revolution."[69]

This sincere faith in the rule of law to restore the legitimacy of the liberal state has proved to be more problematic than most activists have recognized, however. On one hand, legalistic rule following tends to provide a rather blunt instrument for remedying complex social problems. The reason is that official discretion is at once an unavoidable and valuable aspect of legal administration. In the words of Kenneth C. Davis, "only through discretion can the goal of individualized justice be attained.... Rules without discretion cannot fully take into account the need for tailoring results to unique facts and circumstances of particular cases."[70] Where conflict and debate over fidelity to rules become the primary focus of legal interaction, by contrast, policy choices are unlikely to address adequately the actual social problems and injustices at stake. Legalistic rule adherence becomes an end in itself rather than a resource for securing effective and fair results.[71] Moreover, legalistic rule following often only suspends serious moral debate, nurtures unnecessary suspicion among political actors, and exacerbates the sense of unreasonableness in legal administration. As Christopher Stone has argued, rigid insistence on conformity to "rules and regulations, backed by threats of litigation, breeds distrust, destruction of documents, and an attitude that 'I won't do anything more than I am absolutely required to do.' "[72] Even if expanded citizen participation in legal decision making works to enhance the fairness of specific policy debates, the goal of restricting policy to the terms of formal rules—whether specified by legislative statute, court decrees, or agency rule-making processes— may actually inhibit as much as encourage responsible action by regulators and regulated alike.

A variety of scholarly studies illustrate that these conceptual problems have been largely realized in the practice of public interest politics. Bardach and Kagan's *Going by the Book*, for example, provides widespread evidence about the significant impact of liberal public interest–group efforts to place narrow rule formulation and implementation at the center of state regulatory politics. While fully acknowledging the new social benefits gained in many policy areas, they identify a larger pattern of regulatory "unreasonableness" in policy formulation by rule-bound officials. In their words, "Although the scope of the problem is unknown, it is likely that in a very large number of cases regulatory toughness in its legalistic manifestation creates resentment and resistance, undermines attitudes and infor- mation-sharing practices that could otherwise be cooperative and constructive, and diverts energies of both sides into pointless and dispiriting legal routines and conflicts."[73] The costs of such legalistic rule fetishism, then, have not been overregulation so much as ineffica- cious regulation that undermines public faith in government authori- ty. This conclusion is hardly unique; it has been confirmed by numer- ous other studies in policy areas such as air pollution control, environmental impact statements generally, workplace safety and health regulation, consumer protection, and school finance reform.[74]

On the other hand, ironically, the very character of the rules themselves encouraged and embraced by the modern reformers has tended to exacerbate the long-developing dilemmas of legal legitimation in the modern liberal state. Traditionally, the formal liberal legal order has been structured around rules that are inherently "positive," "general," "autonomous," and "public."[75] These elements of formality are important to secure the relative neutrality and objectivity of limited state authority with regard to particular social interests so crucial for classical liberal ideology. However, as the modern state has extended its reach into spheres once considered the domain of market autonomy and not subject to collective control, public law has become increasingly regulatory in function, homogeneous in organization, and purposive in character. More important, the rapid proliferation of rules ever more specific, complex, and technical in character has deprived law of its once esteemed generality, autonomy, and impartiality. As law has increasingly become the product of particularistic ad hoc balancings of narrow interests that resist formulation as general rules, the traditional assumptions of liberal public law no longer appear to be substantiated. Rather than securing an autonomous stance of the state above social conflict, the legal process has become the central arena for its increasingly politicized expressions. As Roberto Unger has summarized, citizens are "condemned to search for a justice they cannot find, and all social arrangements will be rendered suspect by their lack of moral foundation."[76]

We need not agree with Unger's own scenario of "crisis" to understand the relevance of public interest activism to these larger trends in the liberal legal order. Not only has the reformers' obsession with legal rules arguably undercut effective policy making in many cases, but their pervasive pressure for more responsive law has embraced the very ideal of legality only to expose its paradoxical character in practice. The sheer number of rules, regulations, and statutory mandates binding officials has soared nearly out of sight under the activists' pressure. Likewise, the undeniable tendencies to increasing particularism, specificity, technicality, and even arbitrariness have become evident in major legislative statutes such as the Clean Air Act and the Occupational Safety and Health Act, in rules of judicial standing to sue, in private tort law principles of liability, and in numerous areas of administrative law bearing the marks of influence from public interest liberals.[77] Overall, the expansion of liberal state obligations encouraged by the reformers has been paralleled by a decline in the very possibility of creating authoritative, generally applicable rules for mediating social conflict. The more the state promotes individualized social justice, therefore, the less does its traditional mask of formal legal neutrality shield it from responsibility for the fundamental inequalities and deprivations endemic to modern capitalist society. Legalistic politics ends up confounding the dilemmas of liberal state legitimacy rather than resolving them.[78]

The broad terms of these two lines of argument are difficult to verify, of course, and deserve some substantial qualification. While clear cases of legal unreasonableness can be cited, the primary evidence about regulatory action has come from business interests who tend to protest nearly all forms of state control.[79] Likewise, it should be acknowledged that the controversial legalistic obsession with rule following generally has provided the activists in practice more an invaluable instrument of political leverage against opponents than a rigid policy ideal.[80] Finally, scholarly concern for the loss of autonomy and generality in contemporary law must be balanced by recognition that the values of pragmatic, instrumental policy making have always coexisted with formalistic legal pieties throughout American history.[81] Nevertheless, the basic thrust of both developments discussed above rightly emphasizes the liberal reformers' contributions to the increasing inscrutability of modern politics mired in legalistic complexity. Indeed, the most important point to recall is that growing state responsiveness to organized group interests has hardly rendered law any more accessible to the average citizen in everyday life. Given the fact that most citizens are not even aware of elite participation on their behalf, we should be skeptical about claims that public interest advocacy will redress citizen frustrations and serve to legitimate ever-expanding state authority. On the contrary, a more plausible conclusion is that public interest liberalism has contributed to rising citizen expectations about the promises of law at the same time that the legal process itself has become ever more the mysterious, alien, and intrusive domain of specialized activity eerily portended by Kafka long ago.[82]

Social Power and the State. So far, I have emphasized the ethical motivations and theoretical designs behind the development of liberal public interest advocacy. But it is important to recognize that such independent, legalistic, adversarial organizational evolution has reflected the imperatives of political necessity as much as abstract moral preference. The crucial fact to recall is that public interest groups simply were denied a great deal of the access, alliance, and financial support that they sought from legislative, executive, and judicial authorities throughout the 1970s. In particular, the failure to win necessary backing for the proposed agency for consumer advocacy and for fully subsidized group participation in regulatory proceedings greatly impeded the most promising institutional linkages of the reformers to government. And therein lies the central dilemma of the activists: although powerful enough to simply survive on their own, liberal public interest groups have lacked the social resources necessary *either* to compel substantial state alliance *or* to succeed alone in their battle against corporate power.

Two dimensions of this claim about deficient public interest–group power deserve mention. First, despite their impressive private moblization efforts, liberal activists have not been able to match the resources of personnel and money available to other major interest groups in Washington. It is important to recognize that the initial success of public interest groups owed to the unique contextual facts not only of relative economic prosperity, but also of initially ineffective opposition from business groups unprepared for the new social challenge. As circumstances changed during the next decade, however, the meager foundations of the new reform politics become increasingly more apparent. We have discussed how the failure of the state to uphold the New Deal promise of economic prosperity stimulated massive pressures by big business for regulatory relief at the same time that the liberal antigrowth social values faded in relevance to the public. Coordinated by associations such as the Business Roundtable and the Chamber of Commerce, corporations mobilized for action at all points of public interest infiltration—congressional committees, federal courts, regulatory agencies, mass media—to make their case against social regulation. At the same time, conservative "public interest" law firms such as the Pacific Legal Foundation and Rocky Mountain Legal Foundation joined right-wing lobbying groups and PACs in challenging the liberals at their own game of direct action within government.[83] Consequently, business and other conservative opponents actually cultivated a far more dominant organized presence within Washington by the late 1970s than ever before. As one 1981 empirical study illustrates, roughly 70 percent of all organizations represented by lobbyists in Washington are business-and trade-oriented, while public interest groups make up only a paltry 4 percent.[84] Given the facts of far more copious resources in money, expertise, and legal counsel available to most business interests, the contest for influence in government developed into a classic case of elephants dancing among chickens. In sum, if liberal public interest groups generated trends in quasi-corporatist directions during the 1970s, it was, ironically, within primary business sectors that this was most apparent.[85]

Even were public interest activists able to achieve their ideal goal of nearly equalized lobbying resources, they would still lack the essential social foundations to match the status of other dominant groups active within and beyond the formal governmental process. Public interest mobilization of widespread popular support around quality-of-life concerns did force some state accommodation, as Handler argues. But we have seen that the relative salience of such support declined with economic deterioration, and the reformers' insubstantial organizational linkage both vertically to the grass roots and horizontally to other organized social interests allowed them little privileged influence over the public beyond media manipulation already available to state officials. It is especially significant to note in this latter regard the ironic character of the public interest constituency which has guaranteed their relative independence from the state. On one hand, the minimal "checkbook affiliations" of most members in the groups not only fall far short of the movement's ideals of participatory democracy; they deny movement leaders effective control over constituents, which the state might find desirable, as well. In fact, a few simple changes in tax laws and postal rates could destroy the reformers' ability even to mobilize a substantial constituency of supporters at all.[86] On the other hand, this largely middle-class constituency has offered little potential for socially disruptive action such as that which gained at least minimal attention for the representatives of the American underclass in the 1960s. As a result, the reformers simply had few means available to reproduce the favorable climate created by the civil rights movement, antiwar protest, and other forms of liberal populist activity which made their early successes possible.

More important, the liberal "new consumer" advocates also lack the structural foundations of economic control over jobs, commodities, and material welfare that traditionally have provided business its "privileged position" in policy-making forums.[87] The simple fact is that periodic consumer boycotts, muckraking exposure of corporate irresponsibility, and control over technical information hardly provide leverage against the state equal to threats of corporate plant closings and capital flight, farmers' refusals to plant crops, or even the weapon of worker strikes available to labor. Even though many of the reformers' causes continue to command some state attention, therefore, the dependence of state officials on the reformers themselves has remained fairly insignificant. As the Carter administration quickly discovered, cultivating populist appearances does not require devolution of much actual decision-making influence to public interest spokespersons.[88] In short, the equilibrium of fundamental social power necessary to force accommodation by the state simply does not exist. As Alan Cawson has argued, "to the extent that the economic role is the fundamental one, access and mutual support will be granted to the representatives of indispensable economic groups. Thus producer groups will be corporatized as a necessity whilst the expansion and activity of consumer groups will occur largely outside the purview of the state."[89]

It thus should not be surprising that liberal public interest ties to government agencies were loosened, their gains halted, and their past victories jeopardized as the 1970s wore on. From the beginning, the primary reliance on formal legal processes, rules, and rights claims has constituted an attractive but fragile strategy of influence for reform leaders lacking substantial social foundations of power.

Direct-action pressure tactics have provided public interest liberals a host of discrete legal victories, to be sure. But the pragmatic, case-by-case approach to social change required by the legal system has also divided scarce resources and impeded development as a unified social movement, thus leaving the individual groups increasingly vulnerable both to powerful corporate opponents on most specific policy fronts and to changes in general policy priorities by high-level state managers sensitive to growing public anxiety about economic matters. As expansion of equal access increasingly sanctioned undesirable outcomes reflecting the gross inequalities of established power, therefore, so were the inadequacies of the reformers' basic faith in radical pluralism to effectively challenge corporate capitalism clearly exposed. That a more corporatist alternative would have been welcome by most liberal activists is not clear. The crucial point is that they lacked the stature necessary even to open that possibility.[90]

This fragility of public interest linkages to the state was most fully demonstrated during the early Reagan admininstration. As Joel Krieger and Teresa Amott have contended, Reagan's "hypercapitalist" policy goals were largely "decorporatizing" in design.[91] His initial issue agenda emphasized exclusion over cooptation of conflicting interests, withdrawal of the state from economic planning responsibilities, an attack upon welfare state legitimation, and the triumph of ideological over technocratic policy formulation. The new administration boldly alienated labor through snubs to leaders such as Lane Kirkland, cuts in CETA and welfare budgets, and advocacy of a Mexican guest-worker program and lowered minimum wage standards. Even important sectors of capital—small business, Wall Street, farmers—were denied influence at first, although tensions eased as the administration increased access to business interests hurting from economic recession in the early years.

Most dramatic of all, Reagan's "New Beginning" launched a direct attack upon the social regulatory establishment and the radical liberals who supported it. If the reformers' participatory designs undercut effective state leadership, Reagan exercised effective leadership by excluding undesirable participants. Although winning few actual statutory changes, Reagan utilized his avowed election mandate to undercut social regulatory enforcement in four general ways: (1) *budget cuts* in key agencies, including up to 15 percent at the FTC, 30 percent at the CPSC, 22 percent in OSHA, and over 50 percent of the research and development funds and 25 percent of the toxic programs funds at EPA from 1980 levels; (2) *personnel changes* replacing Carter public interest appointees with inexperienced, pro-business sympathizers such as James Watt and Anne Gorsuch (later Anne Burford), replacing lawyers with economists at civil servant levels, and cutting overall staffs (8 percent across the board, 20 percent at CPSC, 30 percent at EPA, and 27 percent of OSHA inspectors) by reductions in force and resignations (2,500 at EPA); (3) *regulatory rollbacks* including elimination of thirty-four different rules affecting the auto industry alone and creation of procedural obstacles to all new regulations such as EO 12291, which mandated economic cost–benefit reviews; and (4) *executive branch reorganization* to centralize overall regulatory management responsibility and accountability in the OMB.[92] As a result, scores of rules were weakened and regulatory enforcement by inspections, violation charges, and prosecution undercut markedly in key areas of social policy.[93] At the same time, public rights of access and support for regular citizen-group participation were circumscribed by discretionary agency policy changes, OMB guidelines, and reinterpretations of FOIA and other statutes. Specific efforts to defund the Left likewise cut the operating budgets of some prominent public interest groups anywhere from 10 percent (League of Women Voters) to 25 percent (Conservation Foundation), and even much more for small legal and research firms.[94] The important implication of these facts is not only that some agencies were "strangled" and "dismantled," as some observers have claimed, but that most reform activists lost their foothold in government.[95]

Public interest liberals have not been rendered wholly ineffective, of course. Public support for most of their causes is far too great, if not very intense, to be defied openly by even a popular president. Indeed, after the initial onslaught, the liberals have proved remarkably successful in fighting further regulatory rollbacks, in protecting extant legislation, in forcing the replacement of imprudent ideologues such as Watt and Burford, in enforcing existing regulatory guidelines, and in winning new amendments to environmental statutes. But the more relevant point is that their tactics are again those primarily of adversarial outsiders. Public media campaigns to expose evil and generate opposition to the Reagan revolution have again become prominent. Expanding membership lists to make up for financial and political support lost from the state has likewise become more important as well as easier. And, of course, "we are back into court," says a NRDC attorney. "We are filing more suits than we were in 1980."[96] In the area of Clean Air Act and Clean Water Act enforcement alone, private actions rose dramatically from a total of 20 notices and 35 actual lawsuits for the three-year period of 1978–1980 to 139 notices and 154 lawsuits in 1984 alone.[97] Other judicial action produced more than a few significant victories, including successful challenges to the NHTSA decision to rescind passive restraint standards, the DOT effort to rescind liquor label standards, and the EPA attempt to alter the definition of "stationary source" covered by the Clean Air Act. Armed with new public support and expanded attorneys' fee entitlements, one clean-water lobbyist went so far as to claim that public interest liberals "are likely to be more effective in opposition than in power."[98]

The bitter irony, however, is that apparent public interest victories in specific battles also eliminated many of the symbols of evil so useful to the liberals' larger war against Reagan's reelection in 1984. For example, the president's appointment of William Ruckelshaus and William Clark to replace Gorsuch and Watt actually enhanced his political standing by making cosmetic concessions to liberals while revitalizing only selective regulatory actions. Reagan's reelection was important not only in that it has encouraged action in such a direction, moreover, but because his likely appointments to the Supreme Court and other federal courts might prove to be the most crushing blow of all to the liberal reformers.[99] In sum, then, the Handler thesis seems correct that the central problem of public interest reform groups is one of their relative powerlessness. But the particular social character of this powerlessness has doomed the liberal reformers' project of democratic legitimation not so much by corporatist cooptation during the 1980s as by their de facto exclusion from the state to a peripheral position at once independent, adversarial, and yet increasingly impotent to initiate further progressive change.

Politics without Parties. The problems of leadership, organization, and power once again call attention to the peculiar disinterest of public interest liberals in the most conventional form of collective action by democratic reform groups—that of partisan electoral politics. In fact, support by Common Cause and other groups for structural reforms in federal campaign laws and internal party organization have actually undercut the leadership and policy functions of the major parties by restricting their control over electoral fund raising and distribution.[100] This is not to agree with critics who blame the much bemoaned decline of modern parties—or at the least the Democratic party—on the liberal reformers. American political parties have withered under pressures of policy failure and institutional change far more pervasive and enduring in nature. Moreover, the proposals for federal campaign reform, for direct presidential election, for greater public disclosure, and for direct primaries are not without significant virtues.[101] Still, critics are right that many such reforms have displayed a costly insensitivity to the value of strong parties typical of the liberal rights–oriented mentality generally.

Even more significant has been the reformers' refusal of direct, consistent partisan support for electoral candidates—presidential, congressional, state, and local—and policy platforms. Their general strategy with regard to elections seems to have been primarily to "let Tweedledee and Tweedledum fight it out, and then attack the winner."[102] The reformers' posture has mirrored that of corporatist clients in this regard, but the logic behind each differs greatly. Public interest activists have eschewed party politics not because it is too democratic and volatile, as incorporatated interests often do, but rather because American parties are seen as too unresponsive, undemocratic, and inert.[103] In the liberal reform view, partisan identification would only limit pragmatic flexibility, drain scarce resources, and threaten cooptation of their primary issues into meaningless personality campaigns. "People do not express themselves through the parties any more," noted liberal direct mail strategist Thomas Matthews in 1980, "because they can no longer see a connection between their own actions and what happens on a grand scale."[104] Much like James Q. Wilson's "amateur democrats" of the previous decade, the reformers seem to believe that effective issue politics transcends partisan commitment.[105]

This attitude is surprising and significant because, as Schattschneider once argued, party politics traditionally has been the most effective vehicle for providing leadership, coordination, and influence around popular issues of general concern. "The big game is the party game because in the last analysis there is no political substitute for victory in election" of officials to provide influential leadership within and without government.[106] Party politics was crucial, after all, to earlier liberal progressive social movements in the Jacksonian, Populist, and New Deal eras. The revitalized Republican party behind Ronald Reagan has provided both crucial means and end for proliferating New Right social groups and resurgent business interests since the late 1970s.[107] Also relevant is the degree to which public interest reformers themselves depended on the New Deal social consensus, the support of liberal majorities in Congress, and President Carter—all secured by the Democratic party. Numerous studies have confirmed the deep division on public-interest issues between legislators from the two dominant parties at both the federal and state levels. Not only do Democrats identify themselves much more closely with the liberal ideology of the reformers than do the more conservative business-oriented Republicans, but the former as a whole have been more than twice as likely to support environmental, consumer, and other public interest–type legislation than the latter.[108] In other words, the new activists have gladly taken what they could get from the Democrats while providing very little formal support to the party in return.

These observations are not intended to refute the reformers' claims that existing electoral processes generally constitute "manipulable forms of false democracy," as one environmentalist has put it.[109] Yet to persist in the belief that direct-action pressure politics and sustained work for elective office are mutually exclusive democratic commitments is naive. Whereas legalistic pressure politics tends to disaggregate interests, issues, and alliances within state and society, party politics holds out the possibility of forging new bonds of power and purpose among disparate groups.[110] It is true that such hopes have not been realized in our modern era of "alienated politics." But strong parties still offer the greatest potential for developing genuinely responsive, democratic, majoritarian structures capable of coordinating diverse social demands into comprehensive programs of progressive political change within and through the state. Likewise, the mutual allegiances and obligations generated by coherent party structures can offer a nonlegalistic supplement to the rule of impersonal rules as a control on the discretionary exercise of state power. Indeed, it is probably only through the development of viable federated party-like forms that democracy can be advanced against the twin anathemas of centralized technocratic elite management and arbitrary pluralistic parasitism within national government. As Walter Dean Burnham summarizes, "something . . . is needed to create a functioning nation, something that produces bonds of sentiment which override citizen pursuits of individual and group interests. . . . The power to decide, to plan, to create comprehensive policy whose legitimacy wins broad public support—in short, to 'steer' under these conditions—requires the creation of an organized political will."[111]

More overt and sustained partisan commitment would not be a panacea, to be sure. Alignment with either party would guarantee neither electoral success nor translation of such success into greater political power. Moreover, formal party affiliation might increase the costs imposed by the electoral triumph of opponents, although the case of labor largely defies this argument.[112] But this does not alter the fact that the liberal reformers' nonpartisan stance is inadequate to the task of promoting a broadly based coalition for democratic change, to which they have proclaimed commitment since the late 1960s. And the costs of continued nonpartisanship are likely to increase in the future. Not only has Republican conservatism redefined the public agenda, but leading voices within the Democratic party are advocating more centralized forms of party reorganization and cooperation with business interests as a way to reverse the trend.[113] As a result, default by progressive-minded activists may jeopardize their own fates as well as that of the Democratic party.

Once again, some signs indicate that many public interest activists have come to a similar realization. Barry Commoner's attempt to develop a third party alternative in 1980 went the way of most such efforts in America, but it did generate greater interest in electoral politics and coalition building among many of the activists. During recent years, Mark Green has exhorted the reform troops to "remember the Democrats," environmentalists have experimented with party support at various levels of government, and talk of rebuilding the moribund Democratic party organization has crept into the reform dialogue.[114] Perhaps most interesting have been the various strategies for developing a "party within a party" advocated by some leaders and groups. Under this strategy, the groups "would unite in a permanent coalition within the Democratic party, supporting a program of economic democracy.... By mobilizing its supporters and launching massive voter-registration drives in these campaigns, it would work to defeat Reagan in 1984 (and his counterpart in 1988), but would not waste time and effort on the presidential primaries."[115] The advantage of this approach is that it might help to redefine and revitalize the Democratic party in future campaigns while enabling public interest activists to pursue their own direct advocacy efforts as they had previously.

Nevertheless, such talk has produced little action. The contributions of public interest groups to electoral politics have been largely nonpartisan, issue-specific, and organized around PACs and endorsements for selective candidates. Most public interest leaders have opted for criticizing President Reagan's attempt to "politicize" the executive establishment from above rather than for helping the Democrats elect leaders who could do the same for different purposes. Even Mark Green still argues that "media politics and citizen politics" actually add up to "the equivalents of a political party" which obviates partisan allegiance.[116] And the reasons why such formal nonpartisanship continue to prevail are quite clear. The sheer weight of past organizational legacy, political success, and leadership priorities as well as state institutional incentives once again have effectively deterred any radical shifts in conviction. In particular, a more overt partisan strategy might jeopardize the tax-exempt status of some

groups, alienate significant portions of present members, and seriously divide the activists among themselves. As a result, the cumulative
contributions of most public interest groups to a more just democratic
order are likely to remain as minimal as Handler's analysis has
predicted. Once again, it seems the fragmenting political structures
and ideological propensities of American liberalism have rendered
largely innocuous potentially progressive reform efforts to expand
popular control over the power of private capital.

Authority and Purpose:
The Elusive Ethical Imperative

Moralists without Morality? The revitalization of citizen faith in
liberal state authority requires more than simply increased institutional
leadership and coordination, we have seen. Nearly everyone agrees
that the dilemma of dwindling government legitimacy reflects at
bottom a crisis of substantive moral purpose.[117] The reformers thus
have spoken often about the need for a transformation in the fundamental values that inform and inspire collective life. "We must
generate a new vision," exhorts John Gardner.[118] Specifically, they
have been convinced that a post–New Deal politics necessitates a
revitalized liberal public ethics. "A revolution is truly needed—in our
values... [and] outlook" as well as in our "economic organization,"
agrees Sierra Club executive Michael McCloskey.[119] Such a new moral
vision is necessary, they rightly claim, to both guide and legitimate
state subordination of private social interests for the collective public
interest of all in society. Without this moral foundation, concludes
Simon Lazarus, the reformers cannot succeed in "vindicating the
populist democratic faith that most Americans still consider the true
source of legitimate public authority."[120]

Despite such lofty aspirations and occasionally moralistic tone,
however, the reformers' pragmatic posture remains quite ambiguous
about the actual moral purposes at the center of the public interest
enterprise. For one thing, their piecemeal, problem-solving organizational
tactics mirror a narrowly interest-based, process-oriented substantive vision. The reformers' self-proclaimed identity as a new consumer movement illustrates the point. "Consumption" is inherently a
private subjective interest orientation, what political theorist Brian
Barry calls a "want-oriented" concept.[121] The prescribed shift in
values from quantity to quality thus may alter the terms of thinking
about individual want satisfaction, but it does not challenge the
primacy of utility maximization as the basis of political claims. While

241

often critical of the selfish interests indulged by others, the liberal activists still voice their own appeals primarily in terms of individual gratification and welfare—thus invoking few standards of objective measure at all.[122] They simply reject one set of preferences for another. "A great many of us know what we want," announces John Gardner. But explication of what they want explains little about what is right, just, or good. Even some of the new consumer claims exalting the guidelines of Maslowian needs reduce the new politics to estimations of greater therapeutic psychological satisfaction.[123]

Environmentalist Hazel Henderson exemplifies the resulting circularity of moral logic in her brief essay "A Discussion of Values."[124] She begins her argument in agreement with another scholar that all "notions of value are arbitrary and culture bound." Yet, she proceeds to excoriate what she defines as the uniquely exploitive values that inform American capitalism. Having undermined all possibilities of objective moral ground, however, her own justification for higher values ends up a prescription for a more reliable calculus of existing American consumer preferences. This not only avoids the challenge of moral argument, but also signals implicit acceptance of market mechanisms over moral judgment generally as well as the priority of specific interests contrary to those the reformers are seeking to advance.[125]

In sum, the new consumer agenda tends to reflect as much as challenge the instrumental, utilitarian, subjectivist interest orientation to political action inherent in capitalist society. Liberals ever since Bentham have tried repeatedly to derive collective normative principles of public happiness from such foundations of rational calculation about individual pleasure. Yet the endless circularity of their laborious dance has rendered their efforts consistently unconvincing. Consumer utility alone, however inner-directed or health conscious, cannot provide the moral criteria necessary to legitimate expansive state action. "From the point of view of ethics," agrees John Schaar, "there is no metaphysical difference between an ethics of pure pleasure seeking and one of health, self-realization, self-denial, or anything else, so long as these refer to nothing outside of the individual."[126] This is why classical liberals have always exalted private freedom and market transactions against collective determination of priorities in the distribution of social goods. Unable to transcend these same subjectivist propensities that they criticize, the reformers' attempt to bridge the gap between private bourgeois and citizen, between narrow self-interest and the collective good, and between markets and politics likewise has often floundered in ethical confusion.

The reformers' prevailing conception of the "public interest"—the axial idea around which their multiple moral claims turn—further reveals this affinity with the logic of the liberal marketplace mentality they aspire to alter. Common usage of the term in political discourse usually implies the invocation of objective value, of substantive right, of moral certitude in word and deed. When we claim that something is "in the public interest," explains Virginia Held in a classic work on the subject, we are "asserting its justifiability."[127] Stephen Bailey likewise contends that "to have this phrase serve their purpose over time, public servants must be able to give it rational content in widely shared value commitments."[128] By contrast, the reform activists have all but severed the concept from any such substantive ethical moorings. "Aware of the decidedly illiberal implications of a priori notions of 'public interest,'" notes consumerist Peter Schuck, most activists believe that the prudent course is to avoid definition of any transcendent objective meaning in the term.[129] "No citizens' movement should assume that it has some divinely inspired grasp of what is in the public interest," instructs the always prudent John Gardner. "We don't define 'the public interest' in the same sense that our group represents it while others don't," agrees another advocate.[130] At best, the reformers have claimed to advance only a particular aspect, rather than a comprehensive moral vision, of *the* public interest. In fact, the activists, ironically, are quick to turn accusations of ideological dogmatism on their critics to avoid all taints of moral idealism or rigidity in their own perspective. "Wherein lies the real public interest?" queries an NRDC editorial. "The Wall Street Journal [is] preying upon a naive assumption of a great many that the public interest is a singular, static ideal when in reality there is more than one public interest in many complex issues."[131]

While the liberal reformers' frequent rejection of ideological rigidity is laudable, it also tends to sap the ideal of "public interest" of its general substantive content. "The concept [is] a processual one," says Schuck, "referring not to the substance of a particular policy decision, but rather to the conditions and procedures under which decisions are arrived at."[132] Another group of reform advocates agrees that the public interest is "the sum total of all interests in the community . . . which are balanced for the public good."[133] The liberal activists' primary ethical responsibility is thus merely to formalize rights of citizen-interest input and to even the balance of forces in the calculus. Since the impersonal and impartial governmental process ciphers the common good automatically, it follows, the criteria for rightful collective choice and evaluation of outcomes are nearly irrelevant. Where "legitimacy of government action derives from...the process employed" and "not from the inherent wisdom of the decision itself," ruminations about collective purpose seem almost pointless.[134] Substantive moral integrity matters little more than institutional coherence in policy making, it seems, as long as the reformers' particular interests receive fair hearing and their rights are respected. In short, the reformers' instrumental normative perspective both confirms and rationalizes their fragmented and fragmenting interest-group impact upon government.

These observations do not deny that public interest activists share certain collective moral impulses, insights, and aspirations of genuine significance. The basic deficiency is neither an excess nor a paucity of moral intention, but rather the inherent narrowness, idiosyncracy, and randomness of their particular ends in relation to any center of ethical gravity. This explains in part the apparent contradiction between charges by conservatives that the reformers are at once "libertarian" and "authoritarian," "selfish" and "moralistic," "nihilistic" and "zealously religious," "amoral" and "ideological."[135] Beneath all the conceptual confusion invoked by such fiery rhetoric lies an acknowledgment that the reformers combine both intense moral conviction and pragmatic skepticism toward ultimate ends in a way typical of most liberal politics. Suspicious of grand designs and motivated by concern for interests over ideas, they thus appear to be ardent moralists without a genuine morality.[136] With "radical" ethical critics such as these, defenders of the status quo should have little to worry about.

The Rediscovery of Natural Right. While public interest liberals appear to lack a comprehensive moral vision of the public good, they nevertheless have acted on behalf of important moral concerns and public interests in an attempt to balance and transform the existing calculus of commitments in American public life. In particular, we have seen that many of their most important substantive commitments derive from a common core of ecologically inspired quality-of-life ethics.[137] This moral orientation has justified the proposed transformation of American values from profits to people, from wealth to health, and from the ethic of private property to the "land ethic."[138] Not only have "rights of nature" defined the most important of the public rights advocated by the new liberals, therefore, but they also provide the most commonly invoked principles of natural right promulgated to legitimate the entire liberal reform enterprise.

This exaltation of nature is hardly novel, of course; it owes much to the long and deeply rooted tradition of what Leo Marx calls "romantic pastoralism" in America.[139] Indeed, such paeans to the regenerative power located within nature's "fresh green breast" have long expressed a sort of mystical underside in our rationalistic liberal tradition. Crèvecoeur's yeoman idyll, Jefferson's agrarian republicanism, Jacksonian radical democracy, the "free soil" ideology of Manifest Destiny, the Populist movement, and numerous other progressive reform movements in the twentieth century have all drawn upon the redemptive promise of nature. At the same time, however, the most recent expression of esteem for nature by public interest liberals has also born the unique stamp of their own historical epoch—in particular, the influence of Bohemian romanticism from the 1950s and the New Left antipathy to modern industrial society in the 1960s.[140] In the words of poet-activist Gary Snyder, the contemporary embrace of nature emerged from a "number of things [that] happened together. An interest in Oriental thought, in Buddhism, in American Indians, in tribalism, in communal living," and the environmental movement generally.[141]

This renewed faith in the capacity of nature to revitalize society has been manifested at three levels of experience. The first and most important concerns the *physical* aspects of biological life. Its primary ethical obligations to safety and survival inspire dramatic counsel of fear and alarm about the wasteful, destructive habits of civilization.[142] Obsessed with "fireballs of nuclear holocaust . . . or the new ice of a glacial era brought on prematurely" as well as everyday dangers in the workplace, at home, and on the highway, Sierra Club leader John Mitchell typically advocates "preservation of the species" as the highest goal of the new reform politics.[143] Scholar-activist Robert C. Mitchell has compiled a lost of common dangers identified in environmental mail solicitations alone:

According to the National Parks and Conservation Association "our National Parks are in danger," . . . the National Audubon Society warns against "sacrificing" our land, water, and air to appease the "furies of inflation"; the Environmental Defense Fund raises the "threat from poisoned air, water and food"; the Natural Resources Defense Council offers itself as an "inspired and effective approach to preserve a livable world"; the Friends of the Earth remind us that [if we] "continue to pollute the air in our major cities . . . there will soon be no such thing as fresh air for us to breathe"; and the National Wildlife Federation seeks to meet "the crisis [of] the continued survival of man and wildlife on this fragile planet."[144]

It is this concern with physical safety and health both within and beyond our productive processes which generates the often embarrassingly extreme rhetoric of the reformers. For example, in 1970 David Brower predicted total "destruction in a decade" and John Platt wrote in *Science* that "we may have less than a 50–50 chance of living until 1980."[145] Yet behind this rhetorical overkill thrives genuine fear and conviction about the threats to the survival of the planet. As Paul Ehrlich, author of the best-selling *The Population Bomb*, has proclaimed, "I am an alarmist, because I'm very goddamned alarmed."[146]

The counsel of nature has been embraced on more affirmative terms as well. For one, nature is exalted as tutor to our *intelligence* about how better to order our created world of convention. Nature's laws are frequently invoked as a prudent counterbalance to the myopic, predatory, and corrupt ways of civilized humans. Generally harmonious, pure, and balanced in a self-sustaining steady-state equilibrium, nature is understood as embodying a transcendent order the truths of which should humble our rationalistic intelligences.[147] "Nature knows best" is thus Barry Commoner's fourth law of ecology.[148] If Kafka is the reformers' favorite poet of civilized darkness, then Wordsworth seems to be their poet of natural light:

> One impulse from a vernal wood
>   May teach you more of man
> Of moral evil and of good
>   Than all the sages can.
> Sweet is the lore that Nature brings
>   Our Meddling intellect
> Misshapes the beautious forms of things:
>   We murder to dissect.[149]

Contemporary ecologist Nancy Newhall agrees, noting that "wilderness has answers to questions that man has not learned how to ask." Influential leader David Brower likewise refers to nature as a "benchmark" and "touchstone." "In wilderness is the only unsullied earth sample of the forces generally at work in the universe," he proclaims.[150]

Nature has also been revered as a source of *spiritual* regeneration. In nature, it is assumed, both head and heart are renewed by contact with a more harmonious order of things; communion with external physical nature and internal psychological nature go hand in hand. As Emerson professed, in nature "I become a transparent eyeball; I am nothing; I see all; the currents of universal being circulate through me; I am part and particle of God."[151] John Muir extolled the wilderness experience of humans in similar terms: "Thousands of tired, nerve-shaken, over-civilized people are beginning to find out that going to the mountains is going home; that wilderness is a necessity; and that mountain parks and reservations are useful . . . as fountains of life." Kenneth Brower likewise defends the sanctity of nature in terms of the rights of future generations of Americans "to see, and enjoy, and be inspired and renewed, somewhere, by those places where the hand of God has not been obscured by the industry of man." Or, as *Ecotactics* contributor Alan Gussow puts it, "in the way food nourishes our body, the environment feeds our dreams."[152] Such a celebration of nature has taken on nearly religious significance for many who regularly worship in the "wilderness cathedral." Indeed, the primary impulses behind the new ecological preservationist ethic, Arthur St. George's opinion study has confirmed, are "religious," "aesthetic," and "spiritual" in character. It is not surprising that John McPhee titled his popular book on the high priest of environmentalism, David Brower, *Encounters with the Archdruid*.[153] If the new ecologically oriented political movement had an official motto, it almost surely would be "in nature we trust."

Nature and Politics. The embrace of physical nature has provided many public interest liberals an Archimedean point upon which to stand in judgment of modern civilization and to measure human achievement in critical terms. The purity and innocence of the natural wilderness has stood as bold contrast to our sins, the imperatives of the despoiled physical environment a warning about our own danger to ourselves. Yet this invocation of nature has to a large extent also tended to reflect and reinforce the inherently narrow, limited, and piecemeal character of the new reform vision. The result has been that the reformers' quest for an improved quality of life has led not to the creative spring found at Thoreau's Walden so much as to an unregenerate winter of perpetual discontent. The implications of this claim are several.

One problem is that the lessons of nature are not particularly clear to the frail human mind. The same mystery that intrigues us also confounds us. This is so primarily because nature is without language. Unlike most divine religions, the religion of nature remains speechless, unwritten, unrevealed. While nature provides a truly magnificent vision worthy of infinite description, it is we who must choose the words of meaning. "Nature never draws the moral, but

247

leaves it for the speculator," instructed Emerson.[154] As a result, nature more often serves as a mirror of our existing intellectual propensities than as a window to moral truth. From Platonic idealists to Enlightenment rationalists, civilized peoples have seen in nature the order that best serves their faith. Hierarchy and equality, change and continuity, freedom and order, justice and force—it is all there to be found. Indeed, the historical legacy of romantic obsessions with nature in America has been highly ambiguous. While many have found in nature reason to tame our human hubris through the pursuit of peace and communion, others have found in the wilderness experience of "natural" life justifications for much more violent and destructive indulgences such as Indian conquest, land appropriation, and wildlife slaughter.[155]

Furthermore, whatever wisdom of the natural world we might discern is of limited relevance to the uniquely moral realm of public life.[156] Of course, nature does provide important sources of knowledge which are useful to intelligent political action. Sensitivity to the scarcity of basic resources, to the costs of careless waste and abuse, to the intrinsic loss or destruction of human life and wildlife, and generally to the obligations derived from our interdependence with the nonhuman world can be vital counterbalances to our homocentric greed and lust for power. Because all levels of life are intricately and often imperceptibly interconnected, we must recognize that "all things affect each other.... that we are indeed part of a vast chain."[157] However, ecological knowledge is of little help in defining the moral imperatives of political authority. Such counsel instead constitutes primarily the amoral imperatives of biological necessity. Our very "freedom is the recognition of necessity," quotes Garrett Hardin from Hegel.[158] In other words, while our knowledge of nature can help demarcate the circle of contingencies and risk probability that constrains our options, it provides little instruction or justification as to the human purposes for which we should act within those constraints.

In one sense, then, this recognition of necessity defines what we cannot choose, the realm where questions of moral right and legitimacy are irrelevant. Consider Jacques Cousteau's appeal that "the ocean can die, these horrors could happen. And there would be no place to hide!"[159] If such necessity were to threaten us—and risk of this is hardly great—there could be no choice of ends, only of means. In a dissolving world, moral authority must bow before the technical counsel of the engineer or doctor. As Richard Neuhaus instructs, "when survival is king, all questions of right and wrong are irrelevant and diversionary:... it is necessary."[160] This fact explains not only ⁻

248

much of the emotional response generated by various visions of eco-catastrophe, but also the frankly authoritarian tendencies of some radical environmentalists. Where survival is seen to be in jeopardy, "freedom in a commons brings ruin to all," and the only hope is "mutual coercion mutually agreed upon by all." This, notes one activist, is the "ecology of revolution. . . . Our politics and our economics must be secondary . . . to the real issue of life and death."[161]

Understood in another sense, the problem of such obsession with the alleged necessity of survival issues is that they tend to exalt life itself as the highest end of political action. "The revolution must be an affirmation of all life. . . . not only human life, but plant and animal life as well," says ecological theorist Tony Wagner in typical fashion.[162] In other words, the primary concern for physical preservation and health is hardly a matter of quality at all; it actually severs the value of life from any other higher purpose or reason. As former Nader ally Joan Claybrook has claimed, "the sanctity of life has the highest value in our society." Such a commitment alone cannot justify positive purposive action, sacrifice for principle, or allegiance to community sustained by the collective cause of justice; it can only inform, qualify, or discount the exercise of moral judgment. "When the survival of the species is at stake," proposes League of Conservation Voters leader Marion Edey, "the question of how we divide up our frantic last-minute spoils is trivial."[163] This ethic assumes that nothing is worth dying for and that every life is worth living. In Arendt's terms, it elevates "mere life" over the "good life" that is the end of political authority. The fetishism of "survival" and "life" affirms hope for our continued existence among other creatures, to be sure; but it contributes only minimally to our capacity to be fully human, to create a more noble world, or to perform exemplary deeds of justice and virtue.[164] In fact, the new ecopolitics has been curiously evasive about precisely those most serious issues of human survival—material poverty, nuclear arms buildup, and American foreign intervention generally—where ethical and ideological values are critical to political choice. All in all, as French writer Andre Gorz has argued, "it is impossible to derive an ethic 'for politics' from ecology."[165]

Such naturalistic obsessions with survival and safety are not only limited in their substantive reach; they have tended to contribute a distinctively prophylactic, defensive character to the new reform politics as well.[166] Consider the most common characterization of the citizen constituency by the reformers. Typically, citizens are portrayed as unwitting victims, hostages, and dupes endangered by the malign forces of moral and physical pollution. An *Ecotactics* essay thus summarizes the appropriate posture for concerned citizens in this way: "I am poor little me. Victim of environmental larceny. Parent and grandparent of victims unto the seventh generation."[167] Nader similarly exhorts that "in a society where power accretes to the victims, you would not just have rights, which we have plenty of, you would have remedies, which we have fewer of." Elsewhere he asks, "Must a legal system not accord victims the power . . . to deter those forces which victimize them?"[168] John Gardner speaks in the same terms: "Individuals are less apt to be victims of tyrants than to be victims of large-scale organization, victims of the tyranny of the formula." And so it goes for more traditional consumer advocates: The "average consumer falls prey almost daily to a long list of silent, unseen injuries," they complain.[169]

Of course, both greater objective levels of risk and expanded knowledge of victimization surely justify increased intolerance of such risks.[170] But the basic point emphasized here is that the ecology-minded reformers, like Thomas Hobbes, seem to believe that trepidation is the best stimulation for public concern. "Fear and liberty are consistent," said Hobbes; and "liberty, or freedom, signifieth, properly, the absence of opposition."[171] The goal of political authority in such classic liberal prescriptions is not so much the expansion of public freedom to act and to choose our collective life as the insulation of familiar private freedoms from the risks of external incursion. The only major difference of conception is that for the new ecologists nature is the esteemed sanctuary of order and value, and our rationalistic civilization the cause of life that is "solitary, poor, nasty, brutish, and short."[172] Still, however, the primary goals of such "defensive liberalism" are safety, security, and stability. Indeed, the same imperatives to self-preservation dominate modern liberal efforts to win public entitlements against the dangers of waste and injury from a hostile world: "An ethic, ecologically, is a limitation on freedom of action in the struggle for existence," defined Aldo Leopold in his popular *Sand County Almanac*.[173]

Much as in classical liberal theory, the call to public life for modern victimized consumers thus has been mostly one of prevention and redress rather than of positive purpose. As Robert C. Mitchell has argued, liberal public interest campaigns focus more on avoiding "public bads" than in promoting "public goods."[174] The highest priorities are to halt abuses, to ward off dangers, to secure against unwarranted intrusions, and to recover denied satisfactions. A "statement of purpose" from Environmental Action exemplifies the point: "We seek to enhance the compatibility of humanity and the environment by preventing pollution, reducing the use of non-renewable resources, encouraging the conservation of energy and materials, and eliminating threats to natural cycles."[175] Such typically negative, if worthwhile, orientations are conveyed in the familiar reform rhetoric and slogans as well. They want to "pull the plug" on the nuclear industry, to "save the whales" and other animals, to "stop the bulldozers," to "stop up" the Alaska pipeline, to "protect the Earth," and to put a "moratorium on growth."

Likewise, establishing "countervailing powers," "civic balance," and "institutional watchdogs" to check the initiative of others is their primary political project. To "cancel, delay, or modify development projects that they oppose" defines the major expenditure of energy and funds, note two regulatory reform observers.[176] Indeed, the legalistic strategy of public interest liberals has been successful largely because law is most useful as a resource to halt or delay rather than to initiate action. This is the essence of Lon Fuller's classic argument that law best enforces the morality of "duty" rather than that of "aspiration"; it is most useful at mandating "thou shalt nots" rather than "thou shalts," and acts of omission rather than acts of commission.[177] The new activists' very understanding of power has reflected this limited, morally reflexive perspective as well: "The idea of empowerment points to a democratic process that needs continued review to determine where excessive or abusive power—by corporations, by government, by coercive institutions—calls for more corrective power by the people," claims Nader.[178] In nearly all cases of concern, correcting for the motives or byproducts of action by others and curing the diseases of modern civilized life take precedent over defining affirmative goals and aspirations for collective endeavor. "Rather than dreaming of taking power, they are working as a mechanism to check power," spokesperson Simon Lazarus noted approvingly in the early 1970s.[179]

This tendency of the professional liberal reformers to prophylactic, preventive politics reflects a marked affinity with the radical naturalism of the New Left in the 1960s. As Marshall Berman has argued, the supposed expansion of consciousness in that decade ironically involved a contraction in vision as well: "It seems virtually impossible for Americans today to feel or even imagine the joy of building, the adventure and romance and heroism of construction," he summarized. Like modern Thoreaus, the young activists rebelled against the indignities of existing political and economic relations. For the radical youths, however, collective action in the pursuit of power seemed to be inherently tied to venality, exploitation, and big endeavors that

251

crush little people's lives. The fundamental ethic was thus for each of us to "do our own thing," to cultivate our own gardens, or at best to try to humanize those who pull the levers of the imperious social machine. Of the New Left generally Berman concludes, "We knew that things needed to be stopped, and how to stop them, but had no idea how to start things" of great political significance.[180]

Such propensities were evident especially in the two most important events of the era in which the public interest movement emerged—the antiwar movement and the campaign to impeach Richard Nixon. The professional liberal reformers who followed seemed to carry on in similar fashion. Only the issues and forums of dissent changed. Operating under the assumptions of what Common Cause activists call the "adversity theory," the reformers have thrived by perpetuating a sense of almost daily crisis.[181] Elaborate dramatizations of physical catastrophes and, more often, near-catastrophes—toxic waste seepage, oil spills, nuclear shutdowns—have provided the bread-and-butter pitch of those committed to life and health. Exposing hidden dangers and transgressions of present arrangements is the basic task of muckrakers with few ideas about what we should be doing instead. Some reformers even blame the absence of major crises for the decline in support for public interest politics during the late 1970s: "The singleness of purpose and passions that illuminated the anti-war protests and the impeachment campaigns have largely dissipated," begins one public interest report in 1977. "At present, there are no pressures, like the Vietnam War, no one figure, like Richard Nixon, whose threat to civil liberties can be welded into a united opposition."[182] We have seen that the biggest catalyst to revival of public interest support and membership has been the electoral triumphs of Ronald Reagan and other conservatives in the 1980s. The threat of James Watt alone is cited for boosting environmental group support by over 25 percent in 1981, support that mostly disappeared with his later removal.[183] In other words, what is curious about the new reform politics is that its very motivation has depended largely on the prosperity of its adversaries.

This logic of the reformers' ecological ethics points yet one step further. Their defense of physical nature against civilization has not only been limited in relevance for purposive moral direction; it also reflects a deeper ambivalence about the fruits of human artifice in general.[184] This is especially true of the new preservationist ethic committed "to wilderness . . . [as] an end in itself and opposition to all development or mechanized intervention in as yet natural areas."[185] The values enshrined here aim less to regenerate mutually beneficial intercourse of humans among themselves and nature than to establish the boundaries of exclusivity between the two, primarily for the benefit of the latter. In other words, the quest for qualitative change in modern society has required a shift in the quantitative balance of human creation and untainted nature upon earth. "Liberate the ecosystem," many proclaimed in the early 1970s. A better society is a shrunken society: "less is more."[186] We have already charted the costs of this position in the reformers' indifference about economic issues. "All production is also destruction," environmentalists are wont to repeat. Since it is "wealth and technology that have made community and self impossible," implies Charles Reich, less of both are desirable.[187] Even more moderate commitments to the middle ground of rural society express much the same sentiment. The demands for simplicity, smallness, and personal independence still imply that diminished—not new or different—forms of human artifice are the keys to securing and enhancing life. Unlike older teleological conceptions of human nature celebrating creative social power, the new liberal ethics has seemed most concerned with recapturing a Paradise Lost. "Orphaned by unwelcome change and then adopted by anxiety," comments George Shulman, "the pastoral impulse seeks to recover the lost inheritance of a true home . . . [and] to judge and devalue the real one, created.[188] The reformers' challenges to blind faith in social salvation through technological progress, physical domination, and commodity consumption are valuable, to be sure. But to suggest that our ideals for improved civilization should be abandoned in deference to nature, and that our creative strivings pose only threats of increased destruction, is quite another matter.

These views have carried over into the sphere of politics in particular. The very image of unregenerate political life portrayed routinely through the words of the reformers is enough to discourage most attentive citizens from conviction and hope.[189] If nature everywhere is pure and innocent, in the political world the activists seem to find only greed, corruption, incompetence, and injustice. Bureaucracy is impenetrable, and bureaucrats are recalcitrant corporate lackeys. Legislators are pictured as media hucksters and the "other government" of Washington lawyers as amoral counselors of sin. In short, the "cancer of corruption" appears to be contagious. "A society is like a fish—it rots from the head down," claims Nader.[190] While this cancer afflicts all government insiders, the public life of virtuous reform-minded outsiders is portrayed as only little more desirable. Like an earlier nature lover, Thomas Jefferson, the new activists tend to confirm that "public employment . . . is but an honorable exile from one's family and affairs" with "few attractions."[191] If fear for physical survival and health is the prime motive to political action, public life itself is nothing but work, sacrifice, discipline, duty, and tedious research to fight impending evils. "It's time consuming, demanding work," warns an FOE membership appeal. "If citizen action is to be successful it requires . . . lots and lots of stamina," admonishes another.[192] This is what Robert Buckhorn implies when he suggests that Nader "doesn't think of himself as a political animal—if anything, he is afraid of politics."[193] In fact, Nader's exhortations to action often resemble Puritan jeremiads replete with exposition upon the sins, hardship, and burdens of public life.[194]

Of course, it may be true that this sober view of politics is preferable to the escapist "cult of easiness" encouraged by consumer society or the uncritical patriotism of the New Right moralists that the reformers criticize. Even so, such attitudes still seem to betray marks of a commitment that lacks redeeming purpose. They suggest the posture of Puritans with little light to oppose to the darkness from which they seek release, or of Sisyphus without cause for smile in his relentless uphill climb. In Hannah Arendt's terms, the new reform politics has been conceived more as a "labor" for existence than as creative action and "public happiness" in the good life. The Greek origin of the word *act, archeim*, itself means "to begin," "to lead," or "to rule." To act, in its most general sense, means "to take initiative, to begin . . . to set something in motion," Arendt observes.[195] For the professional reform elites, however, most of their youthful enthusiasm for new beginnings seems to have withered, and the affirmative convictions about a better world have been dwarfed by resigned defensiveness. The spirit of Roosevelt's exhortation that "the only thing we have to fear is fear itself" appears to have been lost. Encouraging concern for preserving biological nature has taken precedence over fulfillment of human nature as citizens, and the goal of minimizing mortal risks has eclipsed hope for designing immortal grand historical advances in social justice.

In sum, the naturalistic ethic embraced by many movement activists has tended both to reflect and to nurture a general ambivalence about the very promise of just government action discussed earlier. Beneath the democratic rhetoric of many reform leaders has lingered a crisis of confidence about even the possibility for a movement of collective purpose, vision, and grand design which might transcend their piecemeal, legalistic approach. Obsessed with preventing the worst of possibilities under existing arrangements rather than restructuring society itself, the liberal ethic of preservation has ended up being largely conservative in character. The authority of positive political purpose continues to elude the reform activists, and without such moral authority there can be no real gain in freedom. "It is never freedom till you find something you really positively *want to be*," wrote D. H. Lawrence.[196] Without authoritative purpose, there also can be no community. "A community... needs to have something fundamental to do, an organic purpose beyond 'fellowship' that reaffirms the community's need to continue its collective purpose," agrees Lawrence Goodwyn.[197] Given such uncertain and equivocal attitudes of modern liberals about the power and purposes of the state, it thus is not surprising that the unabashed antipathy toward big government voiced by conservatives, however simplistic and contradictory, again triumphed over progressive change in the 1980s.

If the celebration of "nature's way" has yielded more principles of reaction than of action, the appeal to spirituality has constituted more a tonic of consolation than a catalyst to political commitment. However valuable for informing criticism of existing conventions and injustices, nature's promise of peace, solitude, simplicity, health, and immediacy defines all that politics is not and cannot be. "Nature is loved... as the City of God, although, or rather because there is no citizen," instructed Emerson.[198] In other words, the reformers' aesthetic and spiritual dedication to nature is religious in the narrowly critical sense that Marx attacked Christianity.[199] The religion of nature has tapped few social truths; it serves more as a projection of our wishes for heavenly peace so denied by our mortally sinful society. It constitutes an apolitical promise of regeneration which only confounds the already deep divisions between conceptions of the real and ideal, and between spiritual and material life, which characterize liberal culture.[200] The romantic desire to develop our inner rather than social selves, to "flow with the current" of natural order, to take our "modest place in the seemingly stable-state web of living organisms, disturbing as little as possible" all define profoundly passive, antipolitical aspirations for emotional rescue at odds with the reformers' democratic pretenses.[201] At best, the new "anticipatory politics" of promoting health, safety, and life has tended to deal with the symptoms rather than the sources of modern fears. As two poverty lawyers have suggested, the ecological impulse reflects a desire more to relieve ourselves of guilt and anxiety about existing society than to initiate new, more redemptive social relations.[202]

Public interest advocates have from the beginning railed against America's exploitive capitalistic impulses and the regenerative violent lust symbolized by the cowboy. This is apparent in their opposition to the "frontier hangover" of "cowboy economics," of "cowboy-technocrats," and of Ronald Reagan's assumed cowboy identity. Yet far removed from the context of older agrarian radicals, the modern reformers have found in the wilderness no alternative costume of comparable political relevance.[203] In other times, Moses went to the mountaintop to accept God's commandments, the Puritans to build a "city upon a hill," and Martin Luther King to dream of a "beloved community" of justice which must be constructed. More recently, radical ecologists and feminists have developed new perspectives about psychological and physical nature pointing to the need for a thorough reconstruction of human relations among ourselves and with the world. By contrast, David Brower's ecological reform goal is to "let man heal the hurt places, and revere whatever is still miraculously pristine."[204] In nature, the reformers have found a record of reprehensible wrongs, some warnings to abate our carelessness, and some moments of consolation. But the collective political purposes and principles of social justice discovered there have been few. As so often before in America, writes historian Perry Miller, the appeal to nature has "served not so much for individual or artistic salvation as for an assuaging of national anxiety."[205]

Conclusion

It would be somewhat unfair to condemn public interest liberals for failure to live up to the standards implied by their own lofty aspirations. The motivations and results of their actions—including those of strict environmentalists as well as other groups—have transcended in large degree the limits of naturalism explored here. Indeed, the reform activists have been among our best contemporary critics of industrialization, mass culture, and bureaucratic society. Likewise, their manifold contributions to greater safety, security, and fairness for American citizens have been documented throughout this study. In sheer terms of policy achievements, the public interest reform legacy compares quite favorably with that of their liberal precursors. Also, time and experience have led the reformers to consider new commitments deserving much support. However, the liberal activists' rebellion against our inherited political culture appears to have trapped them in a pattern of defensiveness, moral confusion, and dwindling powers of social transformation. Their unease with traditional liberal values and arrangements has been matched by a lack of faith in radical alternatives. As a result, public interest advocates have contributed little either to reviving public faith in progressive politics or to challenging resurgent conservatism within modern America.

The fault is not theirs alone, of course. Our liberal capitalist heritage has provided little in the way of radical democratic parentage. While the modern dissenters have struggled to find cause for conviction, they remain caught in the web of contradictions they seek to break, condemned to repeat the past. Nevertheless, they have fought nobly to affirm the best—faith in open government, the rule of law, individual responsibility—and to repudiate the worst—careless waste, pervasive material greed, structural inequality—in our American legacy. For this alone they deserve praise and support. But whether these commitments can contribute to development of a more comprehensive vision and broader coalition for progressive change remains the greatest challenge facing reform activists.

Postscript

I noted in the Preface that this book developed in large degree from reflections about the legacy of liberal reform politics that evolved out of the 1960s. My discussion of public interest liberalism—admittedly one of the most moderate movements with roots in that era—has allowed me to wrestle at least implicitly with many of the promises and problems surrounding progressive politics in general within contemporary America. Specifically, by delineating at length the most creative and consequential manifestations of public interest advocacy, I have recognized various aspects of the New Left inheritance which also have influenced advocates for many other more or less progressive concerns at home and abroad. But at the same time, my analysis of the important external and self-imposed obstacles impeding the advance of public interest groups need hardly be limited to them alone; such dilemmas have also plagued advocates for other forms of liberal and Left reform politics attempting to challenge the hierarchical structures of power in modern society.

To summarize those themes here would be redundant. Yet it does seem fitting to comment more directly on the larger prospects for progressive political activism in America during the coming years. This invites, first, some speculation about the apparent conservative drift of the national mood during the 1980s which has figured prominently, but received little direct analysis, in the preceding discussion. Second, I offer some suggestions about potential opportunities for a revitalization of Left-oriented politics and the role that public interest liberals might play in such a scenario. My aim is not to predict the political future as much as to offer a brief outline of some factors that are likely to shape the context in which progressive activists will wage their campaigns for political change.

258

Postscript

It is very tempting to take up the issue of conservative revival through lengthy discussion about the nature and impact of Reaganism in the 1980s. Without a doubt, President Reagan's governmental success has been one of the most amazing—and to those on the Left, one of the most disconcerting—phenomena of twentieth-century American politics. Defying the basic axioms of contemporary political science, the president has twice won election by side-stepping party professionals, sharpening ideological debate, and dividing the nation on a host of important social issues.[1] The previous pages have made frequent reference to the ways in which the Reagan administration in particular has both symbolized and consolidated the declining influence of public interest liberals and other progressive policy activists in Washington. Buoyed by high popularity ratings and a short-term political climate of apparent calm, the "Great Communicator" has managed to bury an assault upon the federal regulatory and welfare establishments in bureaucratic obscurity and nostalgic "Happy Days" media gloss. Moreover, some analysts have even interpreted the expressions of public faith in the president's unabashed conservative values and his electoral landslide in 1984 as signs of a long-term realignment in American policy priorities and partisan attachments.[2]

Although the new conservatism has the dizzying spin of a major historical force, however, there are good reasons to believe that this popular phenomenon will not prevail long into the future. First, of course, is the fact that so much has depended on the charismatic personality of the president himself, a fact highlighted by studies repeatedly confirming his high personal popularity even while many of his programs remain markedly unpopular. Consequently, once the mantle of Republican conservatism is passed on to one of the many contending successors, public faith will have to be rewon again largely on new grounds. This raises a second and far more important point. In short, the president and his conservative allies throughout government and society have not actually addressed the sources of the crisis that undercut New Deal liberalism and brought the conservatives to power. Their achievement has not been to end or even to slow the decline of the empire, but only to revitalize citizen *belief* in the old dreams of personal and national triumph which the government simply cannot realize. Even sympathizers admit that the president has appealed more to the desperate hopes of Americans than to their convictions about what is actually attainable.[3] Despite lofty claims of aspiration, the new conservative policy agenda has offered little to deal with, and in fact may have exacerbated further, the complex structural roots of continuing high unemployment, declining produc-

259

tivity, increasing economic inequality, and escalating racial and ethnic frustration at home as well as proliferating military buildup, Third World upheavals, and armed conflicts among nations around the globe. It is true that the president's reign in the mid-1980s has been blessed by a relative respite from the most dramatic domestic ramifications of such problems, but conservative leaders of the future cannot realistically expect the same.[4]

Furthermore, there are good reasons to believe that the diverse array of leaders, organized groups, and mobilized supporters behind the Reagan lurch to the Right will find unity much more difficult to sustain in the future. Above all, it should be recognized that the primary advocates of conservatism in modern America remain almost as divided in substantive belief and fragmented in organization as are their liberal counterparts. As voting analyst Kevin Phillips has argued in a series of influential books, the Republican party that has rallied around Reagan constitutes an uneasy alliance of neoconservative intellectuals, the corporate establishment, small-business owners, New Right moralists, military enthusiasts, and an unstable distribution of working persons across the entire electorate (strongest in the Sun Belt).[5] Although united around apprehensions about American decline and loss of faith in liberals to reverse that decline, the fault lines of dissension among these groups nevertheless remain great on key policy issues and social identity.

The much publicized role of the New Right deserves special mention in this regard. What is most interesting about these groups is that, for all of their radically different aims, they actually mirror the character of rival public interest liberals in some remarkably telling ways. As Richard Viguerie has put it, "all the New Right has done is copy the success of the Old [and New] Left."[6] Indeed, New Right leaders have often been labeled "public interest conservatives."[7] Like their liberal counterparts, New Right groups tend to be mostly elite-dominated, nationally focused, media-oriented, highly adversarial interest-group organizations only very loosely linked to grass-roots constituencies and fiercely jealous of their own autonomy in relation to other organizations (including political parties). There are localist aspects to both movements, but they are not broad or well developed. In fact, public interest conservatives and liberals are alike in that each lack the institutional social foundations typical of their Old Right and Old Left ancestors.

The parallels in substantive orientation between the opposing movements are striking as well. Focusing primarily on social (moral issues of social consumption and reproduction) rather than economic (production) concerns, New Right activists have combined simplistic moralizing, muckraking exposés, and sophisticated pragmatic legal strategy into advocacy for a multitude of diverse issues demanding selective state action much like their more liberal counterparts. In particular, the propensities to prey upon apocalyptic social fears, to focus on narrow aspects of preserving life, and to seek recovery of an idealized past constitute a curious affinity between conservative and liberal reformers.[8] These facts no doubt reveal much about the ubiquitous technobureaucratic forms and psychic apprehensions that dominate America as it drifts toward the twenty-first century. But of more immediate relevance is that many of the same dilemmas I have identified as plaguing public interest liberals—especially concerning their narrow ethical appeal and disaggregating organizational impact— suggest important limitations at the core, if not across the entire spectrum, of modern conservative politics as well. The fact is that Jerry Falwell and other New Right moralists neither have much in common with the corporate managerial elite responsible for much of the antiregulatory backlash nor command much broad public support for their primary issue agenda.[9] Although apparently well entrenched within a solid coalition in the 1980s, therefore, New Right activists before long could well find themselves cast from power into the periphery of organized politics much like those liberals who rode high during the late 1970s.

Finally, the popular roots of partisan allegiance in the nation show few signs of deep or stable transformation.[10] The young have probably been most susceptible to the president's charms and heroic posturing, but their attachments to his policies are weak and their conservatism more a product of personal anxiety about the future than of political conviction. By contrast, most working-class people have voted increasingly Republican for the same reasons that they used to vote Democratic and proudly support liberals—that is, on the basis of perception about who is best able to deliver on basic bread-and-butter issues. The progressive wings of the Democratic party have lost ground in the battle for faith on these issues, but popular perceptions can again surely be altered with new economic developments and effective leadership.[11] Other important factors include that New Right Christian zealotry has prohibited enduring links of the Jewish community to Republican conservatism, that the support of most blacks for progressive candidates and policy proposals seems assured, and that the huge underclass of other poor or excluded citizens remains largely untapped. The core of the New Deal Democratic party—northern Catholics and southern whites—has become a volatile periphery openly hostile to some tenets of progressive liberalism, it is true. But the former still retain sound economic and historical causes for allegiance to Democrats, and Jimmy Carter's narrow victory in 1976 suggests that the white South has not been totally lost.[12] In sum, public support for conservative symbols has undoubtedly grown, but the general mood remains more alienated than truly conservative, more cautious than committed, more hopeful than convinced. It seems that most Americans still want what they have always have wanted—prosperity, security, and peace. Despite the trends of the moment, there simply is little reason to think that progressive activists cannot address these issues in ways that effectively compete with more moderate and conservative rivals in the future.

Whether progressive activists will be able to meet the challenge implied by such potential opportunities raises another set of difficult questions, of course. But there are some reasons for optimism emanating from actual developments among liberal and Left activism in recent years. The most notable fact is that, throughout the nation, myriad progressive groups have been mobilizing and acting on behalf of crucial issues largely outside the glossy mainstream of media politics: the variety of church, campus, and community organizations mobilized around issues of U. S. policy in South Africa and Central America as well as nuclear arms policy; the increasingly effective women's and gay-rights movements; the growing numbers of radical ecologists and advocates of "Green party" politics; the renewed efforts to mobilize blacks, ethnics, and the multitude of the poor by Rev. Jesse Jackson and others; the diverse experiments of working people both in and out of labor unions to reassert themselves; and the legions of intellectuals committed to progressive economic and social policy formulation—all have constituted elements of an increasingly dynamic movement to build an eclectic base of progressive politics in the nation.[13]

Such diverse forms of activism are hardly new, of course. Most of the activists and groups advancing these causes emerged well before the 1980s, and so far have not been able to make much impact on the direction of mainstream public discourse. Indeed, it is highly unlikely that a Left or even progressive liberal agenda will win the support of many Americans any time in the near future. Nevertheless, there have been several important developments in Left politics worth noting that could lead to a more productive working relationship with moderate liberals in coming years. First, years of organizing experience and reflection seem to have nurtured a growing sophistication among many active progressives.[14] Radical advocates have become

262

more technically competent without succumbing to the technocratic impulses of liberal pragmatism and more intellectually coherent without rigidifying into purist dogma. A greater openness to multiple strategies of action on a variety of fronts has signaled both increased flexibility and greater sobriety about the long-term requirements of independent action for political change. Elections are no longer discounted, legal action is valued as a limited strategic resource, and the arts of long-term agenda building have become increasingly respected.[15]

A second, and perhaps more important, development in recent years has been a growing spirit of cooperation and willingness to work together toward common goals among the broad range of diverse groups committed to egalitarian change. Although still hardly unified in values and visions, the Left has become less sectarian and more respectful toward the diverse value orientations necessary for effective progressive advances. This has been demonstrated within the ideological wing of Left advocacy by the increasing dialogue between those progressives of varying types who emphasize traditional structural economic issues and those cultural critics (especially feminists and radical ecologists) who emphasize what used to be considered superstructural issues.[16] Especially encouraging in this regard has been the collapse of the most extreme wings of the disillusioned New Left and parallel rise of more moderate leadership cadres (such as DSOC and NAM) willing to acknowledge the fundamental importance of feminist, ecological, and antimilitarist concerns for social justice. At the level of popular activism, an increasing diversity in Leftist movement building has reflected both these ideological shifts and fundamental changes in society itself. Most important, this has involved a shift from the older focus on radicalizing an immigrant working-class base to an agenda of developing alliances involving non-unionized workers, Leftist professionals, cultural dissidents and antitraditionalists (gays, feminists, utopian ecologists), and nonsocialist "new populist" groups working for progressive change from more traditional church, neighborhood, and other localist bases. Not only has dialogue and coalitional action increased among these diverse groups, but at least some basic consensus has emerged about their shared commitments to protecting individual rights, expanding popular control, and promoting the principle of fairness both in the organization of domestic social institutions and in relations with other nations.[17]

Of course the challenges that confront these diverse groups are quite formidable. Perennial problems still face progressive advocates—

263

especially those of organizational fragmentation, programmatic incoherence, and meager social power with which to fight existing hierarchical structures. The increasing consensus about the need to reappropriate traditional liberal populist discourse for progressive causes could end up coopting both the demands and the identity of Left-oriented political advocates. More important yet, the necessary alliance of the Left with moderate liberal independents and Democrats is likely to remain difficult to achieve. Indeed, the modern legacy of liberal attachment to the cold war, to American world hegemony, and to profit-led economic growth may create a greater obstacle for progressives than that of clearly defined conservative rivals.

It is in this regard that the role of public interest groups and other established liberal reform activists may prove significant. On one hand, they offer to the progressive cause valuable resources of institutional influence and alliance in Washington. In particular, their contribution to battles for legal rights, legislative mandates, and media attention could prove pivotal to both national and local progressive campaigns. On the other hand, liberal reform groups stand to gain much influence in return amid a context of growing success by advocates for egalitarian democratic change within state and society. However, it is also important to recall that the long-developing organizational ties of many public interest liberals to both the established governmental process and a moderate citizen constituency have increasingly rendered their connections to popular movements and progressive ideals difficult to sustain. The bulk of evidence from historical precedent suggests that these latter factors are likely to win out, thus institutionalizing further the role of most public interest liberals as specialized interest-group participants in a perpetually volatile American political system.[18] Yet history does not always repeat itself, and a majority of those reformers whose voices have been heard throughout this book retain a striking independence of will. Many of us thus will be watching for and supporting more creative actions toward democratic change from them in the future.

Notes

Introduction

1. Robert Buckhorn, *Nader: The People's Lawyer*, p. 48.
2. 1977 *ACLU Annual Report*, p. 6.
3. Quoted in Bill Keller, "Environmental Movement Checks Its Pulse and Finds Its Obituaries Are Premature," p. 214; and Timothy Clark, "After a Decade of Doing Battle, Public Interest Groups Show Their Age," p. 1136.
4. Jeffrey Berry, *Lobbying for the People*, p. 7. See also Andrew McFarland, *Public Interest Lobbies: Decision Making on Energy*, pp. 40–41.
5. Mancur Olson, *The Logic of Collective Action*, p. 15. See also Burton Weisbrod et al., *Public Interest Law: An Economic and Institutional Analysis*, pp. 4–29.
6. Council for Public Interest Law, "Survey," January 1980, p. 2. Andrew McFarland defines a public interest group as "one that seems to represent the general interests of the whole public; does *not* chiefly represent some specific economic interest; and is *not* a lobby in one of the following traditional categories: religion, ethnic groups, race, regional interests, women's rights, vocational groups, and perhaps others." Quoted in Clark, "After a Decade," p. 1138. On the difference between public and private interests, see E. E. Schattschneider, *The Semi-Sovereign People*, pp. 22–24.
7. My classification clearly includes opponents of nuclear energy production, but pacifist protestors of nuclear weapons development (the Peace Movement) are more problematic. Many public interest liberals strongly support the latter cause both formally and informally, to be sure. However, because the latter movement arose later in time and extends to a broad diversity of religious and other group organizations outside of traditional public interest activity, the anti-nuclear weapons activists are not considered strictly as part of the study provided here. See Constance E. Cook, *Nuclear Power and Legal Advocacy*.
8. Berry, *Lobbying*, p. 94.
9. This demarcation of liberal public interest activists is important, we shall see, because a host of conservative public interest groups emerged in the 1970s to do battle with them through imitation of their own favorite strategies. For discussion, see Karen O'Connor and Lee Epstein, "Rebalancing the Scales of Justice: Assessment of Public Interest Law." See also the Postscript to this study.

265

10. In this sense, the movement could be understood to constitute the national wing of what Harry Boyte has called the "backyard revolution" in American politics. See Chapter 4 of this volume and Harry C. Boyte, *The Backyard Revolution: Understanding the New Citizen Movement.*

11. See Chapter 5 of this volume for discussion of this topic.

12. Berry's valuable *Lobbying for the People* and Andrew McFarland's fine *Public Interest Lobbies* are two good examples of this approach. For a classic statement of the model, see David Truman, *The Governmental Process.* For the most sophisticated critical discussion, see David Vogel, "Promoting Pluralism: The Politics of the Public Interest Movement," pp. 609–628.

13. See, for example, Weisbrod et al., *Public Interest Law;* Joel Handler, *Social Movements and the Legal System: A Theory of Law Reform and Social Change;* Lettie M. Wenner, *The Environmental Decade in Court;* Bruce A. Ackerman and William T. Hassler, *Clean Coal/Dirty Air.*

14. This approach has been adopted in some degree by Handler, *Social Movements,* and Robert Holsworth, *Public Interest Liberalism and the Crisis of Affluence.* It is encouraged also by Simon Lazarus, *The Genteel Populists,* although formal analysis of "social movements" is not developed in his nonacademic treatment. My analysis largely parallels Jo Freeman's analysis of the women's movement in her *The Politics of Women's Liberation.*

15. John D. McCarthy and Mayer N. Zald, "Resource Mobilization and Social Movements: A Partial Theory," pp. 1212–1241.

16. Sociologists label such groups individually as "social movement organizations" and collectively as a "social movement industry." Ibid., pp. 1218–1219.

17. The most consistent identification of "them" has been by so-called neoconservatives. Public interest activists form the nucleus of the liberal "new class" that so invokes the wrath of such thinkers. For example, Samuel Huntington identifies specifically "cause organizations... such as Common Cause, Nader groups, and environmental groups" as the unified opposition. In Crozier et al., *The Crisis of Democracy,* p. 61.

18. Quoted in Al Gordon, "Public Interest Lobbies: Nader and Common Cause Become Permanent Features," pp. 1202–1203.

19. The Consumers Union, "The Rise of Business Lobbying," in Mark Green and Robert Massie, Jr., eds., *The Big Business Reader: Essays on Corporate America,* p. 255. Influential movement leader David Cohen similarly notes that "there is a historic connecting point between the public interest movement and the rise of issue politics in the late 1960s.... Three areas stand out: the environmental push, Ralph Nader's transformation of the consumer movement, and Common Cause's building on institutional and governmental reform, focusing on abuses of power, money, secrecy." "The Public Interest," p. 5.

20. Berry, *Lobbying,* p. 43. Edgar Shor notes that "a fairly wide consensus exists on the conception of the public good urged upon agencies by consumer advocates, environmentalists, civil rights leaders and champions of the 'disadvantaged' generally." "Symposium: Public Interest Representation and the Federal Agencies," p. 131. Sociologists define social movements themselves in terms of such common ideas. As McCarthy and Zald put it, a social movement is characterized by "a set of opinions and beliefs in a population which represents preference for changing some elements of the social structure and/or reward distribution of a society." "Resource Mobilization," pp. 1217–1218.

21. For a typical statement of this understanding of ideology, see Irving Kristol

and Daniel Bell, eds., "What Is the Public Interest?" *The Public Interest* 1 (Fall 1965), pp. 3–4. Kristol is one of the most outspoken critics inveighing against the alleged ideological tendencies of public interest reformers as well. See as example his *Two Cheers for Capitalism*, pp. 6–7, 40. Public interest liberals themselves demonstrate this attitude toward ideology also. A co-worker of Nader says that "in the radical movement, ideological considerations come first. In the Nader movement, the issue comes first.... the work is done here on the basis that social theory will come out of the accumulation of facts." Quoted in Boyte, *Backyard Revolution*, p. 88.

22. Sheldon Wolin, *Politics and Vision*, pp. 17–21.

23. Charles W. Anderson, "The Logic of Public Problems: Evaluation in Comparative Policy Research," in Douglas Ashford, ed., *Comparing Public Policies: New Concepts and Methods* (Beverly Hills: Sage Publications, 1978), pp. 20, 33. See also Hanna F. Pitkin, *Wittgenstein and Justice* (Berkeley: University of California Press, 1972).

24. My personal contact with public interest leaders has been facilitated through two general endeavors. First, I spent the better part of the summer of 1980 in Washington, D.C., collecting materials and interviewing staff members of over thirty prominent public interest groups. Second, I gained considerable information from personal interviews as well as secondary resources during a year (the 1979–80 academic year) of field research work for Eugene Bardach and Robert Kagan's *Going by the Book: The Problem of Regulatory Unreasonableness*.

25. Clifford Geertz, "Thick Description: Toward an Interpretive Theory of Culture," in *The Interpretation of Cultures* (New York: Basic Books, 1973), pp. 3–20.

26. Ronald Dworkin, *Taking Rights Seriously*. I do not comment directly on Dworkin's specific ideas in my discussion, but only on the faith in legal rights advocacy itself shared by Dworkin with many other liberals. See Peter Gabel's "Book Review," *Harvard Law Review* 91 (1977), pp. 302–315.

27. In this sense, public interest liberals to a large degree have been both handicapped and empowered by what Stuart Scheingold has labeled the "Myth of Rights." *The Politics of Rights: Lawyers, Public Policy, and Political Change.*

28. Quoted from Sierra Club executive director Michael McCloskey's "Foreword," in John G. Mitchell and Constance L. Stallings, eds., *Ecotactics*, p. 11.

Part One: Preface

1. Truman, *The Governmental Process*, pp. 52–56. See also Berry, *Lobbying*, chap. 2.

2. Hayden quoted in Massimo Teodori, *The New Left: A Documentary History*, p. 169.

3. Andrew McFarland calls this "civic skepticism," although he focuses less on the actual causes of this pessimism than emphasized here. See *Public Interest Lobbies*, pp. 12–21. See also Alan Wolfe, *The Limits of Legitimacy: Political Contradictions of Contemporary Capitalism.*

4. The rise of anticorporate campaigns in the 1960s is discussed in excellent fashion by David Vogel, *Lobbying the Corporation*, chaps. 1–2. Quote is from Vogel, p. 30. See Teodori, *The New Left*, pp. 93–120.

Notes to Part One Preface

5. Gitlin quoted in Teodori, *The New Left*, p. 191; see also pp. 169–196, 240–270.

6. For a documentation and defense of such strategy for "poor people's movements," see Frances Fox Piven and Richard A. Cloward, *Poor People's Movements: Why They Succeed, How They Fail*. For critical reflections, see Todd Gitlin, *The Whole World Is Watching: Mass Media in the Making and Unmaking of the New Left*.

7. Staughton Lynd, quoted in Teodori, *The New Left*, p. 231.

8. Robert Rabin, "Lawyers for Social Change: Perspectives on Public Interest Law," p. 207–261.

9. Tigar quoted in Robert Lefcourt, ed., *Law against the People: Essays to Demystify Law, Order, and the Courts*, p. 12.

10. The ideas expressed in this paragraph, especially concerning the levels of generations, owe much to discussions with Charles Halpern and Nan Aron of INSPIRE in July 1980. For a parallel development in the women's movement, see Jo Freeman, *The Politics of Women's Liberation*. It should be noted here that the emergence of the women's movement has been quite influential to public interest activism generally.

11. Sanford Jaffe, *Public Interest Law: Five Years Later*, p. 6.

12. Moore quoted in Vogel, *Lobbying the Corporation*, p. 73.

13. Nader quoted in Buckhorn, *Nader: The People's Lawyer*, pp. 172–173, 204.

14. McCloskey, "Foreword," in Mitchell and Stallings, eds., p. 11.

15. John Gardner, *In Common Cause*, pp. 72–76.

16. Statistics are provided by Jeffrey Berry's surveys, *Lobbying*, pp. 85, 88, 94. See also Joel F. Handler et al., *Lawyers and the Pursuit of Legal Rights*.

17. David Cohen, "The Public Interest," p. 6; Robert Cameron Mitchell, "How 'Soft,' 'Deep,' or 'Left'? Present Constituencies in the Environmental Movement for Certain World Views," p. 346.

18. Berry, *Lobbying*, pp. 84–96, 292.

19. Ibid., p. 102.

20. On the "new class," see B. Bruce-Briggs, *The New Class?* (New Brunswick, N. J.: Transaction Books, 1979).

21. Max Weber, in Hans H. Gerth and C. Wright Mills, eds., *From Max Weber* (New York: Oxford University Press, 1972), pp. 180–194.

Chapter 1. The Campaign for Reform

1. McFarland, *Public Interest Lobbies*, p. 16.

2. Michael McCloskey, "Foreword," in Mitchell and Stallings, eds., p. 11.

3. Gardner, *In Common Cause*, p. 99; idem., "Excerpted Remarks," in Garrett De Bell, ed., *The Environmental Handbook*, p. 4; Ralph Nader, "Introduction," in Mitchell and Stallings, eds., p. 13.

4. Donald Schwartz, quoted in Vogel, *Lobbying the Corporation*, p. 73; David Riley, "Taming GM . . . and Ford, Union Carbide, U.S. Steel, Dow Chemical," in Bruce Wasserstein and Mark Green, eds., *With Justice for Some: An Indictment of the Law by Young Advocates*, pp. 207–243.

5. De Bell, "Foreword," in De Bell, ed., p. xiv; Ralph Nader, ed., *The Consumer and Corporate Accountability*, p. 3.

6. Nader, "Introduction," in Green and Massie, eds., p. 1.

268

7. Jon Breslaw, "Economics and Ecosystem," in De Bell, ed., p. 104; Nader, "Introduction," in Mitchell and Stallings, eds., p. 14. See also Barry Commoner, *The Poverty of Power* (New York: Bantam Books, 1976), pp. 221–249.

8. See Nader, ed., *Consumer and Corporate Accountability*, pp. 5–18; Green and Massie, eds., *Big Business Reader*, pp. 1–56, 475–558; Ralph Nader, Mark Green, and Joel Seligman, *Taming the Giant Corporation*, pp. 198–238.

9. Nader et al., *Taming*, p. 211; Lippmann cited in Green and Massie, eds., *Big Business Reader*, p. 475.

10. Michael Pertschuk and Kenneth M. Davidson, "What's Wrong with Conglomerate Mergers?" in Green and Massie, eds., p. 497.

11. See Nader et al., *Taming*, pp. 150–153; Nader, ed., *Consumer and Corporate Accountability*, pp. 86–126.

12. Beverly C. Moore, Jr., "The Lawyer's Response: The Public Interest Law Firm," in Wasserstein and Green, eds., p. 301.

13. Nader et al., *Taming*, p. 151. See also Thomas Turner, "Ecopornography," in De Bell, ed., pp. 263–267.

14. Adolph A. Berle, Jr., and Gardiner C. Means, *The Modern Corporation and Private Property.* See Pertschuk and Davidson, "What's Wrong with Conglomerate Mergers?" in Green and Massie, eds., pp. 484–493; Nader et al., *Taming*, chap. 4; Donald E. Schwartz, "Toward New Corporate Goals: Co-Existence with Society," pp. 57–104; Vogel, *Lobbying the Corporation*, chap. 3.

15. Nader et al., *Taming*, p. 81.

16. Robert Fellmeth, "The Regulatory–Industrial Complex," in Wasserstein and Green, eds., p. 274. In the same volume, see also David Riley's discussion of management power at Honeywell: "Taming GM," pp. 207–208.

17. Gardner, *In Common Cause*, p. 69.

18. Nader quoted in Lazarus, *The Genteel Populists*, p. 4. The "new orthodoxy" of the reformers is "a cynical vision of government as captive of corporate power," says Lazarus.

19. Common Cause, *Government Subsidy Squeeze*, p. 69.

20. *Media Access Project 1980 Annual Report*, pp. 34–36; quote on p. 35.

21. Mark Green, James Fallows, and David Zwick, *Who Runs Congress?* See also Common Cause, *How Money Talks in Congress*. Gardner quoted in the brochure "Common Cause: Modern Americans Fighting for Principles as Old as the Republic."

22. Mark Green and Andrew Buchsbaum, *The Corporate Lobbies: Political Profiles of the Business Roundtable and the Chamber of Commerce*, pp. 7, 4.

23. *CFA News* 4/5 (1980).

24. Ibid. See also generally Green and Buchsbaum, *The Corporate Lobbies;* and Common Cause, *How Money Talks in Congress*.

25. See Common Cause, *Government Subsidy Squeeze*.

26. The Consumers Union, "The Rise of Business Lobbying," in Green and Massie, eds., p. 253.

27. Ibid., p. 258.

28. Gardner, *In Common Cause*, p. 37.

29. David Cohen, "Reviving the Political Party System." For a scholarly review of these arguments. see Austin Ranney, "Political Parties: Reform and Decline," in Anthony King, ed., *The New American Political System*, p. 89.

30. Gardner quoted in Theodore Jacqueney, "Common Cause Lobbyists Focus on the Structure and Process of Government," p. 1304.

31. Nader, ed., *Consumer and Corporate Accountability*, p. 369; Gardner, *In Common Cause*, p. 20.

32. Schwartz, "Symposium—Federal Chartering of Corporations," p. 73. See also Joseph Onek and Simon Lazarus, "The Regulators and the People," pp. 1070, 1073.

33. Fellmeth, "The Regulatory–Industrial Complex," in Wasserstein and Green, eds., p. 247.

34. For example, Robert Rabin notes that "organizations do not easily depart from established patterns of activity." "Lawyers," p. 244. See also Gardner, *In Common Cause*, p. 99.

35. Joseph Sax, *Defending the Environment: A Handbook for Citizen Action*, pp. 53–62; *Environmental Action Report*, June 1980, p. 11.

36. Donald K. Ross, *A Public Citizen's Action Manual*, p. 225.

37. Gardner quoted in McFarland, "Common Cause," p. 84, unpublished manuscript version of book later published as *Common Cause: Lobbying in the Public Interest*. See Gardner, *In Common Cause*, pp. 80–81.

38. This chant appears frequently in public interest publications.

39. Mark Green, "Why the Consumer Bill Went Down," pp. 198–201. For two interesting interpretations of this problem, see Olson, *The Logic of Collective Action;* Joshua Cohen and Joel Rogers, *On Democracy*, chap. 3.

40. Quoted in McFarland, "Common Cause," p. 84.

41. Edward Berlin et al., "Consumers of the World Unite," in Wasserstein and Green, eds., p. 288.

42. Ralph Nader and Cirardeau Spann, "The Justices Slam the Door," pp. 495–498.

43. Fellmeth, "The Regulatory–Industrial Complex," in Wasserstein and Green, eds., p. 254; Nader et al., *Taming*, p. 132.

44. Justice Skelly Wright quoted in Lazarus, *The Genteel Populists*, p. 243; Nader, "Introduction," in Mitchell and Stallings, eds., p. 15; Fellmeth, "The Regulatory–Industrial Complex," in Wasserstein and Green, eds., p. 254.

45. Lazarus, *The Genteel Populists*, p. 223.

46. Riley, "Taming GM," in Wasserstein and Green, eds., p. 208.

47. Harrison Wellford, "On How to Be a Constructive Nuisance," in De Bell, ed., p. 274; Nader et all, *Taming*, p. 8.

48. Mark Green, *The Other Government: The Unseen Power of Washington Lawyers*. Ralph Nader and Mark Green, eds., *Verdicts on Lawyers*; Eric Van de Loon, "The Law School of Response," in Wasserstein and Green, eds., p. 335.

49. Nader et al., *Taming*, p. 8.

50. Quoted in McFarland, "Common Cause," p. 80. Gardner, *In Common Cause*, pp. 24–25, 33.

51. Nader, ed., *Consumer and Corporate Accountability*, pp. viii–ix.

52. Gardner, *In Common Cause*, p. 18.

53. Sax, *Defending*, p. xi.

54. Gardner, *In Common Cause*, p. 25.

55. Riley, "Taming GM," in Wasserstein and Green, eds., pp. 240–241.

56. Gardner, *In Common Cause*, p. 88; Ralph Nader, "Consumerism and Legal Services: The Merging of Movements," p. 251.

57. Berry, *Lobbying*, p. 34; Council for Public Interest Law, *Balancing the Scales of Justice: Financing Public Interest Law in America*, p. 29.

58. Marion Edey, "Eco-Politics and the League of Conservation Voters," in De Bell, ed., p. 313.

59. McFarland, *Public Interest Lobbies*, p. 2.

60. Gardner, *In Common Cause*, pp. 85–91.

61. *Environmental Action 1979 Annual Report.*

62. Quoted in Boyte, *Backyard Revolution*, p. 92.

63. Jeffrey Berry, "Lessons from Chairman Ralph, Nader's Secrets of Success." See also Gardner, *In Common Cause*, pp. 18–22.

64. Gardner, *In Common Cause*, pp. 74, 91.

65. McCloskey, "Foreword," in Mitchell and Stallings, eds., p. 12; Riley, "Taming GM," in Wasserstein and Green, eds., p. 241.

66. McFarland, *Public Interest Lobbies*, pp. 54–56.

67. Berry, *Lobbying*, p. 28.

68. Big Business Day Bulletin, 1980.

69. Riley, "Taming GM," in Wasserstein and Green, eds., p. 235; Gardner, *In Common Cause*, p. 89.

70. Ralph Nader, "Freedom from Information: The Act and the Agencies"; Schwartz quoted in Vogel, *Lobbying*, p. 78; *Media Access Project 1979 Annual Report.*

71. Nader, "Consumerism," p. 253; Gardner, *In Common Cause*, p. 88.

72. Gardner, *In Common Cause*, p. 89; Riley, "Taming GM," in Wasserstein and Green, eds., p. 243; Lazarus, *The Genteel Populists*, p. xiv.

73. Tony Wagner, "The Ecology of Revolution," in Mitchell and Stallings, eds., p. 45; also, "Editor's Note," p. 5 of same volume.

74. Edey, "Eco-Politics and the League of Conservation Voters," in De Dell, ed., p. 316; David Cohen, "The Neo-Conservatives: Professional Pessimists." Gardner claims that "the light of day has a marvelously cleansing effect on politicians." *In Common Cause*, p. 89.

75. Theodore Jacqueney, "Common Cause," p. 1302.

76. Berry explores this point well in *Lobbying*, p. 179.

77. Wellford, "On How to Be a Constructive Nuisance," in De Bell, ed., pp. 268–284.

78. Amory Lovins, "Energy Strategy: The Road Not Taken," *Foreign Affairs* 55 (October 1976), pp. 68–96.

79. Berry, "Lessons."

80. See Lazarus for extensive critical explication of this theme. *The Genteel Populists*, chaps. 4–5.

81. De Bell, "Eco-Tactics," in De Bell, ed., p. 285.

82. Berlin et al., "Consumers of the World Unite," in Wasserstein and Green, eds., p. 279.

83. *Public Citizen 1979 Annual Report.*

84. See Berlin, et al., "Consumers of the World Unite," in Wasserstein and Green, eds., p. 279; Green, Fallows, and Zwick, *Who Runs Congress?*, p. 1.

85. Hazel Henderson, *Creating Alternative Futures*, p. 7.

86. Gardner, *In Common Cause*, p. 104.

87. Ibid., p. 88; Nader, "Introduction," in Ross, *Action Manual*, p. xiii.

88. De Bell, "Foreword," in De Bell, ed., p. xv; Nader, "Introduction," in Ross, *Action Manual*, p. xv.

89. John G. Mitchell, "Editor's Note," in Mitchell and Stallings, eds., p. 5.

90. Wellford, "On How to Be a Constructive Nuisance," in De Bell, ed., p. 269; Nader, "Introduction," in Ross, *Action Manual*, p. xv.

91. Gardner, *In Common Cause*, p. 78.

92. Ibid., p. 85.

93. Berry, *Lobbying*, p. 60; De Bell, *The Environmental Handbook*, p. 340.

94. Berry, *Lobbying*, pp. 18–44; Council for Public Interest Law, *Balancing the Scales*, pp. 245–261.

95. Berry, *Lobbying*, pp. 72–76; Council for Public Interest Law, *Balancing the Scales*, pp. 226–244; James W. Singer, "Liberal Public Interest Law Firms Face Budgetary, Ideological Challenge," pp. 2052–2056; Clark, "After a Decade." See also Jack L. Walker, "The Origins and Maintenance of Interest Groups in America," pp. 390–406.

96. Berry, *Lobbying*, pp. 45–59; Richard Corrigan, "Public Interest Law Firms Win Battle with IRS Over Exemptions, Deductions," pp. 2451–2459; Charles Goetz and Gordon Brady, "Environmental Policy Foundations and the Tax Treatment of Citizen Interest Groups," pp. 211–231; Oliver A. Houck, "With Charity for All."

97. Nader, "Consumerism," p. 251. See also Robert Leflar and Martin H. Rogol, "Consumer Participation in the Regulation of Utilities: A Model Act," pp. 235–297; Andrew Sharpless and Sarah Gallup, *Banding Together: How Check-offs Will Revolutionize the Consumer Movement*.

98. Nader, "Introduction," in Ross, *Action Manual*, p. xiii.

99. Wellford, "On How to Be a Constructive Nuisance," in De Bell, ed., p. 270.

100. Nader, "Consumerism," p. 253; Gardner, *In Common Cause*, p. 94.

101. Quoted in Berry, *Lobbying*, p. 25.

102. See Council for Public Interest Law, *Balancing the Scales*, pp. 28–29; Nader, "Consumerism," and Nader and Green, eds., *Verdicts on Lawyers* generally; Lazarus, *The Genteel Populists*, chap. 10.

103. Gardner, *In Common Cause*, p. 89.

104. Berry, *Lobbying*, p. 255; Gardner, *In Common Cause*, p. 90.

105. This is the obsessive theme of Lazarus's *The Genteel Populists* in particular.

106. McCloskey, "Foreword," in Mitchell and Stallings, eds., p. 11; Sax, *Defending*, p. 148. The doctrine of public rights is best explained and defended by the arguments of Sax, "The Public Trust Doctrine in Natural Resource Law," p. 471. See also Christopher Stone, *Should Trees Have Standing? Toward Legal Rights for Natural Objects*. Sax concludes his argument about rights for the environment with a general recognition of similar public-rights claims: "Everything that has been said here is adaptable to the problems of housing and welfare, to the proliferation of shoddy merchandise, and the miserable charade that too frequently passes for public regulation of business and the professions." *Defending*, p. 245. See also Nader, "Consumerism," and Wellford, "On How to Be a Constructive Nuisance," in De Bell, ed., p. 270.

107. Paul Ehrlich, "Man's Inalienable Rights," in De Bell, ed., p. 233.

108. Rene Dubos, "Limits of Adaptability," in De Bell, ed., p. 27.

109. Gardner, *In Common Cause*, p. 44; Nader, "A Citizen's Communications Agenda," p. 3; Nader, *Public Interest Perspectives*, p. 2.

110. Gardner, *In Common Cause*, p. 48.

111. Chet Atkins and Wendy Kimball, "State Legislatures," in Mitchell and Stallings, eds., p. 130; Sax, *Defending*, p. 239.

112. See Sax, *Defending*, pp. 158–174; Vogel, "Promoting Pluralism."

113. David Cohen, "Reviving the Political Party System"; Gardner, *In Common Cause*, p. 21.

114. For an overview and analysis of these transformations, see Austin Ranney, "Political Parties: Reform and Decline," in King, ed., pp. 213–248. See also the criticism by Everett Carl Ladd, Jr., "Reform Is Wrecking the U. S. Party System," *Fortune* 96 (November 1977), pp. 177–188.

115. See Joel L. Fleischman and Carol S. Greenwald, "Public Interest Litigation and Political Finance Reform," pp. 114–123.

116. See Berry, *Lobbying*, chap. 8.

117. See Theodore Jacqueney, "Common Cause," pp. 1294–1297. For an overview of the changes within Congress in the last decade, see Laurence C. Dodd and Bruce I. Oppenheimer, eds., "The House in Transition: Change and Consolidation," pp. 31–61; and Robert H. Davidson, "Two Avenues of Change: House and Senate Reorganization," both in Dodd and Oppenheimer, eds., *Congress Reconsidered* (Washington: Congressional Quarterly Press, 1981); James Sundquist, *The Decline and Resurgence of Congress;* Schuck is quoted in "Symposium," *Public Administration Review*, March/April 1977, p. 136. On the influential role of Common Cause, see McFarland, *Common Cause*, chaps. 7–8.

118. Ernest Gellhorn, "Public Participation in Administrative Proceedings," p. 359; Council for Public Interest Law, *Balancing the Scales*, p. 182; Lynn Cunningham et al., *Strengthening Citizen Access and Government Accountability.*

119. *Scenic Hudson Preservation Conference v. FPC* (1965). See Gellhorn, "Public Participation," generally, and "The Judicialization of Politics" in Chapter 2 of this volume.

120. Cunningham et al., *Strengthening*, p. 165. See also Nader, "Freedom from Information."

121. Walter Rosenbaum, *The Politics of Environmental Concern*, p. 268; Paul Culhane, "Natural Resources Policy: Procedural Change and Substantive Environmentalism," in Theodore Lowi and Alan Stone, eds., *Nationalizing Government: Public Policies in America* (Beverly Hills, Calif.: Sage Publications, 1978), p. 212. See also Frederick R. Anderson, *NEPA in the Courts;* Wenner, *The Environmental Decade in Court.*

122. Joseph A. Pika, "Interest Groups and the Executive," in Allen J. Cigler and Burdett A. Loomis, eds., *Interest Group Politics*, p. 307.

123. Cunningham et al., *Strengthening;* Richard Frank et al., *Public Participation in the Policy Formulation Process.* David Vogel explores the "reverse capture" logic in his penetrating essay, "Promoting Pluralism."

124. Juan Cameron, "Nader's Raiders Are inside the Gates," pp. 252–262; *CFA News* 4/5 (1980), p. 4; David Broder, *Changing of the Guard: Power and Leadership in America*, p. 237.

125. See Richard Leighton, "Consumer Protection Agency Propositions: The Origins of the Species," pp. 269–311; Cunningham et al., *Strengthening*, pp. 62–69. Both the titles "Consumer Protection Agency" and "Agency for Consumer Advocacy" have been used in proposed legislation.

126. Nader quoted in Philip Shabecoff, "Bill to Create a Consumer Agency Alive Again, with Good Prospects," p. 37.

127. George McGovern quoted in affirmation by Sax, *Defending*, p. xii.

128. Quoted in Clark, "After a Decade," p. 1141.

129. See Karen Orren, "Standing to Sue," pp. 723–741; Richard Stewart, "The Reformation of American Administrative Law," pp. 1669–1813.

130. 405 U.S. 722 (1972). For discussion, see Culhane, "Natural Resources Policy," in Lowi and Stone, eds., pp. 201–262.

131. Jules Bernstein et al., "Corporate Democracy Act," in Green and Massie, eds., p. 605.

132. See Cunningham et al., *Strengthening*, pp. 244–245; Berlin et al., "Consumers of the World Unite," in Wasserstein and Green, eds., pp. 279–333; Charles Halpern and John Cunningham, "Reflections On the New Public Interest Law: Theory and Practice at the New Center for Law and Social Policy," p. 1116; Stephen C Yeazell, "Group Litigation to Class Action," p. 1067; Barry Boyer and Errol Meidinger, "Privatizing Regulatory Enforcement: A Preliminary Assessment of Citizen Suits under Federal Environmental Laws."

133. Nader et al., *Taming*, p. 8, and the entire work generally. See Vogel, *Lobbying the Corporation*, for a historical analysis of early efforts.

134. Riley, "Taming GM," in Wasserstein and Green, eds., p. 219. See Charles Peters and Taylor Branch, *Blowing the Whistle*.

135. Quote from Moore, "The Lawyer's Response," in Wasserstein and Green, eds., p. 305.

136. Paglin and Shor, "Regulatory Agency Responses," p. 141; Lazarus, *The Genteel Populists*, p. 230.

137. Quoted in Vogel, "Promoting Pluralism," unpublished paper, p. 25. On postal rate reduction, see Clark, "After a Decade," p. 1138.

138. Philip Schrag and Michael Meltsner, "Class Action: A Way to Beat Bureaucracies without Increasing Them," p. 55; Nader, "Consumerism," p. 251; Moore, "The Lawyer's Response," in Wasserstein and Green, eds., p. 306.

139. *Public Citizen 1979 Annual Report* (in the section "Congress Watch").

140. Cunningham et al., *Strengthening*, p. 105, from the case of *Brandenburgh v. Thompson*. The logic of "private attorney general" was articulated best in *Office of Communication, United Church of Christ v. FCC* (259 F 2d 994, 1003 D.C. Cir. 1966): "The theory that the Commission can always effectively represent the listener interests . . . without the aid and participation of legitimate listener representatives [acting as] private attorney general . . . is no longer a valid assumption which stands up under realities of actual experience [and] neither we nor the commission can continue to rely on it."

141. *Alyeska Pipeline Service Co. v. Wilderness Society* 95 S. Ct. 1612 (1975). See Council for Public Interest Law, *Balancing the Scales*, pp. 312–324, 348–350; "Note: Will the Sun Rise Again for the Equal Access to Justice Act?" *Brooklyn Law Review* 48 (Winter 1982), p. 265; Karen O'Conner and Lee Epstein, "Bridging the Gap: Judicial Interest Groups and the Erosion of the Americal Rule Governing Awards of Attorney Fees."

142. Council for Public Interest Law, *Balancing the Scales*, p. 342.

143. For a review of agency funding schemes, see the Paglin and Shor, "Regulatory Agency Responses," pp. 140–148.

144. Onek and Lazarus, "The Regulators and the People," p. 1096.

145. McFarland, *Public Interest Lobbies*, p. 9; Reilly quoted in Keller, "Environmental Movement Checks Its Pulse," p. 216; Nader quoted in *Harvard Law School Record*, 1969, Vol. 29, no. 3.

146. *Environmental Action 1979 Annual Report;* Council for Public Interest Law, *Balancing the Scales*, p. 165.

147. Sax, *Defending*, p. 115; Gerald R. Rosen, "The Growing Clout of 'Do Good' Lobbies," p. 46; Cohen quoted in McFarland, "Common Cause," p. 6.

148. Schwartz quoted in Vogel, *Lobbying the Corporation*, p. 74.
149. Gardner, *In Common Cause*, p. 97; Council for Public Interest Law, *Balancing the Scales*, p. ix.
150. Gardner, *In Common Cause*, p. 110; Riley is quoting A. A. Berle, "Taming GM," in Wasserstein and Green, eds., p. 207.

Chapter 2. The New Liberal Philosophy

1. Vogel, "Promoting Pluralism," p. 616.
2. Nader et al., *Taming*, p. 16.
3. Nader, "Introduction," in Ross, *Public Citizen's Action Manual*, p. vii.
4. "Common Cause: Modern Americans Fighting for Principles" (brochure).
5. For general discussions, see Richard Hofstadter, *The American Political Tradition;* Bernard Bailyn, *The Ideological Origins of American Politics* (Cambridge: Harvard University Press, 1967); Louis Hartz, *The Liberal Tradition in America.* For discussion of Nader as a classical liberal, see Holsworth, *Public Interest Liberalism.*
6. Kenneth and Patricia Dolbeare, *American Ideologies*, p. 81.
7. Riley, "Taming GM," in Wasserstein and Green, eds., p. 208. See also p. 241.
8. Lazarus, *The Genteel Populists*, p. 16.
9. Quoted in Lawrence Goodwyn, *The Populist Moment*, p. 1.
10. Gardner, quoted in McFarland, "Common Cause," p. 80.
11. Richard Hofstadter, *The Age of Reform*, p. 5.
12. Wellford, "On How to Be a Constructive Nuisance," in De Bell, ed., p. 272.
13. Berry, "Lessons." For a general discussion of the instrumentalist perspective in the liberal tradition, see Christopher Lasch, *The Agony of the American Left*, pp. 5–12.
14. Gardner, *In Common Cause*, pp. 38, 41; Hofstadter, *Age of Reform*, p. 262.
15. Lincoln Steffens quoted in Christopher Lasch, *The New Radicalism, 1889–1963*, p. 265.
16. Lazarus, *The Genteel Populists*, p. 10.
17. See Hofstadter's *The Age of Reform*, generally. See also Grant McConnell, *Private Power and American Democracy*, p. 32.
18. Green and Massie, eds., *Big Business Reader;* environmentalist (NRDC) quoted in McFarland, *Public Interest Lobbies*, p. 16. See Beverly C. Moore, "The Lawyer's Response," in Wasserstein and Green, eds., generally.
19. Charles E. Little, "Epilogue," in Mitchell and Stallings, eds., p. 244.
20. Jeffrey Berry, "Lessons."
21. Hofstadter, *Age of Reform*, p. 186; Royce quoted on p. 202.
22. See Lasch generally in *The New Radicalism*, as well as Hofstadter, *Age of Reform*, p. 198. Another interesting source on muckraking is Walter Lippmann, *Drift and Mastery.* See Lazarus, *The Genteel Populists*, p. 94, for a contemporary example.
23. Nader quoted in Charles McCarry, *Citizen Nader*, pp. 218–219. See also Lasch, *Agony of the American Left*, pp. 254, 262; Hofstadter, *Age of Reform*, pp. 201–202.
24. See Hartz, *Liberal Tradition in America;* Michael P. Rogin, *The Intellectuals and McCarthy: The Radical Specter*, pp. 35–58.
25. William James and Charles Sanders Peirce quoted in R. Jeffrey Lustig,

Notes to Chapter 2

Corporate Liberalism: The Origins of Modern American Political Theory, 1890–1920, p. 156.

26. John Dewey, *Reconstruction in Philosophy* (Boston: Beacon Press, 1948), p. 156. See Lustig, *Corporate Liberalism,* pp. 150–194.

27. Sax, *Defending,* p. 235. See John Guinther, *The Moralists and Managers* (New York: Anchor Press, 1976).

28. Gardner, *In Common Cause,* p. 85.

29. On Nader, see Holsworth, *Public Interest Liberalism,* pp. 10–16; Gardner, *In Common Cause,* pp. 87, 101. See also Wellford, "On How to Be a Constructive Nuisance," in De Bell, ed., p. 278.

30. Nader quoted in Jack Newfield, "Nader's Raiders: The Lone Ranger Gets a Posse," p. 56 ff.

31. From "In Common," 1980 Common Cause newsletter.

32. Gardner, *In Common Cause,* pp. 101, 87.

33. Rabin, "Lawyers," p. 232.

34. Richard Pells, *Radical Visions and American Dreams,* p. 10. See also Hofstadter, *Age of Reform,* chap. 4.

35. Robert Wiebe, *The Search for Order, 1877–1920.*

36. See Kristol, *Two Cheers for Capitalism,* esp. chaps. 2, 5, 7. For critical analysis, see Peter Steinfels, *The Neoconservatives,* pp. 283–290; Rogin, *The Intellectuals and McCarthy,* pp. 17, 97–99, 119–120.

37. Roosevelt quoted in Hofstadter, *Age of Reform,* p. 247.

38. Nader, "Introduction," in Green and Massie, eds., p. 5.

39. Pells, *Radical Visions,* p. 47.

40. Lazarus, *The Genteel Populists,* p. 11.

41. For a review of the literature on populism generally, see Goodwyn, *The Populist Moment,* pp. 332–342.

42. Wiebe, *Search for Order,* chap. 6.

43. James Weinstein, *The Corporate Ideal in the Liberal State, 1900–1918,* p. ix; Lasch, *Agony of the American Left,* p. 11.

44. See Paul K. Conkin, *The New Deal.*

45. Goodwyn, *The Populist Moment,* pp. 264–265. See Lustig, *Corporate Liberalism,* generally.

46. The most important work in this regard is Lazarus, *The Genteel Populists.*

47. Riley, "Taming GM," in Wasserstein and Green, eds., p. 241. See also Lazarus, *The Genteel Populists;* Nader et al., *Taming;* Council for Public Interest Law, *Balancing the Scales,* pp. 26–30, for self–conscious contrasts with earlier movements.

48. See McFarland, *Public Interest Lobbies,* pp. 4–24.

49. In this sense, the new reform pragmatism differs from that of corporate liberals in the Progressive and New Deal eras. See Lustig, *Corporate Liberalism.*

50. Gardner, *In Common Cause,* p. 16.

51. Nader, "Introduction," in Green and Massie, eds., p. 5.

52. Green, "Corporate Governance," in Green and Massie, eds., p. 445.

53. Sax, *Defending,* p. 158.

54. Nader quoted in Vogel, *Lobbying,* p. 76; Riley, "Taming GM," in Wasserstein and Green, eds., p. 242.

55. Dahl quoted in Nader et al., *Taming,* p. 123. Riley argues that "there is no good reason in this world why the people should not participate generally in the

276

processes of our private government." "Taming GM," in Wasserstein and Green, eds., p. 218.

56. Nader et al., *Taming*, p. 276.

57. Theodore J. Lowi, *The End of Liberalism*, pp. 292–294; Gus Speth quoted in *Amicus* 1 (4) (Spring 1980), p. 6.

58. For discussion of this distinction, see Paul Weaver, "Regulation, Social Policy, and Class Conflict," p. 45–63. Also see the debate between Mark Green and Ralph Nader ("Economic Regulation vs. Competition," "Winter's Discontent") and Ralph Winter ("Economic Regulation vs. Competition") in *Yale Law Journal* 82 (April 1973), pp. 871–919. For a review of social regulations passed at state and local levels in the Progressive Era, see Bardach and Kagan, *Going by the Book*, chap. 1.

59. Marver Bernstein, *Regulation by Independent Commission;* Weinstein, *The Corporate Ideal in the Liberal State.*

60. Green and Nader, "Economic Regulation vs. Competition," p. 876.

61. Ibid., p. 885.

62. This is not true of all new regulations, of course. Public interest–inspired regulations in auto safety, nuclear power, drug safety, strip-mining restoration, and nursing homes often are industry-specific. The point is that the goals of safety, health, and welfare maximization are comprehensive and all encompassing throughout the economy, while the relevant rules themselves have become increasingly more specific, detailed, and particularistic.

63. Many of the points argued in the next pages are also discussed in Charles Noble, "The Contradictions of Social Regulation: The Case of OSHA," a paper delivered at the American Political Science Association annual meetings, New York, 1981. It should be noted that a major reason for these market-based controls derived from constitutional rulings by the Supreme Court prohibiting regulation of workplace production under congressional commerce clause authority until the late 1930s. For a historical discussion of workplace politics, see Richard Edwards, *Contested Terrain: The Transformation of the Workplace in the Twentieth Century* (New York: Basic Books, 1979).

64. See Noble, "Contradictions of Social Regulation," pp. 7–9. The term "commodification" implies a convergence in the Marxist understandings about "commodity" and "reification" and is generally attributed to the classic essay by George Lukacs, "Reification and the Consciousness of the Proletariat," in *History and Class Consciousness* (Cambridge, Mass.: MIT Press, 1968), pp. 83–222.

65. A contemporary justification for this logic has been provided by Charles Schultze, "The Public Use of Private Interests," *Harper's*, May 1977, pp. 43–62.

66. For a critique of the restrictions imposed on citizen choices by these policies, see David Vogel, "The Inadequacies of Contemporary Opposition to Business," p. 50. See also Ralph Winter, "Economic Regulation vs Competition: Ralph Nader and Creeping Capitalism"; Bardach and Kagan, *Going by the Book*, chaps. 2–3.

67. Weaver, "Regulation," p. 57. "The most primordial fact of American culture remains its emphasis upon production," notes one environmentalist in agreement. See Rosenbaum, *The Politics of Environmental Concern*, p. 112; Noble, "The Contradictions of Social Regulation."

68. Abbey quoted in De Bell, "A Future That Makes Ecological Sense," in De Bell, ed., p. 155.

69. Riley, "Taming GM," in Wasserstein and Green, eds., p. 238.

70. Paul Ehrlich, "Too Many People," in De Bell, ed., p. 239. See also Rosenbaum, *Politics of Environmental Concern*, pp. 54–55, 82–83, 112–113, 273–278. Influential works have included D. H. Meadows et al., *The Limits to Growth;* Barry Commoner, "The Environmental Cost of Economic Growth"; H. E. Daley, ed., *Toward a Steady-State Economy.*

71. Nader et al., *Taming*, p. 17.

72. Paul Ehrlich, "Eco-Catastrophe," in De Bell, ed., p. 175.

73. Andrew Hacker, *The End of the American Era.* Barry Commoner, *The Politics of Energy*, p. 78. See also Tom Hayden, *The American Future: New Visions beyond Old Frontiers.*

74. Leona Train and Robert Rienow, *Moment in the Sun*, p. 233. See especially, also, Hayden, *American Future*, in general; Riley, "Taming GM," in Wasserstein and Green, eds., p. 239; Gardner, *In Common Cause*, p. 106; and elsewhere in most environmental tracts.

75. Environmentalists Hazel Henderson, Barry Commoner, and Kenneth Boulding join Nader and many consumerists in making this point often. A 1972 U. N. study concluding that "it is usually recognized today that high rates of growth do not guarantee the easing of urgent social and human problems" is often cited.

76. Riley, "Taming GM," in Wasserstein and Green, eds., pp. 238–239; "People over profits" was Barry Commoner's Citizens Party chant.

77. John Compton, "Science, Anti-Science, and Human Values," NRDC *Amicus*, Spring 1980, p. 36; Barry Commoner quoted in *Environmental Action* magazine, June 1980, p. 26. The new activists vary significantly in terms of understanding relations with each other and nature, although most agree about the need to oppose human domination over nature. For an overview of these philosophical debates, see David L. Sills, "The Environmental Movement and Its Critics," pp. 16–26. See also Holsworth, *Public Interest Liberalism*, for an interesting, if somewhat presumptive, discussion of Nader and other environmentalists.

78. Kenneth Boulding, "The Economics of Spaceship Earth," in De Bell, ed., p. 97. See Sills, "The Environmental Movement," pp. 24–26.

79. Nader quoted in Buckhorn, *Nader*, p. 293.

80. The term "socialist of the heart" was coined long ago by George Mosse. The quote is from Gardner, *In Common Cause*, p. 105. This moral appeal for middle-class Americans to restrain their appetites for wealth is hardly new in American history, but, except for mandarins such as Veblen, has been relatively novel within the twentieth-century reform tradition. See Holsworth, *Public Interest Liberalism*, pp. 73–93; David E. Shi, *The Simple Life: Plain Living and High Thinking in American Culture.*

81. Karl Marx, "On the Jewish Question," in Robert Tucker, *The Marx–Engels Reader* (New York: Norton, 1978), p. 43.

82. Charles Reich, *The Greening of America*, pp. 87–89. Reich is an influential theorist for the movement. Vogel makes this general point as well in "Promoting Pluralism."

83. Lazarus, *The Genteel Populists*, p. 191.

84. McFarland, *Public Interest Lobbies*, pp. 16–17.

85. Lippmann, *Drift and Mastery*, p. 50.

86. Gardner, *In Common Cause*, pp. 20–21; Sax, *Defending*, p. 64.

87. Riley, "Taming GM," in Wasserstein and Green, eds., p. 243.

88. Sax, *Defending*, p. 68. Reich argues in "The New Property" that "the

public interest state was the end point" of earlier reform, "but somehow the result is different from what the reformers wanted." p. 771.

89. Quote by Wellford, "On How to Be a Constructive Nuisance," in De Bell, ed., p. 272; Gardner, *In Common Cause*, p. 75.

90. Cunningham et al., *Strengthening*, p. x. Activists thus often speak of their focus on "government between elections."

91. Quoted in Newfield, "Nader's Raiders," p. 491. This attitude likewise is echoed often in the perennial complaints of ecologists such as this one: "When Washington is called to help out... it often has proved ham-handed and entangled in its own archaic bureaucracy. The end result is that nobody in authority has been able to take care of the country's mounting needs." John Fischer, "Survival U: Prospectus for a Really Relevant University," in De Bell, ed., p. 144.

92. David Schuman, *The Ideology of Form: The Influence of Organizatons in America*.

93. Cohen, "The Public Interest," quoting an affidavit submitted by Arthur H. Miller in the *Buckley v. Valeo* lawsuit, pp. 5, 3. See Vogel, "Promoting Pluralism," for a similar view.

94. Henderson, *Creating Alternative Futures*, p. 280. See also Halpern and Cunningham, "Reflections," p. 1079.

95. Sax, *Defending*, p. 82; Nader, "Introduction," in Green and Massie, eds., p. 5.

96. John Gardner quoted in McFarland, "Common Cause," p. 85.

97. Moore cited in Vogel, *Lobbying the Corporation*, p. 80.

98. Vogel, "Promoting Pluralism," p. 610.

99. Halpern and Cunningham, "Reflections," p. 1109.

100. Sax, *Defending*, p. 189.

101. Tom Hayden, *The American Future*, p. 178. Consumerist and former FTC Commissioner Michael Pertschuk says this of Nader and the public interest movement generally: "Nader's popular appeal was built upon his attack on unresponsive government bureaucracy as well as on business. In seeking to restructure regulatory schemes, he had always pressed for new forms of direct citizen participation, such as rights of petition, bureaucratic accountability to direct citizen's action, or self-help remedies like consumer class actions, which bypass bureaucracies." Pertschuk, *Revolt against Regulation: The Rise and Pause of the Consumer Movement*, p. 131. See also Henderson, *Creating Alternative Futures*, p. 280. She argues that most groups "share the same demand for greater participation in the decisions affecting their lives" which springs from "disaffection with large bureaucracies of both business and government."

102. Samuel Hays, *The Gospel of Efficiency*, p. 125. See Wiebe, *Search for Order*, chap. 5.

103. Mark Green, *Winning Back America*, p. 119.

104. The reference to Weber is significant. Weber was deeply ambivalent about the implications of modern bureaucratic development. On one hand, he lamented the dehumanizing, impersonal "shell of bondage" and "iron cage" that bureaucratic organizations imposed on both public and private life. On the other, bureaucratic forms, he argued, are more "technically expedient" than other forms of interaction. Bureaucracy organizes collective endeavors with greater speed, precision, continuity, and coordinated unity amid modern complex productive and managerial relations. The new reformers share Weber's lament about the threat

to freedom and community, yet they challenge his assumptions about the benefits of efficiency and technical expediency. Bureaucracy is found wanting in both respect in their eyes. Arthur Mitzman, *The Iron Cage* (New York: Grosset and Dunlap, 1969), esp. pp. 171–191. See Green and Massey, eds., *Big Business Reader,* p. 28; Ross, *Public Citizen's Action Manual,* p. 169.

105. Martin Carnoy and Derek Shearer, "Democratic Technology," in Green and Massie, eds., p. 369. Common Cause, *Government Subsidy Squeeze.* An EDF report agrees that "when benefits as well as costs are calculated, protecting the environment is a sound economic investment, and far less costly in the long run than in not protecting it." *EDF Annual Report, 1979.* See also Nader et al., *Taming,* p. 217; Gardner, *In Common Cause,* p. 8; James Ridgeway, *The Politics of Ecology,* chaps. 5–6.

106. Carnoy and Shearer, "Democratic Technology," in Green and Massie, eds., p. 369. These themes are developed widely by Barry Commoner, David Noble, Stanley Boyle, and John Blair. See Martin Carnoy and Derek Shearer, *Economic Democracy,* for an overview.

107. Gardner, *In Common Cause,* p. 17.

108. Carnoy and Shearer, "Democratic Technology," in Green and Massie, eds., p. 368.

109. Crozier et al., *The Crisis of Democracy,* p. 45.

110. Gardner, *In Common Cause,* p. 17. Edgar Shor argues that "representativeness" has replaced "efficiency" as the new touchstone of legitimacy. "Symposium," p. 132. See De Bell, ed., *The Environmental Handbook,* pp. 96–102, 102–112, 153–157. See also Henderson, *Creating Alternative Futures,* chaps. 2–6.

111. John Kenneth Galbraith, *The New Industrial State.* Galbraith has been a very influential force on public interest thinking and is quoted often in the works of the activists. Whether bureaucracies are necessary, however, somewhat separates the reformers and Galbraith. Quote is from *In Common Cause,* p. 106.

112. Robert Dahl in Ralph Nader and Mark Green, eds., *Corporate Power in America* (New York: Grossman, 1973), pp. 23–24.

113. Henderson, *Creating Alternative Futures,* p. 31. See also Carnoy and Shearer, *Economic Democracy,* esp. p. 298. John Compton notes in *Amicus,* Spring 1980, that "it is a mistake to join either the opponents or proponents of scientific and technical developments in their own simplistic terms." p. 34.

114. See essays by Jon Breslaw, Boulding, and De Bell in De Bell, ed., *The Environmental Handbook,* pp. 102–112, 96–101, 153–160; also, Henderson, *Creating Alternative Futures,* and Barry Commoner, *The Closing Circle.* This is what Nader means when he argues that "the quality of life is deteriorating in so many ways that the traditional measurements of the standards of living...have come to sound increasingly phony." Nader, ed., *Consumer and Corporate Accountability,* p. 4.

115. Barry Weisberg, "The Politics of Ecology," in Robert Disch, ed., *The Ecological Conscience* (Englewood Cliffs, N.J.: Prentice-Hall, 1970), p. 1154.

116. David Dellinger, "The Anti-Nuclear Movement," in Michio Kaku and Jennifer Trainer, eds., *Nuclear Power: Both Sides,* p. 233.

117. Tocqueville, *Democracy in America,* esp. pp. 667–705.

118. See Samuel P. Hays, "Political Parties and the Community/Society Continuum"; also William A. Williams, *The Contours of American History,* pp. 345–412. Hofstadter, *Age of Reform,* p. 11.

119. Hays, "Political Parties," p. 170. One debatable exception to this trend was the federalistic design of the Wagner Act.
120. Schwartz, "Symposium," p. 86.
121. Cunningham et al., *Strengthening*, pp. ix–xvii.
122. Schwartz, "Symposium," p. 78. See also Vogel, *Lobbying*, p. 20.
123. Nader, "Consumerism and Legal Services," p. 251.
124. Quoted in Nader et al., *Taming*, p. 222.
125. Berkeley People's Architecture, "Cities," in De Bell, ed., pp. 236–237; Green, "The Road to Monopoly," in Green and Massie, eds., pp. 503, 475–533 generally.
126. David Riley, "Taming GM," in Wasserstein and Green, eds., p. 241; Cunningham et al., *Strengthening*, p. xi.
127. Gardner, *In Common Cause*, p. 109.
128. Schwartz, "Symposium," p. 28.
129. Lasch, *New Radicalism*, p. 174.
130. See Wiebe, *Search for Order*, pp. 152–160; Hays, *Gospel of Efficiency*, pp. 122–146, 261–676; Lasch, *New Radicalism*, pp. 141–180.
131. McCarthy quoted in McConnell, *Private Power*, p. 43. For a recent expression, see Lloyd Cutler and David Johnson, "Regulation and the Political Process," p. 1395. Ackerman and Hassler, *Clean Coal/Dirty Air*, chap. 1.
132. E. F. Schumacher, *Small is Beautiful: Economics as if People Mattered*, p. 158; Sax, *Defending*, p. 60; Ackerman and Hassler, *Clean Coal/Dirty Air*, chap. 2; Robert D. Putnam, "Elite Transformation in Advanced Industrial Societies," *Comparative Political Studies* 10 (October 1977), pp. 383–412.
133. Frank et al., *Public Participation*, p. 15. Environmentalist Robert Rienow notes that "the economist prodding the nation to growth is not disturbed by the beer-can littered landscape or the unsightliness of the strip mining location"; quoted in Rosenbaum, *The Politics of Environmental Concern*, p. 65.
134. David Riley, "Taming GM," in Green and Wasserstein, eds., p. 237.
135. Friends of the Earth Foundation pamphlet, 1980, p. 5. This theme is frequently acknowledged by Barry Commoner, John Compton, Tom Hayden, John Gardner, and others.
136. Frank et al., *Public Participation*, p. 14; Cunningham et al., *Strengthening*, p. xi.
137. Sax, *Defending*, p. 56.
138. Lazarus, *The Genteel Populists*, pp. 242–244.
139. Halpern and Cunningham, "Reflections," p. 1098.
140. Paul Brooks, "Notes on the Conservation Revolution," in Mitchell and Stallings, eds., p. 41. See McFarland, *Public Interest Lobbies*, p. 18; Ackerman and Hassler, *Clean Coal/Dirty Air*, pp. 4–12.
141. Croly quoted in McConnell, *Private Power and American Democracy*, p. 42.
142. Gladden quoted in Lasch, *New Radicalism*, p. 163. See Rogin, *The Intellectuals and McCarthy*, p. 193.
143. Bellamy quoted in Wiebe, *Search for Order*, p. 138. See Lustig, *Corporate Liberalism*, pp. 150–194.
144. Wiebe, *Search for Order*, pp. 161–162. For recent defenses of socialized professional consensus, see James Q. Wilson, *The Amateur Democrat;* Nelson W. Polsby and Aaron Wildavsky, *Presidential Elections: Strategies of American Electoral Politics.*

145. Gardner, *In Common Cause*, p. 38. This is not to agree with conservatives that the new liberal reformers monopolize intransigence in modern public life. Corporate and state officials are often even more rigid, but they do not defend conflict as a principle.

146. Nader, "We Need a New Kind of Patriotism," *Life*, July 9, 1971. Council for Public Interest Law, *Balancing the Scales*, p. xi; Nader et al., *Taming*, p. 225.

147. Odom Fanning, *Man and His Environment: Citizen Action*, pp. 2, 226. Hazel Henderson likewise extols "creative social conflict," *Creating Alternative Futures*, pp. 237–267.

148. Gardner, *In Common Cause*, p. 107.

149. Sax, *Defending*, p. 107; Cohen, "The Public Interest," p. 8.

150. Nader quoted in Buckhorn, *Nader*, p. 294; Gardner quoted in McFarland, "Common Cause," p. 83.

151. Nader et al., *Taming*, p. 122.

152. Gardner, *In Common Cause*, p. 22. Neoconservative writers in particular have railed against the adversary ideals of modern liberals in *The Public Interest* and *Commentary*.

153. Lazarus, *The Genteel Populists*, p. 79.

154. Buckhorn, *Nader*, pp. 35, 290.

155. Ibid., pp. 264–265. The *1979 ACLU Annual Report* warned as well that "the ACLU itself should be watched closely . . . to be sure we don't mute our voices out of reluctance to criticize old friends."

156. Vogel, "Promoting Pluralism."

157. Gardner quoted in McFarland, "Common Cause," p. 85.

158. Lazarus, *The Genteel Populists*, pp. 188–189. By "academic pluralists" I do not suggest a monolithic club of thinkers with wholly uniform ideas. I refer to the similarities in perspective of Seymour Martin Lipset, Daniel Bell, Giovanni Sartori, William Kornhauser, Edward Shils, and David Truman. What distinguishes these thinkers is their forthright advocacy of *pluralism* as a prescriptive theory rooted in particular sociological assumptions about the nature of social interaction. By contrast, many theorists of *community power* (Polsby), *polyarchy* (Dahl), and *interest-group liberalism* who generally use pluralism as an analytic tool of interpretation are not necessarily included. See Rogin, *The Intellectuals and McCarthy*, chap. 1.

159. Lazarus, *The Genteel Populists*, pp. 170–175; Gardner, *In Common Cause*, pp. 80–83; Gordon Harrison and Sanford Jaffe, *The Public Interest Law Firm: New Voices for New Constituencies*, p. 8.

160. Gardner, *In Common Cause*, p. 81.

161. See Sandor Halebsky, *Mass Society and Political Conflict: Toward a Reconstruction of Theory*; Michael Rogin, "Non-Partisanship and the Group Interest," pp. 112–141.

162. Gardner, *In Common Cause*, pp. 105–106.

163. *Environmental Action, 1979 Annual Report*.

164. There are two ways in which the political process is not directly majoritarian. First, as many pluralists since Schumpeter have argued, the electorate is poorly informed, apathetic, and deferential to leaders. Second, the state does not directly determine policy; rather, it formulates policy as *one* of many participants in the process, although it is headed by *elected* actors with some final authoritative decision-making power in many areas.

165. Common Cause, *Government Subsidy Squeeze*, p. 12.

166. Gardner, *In Common Cause*, p. 104.

167. C. Wright Mills, "The Social Scientist's Task," in Henry Kariel, ed., *Frontiers of Democratic Theory* (New York: Random House, 1970), p. 427.

168. David Trubeck, "Complexity and Contradictions in the Legal Order," p. 563.

169. Tocqueville, *Democracy in America*, p. 270; Hartz, *Liberal Tradition*, pp. 48–49, 102–106. See also Scheingold, *The Politics of Rights*.

170. Jerold S. Auerbach, *Unequal Justice: Lawyers and Social Change in Modern America*, pp. 102–230.

171. Trubeck, "Complexity and Contradictions," p. 564. See also Lazarus, *The Genteel Populists*, chap. 10; Trubeck et al., "Legal Services and the Administrative State," unpublished paper, November, 1978.

172. See Donald Horowitz, "The Courts as Guardians of the Public Interest," pp. 149–150.

173. The literature on the subject is vast. Three varied accounts include Arthur S. Miller, *The Supreme Court and American Capitalism;* Morton Horwitz, *The Transformation of American Law, 1780–1860* (Cambridge: Harvard University Press, 1977); Arnold M. Paul, *Conservative Crisis and the Rule of Law.* See also Michael W. McCann, "Resurrection and Reform: The Changing Status of Property in the American Constitutional Tradition," pp, 143–176.

174. Lefcourt, ed., *Law against the People*, p. 6. See also Auerbach, *Unequal Justice.*

175. Council for Public Interest Law, *Balancing the Scales*, p. 29. See also Ackerman and Hassler, *Clean Coal/Dirty Air,* chap. 1.

176. McCann, "Resurrection and Reform," pp. 147–157.

177. Ibid., p. 148.

178. *U. S. v. Carolene Products Co.*, 304 U.S. 144, 58 S.Ct. 778, 82 L. Ed. 1234 (1938).

179. Lazarus, *The Genteel Populists*, p. 236. See also Jonathan Casper, "The Supreme Court and National Policy Making," p. 50; Rabin, "Lawyers for Social Change"; Scheingold, *The Politics of Rights.*

180. Clement Vose, "Litigation as a Pressure Group Activity," *The Annals of the American Academy of Political and Social Science* 319 (1958), p. 25.

181. See Rabin, "Lawyers for Social Change," generally.

182. Lazarus, *The Genteel Populists*, pp. 244–245, and chap. 10 generally.

183. This is the most convincing aspect of David Vogel's general argument about the continuity of modern reform and older business political tactics. See "Promoting Pluralism." See also Gabriel Kolko, *The Triumph of Conservatism;* Weinstein, *The Corporate Ideal in the Liberal State.*

184. Harrison and Jaffe, *Public Interest Law Firm*, p. 8; Council for Public Interest Law, *Balancing the Scales*, p. 30.

185. Anderson, *NEPA and the Courts.*

186. Richard Kazis and Richard L. Grossman, *Fear at Work: Job Blackmail, Labor and the Environment*, p. 32.

187. Richard Liroff, *A National Policy for the Environment: NEPA and Its Aftermath*, p. 88. For an overview on environmental issues, see Wenner, *The Environmental Decade in Court.* Wenner points out, however, that environmental disputes still account for only 1 percent of all federal cases, p. 24.

188. "Public Access to Information," *Northwestern Law Review* 68 (May 1973),

p. 177. Ironically, much of this litigation has been inspired by businesses spying on one another.

189. Abram Chayes, "The Role of the Judge in Public Law Litigation," p. 1303. While *direct* public interest legal action has contributed to increased litigation, most of the increase is by government suits under *indirect* reform pressure for greater state regulation. See Michael Wines, "Auchter's Record at OSHA Leaves Labor Outraged, Business Satisfied," *National Journal*, October 1, 1983, pp. 2008–2013.

190. Schrag and Meltsner, "Class Action," p. 57.

191. Schwartz, "Symposium," p. 79; Ridgeway, *The Politics of Ecology*, p. 198. See also Horowitz, "The Courts as Guardians."

192. Onek quoted in Richard E. Cohen, "Public Interest Lawyers Start Looking Out for Their Own Interests," p. 861.

193. For a negative view of this, see Donald Horowitz, *The Courts and Social Policy;* idem., "The Courts as Guardians," p. 150; Lazarus, *The Genteel Populists*, pp. 230, 238. See Sax, *Defending*, chap. 7, on the consequences of public rights for court action.

194. Chayes, "Role of the Judge," p. 1289. See also Owen Fiss, "The Supreme Court 1978 Term–Foreword: The Forms of Justice," pp. 1–58.

195. Nathan Glazer, "Toward an Imperial Judiciary?"; Horowitz, *Courts and Social Policy*.

196. Sax, *Defending*, pp. 151, 61, 57, 157.

197. Lazarus, *The Genteel Populists*, p. 262.

198. Stewart, "The Reformation of American Administrative Law," pp. 1667–1814. See also Ernest Gellhorn, "Public Participation," pp. 359–404; Roger C. Cramton, "The Why, Where, and How of Broadened Public Participation in the Administrative Process," pp. 525–550; Comment, "Public Participation in Federal Administrative Proceedings," pp. 702–845; Shor, ed., "Symposium: Public Interest Representation," pp. 131–154. For a discussion of "post-formalism" in law, see Trubeck, "Complexity and Contradictions"; Roberto Unger, *Law in Modern Society*, chaps. 2–3.

199. Stewart, "Reformation," pp. 1670–1687, esp. 1675; Ackerman and Hassler, *Clean Coal/Dirty Air*, p. 6.

200. Stewart tangentially discusses both public interest activists and the implications of their reforms throughout his article. For assessment, see Stewart, "Reformation," esp. pp. 1748–1790.

201. Garrett Hardin, "The Tragedy of the Commons," in De Bell, ed., p. 40. For detailed discussion, see Trubeck, "Complexity and Contradictions"; Lazarus, *The Genteel Populists*, chaps. 1–3; Sax, *Defending*, chaps. 3–5; Fellmeth, "The Regulatory–Industrial Complex," in Wasserstein and Green, eds.; Wellford, "On How to Be a Constructive Nuisance," in De Bell, ed., p. 274.

202. Cutler and Johnson, "Regulation and the Political Process," pp. 1402–1403. See, also, Harrison and Jaffe, *Public Interest Law Firm*, p. 38; Richard Funston, "The Judicialization of the Administrative Process," pp. 38–60.

203. Stewart, "Reformation," p. 1760.

204. Ernest Gellhorn writes that "public intervenors in trial type proceedings should be accorded full participation with all the rights of other parties, if they can make a serious showing of the need to participate." "Public Participation," p. 384. Moore quote from "A Lawyer's Response," in Wasserstein and Green, eds., p. 310.

205. A brief account of this development is available in Horowitz, "Courts as Guardians," pp. 149–150. See also Cunningham et al., *Strengthening*, pp. 150–155.

206. For detailed discussion, see Frank et al., *Public Participation*, pp. 36–46. For an interesting perspective on these and future trends, see Martin Shapiro, "Administrative Discretion: The Next Stage," unpublished paper delivered at the Western Political Science Association, Seattle, March 27, 1983.

207. Horowitz, "Courts as Guardians," p. 151. See also Stewart, "Reformation," p. 1670.

208. Shor, ed., "Symposium," generally. The federal judiciary has generally confirmed that administrative enforcement mechanisms can be considered a court for purposes of the statutory bar, if the agency has equivalent powers and procedures. *Baughman v. Bradford Coal* 592 F.2d 215 (3rd Cir.).

209. Mark Nadel and David Vogel, "Who Is a Consumer? An Analysis of the Politics of Consumer Conflict," p. 37. See also Green, "Why the Consumer Bill Went Down." Green says that "the purpose of the consumer advocacy office was to make regulation work better by making the adversary process work better," p. 198.

210. David Riley, "Taming GM," in Wasserstein and Green, eds., p. 217.

211. Lazarus, *The Genteel Populists*, chap. 10. Lazarus argues that, in contrast, "participatory democracy has not been and cannot be a corrective for the undemocratic features of most large-scale bureaucratic decision making," p. 48.

212. Schrag and Meltsner, "Class Actions," pp. 55–61.

213. John Denvir, "Towards a Political Theory of Public Interest Litigation," p. 1160; Sax, *Defending*, p. 57.

214. Horowitz, "Courts as Guardians," p. 151.

215. For example, Gardner's reform discourse (*In Common Cause*) utilizes little specifically legal language and few direct judicial analogies. However, the structural reforms in state processes which he proposes closely parallel the "court" model of government.

216. Sax, *Defending*, p. 82; Harrison and Jaffe, *The Public Interest Law Firm*, p. 38; Halpern and Cunningham, "Reflections," pp. 1101, 1109.

217. Donald Black, "The Mobilization of Law," pp. 125–150.

218. Sax, *Defending*, pp. 57–60. Harrison and Jaffe agree that "there is a sense in which the courts are more responsive than legislatures to the insistence that policy issues be dramatized, debated, and decided." *The Public Interest Law Firm*, p. 8.

219. Ralph Nader, *Public Interest Perspectives: The Next Four Years*, p. 2. Joseph Sax agrees in similar terms: "An essential format for reasserting participation in the governmental process is in the courtroom . . . because the court preeminently is a forum where the individual citizen or community group can obtain a hearing on equal terms with the highly organized and experienced interests that have learned so skillfully to manipulate legislative and administrative institutions." *Defending*, p. xviii. See also Chayes, "Role of the Judge," pp. 1308–1319, and Gellhorn, "Public Participation," pp. 362–372.

220. Nader, *Public Interest Perspectives*, p. 2.

221. See Halpern and Cunningham, "Reflections," pp. 1098–1099. "Each [group] is privately funded and essentially independent of corporate, bureaucratic, or political control." See also Nader, "Consumerism and Legal Services."

222. Chayes, "Role of the Judge," p. 1309. See also Harrison and Jaffe, *The Public Interest Law Firm*, p. 38.

223. Berry, *Lobbying*, p. 267.
224. "Regulatory-Industrial Complex," in Wasserstein and Green, eds., p. 275. See also Moore, "The Lawyer's Response," in Wasserstein and Green, eds., p. 310.
225. Liroff, *A National Policy*, p. 151. See Nader in Sax, *Defending*, p. xviii. Quote from Lazarus, *The Genteel Populists*, pp. 250–251.
226. Frank et al., *Public Participation*, p. 79.
227. Sax, *Defending*, p. 58. See Scheingold on rights as a resource in *The Politics of Rights*, pp. 83–96, 203–218.
228. Justice Brennan quoted in Eric Van DeLoon, "The Law School Response," in Wasserstein and Green, eds., p. 335.
229. NRDC membership solicitation letter. Halpern and Cunningham, "Reflections," p. 1102. See also Eric Van de Loon, "The Law School Response," in Wasserstein and Green, eds., p. 341, and generally F. Raymond Marks, et al., *The Lawyer, the Public, and Professional Responsibility.*
230. Lazarus, *The Genteel Populists*, p. 215.
231. Chayes, "Role of the Judge," p. 1308; Lazarus, *The Genteel Populists*, p. 245; Harrison and Jaffe, *The Public Interest Law Firm*, p. 14.
232. Sax, *Defending*, p. 221; Lon Fuller, *The Morality of Law.*
233. Chayes, "Role of the Judge," p. 1308.
234. Lazarus and Denvir suggest this throughout their discussions.
235. Sax, *Defending*, pp. 107, 112; Lazarus, *The Genteel Populists*, pp. 244–248. Quote from Denvir, "Towards a Political Theory," p. 1160.
236. Sax, *Defending*, p. 112. The use of the term "reduce" is interesting in its ambiguity here. Discussion of the typical case-by-case, instrumental approach is included in the second half of this book.
237. Chayes, "Role of the Judge," p. 1308; Sax, *Defending*, pp. 228, 112.
238. Denvir, "Towards a Political Theory," p. 1157. See also Wellford, "On How to Be a Constructive Nuisance," in De Bell, ed., pp. 270–275; Nader, "Freedom from Information," generally.
239. Lazarus, *The Genteel Populists*, p. 253.
240. See Dworkin, *Taking Rights Seriously*, esp. chaps. 2–4. On the connection between formal law and reform politics, see Theodore Lowi, *The Politics of Disorder.*
241. Henderson, *Creating Alternative Futures*, p. 80. For discussion of the morality of law, see Fuller, *The Morality of Law.*
242. Harrison and Jaffe, *The Public Interest Law Firm*, p. 32.
243. Lazarus, *The Genteel Populists*, p. 238; Harrison and Jaffe, *The Public Interest Law Firm*, p. 14. The District of Columbia Circuit Court ruled in *Environmental Defense Fund v. Ruckelshaus* (1971) that "courts should require administrative officers to articulate the standards and principles that govern their discretionary decisions in as much detail as possible. Rules and regulations should be freely formulated by administrators, and revised when necessary. Discretionary decisions should more often be supported with findings of fact and reasoned opinions."
244. Lazarus, *The Genteel Populists*, p. 248, for example.
245. Alexander Hamilton, "Federalist 78," in Clinton Rossiter, ed., *The Federalist Papers* (New York: Mentor, 1961), pp. 464–472.
246. Denvir, "Towards a Political Theory," p. 1157. See also Lazarus, *The Genteel Populists*, p. 248.

Notes to Part Two Preface

247. See Philippe Nonet and Philip Selznick, *Law and Society in Transition: Toward Responsive Law;* Unger, *Law in Modern Society;* Andrew Frazer, "The Legal Theory We Need Now," pp. 147–188.
248. Nonet and Selznick, "Law and Society in Transition," p. 6.

Part Two: Preface

1. Richard Flacks, "Populism in Search of the People," pp. 26–27.
2. Quoted in Linda E. Demkovich, "Consumer Leaders Hope That Carter Will Go to Bat for Them," p. 1743.
3. Harris poll cited in Buckhorn, *Nader,* pp. 276–277.
4. "Louis Harris Survey," in *Seattle Times,* March 29, 1971, p. A15; Buckhorn, *Nader,* pp. 276–277.
5. Hazel Erskine, "The Polls: Pollution and Its Costs," p. 121.
6. Cited in Rosenbaum, *Politics of Environmental Concern,* pp. 83–86.
7. Cited in "Opinion Roundup—Environmental Update," *Public Opinion,* 1982, p. 18. See also *State of the Environment—1982* (Washington, D.C.: Conservation Foundation, 1982), pp. 424–428.
8. 1976 survey cited in Cunningham et al., *Strengthening* , p. x. Quote is from Seymour M. Lipset and W. Schneider, "The Public View of Regulation," *Public Opinion* 2 (January/February 1979), p. 6.
9. Cunningham et al., *Strengthening,* p. xi.
10. Paul A. Beck and M. Kent Jennings, "Political Periods and Political Participation," *American Political Science Review* 73 (1979), p. 748.
11. Cunningham et al., *Strengthening,* p. ix.
12. Lazarus, quoted in Clark, "After a Decade," p. 1140.
13. Ibid., p. 1136.
14. Ibid., pp. 1140–1141; see also Keller, "Environmental Movement Checks Its Pulse and Finds Obituaries Are Premature," pp. 211–216. On the revitalization of business groups, see Boyte, *Backyard Revolution,* chap. 1; Green and Buchsbaum, *The Corporate Lobbies.*
15. Clark, "After a Decade," p. 1136.
16. Green, *Winning Back America,* p. xi.
17. See Chapter 3 of this volume for discussion of changing issue saliency.
18. Quoted in Lazarus, *The Genteel Populists,* pp. xv–xvi.
19. Clark, "After a Decade," pp. 1136, 1139; Keller, "Environmental Movement," generally.
20. Richard Cohen, "Public Interest Lawyers," p. 860.
21. Clark, "After a Decade," p. 1139; Singer, "Liberal Public Interest Law Firms," p. 2054.
22. See Alan Crawford, *Thunder on the Right: The "New Right" and the Politics of Resentment.* For one public interest leader's views of this conservative onslaught, see Mark Green's *Winning Back America.* See Chapter 5 and Postscript of this book for further discussion.
23. Clark, "After a Decade," pp. 1136–1139; Keller, "Environmental Movement," p. 214; Susan J. Tolchin and Martin Tolchin, *Dismantling America.*
24. Keller, "Environmental Movement," p. 211; McFarland, *Common Cause,* p. 39.

25. See, for example, Boyte, *Backyard Revolution.*
26. Pertschuk, *Revolt against Regulation;* Green, *Winning Back America,* p. 345.

Chapter 3. The Political Economy of Social Reform

1. Every theory of collective action has appealed to some overriding functional image of the constituent social person—whether it be to people as economic producers (farmers, entrepreneurs, workers), religious enthusiasts (Augustinian saints, Puritans), or skilled professionals (Plato's guardians, American Progressives) —from which individuals can develop their identities as public actors and citizens. Public interest liberalism is no exception.
2. Two useful general treatments of the label's applications are covered by the essays in Mary Gardiner Jones and David M. Gardiner, eds., *Consumerism: A New Force in Society,* and Lucy Black Creighton, *Pretenders to the Throne: The Consumer Movement in the United States.*
3. Donald Ross notes that "anyone who buys anything at any time is a consumer.... Because consumer abuse affects everyone, it is an excellent issue around which to rally support and build a community organization." *A Public Citizen's Action Manual,* p. 1. See Buckhorn, *Nader,* pp. 280–281.
4. See Mark Nadel, *The Politics of Consumer Protection.*
5. Commoner cited in Rosenbaum, *Politics of Environmental Concern,* p. 69. Allan Schnaiberg's assessment of the environmental movement also confirms that most activities of environmental groups fall within the general category of "consumer-oriented." Both what he calls "cosmetologists" and "meliorists," and to an extent "reformists" as well, fit this label. *The Environment: From Surplus to Scarcity.*
6. Mihajlo Mesarovic and E. Pertel, *Mankind at the Turning Point.* (New York: New American Library, 1974). See also Fred Hirsch, *The Social Limits to Growth.* Allan Schnaiberg writes that "one way of conceptualizing most environmental politics is that they are aimed at reducing environmental usage of particular resources." Quoted in David Sills, "Environmental Movement," p. 26.
7. Garrett De Bell, "Energy," in De Bell, ed., p. 67. See also James S. Rummonds, "A Challenge to the Law," in Mitchell and Stallings, eds., p. 120.
8. Cited in Halpern and Cunningham, "Reflections," p. 1100. See also Sax, *Defending,* p. xix.
9. Edmond Cahn, "Law in the Consumer Perspective," *University of Pennsylvania Law Review* 112 (1963), pp. 1–21. See also idem., *The Predicament of Democratic Man* (New York: Delta, 1961).
10. Edgar Cahn and Jean Cahn, "Power to the People or to the Profession? The Public in Public Interest Law," p. 1006.
11. Lazarus, *The Genteel Populists,* p. 151. Chief Justice Warren Burger has affirmed likewise in defense of the concept of the "private attorney general" that "consumers are generally among the best vindicators of the public interest." Cited in Sax, *Defending,* pp. ix, 242–244.
12. Ralph Nader, "The Consumer Movement Looks Ahead," p. 284; Nader, ed., *The Consumer and Corporate Accountability.* See Holsworth, *Public Interest Liberalism,* chaps. 3 and 4.
13. Henderson, *Creating Alternative Futures,* pp. 277–279.

14. Gardner, *In Common Cause*, pp. 47, 75.
15. Riley, "Taming GM," in Wasserstein and Green, eds., p. 208, 240–243. See also Bo Burlingham, "Popular Politics, The Arrival of Ralph Nader," pp. 5–15.
16. Berlin et al., "Consumers of the World Unite," in Wasserstein and Green, eds., pp. 279–298.
17. Walter Weyl, *The New Democracy* (New York: 1914), p. 251. Wilson cited in Hofstader, *Age of Reform*, p. 170.
18. Lippmann, "Caveat Emptor," in *Drift and Mastery*, p. 55.
19. Hofstadter, *Age of Reform*, pp. 172–173.
20. The quote is from Nader, and cited in Burlingham, "Popular Politics," p. 9. On the evolution and appeal of consumerism, see Nadel, *Politics of Consumer Protection*; Ralf Dahrendorf, *Class and Class Conflict In Industrial Society*.
21. On the evolution of consumerism within organized labor, see J. David Greenstone, *Labor in American Politics*, chaps. 1, 2, 11. On initial struggles over goals, see Rogin, "Non-partisanship and the Group Interest," pp. 112–141.
22. Berlin et al., "Consumers of the World Unite," in Wasserstein and Green, eds., p. 280; Henderson, *Creating Alternative Futures*, pp. 277–279.
23. See Christopher Lasch, *The Culture of Narcissism*, pp. 127–151. Charles Reich describes these "post-bourgeois" values of consumers with new tastes and wants: "We are producing consumers who are increasingly dissatisfied, no matter what they get." The "popular thinking about the ecology 'crisis' rests largely upon the discovery of new discomforts," adds Richard Neuhaus. *In Defense of People*, p. 133.
24. Riley, "Taming GM," in Wasserstein and Green, eds., p. 238.
25. Boulding, "Spaceship Earth," in De Bell, ed., p. 98. See also Hayden, *American Future*, p. 12.
26. Henderson, *Creating Alternative Futures*, pp. 277–278.
27. Ibid., pp. 347–350.
28. Nader, ed., *Consumer and Corporate Accountabilty*, p. 212.
29. Ibid., p. 374. For a slightly different view, see Holsworth, *Public Interest Liberalism*.
30. Denton Morrison, "The Environmental Movement: Conflict Dynamics," pp. 74–85. The most important and persistent critics are neoconservative economists and social thinkers. See the debate in *Daedalus* 90 (Fall 1974), on "The No-Growth Society." For an early statement of the backlash, see Jeanne Briggs, "The Price of Environmentalism: The Backlash Begins," *Forbes*, June 1977, pp. 36–40.
31. For a review, see Volkmar Lauber, "Ecology Politics and Liberal Democracy," pp. 199–217.
32. Kristol, *Two Cheers for Capitalism*, p. 253; Daniel Bell, "The Prospects of American Capitalism," in *The End of Ideology* (New York: The Free Press, 1962), pp. 75–94.
33. Keith Pavitt, "A European View of the 'Environmental Crisis,'" in Robert C. Axtmann, ed., *Rescuing Man's Environment* (Princeton: Princeton University Press, 1972), p. 129. See Vogel, "The Inadequacies of Contemporary Opposition to Business," p. 52.
34. Quoted in Mary Douglas and Aaron Wildavsky, *Risk and Culture: An Essay in the Selection of Technological and Governmental Dangers*, pp. 136–137.
35. Arlie Schardt quoted in Rosen, "Growing Clout," p. 119. Andrew McFarland argues in similar fashion that "the real values of the low-growth position, then, are its criticisms of existing practices and its initiation of new ideas into the

discussion of energy policy." *Public Interest Lobbies*, p. 53. See Kazis and Grossman, *Fear at Work*, pp. 141–150.

36. Henderson, *Creating Alternative Futures*, p. 117. See, for example, Mark Green, *Winning Back America*, pp. 37–117.

37. Survey cited in Henderson, *Creating Alternative Futures*, p. 3.

38. Ibid., p. 395. The figures were 79 percent to 17 percent. Likewise, by 76 percent to 17 percent, the majority opted for "learning to get our pleasures out of non-material experiences" rather than "satisfying our needs for more goods and services."

39. Hazel Erskine, "The Polls: Hopes, Fears, and Regrets," *Public Opinion Quarterly* 37 (Spring 1973), pp. 132–145; quote on p. 133.

40. Frederick Buttel and William Flinn, "Economic Growth versus the Environment: Survey Evidence," pp. 410–420.

41. Ibid., pp. 416–418.

42. Harris poll cited in Henderson, *Creating Alternative Futures*, p. 395. The 1981 polls are by Newsweek/Gallup and New York Times/CBS News and are cited in *The State of the Environment 1982* (Conservation Foundation), pp. 426–427; Robert C. Mitchell, "Silent Spring/Solid Majorities," p. 16.

43. Lauber, "Ecology Politics"; Hirsch, *Social Limits to Growth*; E. J. Mishan, *Technology and Growth* (New York: Praeger, 1969).

44. Ronald Inglehart, *The Silent Revolution: Changing Values and Political Styles among Western Publics*. For related arguments, see Daniel Yankelovich, *New Rules: Searching for Fulfillment in a World Turned Upside Down* (New York: Random House, 1981); and the chapter "Public Opinion" by C. Everett Ladd in Norman J. Vig and Michael E. Kraft, *Environmental Policy in the 1980s: Reagan's New Agenda*, pp. 58–63.

45. Statistics cited in Eugene Bardach and Robert A. Kagan, *Going by the Book*, p. 26; "Business Bulletin," *Wall Street Journal*, June 27, 1985, p. 1; Michael Wines, "They're Still Telling OSHA Horror Stories, but the Victims Are New," *National Journal*, November 7, 1981, p. 1989.

46. Murray C. Weidenbaum, *The Future of Business Regulation*. For review, see Timothy B. Clark, "The Costs and Benefits of Regulation—Who Knows How Great They Really Are?" *National Journal*, December 1, 1979, pp. 2023–2027. See also Bardach and Kagan, *Going by the Book*, p. 16.

47. See Edward F. Denison, *Accounting For Slower Economic Growth* (Washington, D.C.: Brookings Institution, 1979). For further studies, see Clark, "Costs"; Lester Thurow, *The Zero-Sum Society*. For rebuttal, see Mark Green and Norman Waitzman, *Business War on Law: An Analysis of The Benefits of Federal Health/Safety Enforcement*.

48. Kennedy quoted in Bardach and Kagan, *Going by the Book*, p. 49. See pp. 215–227, 47–51. The full analysis can be found in Murray C. Weidenbaum and Robert de Fina, *The Cost of Federal Regulation of Economic Activity*.

49. Helen M. Ingram and Dean E. Mann, "Environmental Policy: From Innovation to Implementation," in Theodore Lowi and Alan Stone, eds., *Nationalizing Government: Public Policies in America* (Beverly Hills: Sage, 1978), pp. 131–162. See also Eugene Bardach and Lucian Pugliaresi, "The Environmental Impact Statement versus the Real World," pp. 22–38.

50. Ackerman and Hassler, *Clean Coal/Dirty Air.*

51. William K. Tabb, "Government Regulation: Two Sides to the Story," *Challenge*, November/December 1980, p. 48; Green and Waitzman, *Business War*

on Law. See also "Benefits of Environmental Health, Safety; Regulation," Senate Committee on Governmental Affairs, 96th Congress 2d Session, March 25, 1980 (Washington: U. S. Government Printing).

52. Kazis and Grossman, *Fear at Work*, pp. 133–134. See also Michael G. Royston, "Making Pollution Prevention Policy," *Harvard Business Review*, November/December 1980, p. 6.

53. *EDF 1977 Annual Report*, p. 1. See Henderson, *Creating Alternative Futures*, p. 73, and chaps. I–IV generally, for review of the arguments. See also, Arlie W. Schardt, "A Sound Economy and a Healthy Environment: Both Are Possible," EDF Letter, May/June 1978; Sam Love, "'To Hell with Shell': Memories of a Boycott," *Environment Action* 5 (July 7, 1973), pp. 13–15; "Waste in the West: Part I and II," *NRDC Newsletters* 6–7 (1977–1978); Ruth Ruttenberg, "Regulation Is the Mother of Invention," *Working Papers for a New Society*, May/June 1981, p. 43.

54. Steven Kelman, *What Price Incentives? Economists and the Environment;* idem., "Cost/Benefit Analysis: An Ethical Critique," pp. 33–40.

55. Thurow, *Zero-Sum Society*, p. 7; Samuel Bowles, David Gordon, and Thomas Weisskopf, *Beyond the Wasteland: A Democratic Alternative to Economic Decline*, pp. 43–45.

56. Cited in Bowles et al., *Beyond the Wasteland*, pp. 38–39, 45.

57. This is the central thesis of Bowles et al., *Beyond the Wasteland.* See also the Commerce Department's *Economic Report*, 1982, B-45; Barry Bluestone and Bennett Harrison, *The Deindustrialization of America: Plant Closings, Community Abandonment, and the Dismantling of Basic Industry;* Seymour Melman, *Profits without Production* (New York: Knopf, 1983). On the effects of regulatory cutbacks in the auto industry, see Michael Wines, "Regulatory Plan to Relieve Auto Industry of Regulatory Burden Gets Mixed Grades," *National Journal*, July 23, 1983, pp. 1532–1537.

58. The surveys cited here are discussed in Mitchell, "Silent Spring," pp. 16–18; Everett Carl Ladd, "Clearing the Air: Public Opinion and Public Policy on the Environment," p. 18; Michael Pertschuk, "Consumers Ask Government to Police the Marketplace," *New York Times Magazine*, May 29, 1983. On deregulation, see Louis Harris, "Views of Government Regulation of Business," *The Harris Survey*, August 10, 1981, p. 1. On the lack of public sophistication, see Tolchin and Tolchin, *Dismantling America*, pp. 264–265.

59. "People over profits" was Barry Commoner's campaign slogan. The reformers see politics as "an endless succession of quasi-conspiracies against the will and interests of 'the people,' the masses, the public, or some similar concept," argues Lazarus. *The Genteel Populists*, p. 10. The most concise statement of this perspective is by Green and Nader, "Economic Regulation vs. Competition."

60. Moore, "Lawyer's Response," in Wasserstein and Green, eds., p. 304.

61. Quoted in Bardach and Kagan, *Going by the Book*, p. 45.

62. Relevant analyses on the structure of modern capitalism include the following sources: Paul A. Baran and P. M. Sweezy, *Monopoly Capital: An Essay on the American Economic Social Order* (New York: Modern Reader Paperbacks, 1966); James O'Connor, *The Fiscal Crisis of the State;* Harry Braverman, *Labor and Monopoly Capital: The Degradation of Work in the Twentieth Century;* Paul Blumberg, *Inequality in an Age of Decline;* Bowles et al., *Beyond the Wasteland.* For a macroeconomic approach to ecological politics, see Schnaiberg, *The Environment.*

63. This is Lester Thurow's central point in *Zero-Sum Society,* chaps. 4–5.
64. Lazarus, *The Genteel Populists,* pp. 147–153. See Blumberg, *Inequality,* pp. 180–200.
65. Cited in Lazarus, *The Genteel Populists,* p. 138; see chap. 6 generally.
66. Nadel and Vogel, "Who Is a Consumer?" p. 1.
67. On the logic of the problem see Bruce Hannen, "Energy Conservation and the Consumer," *Science* 189 (July 11, 1975), pp. 95–102.
68. See Kazis and Grossman, *Fear at Work,* pp. 8–9.
69. Marjorie Boyd, "The Protection Consumers Don't Want," pp. 30–31.
70. See Blumberg, *Inequality,* pp. 135–146; Seymour Melman, *The Permanent War Economy: American Capitalism on the Decline* (New York: Simon and Schuster, 1974).
71. For two perspectives, see Thurow, *Zero-Sum Society;* Alan Wolfe, *America's Impasse* (New York: Pantheon, 1981).
72. Milton Friedman, "Consumer Responses to Open Dating and Nutrient Labelling," in David A. Aaker and George S. Day, eds., *Consumerism* (New York: Free Press, 1974), p. 209. See generally Boyd, "Protection," pp. 29–34.
73. Most of these analyses are done by conservative muckrakers and often tend to be polemical. See Bernard Frieden, *The Environmental Protection Hustle;* William Tucker, "Environmentalism and the Leisure Class," pp. 49–80; idem., *Progress and Privilege: America in the Age of Environmentalism.*
74. See Bardach and Kagan, *Going by the Book,* pp. 26–28.
75. Hayden, *The American Future,* p. 36.
76. Christopher Stone writes in *Should Trees Have Standing?* that the dominant motive of conservationists "has been to conserve them [resources] *for* us—for the greatest good of the greatest number of human beings." p. 463. Yet the identity of "us" who benefit is obscured by emphasis on "the people" and the "public." This point about the upper-income, middle-class biases of the new politics has been recognized by both sympathetic (Lazarus, McFarland, Holsworth) and hostile (Kristol, Frieden, Winter) critics.
77. Hugh Stretton, *Capitalism, Socialism and the Environment,* p. 58.
78. Two activist lawyers agree that middle-class consumer politics has overwhelmed attention to the "passive and helpless... consumers of governmental goods and services." Cahn and Cahn, "Power to the People," p. 1005. See also "Some Leftists Hit the Ecology Movement as Unfair to the Poor," *Wall Street Journal,* June 23, 1972, p. 1.
79. Rosenbaum, *Politics of Environmental Concern,* p. 74.
80. William Tucker, "The Environmental Era," *Public Opinion* 5 (February/March 1982), p. 46. See also idem., "Environmentalism and the Leisure Class"; Frieden, *The Environmental Protection Hustle;* Ralph Winter, *The Consumer Advocate versus the Consumer.*
81. EPA study cited in Kazis and Grossman, *Fear at Work,* p. 19; Data Resources, Inc., *The Macroeconomic Impact of Pollution Control Programs* (Washington D.C.: U.S. E.P.A., 1981), p. 2. See also Green and Waitzman, *Business War on Law,* pp. 77–78; Henderson, *Creating Alternative Futures,* chaps. 1–4. On the "cleanup industry," see Keller, "Environmental Movement," p. 215.
82. Council on Wage and Price Stability study cited in Bowles et al., *Beyond the Wasteland,* p. 45; Data Resources Inc., *The Macroeconomic Impact,* pp. 17–18; James C. Miller III, "Lessons of the Economic Impact Statement Program," *Regulation,* July 1977, p. 15.

83. Mitchell, "Silent Spring," p. 55. See also Erskine, "The Polls: Pollution," pp. 121–123.
84. Cited in Conservation Foundation, *The State of the Environment—1982*, p. 426.
85. Ladd, "Clearing the Air," p. 18.
86. See Greenstone, *Labor in American Politics*, chap. 11. This new commitment was exemplified by the role of United Steelworkers of America and other labor groups in founding a leading public interest group, Consumer Federation of America, during the late 1960s.
87. Letter from Lane Kirkland concerning Solidarity Day protests, August 12, 1981. See generally, Noble, "The Contradicton of Social Regulation"; Gladwyn Hill, "Labor and Ecology Block," *New York Times* (September 9, 1976), p. a27; Kazis and Grossman, *Fear at Work*.
88. See Council for Public Interest Law, *Balancing The Scales;* Harrison and Jaffe, *The Public Interest Law Firm;* Weisbrod et al., *Public Interest Law*, chaps. 9, 10; Fred Heistand, "The Politics of Poverty Law," in Green and Wasserstein, eds., pp. 160–189; Lazarus, *The Genteel Populists*, pp. 142-143.
89. On the effects of the corporate campaign, see Tolchin and Tolchin, *Dismantling America;* Pertschuk, *Revolt against Regulation*. For a discussion concerning how "symbolic" politics distorts specific policy debates and public perceptions, see Murray Edelman, *The Symbolic Uses of Politics*.
90. Charles Reich wrote in the late 1960s that "no such luxury" of the new consumerism "was possible during most of man's history. It is wealth and technology that have made community and self possible." Richard Neuhaus concluded that "the notion of a post-scarcity world is the cornerstone assumption of the greening of America." *In Defense of People*, p. 131. The critical implications of the Faust image are explored by Marshall Berman, *All That Is Solid Melts into Air: The Experience of Modernity* (New York: Simon and Schuster, 1982), pp. 37–71.
91. Figures illustrating the decline vary among studies, sometimes to significant degrees. The indicators cited here are taken from three different sources representing three unique political perspectives. The basic liberal text is Thurow, *The Zero-Sum Society*. The conservative source is "The Shrinking Standard of Living," *Business Week*, January 28, 1980, pp. 72–78. See also The Business Week Team, *The Reindustrialization of America* (New York: McGraw-Hill, 1982). The Leftist analysis is from Elliot Currie, Robert Dunn, and David Fogarty, "The New Immiseration: Stagflation, Inequality, and the Working Class," pp. 7–32. See also Blumberg, *Inequality;* Cohen and Rogers, *On Democracy*, chaps. 2–3; Bowles et al., *Beyond the Wasteland*.
92. "The Shrinking Standard of Living," p. 73.
93. Conventional business interests ("Capital Crisis," *Business Week*, September 28, 1974, pp. 42–48) and Leftist analysts agree on the basic issue. The latter, however, tend to emphasize the structural conflict between oversupply and surplus of capital in high-profit sectors which outrun consumptive market capacity, thus resulting in stagflation. As long as prices, profits, and production levels are administered in the oligopolistic corporate sector, the expenditure of capital is far out of line with social needs—hence, the problem of "liquidity" shortage and vulnerability in crucial industries (housing, automobiles, stock firms) as well. See James O'Connor's argument in *The Fiscal Crisis of the State* for a useful if abstract treatment of the issues. The argument by Bowles et al. in *Beyond the Wasteland* is the most balanced and detailed on the subject. On recent corporate

trends, see Kenneth M. Davidson, *Mega-Mergers: Corporate America's Billion-Dollar Take-Overs* (Cambridge: Ballinger, 1985).

94. Yankelovich quoted in William Bowen, "The Decade Ahead," *Fortune,* October 8, 1979, p. 88.

95. Harris polls questioning citizens' estimates of the "two or three biggest problems facing people like yourself" between 1970 and 1976 alone reveal a rise in economic concerns from 52 to 85 percent, while concerns for health care (8 to 5 percent), energy (28 to 18 percent), and ecology (41 to 6 percent) fell markedly. See Francis Sandbach, *Environment, Ideology, and Policy,* p. 8. *Los Angeles Times* polls reflected much the same trend in 1984. In response to questions concerning the "two most important issues" facing Congress, a variety of economic concerns ranked at the top, while environmentalism ranked only tenth in salience (4 percent mentioned it). Cited in Scott Keeter, "Public Opinion in 1984," in Gerald Pomper et al., *The Election of 1984: Reports and Interpretations,* p. 96. These results can be contrasted with polls ranking environmentalism second on the same scale in 1971. See Erskine, "The Polls: Pollution," p. 125.

96. See Schnaiberg, *The Environment,* chap. 5.

97. Stretton, *Capitalism, Socialism and the Environment,* p. 51.

98. Richard Kazis and Richard Grossman, "The Future of the Environmental Movement," in Gartner et al., eds., p. 217.

99. See, for example, Bowles et al., *Beyond the Wasteland,* pp. 122–178.

100. Charles Lindblom poses the issue this way: "Can even a highly competent informed consumer vote for precisely the product he wants? Only if the corporation has taken the initiative to put the product on the market. Although the consumer wields a power veto, the initiative is largely in corporate hands." *Politics and Markets,* p. 153.

101. See Stuart Ewen, *Captains of Consciousness: Advertising and the Social Roots of the Consumer Culture;* Galbraith, *The New Industrial State;* Rick Wolff, "Economics, Advertising, and Consumer Culture," *Monthly Review* 29 (March 1978), pp. 49–55.

102. This argument is made in comprehensive fashion by Allan Schnaiberg, *The Environment.* Indeed, his image of "tail wagging" is the subtitle to his analysis of consumption as a political issue (chap. 4).

103. The embarassingly ironic twist to these facts is that some older environmental groups owned stocks and bonds in Exxon, General Motors, Tenneco, and other corporations until the late 1970s. Noted in Wendell Berry, *The Unsettling of America: Culture and Agriculture,* p. 17.

104. For a review, see Blumberg, *Inequality,* chaps. 3–4; Richard Barnett, *The Lean Years: Politics in the Age of Scarcity,* pp. 273–275, 241, 265.

105. Schnaiberg argues that "a piecemeal attack on environmental problems such as air pollution, water pollution, and energy consumption is ultimately not as effective as a close examination of total production in modern societies." *The Environment,* p. 25. As long as social regulation leaves the control of investment primarily in the hands of private capital, such transfers in investment priorities between productive sectors will be avoided or skewed for private particularistic purposes. Investment continues to flow to high-profit sectors—increasingly costly fossil fuel extraction, high-price luxury goods for the rich, low-price commodity fads for all—while administered prices of basic necessities rise rapidly to pay for the costs of dwindling or inaccessible resources; hence the irony that prices of stereo equipment and recreational activities remain bargains while the costs of

housing, health, and heating soar. The point is that social regulation of capitalist producers without economic regulation to control prices and distribute costs according to publicly determined criteria results in leaving most consumers to bear the brunt of sacrifices in unnecessarily burdensome ways. The new consumer demands for social quality do not cut painlessly into corporate profits and the wealth of the rich, but they are channeled into direct conflict with the basic material needs of American workers and the poor.

106. Lazarus's attack upon grand designs is a classic statement of the perspective. See *The Genteel Populists*.

107. See Wendell Berry, *The Unsettling of America*, for one inspiring view. Also relevant is Timothy Luke, "Notes for Deconstructionist Ecology," *New Political Science* 11 (Spring 1983), p. 21.

108. David Vogel, "Inadequacies," implies a similar criticism. On the attitudes of modern corporate captains, see Leonard Silk and David Vogel, *Ethics and Profits: The Crisis of Confidence in American Business* (New York: Simon and Schuster, 1976). It is important to emphasize, however, that business interests have used the claim about capital crisis as a crucial plank in their antiregulatory and antilabor campaigns.

109. Goodwyn, *The Populist Moment*, p. 84.

110. Quoted in Rogin, *The Intellectuals and McCarthy*, p. 170.

111. See Douglass C. North, "Was the New Deal a Social Revolution?" in North, ed., *Growth and Welfare in the American Past*, 2d ed. (Englwood Cliffs, N.J.: Prentice-Hall, 1974), pp. 164–169.

112. See Alan Gartner, Colin Greer, and Frank Riessman, eds., *What Reagan Is Doing to Us* (New York: Harper and Row, 1982). On the sources of the president's appeal, see Wilson Carey McWilliams, "The Meaning of the Election," in Pomper et al., *The Election of 1984*, pp. 157–184.

113. Williams, *The Contours of American History*, pp. 396–397.

114. Dahrendorf, *Class and Class Conflict*. For relevant application, see Greenstone, *Labor in American Politics*, chap. 11. See also Daniel Bell, *The End of Ideology* (New York: The Free Press, 1962), pp. 211–272.

115. Quote from David Shuman, *Ideology of Form*, p. 87. See generally Richard Sennett and Jonathan Cobb, *The Hidden Injuries of Class* (New York: Vintage, 1972).

116. On job insecurity and the structure of the labor market in an age of decline, see Blumberg, *Inequality*, chaps. 2, 6.

117. The classic work on the subject is Braverman's *Labor and Monopoly Capital*. See also *Work in America* by the HEW Task Force (Cambridge: MIT Press, 1973).

118. Schnaiberg, *The Environment*, pp. 372–374. On the relations among work, skill, and political confidence, see Paul Blumberg, *Industrial Democracy* (New York: Schocken Books, 1968). See also Carol Pateman, *Participation and Democratic Theory* (Cambridge: Cambridge University Press, 1970), p. 99.

119. Vernon Jordan quoted in Tucker, "The Environmental Era," p. 46. See generally Manning Marable, *From the Grassroots* (Boston: South End Press, 1980), p. 91; Lasch, *Agony of the American Left*, chap. 4. Most public interest groups are estimated to have less than 1 percent black membership.

120. See Donald J. Treiman and Heidi I. Hartmann, eds., *Women, Work, and Wages: Equal Pay for Jobs of Equal Value* (Washington, D.C.: National Academy Press, 1981); Anne Phillips and Barbara Taylor, "Sex and Skill: Notes toward a

Feminist Economics," *Feminist Review* 6 (1980), pp. 79–88. For the radical position, see Zillah R. Eisenstein, ed., *Capitalist Patriarchy and the Case for Socialist Feminism* (New York: Monthly Review Press, 1970).

121. Boyd, "Protection," p. 31.

122. See Martin Bronfenbrenner, "The Consumer," in James McKie, ed., *Social Responsibility and the Business Predicament* (Washington, D.C.: Brookings, 1974), pp. 187–188.

123. Holsworth, *Public Interest Liberalism*, p. 64, and chap. 4 generally. This view can be easily exaggerated and must be considered within the light of the overall rather sympathetic perspective adopted throughout my discussion.

124. Richard Neuhaus's extreme strictures do contain some truth: "Those who condemn the consumer society are consumers too; the counter-market is no less adept at manipulating, by invention and titillation, the appetite of its consumer slaves." *In Defense of People*, p. 51.

125. See the provocative argument of political scientist Timothy Luke in "Informationalism and Ecology," *Telos* 56 (Summer 1983), p. 59.

126. Lasch, *New Radicalism*, pp. ix–xxviii.

127. Hugh Stretton agrees, noting that "without a reorganization of production ... mild reformations of current industrial production systems will merely shift us from one problem to another." *Capitalism, Socialism and the Environment*, p. 25. See Vogel, "Inadequacies." For examples of increased compromise, see the essays by environmentalists in Kent Galbreath, ed., *Business and the Environment: Toward Common Ground* (Washington, D.C.: The Conservation Foundation, 1984).

128. See Nader's comments in "Alternatives for American Growth: A Conversation with Ralph Nader and Herman Kahn," *Public Opinion* 2 (August/September 1979), pp. 10–15.

129. This forced the context of environmentalist thinking from "surplus" to "scarcity," as Schnaiberg puts it. *The Environment*.

130. Simon Lazarus, *The Genteel Populists*, p. 160.

131. See Richard Grossman and Gail Banekes, *Energy, Jobs, and the Economy*.

132. The most influential leaders and spokespersons for this wing include Amory Lovins, E. F. Schumacher, Barry Commoner, Hazel Henderson, and, to a lesser extent, Ralph Nader. See David Dickson, *The Politics of Alternative Technology*. See Carnoy and Shearer, *Economic Democracy*, chap. 5, and Schnaiberg, *The Environment*, chap. 8, for optimistic assessments.

133. For a sympathetic review of the arguments and their chances of winning support, see Flacks, "Populism in Search of the People," pp. 26–35.

134. Green, *Winning Back America*, pp. 38–118. See Michael Pertschuk, "Consumers and Government to Police the Marketplace," *New York Times*, June 29, 1983, p. A29; Keller, "Environmental Movement," p. 211.

135. See David Sills, "Environmental Movement," p. 20.

136. This discussion owes much to Stuart Hill and David Orr, "Leviathan, the Open Society and the Crisis of Ecology," pp. 457–468. See also Holsworth, *Public Interest Liberalism*, chap. 6.

137. Garrett Hardin, "The Tragedy of the Commons," in Hardin and Baden, eds., *Managing the Commons*, pp. 16–30.

138. Ernest Callenbach, *Ectopia*, pp. 55–56, 118. See generally pp. 55–60, 114–121. This novel has enjoyed great popularity with environmentalists and is endorsed by both Nader and Friends of the Earth on its cover.

139. For hopeful proposals and projections, see Schnaiberg, *The Environment;* Kazis and Grossman, *Fear at Work;* Green, *Winning Back America.*

140. Andrew McFarland, "'Third Forces' in American Politics: The Case of Common Cause," in Jeff Fishel, ed., *Parties and Elections in an Anti-Party Age* (Bloomington: University of Indiana Press, 1978), p. 323. Conversations with activists during recent years have confirmed this point repeatedly.

141. The conservative maintenance incentives within large bureaucratic organizations are further discussed in the next chapters. Here, it is enough to quote Robert Mitchell's inside perspective that public interest liberals constitute a "reformist movement which harbors a vision of an 'appropriate' society which is neither too deep nor too left to alienate . . . its constituency." Quoted in Keller, "Environmental Movement," p. 1981.

142. Fuller, *The Morality of Law,* pp. 170–177. A similar view is implied in the analysis by Donald Horowitz, *The Courts and Social Policy.*

143. Harrison and Jaffe, *The Public Interest Law Firm,* p. 143; Weisbrod et al., *Public Interest Law,* pp. 28–29.

144. See Martin Shapiro, "The Constitution and Economic Rights," in M. Judd Harmon, ed., *Essays on the Constitution of the United States* (Port Washington, N.Y.: Kennikat Press, 1978), pp. 74–98.

145. Henderson, *Creating Alternative Futures,* p. 137.

Chapter 4. The Forms of Organized Citizen Action

1. Nader, "Consumerism and Legal Services," p. 251.

2. Tocqueville, *Democracy in America,* pp. 691–692.

3. John Gardner, *Excellence,* chaps. 12–13; *In Common Cause,* pp. 29-32.

4. Ross, *A Public Citizen's Action Manual,* p. 1. See also, for example, Gardner, *In Common Cause,* p. 73.

5. Green, *Winning Back America,* p. 326. Richard Frank, Joseph Onek, and James Steinberg, *Public Participation in the Policy Formulation Process,* pp. 13–14.

6. Sierra Club pamphlet, "Why the Sierra Club?"

7. Gardner, *In Common Cause,* p. 104; Henderson, *Creating Alternative Futures,* p. 7.

8. Nader cited in Buckhorn, *Nader,* p. 271; see also "Introduction," in Ross, *Public Citizen's Action Manual,* pp. viii–xiv; Sax, *Defending,* p. xix; Council for Public Interest Law, *Balancing the Scales,* p. 116.

9. Gardner, *In Common Cause,* pp. 85–91; Nader, "Consumerism and Legal Services," p. 251.

10. Pertschuk, "Consumers Ask Government," *New York Times,* June 29, 1983, p. A29.

11. David Truman, *The Governmental Process.*

12. E. E. Schattschneider, *The Semi–Sovereign People,* p. 35; McConnell, *Private Power and American Democracy;* Lowi, *The End of Liberalism.*

13. Murray Edelman, *The Symbolic Uses of Politics;* idem., *Politics as Symbolic Action: Mass Arousal and Quiescence* (Chicago: Markham, 1971).

14. Olson, *The Logic of Collective Action.*

15. Robert C. Mitchell, "National Environmental Lobbies and the Apparent

Illogic of Collective Action," pp. 87–121. Total numbers of members have varied over time and with different estimators; the figure of five million is a conservative one.

16. Terry Moe, *The Organization of Interests: Incentives and the Internal Dynamics of Political Interest Groups;* James Q. Wilson, *Political Organizations.*

17. For discussion of this argument, see Brian Barry, *Sociologists, Economists, and Democracy,* pp. 173–180. See also traditional criticisms of utilitarian theory such as John Plamenatz, *The English Utilitarians* (Oxford: Basil Blackwell, 1958), pp. 173–175. I tend to agree with the critics in this debate, but I still address the insights of rational choice theorists because, first, their approach has dominated social science perspectives on social reform movements and, second, they share much in common with the reform activists' own professional, market-based assumptions about political motivation and organizational forms.

18. Peter B. Clark and James Q. Wilson, "Incentive Systems: A Theory of Organizations," pp. 219–266; Robert H. Salisbury, "An Exchange Theory of Interest Groups," pp. 1–32.

19. Terry Moe, "Toward a Broader View of Interest Groups," pp. 531–543. See also idem., *The Organization of Interests.* Salisbury speaks similarly of "expressive" motives ("Exchange Theory," p. 16), and Wilson of a "sense of guilt" (*Political Organizations,* pp. 26–28).

20. Moe, *The Organization of Interests,* p. 144.

21. Berry, *Lobbying,* p. 43.

22. Constance E. Cook, "Membership Involvement in Public Interest Groups"; McFarland, *Public Interest Lobbies,* chap. 2; Arthur St. George, "The Sierra Club, Organizational Commitment, and the Environmental Movement in the United States"; William Devall, "The Governing of a Voluntary Organization: Oligarchy and Democracy in the Sierra Club"; Mitchell, "National Environmental Lobbies"; Handler, *Social Movements and the Legal System,* chap. 1.

23. The central theme here is the conflict between the ends of greater participatory democracy and more effective resource mobilization for professional advocates within the structure of the modern state.

24. The core of the following information is derived from publications and interviews collected from Common Cause in July 1980. Andrew McFarland kindly allowed me access at early stages to his comprehensive study, later published as *Common Cause: Lobbying in the Public Interest.* See also Theodore Jacqueney, "Common Cause Lobbyists," pp. 1294–1301; Mary Topolsky, "Common Cause?" pp. 35–39; David Cohen, "Comments on Andrew McFarland Paper," unpublished paper; Phil Mundo, "The Important Differences among Interest Groups: The Cases of the UAW and Common Cause," unpublished paper, University of California, Berkeley, 1980; Cook, "Membership Involvement."

25. Gardner, *In Common Cause,* p. 122.

26. McFarland, *Common Cause,* pp. 62, 99.

27. Topolsky, "Common Cause?" p. 37. She adds that "state organizations...enjoy little autonomy from the central office and are required to have their programs examined by the national board for conformity with national priorities." The acronym "PAC" used here refers to common cause program action committees, and not to political action committees.

28. McFarland, "Complexity," p. 30. McFarland calls conflicts over state organizational independence the Achilles heel of Common Cause. Idem., *Common Cause,* pp. 102–104.

29. McFarland, "Complexity," p. 18.
30. See Truman, *The Governmental Process*, pp. 197–199.
31. This fact of minority referenda power is important for my argument in subsequent chapters about the limits of the public interest agenda.
32. McFarland, "Complexity," p. 21. See also idem., *Common Cause*, pp. 61–107.
33. Cook, "Membership Involvement," pp. 6–10. See also Handler, *Social Movements and the Legal System*, chap. 1.
34. This is the theme of Topolsky's argument in "Common Cause?" although I find her analysis unjustly critical and lacking in attention to the larger social context.
35. McFarland, "Complexity," p. 23. See also idem., *Common Cause*, p. 100.
36. Berry, *Lobbying*, p. 193.
37. Rabin, "Lawyers for Social Change," pp. 232, 252, 258. See also Alan Morrison's comments in Clark, "After a Decade," p. 1137.
38. Nan Aron and Debora Clovis, *Survey of Public Interest Law Centers*, p. 14.
39. Berry, *Lobbying*, p. 186.
40. For a discussion of Nader's group structure, see McFarland, *Public Interest Group Lobbies*, pp. 67–77. See also Bo Burlingham, "Popular Politics."
41. St. George, "The Sierra Club," p. 39. See Devall, "The Governing of a Voluntary Organization."
42. St. George, "The Sierra Club," pp. 184–185. St. George makes two additional observations. Participation of members is significant in nonpolitical functions—educational programs, recreational outings. Also, there is evidence that many of the members are highly politically active outside the group. They vote, discuss issues, and contact public officials often. Yet, this reflects, he suggests, more their socioeconomic status than their membership in the groups per se.
43. Berry, *Lobbying*, pp. 188–190.
44. See Michael Hayes, "Interest Groups: Pluralism or Mass Society?"
45. Ross, *Public Citizen's Action Manual*, p. 223. See also Gardner, *In Common Cause*, p. 91.
46. Cook, "Membership Involvement," p. 19.
47. Lazarus, *The Genteel Populists*, p. 49.
48. See Berry, *Lobbying*, pp. 190–191. See also Judith Turner, "League of Women Voters Backs Study with Lobbying Influence Policy," *National Journal*, May 20, 1972, pp. 860–870.
49. Cook, "Membership Involvement," p. 19.
50. Hinerfield quoted in Cook, "Membership Involvement," p. 7.
51. McFarland, *Public Interest Lobbies*, pp. 77–83.
52. Bo Burlingham, "Popular Politics," pp. 10–12.
53. Ken Thomson, "Congress Watch Locals," *Citizen Participation* 1, November/December 1979.
54. Arthur St. George and William Devall document these relations. On environmental organizations generally, see Rosenbaum, *Politics of Environmental Concern*, chap. 3; Schnaiberg, *The Environment*, chap.VIII; Mitchell, "National Environmental Lobbies."
55. A 1981 *Congressional Quarterly* article noted that recent "techniques employed by the environmental lobby are the same modern practices employed by business." Keller, "Environmental Movement," pp. 1101–1102.
56. Cohen, "The Public Interest," p. 8.

57. Gardner, *In Common Cause*, p. 76. Conway quote is from Topolsky, "Common Cause?" p. 35.

58. Tocqueville, *Democracy in America*, pp. 62–63.

59. Ibid, p. 162. See also, Aristotle, *The Politics*, bk. VII, sec. 1, and *Ethics* IX, sec. 3.

60. Tocqueville, *Democracy in America*, pp. 189–195.

61. Ibid., pp. 69, 512–513.

62. Ibid., pp. 61–72.

63. Ibid., pp. 63, 87–98, 667–705.

64. See Schuman, *The Ideology of Form*, pp. 142–153; Goodwyn, *The Populist Moment*, esp. chap. 9.

65. Allan Schnaiberg summarizes that "with the partial exception of the nuclear power controversies, the social protest action now takes place in congressional hearings, regulatory commissions hearings and reports of environmental impact meetings, and in legislative lobbying and formal litigation." *The Environment*, p. 389. On the other hand, an important element of public interest legal advocacy has included proposals for more informal, localized forms of dispute resolution, ombudsman representation, and lay judicial proceedings. See Cahn and Cahn, "Power to the People or Power to the Profession?" See also Council for Public Interest Law, *Balancing the Scales*, pp. 355–358; Cunningham et al., *Strengthening*, chap. 1.

66. Quoted in Neal Pierce, "Sierra Club Tilting at Watt Futile?" *San Francisco Chronicle*, March 14, 1981.

67. Topolsky, "Common Cause?" p. 37.

68. Henderson, *Creating Alternative Futures*, p. 375. See also Ralph Nader, "A Citizen's Communications Agenda: Access in the Eighties," *Citizen Participation* 1 (May/June 1980), pp. 3–4, 16.

69. The obvious distinctions between the conventional settings of private living rooms or nature trails to which most public interest members confine their contributions and the action-oriented public spaces of community life celebrated by new populists often are ignored by many who are more optimistic about the new politics than myself. For a similar view, see Hayes, "Interest Groups."

70. Political theorist Sheldon Wolin has commented similarly in a *democracy* editorial that "the new politics has special conceptions of membership, participation, and civic virtue: a member is anyone entered on a computerized mailing list; participation consists of signing a pledge to contribute money; civic virtue is actually writing the check." "Editorial," *democracy* 2 (July 1982), p. 2.

71. For Walzer's argument, see his "A Day in the Life of a Socialist Citizen," in *Obligation: Essays on Disobedience, War and Citizenship* (Cambridge: Harvard University Press, 1970), pp. 229–238. The original statement of the view is attributed to Oscar Wilde. The term "checkbook affiliation" derives from Michael Hayes's provocative article "Interest Groups: Pluralism or Mass Society?" The marginality of such affiliations is suggested by evidence that up to half of new members each year do not renew their memberships. See McFarland, *Common Cause*, p. 46.

72. On the effects of life dominated by modern technological and bureaucratic forms, see Hannah Arendt, *The Human Condition*, esp. pp. 86–87, 128–129; Jacques Ellul, *The Technological Society;* Michael Parenti, *Power and the Powerless*, (New York: St. Martin's, 1978); Christopher Lasch, *The Culture of Narcissism;* idem., *The Agony of the American Left*. On the theme of fragmentation in

particular, see Ira Katznelson, *City Trenches: Urban Politics and the Patterning of Class in the United States* (Chicago: University of Chicago Press, 1981).

73. Christopher Lasch argues that "the new class can become an influence only if it operates outside of the existing structure of economic power, and only if it allies itself with... the unions." *Agony of the American Left*, p. 196. Tocqueville's general reticence about such issues is often exaggerated, but his moderate response to the problems of wage-labor dependency renders his own political prescriptions for "associations" somewhat insubstantial. This does not undermine the validity of his more general insights into the nature of political identity and forms. See *Democracy in America*, p. 556.

74. Tocqueville, *Democracy in America*, p. 292; see generally pp. 47–48, 442–451, 290–301. See also Eric Hobsbawm, "Religion and the Rise of Socialism," *Marxist Perspectives*, 1, 1978, p. 26; E. P. Thompson, *The Making of the English Working Class* (New York: Vintage, 1966).

75. Tocqueville, *Democracy in America*, pp. 521, 174–179. See also John S. Saloma III and Frederick H. Sontag, *Parties: The Real Opportunity for Effective Citizen Politics*. The essays on "Party Prospects" in *democracy*, 2 (3) (July 1982) are interesting on the subject. Barry Commoner's Citizens Party represents an effort to transcend these nonpartisan foundations, but it generally attempted to build from scratch rather than from existing organizational links.

76. John Gardner, *In Common Cause*, p. 27.

77. David Vogel makes a similar point in "The Inadequacies of Contemporary Opposition to Business." For more theoretical development of the idea, see Lasch, *Agony of the American Left*, chaps. 1 and 5; Goodwyn, *The Populist Moment;* Michael Walzer, "The Pastoral Retreat of the New Left," pp. 406–411. Again, however, it is Tocqueville who said it first and said it best: "To create a national representation of the people in a very centralized country does, therefore, diminish the extreme evils which centralization can produce but does not entirely abolish them." *Democracy in America*, p. 693.

78. Vogel, "Inadequacies," pp. 52–69; Paul Weaver, "Regulation."

79. See Boyd, "Protection"; Winter, *The Consumer Advocate versus The Consumer.*

80. Walsen H. Nielson, *The Endangered Species* (New York: Columbia University Press, 1979).

81. Despite the facts, this rallying claim still remains a staple of public interest reform rhetoric. See, for example, Green, *Winning Back America*, pp. 326–330; Pertschuk, *Revolt against Regulation*, pp. 126–151.

82. Lasch, *Agony of the American Left;* Goodwyn, *The Populist Moment;* Richard Flacks, "Making History and Making Life: Dilemmas of an American Left," pp. 263–280; Maurice Pinard, *The Rise of a Third Party: The Social Credit Party in Quebec in the 1962 Federal Election* (Englewood Cliffs, N.J.: Prentice-Hall, 1971).

83. Boyte, *Backyard Revolution*, p. 41. Michael Walzer likewise has concluded that the new liberals "are more likely to identify and represent a constituency than to mobilize its members for active struggle." "Pastoral Retreat," p. 408.

84. See Mitchell, "National Environmental Lobbies," pp. 102–112; Harriet Tillock and Denton E. Morrison, "Group Size and Contributions to Collective Action," in Louis Kreisberg, ed., *Research on Social Movements, Conflicts, and Change* (New York: JAI Press, 1979); Berry, *Lobbying*, pp. 41–43; St. George, "The Sierra Club," pp. 85–98.

85. Mitchell, "National Environmental Lobbies," pp. 107–110; Tillock and Morrison,

"Group Size," p. 21; Berry, *Lobbying*, pp. 37–41; McFarland, *Common Cause*, chap. 2; Cook, "Membership Involvement," pp. 3–6.

86. Russell Hardin and Robert C. Mitchell have carried on a continuous debate about the "rational" character of "purposive" incentives. My own view is that Hardin is correct that Mitchell wrongly collapses ethical and self-interested rational motivations into one category, although Hardin errs in emphasizing the exclusive, zero-sum relations between these motivations. As argued here, *both* ethical and rational concerns are at stake, although the primary issue is one of the structural context in which decisions are made. See Mitchell, "National Environmental Lobbies"; Hardin, "Comments", in Clifford S. Russell, ed., *Collective Decision Making*, pp. 122–130; Barry, *Sociologists, Economists, and Democracy*, pp. 40–46.

87. Gardner, *In Common Cause*, pp. 118–119.

88. See Barry, *Sociologists, Economists, and Democracy*, pp. 33–46; William Browne, "Benefits and Membership," *Western Political Quarterly* 29 (1976), p. 269. It is worth mentioning that many public interest activists, despite their participatory rhetoric, accept the illogic of "collective action" posited by rational choice theories, thus making these theories self-fulfilling to a degree. See, for example, Nader, "Consumerism and Legal Services," p.251; Hardin, "Tragedy of the Commons."

89. Topolsky, "Common Cause?" Public interest membership parallels what Alan Wolfe has called "alienated politics." *The Limits of Legitimacy*, chap. 9. On the politics of symbolic gratification, see Edelman, *The Symbolic Uses of Politics*.

90. W. Lance Bennett, *The Political Mind and the Political Environment*, chaps. 4–7. Roberta Ash Gardner's historical study of early reform movements likewise concludes that "as long as any of the strategies failed to change individual and group self-images, daily routines, and lifestyles, they could not succeed as organizing strategies." *Social Movements in America*, p. 139.

91. Tocqueville, *Democracy in America*, p. 339.

92. Charles Little notes that "when wars are imposed from the top down, you don't win. If there is a lesson from the Sixties, that is it. . . . It is the aggregate of individual actions that weigh the most in any emergency." "Epilogue," in Mitchell and Stallings, eds., p. 246. For an academic analogue to this position, see Frances Fox Piven and Richard A. Cloward, *Regulating the Poor* (New York: Vintage, 1971). For critical reviews, see E. J. Hobsbawm, "Should the Poor Organize?" *New York Review of Books*, March 23, 1978, p. 44; Jeff Lustig, "Community and Social Class," *democracy*, April 1981, pp. 94–111.

93. Henderson, *Creating Alternative Futures*, chaps. 13, 22.

94. Charles Little, "Epilogue," in Mitchell and Stallings, eds., pp. 246–247.

95. See Buckhorn, *Nader*, p. 259.

96. Gardner, *In Common Cause*, pp. 79, 99, 78.

97. Ibid., p. 111. See also pp. 106–107.

98. John Denvir, "Towards a Political Theory," p. 1160.

99. Ross, *Public Citizen's Action Manual*, p. xv. Joseph Sax adds that "the citizen is perfectly capable of fighting his own battles." *Defending*, p. 56.

100. Quotes from Mitchell and Stallings, eds., *Ecotactics*, pp. 12, 18, 70, 81, 247–248.

101. Gardner, *In Common Cause*, p. 92.

102. Cited in Buckhorn, *Nader*, p. 271.

103. On the impersonal dependence on law, see John T. Noonan, Jr., *Persons and Masks of the Law* (New York: Farrar, Straus, and Giroux, 1976).

104. See Chapter 5 of this volume for further discussion.

105. Mitchell and Stallings, eds., *Ecotactics*, pp. 66, 713. Gardner argues further that "there is a longing for authenticity, for immediate experience, for the emotional, symbolic, nonrational elements of life." *In Common Cause*, p. 106.

106. Henderson, *Creating Alternative Futures*, pp. 231–232; Gardner, *In Common Cause*, p. 89.

107. Cited in Bo Burlingham, "Popular Politics," p. 12.

108. St. George, "The Sierra Club."

109. Lazarus, *The Genteel Populists*, chap. 4.

110. Nader, "Introduction," in Ross, *Public Citizen's Action Manual*, p. viii. Schwartz, "Symposium," p. 78.

111. Moore, "The Lawyer's Response," in Wasserstein and Green, eds., p. 235; Cliff Humphrey, "Doing Ecology Action," in Mitchell and Stallings, eds., p. 67. These antiorganizational tendencies are especially true of environmentalists. David Lowenthal says that "the environmental cause exemplfies the antiinstitutional bias characteristic of American reformism." Cited in David Sills, "Environmental Movement," p. 20. Leo Marx also notes that "a certain innocent trust in the efficacy of words, propaganda, and rational persuasion always has characterized the conservation movement in this country." "American Institutions and Ecological Ideals," *Science*, November 1970, pp. 945–953.

112. Henderson, *Creating Alternative Futures*, p. 234.

113. Gardner, *In Common Cause*, p. 93.

114. Ibid., p. 95. See also Nader, "Introduction," in Ross, *Public Citizen's Action Manual*, p. xiii.

115. Wellford, "On How To Be a Constructive Nuisance," in De Bell, ed., p. 269.

116. See Salisbury, "An Exchange Theory of Interest Groups."

117. Humphrey, "Doing Ecology in Action," in Mitchell and Stallings, eds., p. 69; McCarthy and Zald, "Resource Mobilization," pp. 1228, 1231.

118. On the idea of political entrepreneurs, see Salisbury, "An Exchange Theory of Interest Groups." Michael Pertschuk uses this same term in a less academic sense. *Revolt against Regulation*, pp. 13–45. On politics as a consumer commodity, see Walter Dean Burnham, "Party Systems and the Political Process," in William H. Chambers and Walter Dean Burnham, eds., *The American Party Systems* (New York: Oxford University Press, 1967), pp. 300–301; Burlingham, "Popular Politics," p. 12.

119. Hayes, "Interest Groups"; William Kornhauser, *The Politics of Mass Society;* Robert Nisbet, *The Quest for Community* (New York: Oxford University Press, 1953). For critical discussion, see Halebsky, *Mass Society and Political Conflict.*

120. Kornhauser, *The Politics of Mass Society*, p. 73.

121. The tradition to which I refer owes most to Karl Marx. See "The 18th Brumaire of Louis Bonaparte" in particular. Contemporary exponents of such ideas in this tradition include Lasch, Wolfe, Parenti, and Halebsky. For a parallel argument that is consciously non-Marxist, see Harry C. Boyte and Sara M. Evans, "Strategies in Search of America: Cultural Radicalism, Populism, and Democratic Culture," *Socialist Review* 75/76 (May/August 1984), pp. 73–102.

122. Halebsky, *Mass Society and Political Conflict*, chaps. 5–6. For other

somewhat parallel discussions, see Anthony Oberschall, "The Los Angeles Riot," *Social Problems* 15 (Spring 1968), pp. 322–342; Charles Tilly, "Does Modernization Breed Revolution?" *Comparative Politics* 5 (April 1973), pp. 425–447; Donald Von Eschen, Jerome Kirk, and Maurice Pinard, "The Organizational Substructure of Disorderly Politics," *Social Forces* 49 (June 1971), p. 529; Flacks, "Making History."

123. Halebsky, *Mass Society and Political Conflict*, p. 126. In this sense, McFarland is right that public interest groups are democratic according to the polyarchal model, though they are not so according to the populist ideals they themselves extol. See his *Common Cause*, chap. 5.

124. See Lasch, *Agony of the American Left;* idem., *Culture of Narcissism*, for general discussion.

125. Alexis de Tocqueville, *The Old Regime and the French Revolution*, trans. Stuart Gilbert (New York: Anchor, 1955), p. 275.

126. Tocqueville, *Democracy in America*, pp. 429–430, 488, 691–692.

127. See Gardner, *In Common Cause;* De Bell, ed., *The Environmental Handbook;* Wasserstein and Green, eds., *With Justice for Some* for typical examples of such public interest "populist" rhetoric. Joel Handler concludes that "the structures of advanced capitalism are in place—massive bureaucracies and large, powerfully organized economic, social, and political interests. . . . These are the brutal facts facing 'dispersed nonspecialized, non-hierarchichal, voluntaristic units,' and just how are they going to mount this kind of campaign?" How indeed? *Social Movements and the Legal System*, p. 232.

128. Scheingold, *Politics of Rights*, p. 215. The following is based on my extensive survey of existing literature on rights and citizen participation. McCann, "Citizen Access and Citizen Participation: A Comparative Perspective," Boalt Law School, 1980 (unpublished).

129. Black, "The Mobilization of the Law," p. 133. Joel Handler's *Social Movements and the Legal System* comes to a similar conclusion.

130. Joel Handler, "Controlling Official Behavior in Welfare Administration," *California Law Review* 54 (1966), p. 479; idem., *Social Movements and the Legal System;* Neal Milner, "The Dilemmas of Legal Mobilization: Ideologies and Strategies of Mental Patient Liberation Groups," unpublished paper presented at the Western Political Science Association meetings, Sacramento, March 1984; Richard Elmore and Milbrey W. McLaughlin, *Reform and Retrenchment: The Politics of California School Finance Reform* (Cambridge, Mass.: Ballinger, 1982); Nader, "Freedom from Information"; Andrew Gordon, John Heinz, Margaret Gordon, Stanley Divorski, "Research Study: Public Access to Information," *Northwestern Law Review* 68 (May/June 1973), pp. 177–462.

131. Scheingold, *The Politics of Rights*, pp. 214, 119.

132. Anna Jackson and Angus Wright, "Nature's Banner: Environmentalists Have Just Begun to Fight." Quoted in "The Specter of Environmentalism: The Threat of Environmental Groups," Republican Study Committee Special Report, 1982.

133. See Scheingold, *Politics of Rights*, especially pp. 209–219; Lasch, *Agony of the American Left*, chap. 1.

134. Fiss, "The Supreme Court 1978 Term—Foreword: The Forms of Justice," p. 44.

135. Henderson, *Creating Alternative Futures*, pp. 374–375.

136. Jo Freeman, *The Politics of Women's Liberation*, p. 100.
137. See Green, *Winning Back America*, pp. 326–335.
138. Stewart, "The Reformation of American Administrative Law," p. 1806.
139. See Kristol, *Two Cheers for Capitalism*, chaps. 2–7. Bo Burlingham likewise jabs from the Left that "they don't organize citizens. . . . Instead, they act on behalf of the public, an abstract entity with which they have no direct contact." "Popular Politics," p. 12.
140. David Sanford, *Me and Ralph: Is Nader Unsafe for America?*; Dan M. Burt, *Abuse of Trust* (Chicago: Regnery Gateway, 1982).
141. See McFarland, "Complexity" and *Common Cause* for defense of this position. On the concept of "representation" generally, see Hanna Pitkin, *The Concept of Representation* (Berkeley: University of California Press, 1967).
142. Claybrook quoted in Gordon, "Public Interest Lobbies," p. 1197.
143. See, for example, Pertschuk, *Revolt against Regulation*, pp. 126–135.
144. *1979 EDF Annual Report*.
145. Booth quoted in Green, *Winning Back America*, p. 329.
146. Lazarus, *The Genteel Populists*, p. 165.
147. Peterson quoted in "Consumer Activists Now Seen as Part of the Establishment," Associated Press report in *Seattle Times*, March 1, 1983, p. D21.
148. Edey and Green quoted in Green, *Winning Back America*, p. 330; Mitchell quoted in Keller, "Environmental Movement," p. 214. See also Pertschuk, *Revolt against Regulation*, pp. 119–156.
149. See Salisbury on this logic. "An Exchange Theory of Interest Groups."
150. Robert Michels, *Political Parties* (New York: Collier, 1962), p. 15. See also F. Stuart Chapin and John Tsouderos, "The Formalization Process in Voluntary Organizations," *Social Forces* 34 (May 1956), pp. 342–344. Sheldon Wolin's discussion of organization is useful as well. *Politics and Vision*, chap. 10.
151. Quote from McCarthy and Zald, "Resource Mobilization," p. 1226. See also Berry, *Lobbying*; Handler, *Social Change and the Legal System*; Wilson, *Political Organizations*; John D. McCarthy and Mayer N. Zald, *The Trend of Social Movements in America: Professionalization and Resource Mobilization* (Morristown, N.J.: General Learning Press, 1973).
152. Cahn and Cahn, "Power to the People or to the Profession?"
153. Scheingold, *Politics of Rights*, p. 141. See also Handler, *Social Movements and the Legal System*, pp. 29–32.
154. Weisbrod, "The Public Interest Law Firm: A Behavioral Analysis" in Weisbrod et al., *Public Interest Law*, chap.1; Stewart, "Reformation of American Administrative Law," p. 1791.
155. Handler, *Social Movements*, pp. 29–32; Scheingold, *Politics of Rights*, p. 142. See also William Simon, "The Ideology of Advocacy: Procedural Justice and Professional Ethics," *Wisconsin Law Review* 78 (1978), pp. 29–144. The irony of these facts is striking. A movement that began from a populist critique of professional elite hierarchy ends up itself as a professional elite movement. James Ridgeway goes so far as to say that "in reality, they are working towards a new definition of the governmental system, in which lawyers are a commanding elite." Quoted in Sanford, *Me and Ralph*, p. 37.
156. Handler, *Social Movements*. See Lasch, *Agony of the American Left*, chap. 1.
157. Flacks, "Making History and Making Life," p. 270.

158. Ibid., pp. 270, 279.
159. Nader, "Introduction," in Ross, *Public Citizen's Action Manual*, p. xiv. See also Buckhorn, *Nader*, pp. 271–273.
160. Henderson, *Creating Alternative Futures*, pp. 227–228, 248, 376.
161. Gardner, *In Common Cause*, p. 92.
162. Cited in Holsworth, *Public Interest Liberalism*, p. 105; see pp. 106–118 generally. My discussion also owes much to the excellent analysis of Hill and Orr, "Leviathan," pp. 457–465.
163. Robert Heilbroner, *An Inquiry into the Human Prospect* (New York: Norton, 1974), p. 160.
164. William Ophuls, "Reversal in the Law of Tao: The Imminent Resurrection of Political Philosophy," in Stuart Nagel, ed., *Environmental Politics* (New York: Praeger, 1974), p. 40. For a critique see Holsworth, *Public Interest Liberalism*, chap. 6; John Schaar, "Power and Purity," *American Review* 19 (January 1974), pp. 152–179.
165. Cohen, "The Public Interest," p. 8. Morrison quoted in Keller, "Environmental Movement," p. 212.
166. Berry, "Lessons From Chairman Ralph"; Mark Green cited in Clark, "After a Decade," p. 1136. Harry Boyte acknowledges that "the focus on results— and the frequent disavowal of broader goals—accents a tendency toward professionalism and staff domination." Cited in James Green, "Populism, Socialism, and the Promise of Democracy," *Radical Historical Review* 24 (Fall 1980), pp. 35–36. Bo Burlingham adds also that "given their emphasis on professionalism and full-time 'public citizens,' the work falls almost exclusively on the staff." Despite "Nader's participatory vision of the better society," he notes, "the consequence seems built into the PIRG [and other Nader-type] operations." "Popular Politics," p. 11. See also Schnaiberg, *The Environment*, pp. 367, 388.
167. Jack Walker, "The Mobilization of Political Interests," paper delivered at the 1983 APSA meeting in Chicago, p. 30. See also McCarthy and Zald, "Resource Mobilization." But the recent conservative assault upon such government funds will effect these trends significantly. See Rochelle Stanfield, "'Defunding' the Left," and Chapter 5 of this volume.
168. These are the terms of strategy specifically encouraged by direct mail adviser Roger Craver in Clark, "After a Decade," p. 1139. On recent changes within environmental groups toward a more managerial orientation, see Beverly Beyette, "Earth's Observance: The Day Politics Stood Still," *Los Angeles Times*, May 30, 1985, p. 18.
169. See Scheingold, *The Politics of Rights*, and his later "The Politics of Rights Revisited," in James C. Foster, ed., *Governing through the Courts* (Beverly Hills: Sage, 1981), pp. 193–224. See also Denvir, "Towards a Political Theory of Public Interest Group Litigation"; Handler, *Social Movements*, chaps 1, 6; Sax, *Defending*.
170. Black, "The Mobilization of Law."
171. Butler quoted in Clark, "After a Decade," p. 1141. Michael Walzer likewise has argued that state mediation by laws "shape[s] the issues of particular struggles, and shape[s] it in ways that make advocacy and legal representation... more important than political mobilization." Most citizens, he says, "sit and wait, while the organizers and the lawyers do their work." "The Pastoral Retreat of the New Left," p. 408.

Chapter 5. Legitimacy and the Modern Liberal State

1. Goethe, *Faust*, Part III, Act 2.
2. Gardner, *In Common Cause*, p. 25.
3. Nader et al., *Taming the Giant Corporation*, p. 65. Andrew Hacker makes a similar claim that "neither our constitutional law nor our political theory can account for corporate presence in social power." Hacker, ed., *The Corporation Take-Over* (Garden City, N.Y.: Anchor, 1965), p. 8.
4. William James, "The Sentiment of Rationality," in his *Essays on Faith and Morals* (Cleveland: World, 1962), p. 83.
5. Cohen, "The Neo-Conservatives: Professional Pessimists."
6. Gardner, *In Common Cause*, p. 27.
7. John Platt, *Perception and Change: Projections for Survival* (Ann Arbor: University of Michigan Press, 1970), p. 162, and pp. 160–178 generally.
8. Neoconservative writers especially have been concerned about the "crisis" of legitimacy. See, for example, Samuel Huntington's classic chapter in Crozier et al., *The Crisis of Democracy*, pp. 59–65, 74–85; Kristol, *Two Cheers for Capitalism*. For an overall view, see Steinfels, *The Neoconservatives*. For parallel, if more critical, arguments from the Left, see Wolfe, *The Limits of Legitimacy;* Jurgen Habermas, *Legitimation Crisis* (Boston: Beacon Press, 1975).
9. Gardner, *In Common Cause*, p. 99. See also Nader, "Introduction," in Mitchell and Stallings, eds., p. 16.
10. Renewal and rebirth are favorite themes of Gardner (*Self Renewal: The Individual and the Innovative Society*, New York: Harper and Row, 1964), Nader ("Introduction," in Ross, *Action Manual*), and environmentalists generally who look to nature for transformative powers (see "Authority and Purpose," this chapter).
11. Frank et al., *Public Participation*, p. 1.
12. The following works have been most influential for my understanding of authority and legitimacy: John Schaar, "Legitimacy in the Modern State," pp. 276–327; Hannah Arendt, "What Is Authority?" in *Between Past and Future* (New York: Meridian, 1961), pp. 91–141; Carl Friedrich, "Authority, Reason, and Discretion," in Carl Friedrich, ed., *NOMOS 1: Authority* (Cambridge, Mass.: Harvard University Press, 1958), pp. 28–48; Bertrand de Jouvenel, *Sovereignty: An Inquiry into Political Good*, trans. J. F. Huntington (Chicago: University of Chicago Press, 1957); Richard S. Peters, "Authority," in Anthony Quinton, ed., *Political Philosophy* (Oxford: Oxford University Press, 1967), pp. 83–96; Habermas, *Legitimation Crisis;* Wolfe, *Limits of Legitimacy.*
13. Council for Public Interest Law, *Balancing the Scales*, p. ix. See also Riley, "Taming GM," in Wasserstein and Green, eds., pp. 207–210, 240–243.
14. Schaar, "Legitimacy," p. 313. On the idea of transactional relations, see James Macgregor Burns, *Leadership* (New York: Harper and Row. 1978).
15. Friedrich, "Authority," p. 34; Gardner, *In Common Cause*, p. 108.
16. De Jouvenel, *Sovereignty*, p. 35. See Scharr, "Legitimacy," pp. 291–293.
17. De Jouvenel, *Sovereignty*, p. 35.
18. Cohen, "The Neo-Conservatives." See also Nader, "We Need a New Kind of Patriotism."

19. Gardner, *In Common Cause*, pp. 102, and 99–107 generally; Ross, *Public Citizen's Action Manual*, p. 171; Sax, *Defending*, chaps. 4–8.

20. Arendt, "What Is Authority?" p. 97.

21. Harris and NORC polls discussed in Seymour M. Lipset and William Schneider, "Confidence in Confidence Measures," *Public Opinion* 6 (August/September 1983), p. 42; Arthur Miller, "Is Confidence Rebounding?" *Public Opinion* 6 (June/July, 1983), p. 20. See generally, Lipset and Schneider, *The Confidence Gap: Business, Labor, and the Public Mind* (New York: The Free Press, 1983).

22. The debate over realignment has flourished in recent years. For example, see the debate between Richard M. Scammon and Ben J. Wattenberg ("Is It the End of an Era?") and Everett Carl Ladd ("Realignment? No. Dealignment? Yes.") in *Public Opinion* 3 (August/September 1980), pp. 2–15, 54–55.

23. Nader quoted in Theodore Jacqueney, "Nader Network Switches Focus to Legal Action, Congressional Lobbying," p. 842.

24. Notable examples include Nadel, *The Politics of Consumer Protection;* Rosenbaum, *The Politics of Environmental Concern;* Berry, *Lobbying;* McFarland, *Public Interest Lobbies*.

25. Robert Dahl, *Who Governs?* (New Haven: Yale University Press, 1961); Truman, *The Governmental Process*. This point provides a central theme of Vogel's analysis in "Promoting Pluralism."

26. Hayes, "Interest Groups: Pluralism or Mass Society?" pp. 110–125; Douglas and Wildavsky, *Risk and Culture;* Walker, "Origins and Maintenance of Interest Groups"; Vogel, "Promoting Pluralism." On the politics of clientelism, see Lowi, *The End of Liberalism*, pp. 31–65.

27. Handler, *Social Movements*, pp. 222–233. Vogel suggests some of the same assumptions about corporatism in his original 1977 paper, "Promoting Pluralism," delivered at the American Political Science Association annual meetings, although they were deleted from the published version. Graham Wilson has noted that there is a "respectable argument" that public interest groups may encourage corporatism. See Graham Wilson, "Why Is There No Corporatism in the United States?" in Gerhard Lehmbruch and Philippe Schmitter, eds., *Patterns of Corporatist Policy Making* (Beverly Hills: Sage Publications, 1982), p. 233.

28. Philippe Schmitter, "Still the Century of Corporatism?" p. 95.

29. Handler, *Social Movements*, pp. 228–229. It should be noted in fairness to Handler's excellent book that his analysis of social movements includes groups oriented toward civil rights and welfare (poverty) as well as the more middle-class public interest groups that concern me here. My analysis suggests that the different social foundations of these groups has led to divergent relations with the state, although none approach the corporatist form of mutual interdependence.

30. Ibid.

31. President Carter quoted in Demkovich, "Consumer Leaders Hope That Carter Will Go to Bat for Them," p. 1136.

32. The activist is Ray Calamaro, a former lawyer for the Committee for Public Justice serving as assistant attorney general for legislative affairs under Carter. Quoted in Juan Cameron, "Nader's Raiders Are inside the Gates," p. 262. See Clark, "After a Decade," pp. 1136.

33. Clark, "After a Decade," pp. 1139–1141; Singer, "Liberal Public Interest Law Firms," p. 2054.

34. Wilson, "No Corporatism"; Robert H. Salisbury, "Why No Corporatism in America?" pp. 213–230.

35. Eric Nordlinger, *On the Autonomy of the Democratic State*, p. 186. On the fate of the National Industrial Recovery Act, see Ellis W. Hawley, *The New Deal and the Problem of Monopoly* (Princeton: Princeton University Press, 1966), pp. 111–130.

36. Wilson, "No Corporatism?" pp. 221–226; Salisbury, "Why No Corporatism in America?" pp. 215–218. The concept of "demand constraints" is advanced by Cohen and Rogers, *On Democracy*, pp. 51–62.

37. See Louis Hartz, *The Liberal Tradition in America*.

38. See Allan J. Cigler and John Mark Hansen, "Group Formation through Protest: The American Agriculture Movement," in Cigler and Loomis, eds., pp 84–109.

39. See Teresa Amott and Joel Krieger, "Thatcher and Reagan: State Theory and the 'Hyper-Capitalist' Regime," p. 10–13; Wilson, "No Corporatism?" On the relationship between Social Democratic parties and corporatist developments generally, see Gerhard Lehmbruch, "Concertation and the Structure of Corporatist Networks," in John H. Goldthorpe, ed., *Order and Conflict in Contemporary Capitalism* (Oxford: Clarendon Press, 1984), pp. 60–80.

40. On the concept of "iron triangles," see Hugh Heclo, "Issue Networks and the Executive Establishment," in King, ed., pp. 87–124.

41. For other versions of such more refined classification schemes, see John T. S. Keeler, *The Politics of Neo-Corporatism in France: Farmers, the State and Agricultural Policymaking in the Fifth Republic*, forthcoming from Oxford University Press, pp. 5–21; Lehmbruch, "Concertation," in Goldthorpe, ed.

42. See Chapters 3 and 4 of this manuscript. Salisbury, "Why No Corporatism in America?" p. 215.

43. Cited in McFarland, *Common Cause*, p. 118.

44. Ecologist quote is from Jeffrey Lustig, "Community and Class," *democracy* 1 (April 1981), p. 101. See also Buckhorn, *Nader*, pp. 264–265.

45. Jaffe, *Public Interest Law: Five Years Later*, p. 36; Onek and Lazarus, "The Regulators and the People," p. 1088. See also R. Cohen, "Public Interest Lawyers," p. 860.

46. On the financial status of advocates for the disadvantaged, see Nan Aron and Debora Clovis, *Survey of Public Interest Law Centers*, p. 17. Their findings indicate that the relative portion of total assets received from the government is substantial—42 percent for general minority rights, 63 percent for children's rights, 70 percent for poverty rights, and 74 percent for handicapped rights.

47. Walker, "Origins," pp. 399–400.

48. Weisbrod's 1975 survey of seventy-two public interest law firms found that only 11 percent of all revenues received came from government, and 9 percent from the federal government in particular. "Financing Public Interest Law," in Weisbrod et al., *Public Interest Law*, p. 535. The Council for Public Interest Law 1980 survey generally confirms this point on environmental (3 percent) and "other" (1 percent) groups, but not so much for consumer (60 percent) and multiissue (36 percent) organizations. But this survey is not very representative in these latter categories in that it includes several local and marginal groups while excluding the most important national organizations with which I am concerned (CFA, Public Citizen).

49. Berry, *Lobbying*, p. 28. See Chapter 4 of this volume for discussion.

50. Walker, "Origins," p. 400; Berry, *Lobbying*, p. 72.

51. Karen O'Connor and Lee Epstein, "Bridging the Gap between Congress and the Supreme Court"; "Note: Awards of Attorney's Fees to Unsuccessful Environmental Litigants," *Harvard Law Review* 96 (January 1983), pp. 677–696.

52. See Tolchin and Tolchin, *Dismantling America*, chaps. 2–6.

53. Sax, *Defending*, pp. 57, 60. The image is suggested by Coffee, "Rescuing the Private Attorney General: Why the Model of Lawyer as 'Bounty Hunter' Is Not Working," *Maryland Law Review* 42 (1983), pp. 215, 238. See generally the fine discussion by Barry Boyer and Errol Meidinger, "Privatizing Regulatory Enforcement."

54. Thomas Gais, Mark Peterson, and Jack Walker, "Interest Groups, Iron Triangles, and the President in American National Government," paper delivered at the 1982 annual meeting of the Midwest Political Science Association, p. 12.

55. Tolchin and Tolchin, *Dismantling America*, chap. 5; Cameron, "Nader's Raiders," pp. 256–259; Clark, "After a Decade," pp. 1140–1141.

56. See Lowi, *The End of Liberalism;* Heclo, "Issue Networks," in King, ed.

57. Cutler and Johnson, "Regulation and the Political Process," pp. 1395–1418. On antiexecutive attitudes in particular, see Gardner, *In Common Cause*, pp. 82–84, 109. The hostility to executive oversight is confirmed in Tolchin and Tolchin, *Dismantling America*, chaps. 2–3; Green, *Winning Back America*, pp. 118–164; Phillip Keisling, "The Reagan Chainsaw Massacre," pp. 25–31.

58. Bruce Ackerman and James Sawyer, "The Uncertain Search for Environmental Policy: Scientific Factfinding and Rational Decisionmaking along the Delaware River," p. 428. See also Christopher Stone, *Where the Law Ends: The Social Control of Corporate Behavior*, pp. 93–110; Horowitz, *Courts and Social Policy;* Ackerman and Hassler, *Clean Coal/Dirty Air,* chaps 3, 7; R. Shep Melnick, *Regulation and the Courts: The Case of the Clean Air Act.*

59. On the concept of "elastic nets," see A. Grant Jordan, "Iron Triangles, Woolly Corporatism, and Elastic Nets: Images of the Policy Process," *Journal of Public Policy* 1 (February 1981), pp. 95–125. See also Heclo, "Issue Networks," in King, ed.

60. Mancur Olson, *The Logic of Collective Action*, p. 124; idem., *The Rise and Decline of Nations: Economic Growth, Stagflation, and Social Regulation.* See also Samuel Beer, "In Search of a New Political Philosophy," in King, ed., p. 22; McConnell, *Private Power and American Democracy*, p. 362.

61. Heclo, "Issue Network," in King, ed., p. 89. One compelling neo-Marxist account of the modern state dilemma is Wolfe, *The Limits of Legitimacy*, pp. 247–287, 322–347.

62. Lowi, *The End of Liberalism*, p. 63. See also Schattschneider, *The Semi-Sovereign People*, pp. 30–36, 47–61.

63. Nordlinger, *Autonomy of the Democratic State*, p. 155.

64. Lowi, *The End of Liberalism*, p. 59.

65. See the argument of Samuel Huntington in Crozier et al., *Crisis of Democracy*, pp. 59–65, 74–85. He specifically blames liberal public interest groups for the "democratic surge" that undercut state authority in the 1970s (p. 61).

66. Schwartz quoted in Vogel, *Lobbying the Corporation*, p. 74. On social movement reliance on formal law, see Lowi, *The Politics of Disorder.*

67. Harrison and Jaffe, *The Public Interest Law Firm*, p. 39.

68. James S. Rummonds, "A Challenge to the Law," in Mitchell and Stallings, eds., p. 120.

69. Moore, "The Lawyer's Response," in Wasserstein and Green, eds., p. 333.

70. Kenneth C. Davis, *Discretionary Justice: A Preliminary Inquiry*, pp. 19, 17, 49. See also Judith N. Shklar, *Legalism* (Cambridge: Harvard University Press, 1964).

71. Nonet and Selznick, *Law and Society in Transition*, p. 15; Philip Selznick. "The Ideal of Legality," in *Law, Society, and Industrial Justice* (New York: Russell Sage Foundation, 1969), pp. 11–18; Shklar, *Legalism*.

72. Stone, *Where the Law Ends*, p. 104. See also Bardach and Kagan, *Going by the Book*, chaps. 2–4.

73. Bardach and Kagan, *Going by the Book*, p. 119. See also Stone, *Where the Law Ends*, pp. 93–121.

74. Ackerman and Hassler, *Clean Coal/Dirty Air;* Bardach and Pugliaresi, "Environmental Impact Statement"; Steven Kelman, *Regulatory America, Regulatory Sweden: A Comparative Study of Occupational Safety and Health Regulation;* Stephen Breyer, "Analyzing Regulatory Failure: Mismatches, Less Restrictive Alternatives, and Reform," pp. 547–609; Richard F. Elmore and Milbrey W. McLaughlin, *Reform and Retrenchment: The Politics of California School Finance Reform* (Cambridge: Ballinger Publishers, 1982).

75. Unger, *Law in Modern Society*, chaps. 2–3; Duncan Kennedy, "Legal Formality," pp. 351–398.

76. Unger, *Law in Modern Society*, pp. 66–88, 196–201, 240.

77. Orren, "Standing to Sue"; Henry P. Monaghan, "Constitutional Adjudication: The Who and When," *Yale Law Journal* 82 (1973), p. 1363; Horowitz, *Courts and Social Policy*, p. 19; Nonet and Selznick, *Toward Responsive Law;* Henry Friendly, *The Federal Administrative Agencies: The Need for Better Definition of Standards* (Cambridge, Mass.: Harvard University Press, 1962).

78. Stewart, "Reformation of American Administrative Law," p. 1805. This fact of declining generality may be progressive, of course, in that it both encourages individualized justice and hastens the "crisis" of liberalism. For a Marxist view, see Nicos Poulantzas, *State, Power, Socialism*.

79. This point significantly qualifies the argument of Bardach and Kagan, *Going by the Book*.

80. See, for example, the comments of environmental leader Jonathan Lash in Rochelle L. Stanfield, "Ruckelshaus Casts EPA as 'Gorilla' in State's Enforcement Closet," p. 1037.

81. Harry N. Scheiber, "Instrumentalism and Property Rights," *Wisconsin Law Review* 1 (1975), pp. 1–18; Stephen Diamond, "Legal Realism and Historical Method," *Michigan Law Review* (January 1979), pp. 784–794; Robert Summers, *Instrumentalism and American Legal Theory* (Ithaca, N. Y.: Cornell University Press, 1982).

82. See Kafka, "Before the Law" and "The Penal Colony," in *The Penal Colony*, trans. Willa and Edwin Muir (New York: Schocken, 1969), pp. 148–150, 191–230. Such inscrutability may account largely for the decline of faith in legal institutions. See Scheingold, *The Politics of Rights;* Austin Sarat and Richard Grossman, "Courts and Conflict Resolution: Problems in the Mobilization of Adjudication," p. 1215; Stewart, "Reformation of American Administrative Law," p. 1767.

83. On public opinion changes, see Anthony Downs, "Up and Down with Ecology: The 'Issue Attention Cycle,'" pp. 38–50. On agency rebuffs, see Paglin and Shor, "Regulatory Agency Responses." On growing business power, see Burdett A. Loomis, "A New Era: Groups and the Grass Roots," in Cigler and

Loomis, eds., pp. 169–190; Boyte, *Backyard Revolution*, chap. 1. A *Fortune* article in 1978 contended that "the business community has become the most effective special interest lobby in the city [Washington]. Suddenly, business seems to possess all the primary instruments of power, the leadership, the strategy, the support groups, the campaign money—and now a will to use them." Walter Guzarri, "Business Is Learning How to Win Washington," March 28, 1978, p. 53. On conservative public interest law, see Tamar Lewin, "War of the White Knights," *The National Law Journal* 2 (December 24, 1979), p. 15; Singer, "Liberal Public Interest Law Firms," pp. 2052–2056; O'Connor and Epstein, "Rebalancing the Scales of Justice."

84. Kay Lehman Scholzman, "What Accent the Heavenly Chorus? Political Equality and the American Pressure System," p. 1021.

85. See Tolchin and Tolchin, *Dismantling America*, chap. 5. As argued before, however, business relations still remain far too volatile, adversarial, and informal to qualify as even moderately corporatist.

86. See Berry, *Lobbying*, pp. 45–59.

87. See Charles Lindblom, *Politics and Markets;* Ralph Milliband, *The State in Capitalist Society.* The even greater economic powerlessness of disadvantaged groups impedes their potential corporatist development as well, although Handler may be correct that episodic social disruptions force more sustained relations of interdependency between such groups and the state (relative to public interest groups).

88. Tolchin and Tolchin, *Dismantling America*, pp. 43–109; Green, *Winning Back America.*

89. Alan Cawson, "Pluralism, Corporatism, and the Role of the State," *Government and Opposition* 13 (Spring 1978), p. 192.

90. Handler recognizes that the reformers' dependence on legalistic tactics reflects their relative social powerlessness, but he does not acknowledge the ways in which this powerlessness actually impedes corporatist integration into the state.

91. Amott and Krieger, "Thatcher and Reagan," pp. 13–26.

92. The literature documenting these changes is vast. See, for example, the essays in Norman J. Vig and Michael E. Kraft, *Environmental Policy in the 1980s: Reagan's New Agenda;* Lawrence Mosher, "Environmentalists Sue to Put an End to 'Regulatory Massive Resistance,'" pp. 2233–2234; idem., "Move Over, Jim Watt, Anne Gorsuch Is the Latest Target of Environmentalists," pp. 1899–1902; idem., "More Cuts in EPA Research Threaten Its Regulatory Goals, Critics Warn," pp. 635–639; Tolchin and Tolchin, *Dismantling America*, pp. 1–109; George Eads and Michael Fix, "Regulatory Policy," in John A. Palmer and Isabel V. Sawhill, eds., *The Reagan Experiment* (Washington D.C.: The Urban Institute Press, 1982), p. 140; Kazis and Grossman, *Fear at Work.*

93. See especially Tolchin and Tolchin, *Dismantling America.*

94. Cohen and Rogers, *On Democracy*, p. 26; Tolchin and Tolchin, *Dismantling America*, pp. 73–79; 90–96, 199–202. See generally Sierra Club, *Poisons on the Job: The Reagan Administration and American Workers;* Friends of the Earth, *Ronald Reagan and the American Environment;* Jonathon Lash et al., *Season of Spoils: The Reagan Administration Attack on the Environment.* On funding cuts, see Stanfield, "'Defunding' the Left," pp. 1374–1378; Keller, "Environmental Movement," pp. 211–216; Michael Wines, "Lobbyists United to Lobby Against OMB's Proposed Cuts on Lobbying," *National Journal*, February 19, 1983, pp.

370–372; idem. "OMB Pulls Back Its Political Advocacy Rule," *National Journal*, March 19, 1983, p. 324.

95. See "Editorial," *New York Times*, June 4, 1981, p. A22; Keller, "Environmental Movement," p. 211.

96. Quoted in Keller, "Environmental Movement," p. 213. On the actual increase of lawsuits, see Michael Wines, "Administration, Critics Play Legal Cat and Mouse Game on Agency Rules," *National Journal*, December 18, 1982, pp. 2157–2160; Boyer and Meidinger, "Privatizing."

97. Boyer and Meidinger, "Privatizing," pp. 48–49.

98. Jonathan Lash quoted in Mosher, "Enviromentalists Sue," p. 2233.

99. Not only is Reagan likely to fill several Supreme Court positions, but, more important, he will be able to replace nearly half (about 320 of 744 total) of the active federal judgeships before his term ends. As an American Bar Association analysis has documented, these posts are going primarily to affluent white males with clearly conservative ideological biases. Reported in Robert Friedman and Stephen Wermeil, "Reagan Appointments to the Federal Bench Worry Liberals," *Wall Street Journal*, September 6, 1985, pp. 1, 13.

100. Even McFarland admits as much. *Common Cause*, p. 159. See Gary Jacobson, *Money in Congressional Elections* (New Haven: Yale University Press, 1980).

101. For conservative perspectives, see Jeanne Kirkpatrick, *Dismantling the Parties* (Washington, D.C.: American Enterprise Institute, 1978); Everett Carl Ladd, Jr., "Reform Is Wrecking the U.S. Party System," *Fortune*, 96 (November 1977). For alternative liberal views on party decline, see the essays by Burnham, Connolly, and Polsky in the "Party Prospects" issue of *democracy* 2 (July 1982), pp. 7–27, 42–51 and the essays in Thomas Ferguson and Joel Rogers, eds., *The Hidden Election: Politics and Economics in the 1980 Presidential Campaign* (New York: Pantheon Books, 1981). See McFarland, *Common Cause*, chap. 7, for a sympathetic treatment of the reform proposals.

102. John Atlas, Peter Dreier, and John Stephens, "A Party for Change," in Gartner et al., eds., p. 337.

103. Ibid. See, for example, Nader, "The Consumer Movement Looks Ahead," p. 271; Gardner, *In Common Cause*, pp. 117–118; De Bell, ed., *The Environmental Handbook*, pp. 312–318.

104. Quoted in Clark, "After a Decade," p. 1139.

105. Wilson, *The Amateur Democrat*. A qualified exception among the reformers has been David Cohen and other Common Cause activists. See Cohen, "Reviving the Political Party System."

106. Schattschneider, *The Semi-Sovereign People*, p. 58.

107. See, for example, Walter Dean Burnham, *Critical Elections and the Mainsprings of American Politics* (New York: Norton, 1970); Saloma and Sontag, *Parties: The Real Opportunity for Effective Citizen Politics*. On the New Right and the Republican party, see Crawford, *Thunder on the Right*, pp. 225–244.

108. It is true that Democratic administrations have been disappointing to the liberals, and that the Nixon and Ford administrations did not differ radically from the Democrats in their domestic policy orientation. However, not only has there been much greater general issue and value agreement on balancing social and economic priorities between liberal reformers and Democratic legislators, but the entire regulatory ethic itself has depended on the New Deal consensus created and sustained by the Democratic legacy. For empirical evidence about

both policy and ideological bonds between Democrats and the reformers, see Riley Dunlap and Michael Allen, "Partisan Differences on Environmental Issues, a Legislative Roll Call Analysis," *Western Political Science Quarterly* 19 (September 1976), pp. 384–397; Jerry W. Calvert, "Legislators' Party Affiliation and Environmental Voting," paper delivered at the 1985 annual meeting of the Western Political Science Association, Las Vegas, Nevada.

109. For a provocative analysis of this theme, see Jacques Ellul, *The Political Illusion*, trans. Konrad Kellen (New York: Knopf, 1972).

110. See Gerhard Lehmbruch, "Liberal Corporatism and Party Government," in Schmitter and Lehmbruch, eds., *Trends toward Corporatist Intermediation*, pp. 147–183; Wolfe, *Limits of Legitimacy*, pp. 271–278, 305–313; Shattschneider, *Semi-Sovereign People*, pp. 47–62; Saloma and Sontag, *Parties*.

111. Walter Dean Burnham, "The Constitution, Capitalism, and the Need for Rationalized Regulation," in Robert A. Goldwin and William A. Schambra, eds., *How Capitalistic Is the Constitution?* (Washington D.C.: American Enterprise Institute, 1982), pp. 97, 95.

112. For an optimistic view, though, see Atlas et al., "Party for Change," in Gartner et al., eds. Whether the middle-class liberals can contribute to Rev. Jesse Jackson's vision of a Rainbow Coalition remains to be seen as well.

113. See Andrew J. Polsky, "Political Parties and the New Corporatism," *democracy* 2 (July 1982), pp. 42–51. See also Robert Lubar, "Making Democracy Less Inflation Prone," *Fortune*, September 22, 1980, p. 83; Everett C. Ladd,"How to Tame the Special Interest Groups," *Fortune*, October 20, 1980, pp 66–80.

114. Green, *Winning Back America*, pp. 330–335. The Sierra Club for the first time endorsed a presidential candidate in 1984. See Staff Report, "Sierra Club Endorses Mondale/Ferraro," *Sierra* 69 (September/October 1984), pp. 38–40. Some activists, including most notably Mark Green, have attempted to win electoral office themselves. The new attitude is captured in the words of liberal lawyer Bruce Morrison: "I had always been skeptical of electoral politics because of the compromise it involved. . . . But Reagan cleared the air by polarizing the country. It became important and more possible to run a progressive campaign than before." Quoted in John Judis, "Look Left among the Democrats," *In These Times*, June 30–July 13, 1982. See also Cohen, "Reviving the Political Party System."

115. Atlas et al., "Party for Change," in Gartner et al., eds., p. 338.

116. Green, *Winning Back America*, p. 330. The Wilderness Society, to name one group, could not be counted on to join a move to formal Democratic alliance, given the fact that over one-half of their constituents voted for Reagan in 1980. Keisling, "The Reagan Chainsaw Massacre."

117. "Law, to be stable, must be based on ethics," says Garrett Hardin in the introduction to Stone, *Should Trees Have Standing?*, p. xii. In earlier America, Christian religious values defined the ethical imperatives that checked as well as supported the privativistic, selfish propensities of market society. The need to replace, redefine, or supplement these long-withered moral constraints of community and common purpose with new political values defines the important issue here.

118. Gardner, *In Common Cause*, p. 101.

119. McCloskey, "Foreword," in Mitchell and Stallings, eds., p. 11.

120. Lazarus, *The Genteel Populists*, chap. 7.

121. Brian Barry, *Political Argument* (London: Routledge and Kegan Paul,

1965). Barry distinguishes between "want-oriented" and "ideal-oriented" appeals.

122. Garrett Hardin and other technocratic environmentalists are the most extreme examples of these tendencies. See Holsworth, *Public Interest Liberalism*, esp. chaps. 4, 6. My analysis parallels that of Holsworth on these issues, although we divide on some others.

123. Gardner, *In Common Cause*, p. 103. See John Schaar, *Escape from Authority* (New York: Basic Books, 1961), for a classic treatment of this theme. See also Phillip Rieff, *The Triumph of the Therapeutic* (New York: Harper, 1966).

124. Henderson, *Creating Alternative Futures*, pp. 77–80.

125. For a revisionist view of markets as tools of authoritative public value allocation, see Charles Schultze, *The Public Use of Private Interest* (Washington, D.C.: Brookings Institute, 1977).

126. Schaar, *Escape from Authority*, p. 154. See generally pp. 142–158.

127. Virginia Held, *The Public Interest and Individual Interests* (New York: Basic Books, 1973). See also Richard Flatham, *The Public Interest* (New York: Wiley, 1965).

128. Stephen Bailey, "The Public Interest: Some Operational Dilemmas," in Carl Friedrich, ed., *NOMOS V: The Public Interest*, p. 62.

129. Peter Schuck quoted in Sanford, *Me and Ralph*, p. 46.

130. Gardner, *In Common Cause*, p. 83; David Cohen quoted in Gordon, "Public Interest Lobbies," p. 1197. See also, Weisbrod et al., *Public Interest Law*, pp. 26–29; Harrison and Jaffe, *The Public Interest Law Firm*, p. 8; Halpern and Cunningham, "Reflections on the New Public Interest Law," p. 1098; Lazarus, *The Genteel Populists*, p. 153.

131. Peter Borelli, "Say 'Conservation,' Not 'War,'" in *Amicus*, April 1980, p. 5.

132. Schuck quoted in Sanford, *Me and Ralph*, p. 49.

133. Marks, Leswing, and Fortinsky, *The Lawyer, the Public, and the Professional Responsibility*, p. 51.

134. See Moore, "The Lawyer's Response," in Wasserstein and Green, eds., p. 315; Frank et al., *Public Participation*, pp. 13–14. Harrison and Jaffe affirm that "a central idea of our democratic society is that the general interest or common good will emerge out of the conflict of special interests." *The Public Interest Law Firm*, p. 8.

135. See, for example, Kristol, *Two Cheers for Capitalism*.

136. See Holsworth, *Public Interest Liberalism*, for a related but somewhat different argument.

137. The activists are seeking to develop "a new metaphysics, epistemology, cosmology, and environmental ethic of person/planet," says William Devall. "The Deep Ecology Movement," pp. 299–332.

138. For a classic statement of the "land ethic," see Aldo Leopold, *A Sand County Almanac* (New York: Oxford University Press, 1966). See Henderson, *Creating Alternative Futures*, for a popular version of the vision.

139. Leo Marx, *The Machine in the Garden* (London: Oxford University Press, 1964); idem., "American Institutions and Ecological Ideals."

140. See Bennett Berger, "Alternative Life Styles and the Quality of Life," in Clarke and List, *Environmental Spectrum*, pp. 11–124. See also Morris Dickstein, *Gates of Eden: American Culture in the Sixties* (New York: Basic Books, 1972).

141. Quoted in Peter R. Janssen, "The Age of Ecology," in Mitchell and Stallings, eds., p. 55.

142. The ruling party in *Ecotopia* is called the "Survivalist party."

143. Mitchell and Stallings, eds., *Ecotactics*, pp. 34–35, 155.

144. Robert C. Mitchell, "National Environmental Lobbies," pp. 113–114.

145. Platt article reprinted in his *Perception and Change: Projections for Survival* (Ann Arbor: University of Michigan Press, 1970), pp. 160–178; quote on p. 162. See also Rosenbaum, *Politics of Environmental Concern*, p. 64; De Bell, ed., *Environmental Handbook*, p. 161.

146. Paul Ehrlich, "A Playboy Interview," in *Project Survival* (Chicago: The Playboy Press, 1971), p. 77.

147. See Murray Bookchin, "Ecology and Revolutionary Thought," *Motive*, April/May 1974, pp. 330–341; N. Scott Momaday, "An American Land Ethic," in Mitchell and Stallings, eds., pp. 97–105.

148. Cited in Renee Dubos, "Humanizing the Earth," *Science* 179 (1973), pp. 769–772. See Commoner, *The Closing Circle*, pp. 37–41.

149. William Wordsworth, "The Tables Turned," (1798), in M. H. Abrams, ed., *The Norton Anthology of English Literature* (New York: Norton, 1968), p. 1262.

150. Newhall and Brower quoted in Kenneth Brower, "Wilderness," in De Bell, ed., pp. 147–148.

151. Alfred R. Ferguson, ed., *The Collected Works of Ralph Waldo Emerson* (Cambridge, Mass.: Belknap Press, 1971), p. 10.

152. Brower quoted in Neuhaus, *In Defense of People*, p. 143; Kenneth Brower, "Wilderness," in De Bell, ed., p. 150; Gussow, "Who Needs Nature?" in Mitchell and Stallings, eds., p. 240. Kenneth Boulding appeals likewise to the "restoration of a depleting psychic capital" in nature in "The Economics of Spaceship Earth," in De Bell, ed., p. 98.

153. See Richard Meir, "The Other Side of Pollution," in E. Pohlman, ed., *Population: A Clash of Prophets* (New York: New American Library, 1973), p. 215; St. George, "Sierra Club"; John McPhee, *Encounters with the Archdruid*.

154. Emerson in Edward C. Lindeman, ed., *Basic Selections from Emerson* (New York: Mentor, 1954), p. 193.

155. For a survey of the diversity in America alone, see Marx, *The Machine in the Garden*. On the destructive, repressive link to nature in particular, see Richard Slotkin, *Regeneration through Violence: The Mythology of the American Frontier, 1600–1860* (Middletown, Conn.: Wesleyan University Press, 1974).

156. For an overview of attempts to develop a moral philosophy from nature and wilderness, see Roderick Nash, *Wilderness and the American Mind*, especially chap. 13.

157. See, for example, Gussow, "Who Needs Nature?" in Mitchell and Stallings, eds., pp. 240–241.

158. Hardin, "The Tragedy of the Commons," pp. 48–49. The imperative of "necessity" here refers more to the substance than to the style of claims. See Hannah Arendt's interesting discussion in *The Human Condition*.

159. Quoted in Mitchell, "National Environmental Lobbies," p. 114.

160. Neuhaus, *In Defense of People*, p. 117.

161. Wagner, "The Ecology of Revolution," in Mitchell and Stallings, eds., pp. 45–47.

162. Ibid., pp. 49, 47.

163. Claybrook quoted in Letter to the Editor, *Regulation*, March/April 1979, p. 4; Marion Edey, "Eco-Politics and the League of Conservation Voters," in De Bell, ed., pp. 315–316.

164. Arendt, *The Human Condition*, pp. 84–88.

165. Andre Gorz, *Ecology as Politics*, p. 16. For parallel arguments, see Neuhaus, *In Defense of People;* Luke, "Informationalism and Ecology;" Hans M. Enzensburger, "Critique of Political Ecology," pp. 3–32.

166. See Holsworth, *Public Interest Liberalism*, chap. 3. Holsworth does not make the link between ecology and defensiveness per se suggested here; he instead focuses on "liberalism" as the key.

167. Little, "Epilogue," in Mitchell and Stallings, eds., p. 244.

168. Nader quoted in Lazarus, *The Genteel Populists*, p. 21; in Handler, *Social Movements and the Legal System*, p. 4.

169. Gardner quoted in Topolsky, "Common Cause?" p. 38; Moore, "The Lawyer's Response," in Wasserstein and Green, eds., p. 300.

170. See Bardach and Kagan, *Going by the Book*, p. 12.

171. Thomas Hobbes, *Leviathan* (London: Collier Books, 1962), pp. 7, 159–162. See Holsworth, *Public Interest Liberalism*, for a parallel argument about such "defensive liberalism" (chap. 3), although his own discussion of the link between Hobbes and ecology is applied to other concerns (chap. 6).

172. John Gardner says that "people value a degree of safeness.... Because order offers some measure of predictability, most Americans seek order and fear disorder." Quoted in Topolsky, "Common Cause?" p. 37. Critic William Tucker complains that "to say that one is an environmentalist... is to say that one has achieved enough well-being from the present system and that one is now content to let it remain as it is." "Environmentalism and the Leisure Class," p. 80. A more sophisticated version of this view is advanced in Douglas and Wildavsky, *Risk and Culture*. I endorse neither of these two latter assessments except with regard to the narrow point of "defensiveness" discussed here.

173. Leopold, *Sand County Almanac*, p. 217. The term "defensive liberalism" is borrowed from Robert Holsworth's discussion of Nader, *Public Interest Liberalism*.

174. Mitchell, "National Environmental Lobbies."

175. *Environmental Action 1979 Annual Report*.

176. Bardach and Pugliaresi, "The Environmental Impact Statement," pp. 22–38.

177. Fuller, *The Morality of Law*. See also Stone, *Where the Law Ends*, p. 101.

178. Nader quoted in Holsworth, *Public Interest Liberalism*, p. 43. Garrett De Bell is less subtle: "All power pollutes," he says. De Bell, ed., *The Environmental Handbook*, p. 66.

179. Lazarus, *The Genteel Populists*, p. 271.

180. Marshall Berman, "Buildings are Judgement or 'What man Can Build,'" p. 36. See also idem., *All That Is Solid*, pp. 37–71, 290–312.

181. On adversity theory, see McFarland, *Common Cause*, p. 13. See also Jules Maddox, *The Doomsday Syndrome* (New York: McGraw-Hill, 1972). Robert Mitchell's "National Environmental Lobbies" is relevant here.

182. *1977 ACLU Annual Report*.

183. David Darlington, "Thank You, Secretary Watt: Boom Times at the Sierra Club," *New West Magazine*, August 1981; Keller, "Environmental Movement." On the direct costs of this reactive symbolic politics, see Keisling, "The Reagan Chainsaw Massacre"; Phillip Shabecoff, "Watt, Burford May Have Taken Environmentalists' Momentum," *New York Times*, September 23, 1983.

184. Notable counterexamples from within the environmental leadership ranks include Wendell Berry, *The Unsettling of America*, and E. F. Schumacher, *Good Work* (New York: Harper and Row, 1979).

185. St. George, "Sierra Club," p. 126.
186. Janssen, "The Age of Ecology," in Mitchell and Stallings, eds., p. 56; De Bell, "A Future That Makes Sense," in De Bell, ed., pp. 153–158.
187. Gorz, *Ecology as Politics*, p. 20. Reich, *The Greening of America*. See the essays in Mitchell and Stallings, eds., *Ecotactics*, and De Bell, ed., *The Environmental Handbook* generally.
188. George Shulman, "The Pastoral Idyll of democracy," *democracy* 3 (Fall 1983), p. 45, 34–54 generally. The argument advanced here is not intended to suggest that attention to nature per se is not useful for restructuring our thinking about social and political life. Feminist theorists in particular have addressed questions of both psychological and physical nature to provide support for a radical reconstruction of society, often with quite impressive results. See, for example, Mary Midgely, *Beast and Man: The Roots of Human Nature* (Ithaca: Cornell University Press, 1976); Carolyn Merchant, *The Death of Nature: Women, Ecology, and the Scientific Revolution* (San Francisco: Harper and Row, 1980); Isaac Balbus, *Marxism and Domination: A Neo-Hegelian, Feminist, Psychoanalytic Theory of Sexual, Political, and Technological Liberation* (Princeton: Princeton University Press, 1982). See also Murray Bookchin, *The Ecology of Freedom: The Emergence and Dissolution of Hierarchy* (Palo Alto, Calif.: Cheshire Books, 1982).
189. For an interesting essay on this subject, see John Schaar, "Power and Purity," *American Review: No. 19* (Toronto: Bantam Books, 1974), pp. 152–179.
190. Quoted in Buckhorn, *Nader*, p. 293.
191. Adrienne Koch and William Peden, eds., *The Life and Selected Writings of Thomas Jefferson* (New York: Modern Library, 1964), pp. 522–525, 527, 596, 626.
192. From collected FOE and Common Cause membership solicitations. See also Holsworth, *Public Interest Liberalism*, chap. 3.
193. Buckhorn, *Nader*, p. 259. See chaps. 14–16 generally.
194. See, for example, Nader "Introduction," Mitchell and Stallings, eds., pp. 13–19.
195. Arendt, *The Human Condition*, p. 157. See chap. 5 generally.
196. D. H. Lawrence, "The Spirit of Place," in *Studies in Classic American Literature* (New York: Viking Press, 1971), p. 3
197. Goodwyn, *The Populist Moment*, p. 307.
198. Ralph Waldo Emerson, "Nature," in *Emerson's Essays* (New York: Thomas Y. Crowell Co., 1951), p. 387.
199. Karl Marx, "The German Ideology," in Tucker, ed., *The Marx-Engels Reader*, pp. 146–200.
200. See Roberto M. Unger, *Knowledge and Politics* (New York: The Free Press, 1975).
201. Quoted from Callenbach, *Ecotopia*, p. 55.
202. Cahn and Cahn, "Power to the People."
203. See Shulman, "Pastoral Idyll."
204. David Brower, "A Time for Sarsaparilla," in De Bell, ed., p. 10.
205. Perry Miller, "Nature and National Ego," in *Errand into the Wilderness* (Cambridge: Harvard University Press, 1976), p. 211.

Postscript

1. On the achievement and implications of Reagan's victories, see the essays in Thomas Ferguson and Joel Rogers, eds., *The Hidden Election: Politics and Economics in the 1980 Election* (New York: Pantheon Books, 1981); Pomper et al., *The Election of 1984*.

2. On the issue of realignment, see the argument of Richard M. Scammon and Ben J. Wattenberg, "Is It the End of An Era?" *Public Opinion* 3 (August/ September 1980), pp. 2–15; Gerald Pomper, "The Presidential Election," in Pomper et al., *The Election of 1984*, pp. 84–89.

3. Kevin P. Phillips, *Post-Conservative America: People, Politics, and Ideology in a Time of Crisis* (New York: Random House, 1982); Crawford, *Thunder on the Right*.

4. For arguments in defense of this claim, see Alan Gartner, Colin Greer, and Frank Riessman, eds., *What Reagan Is Doing to Us* (New York: Harper and Row, 1982); Gartner et al., eds., *Beyond Reagan*. For an interesting view, see Christopher Lasch, "The Politics of Nostalgia," *Harper's*, November 1984, p. 70.

5. Phillips, *Post-Conservative America*. See also the interesting analysis by Wilson Carey McWilliams. "The Meaning of the Election," in Pomper, *The Election of 1984*, pp. 157–183.

6. Viguerie cited in Michael Lienesch, "Right-Wing Religion: Christian Conservatism as a Political Movement," *Political Science Quarterly* 97 (Fall 1982), p. 410. This article by Lienesch supports my point generally. See also Crawford, *Thunder from the Right;* Richard J. Neuhaus, *The Naked Public Square* (Grand Rapids, Mich.: Eerdmans, 1984).

7. See, for example, O'Conner and Epstein, "Rebalancing the Scales"; Hauck, "With Charity for All."

8. On the substance as well as organization of New Right politics, see Lienesch, "Right-Wing Religion"; Crawford, *Thunder from the Right*.

9. On the question of public opinion toward the New Right, see William Schneider, "Opinion Outlook: Reagan May Find That Presidential Politics and Religion Really Don't Mix," *National Journal*, September 8, 1984, pp. 1690–1691.

10. The general discussion of public opinion and partisan attachment presented in this paragraph owes much to Pomper, "The Presidential Election," pp. 60–90, and McWilliams, "The Meaning of the Election," pp. 157–183, both in Pomper et al., *The Election of 1984*.

11. See Pomper, "The Presidential Election," in Pomper et al., pp. 87–89.

12. McWilliams, "The Meaning of the Election," in Pomper et al., pp. 166–177.

13. For a generally optimistic view of the progressive implications in these very diverse forms of activism, see Boyte, *Backyard Revolution*.

14. This alleged sophistication itself is quite controversial. See, for example, the conflicting views of Harry Boyte ("Populism and the Left") and Jeffrey Lustig ("Community and Social Class") in *democracy* 2 (April 1981), pp. 52–66, 96–110.

15. For an interesting collection of diverse essays illustrating the flexible, multidimensional approaches recently accepted and implemented by a variety of liberal and Left activists, see Gartner et al., eds., *Beyond Reagan*.

16. Stanley Aronowitz makes the distinction between the "ideological" and "popular" left in his two essays "Remaking the American Left: Currents in American Radicalism," *Socialist Review* 67 (January/February 1983), pp. 9–51;

"Socialism and Beyond: Remaking the American Left, Part Two," *Socialist Review* 69 (May/June 1983), pp. 7–42. The arguments in these articles have been most influential to my own analysis in these concluding pages. See also Mark Gann, ed., *The Future of American Democracy: Views from the Left* (Philadelphia: Temple University Press, 1983).

17. Aronowitz, "Remaking the American Left." See also Harry C. Boyte and Sara M. Evans, "Strategies in Search of America: Cultural Radicalism, Populism, and Democratic Culture," *Socialist Review* 75–76 (May/August 1984), pp. 73–100.

18. For pessimistic assessments of liberal cooptive tendencies in America, see Lasch, *Agony of the American Left;* Carl Boggs, "The New Populism and the Limits of Structural Reforms," *Theory and Society* 12 (1983), pp. 349–357.

Bibliography

Public Interest Liberalism: Primary Sources

Aron, Nan, and Debora Clovis. *Survey of Public Interest Law Centers*. Washington, D.C.: Council for Public Interest Law, 1980.

Berry, Jeffrey. "Lessons From Chairman Ralph: Nader's Secrets of Success." Reprint from *Citizen Participation* 1 (1979).

Cahn, Edgar, and Jean Cahn. "Power to the People or to the Profession? The Public in Public Interest Law." *Yale Law Journal* 79 (1970), pp. 1005–1048.

Callenbach, Ernest. *Ectopia*. New York: Bantam, 1975.

Cohen, David. "The Neo-Conservatives: Professional Pessimists." Common Cause reprint from *Congress Monthly* (1980).

———. "The Public Interest." Unpublished paper delivered at the Kennedy Institute of Politics, June 20, 1975.

———. "Reviving the Political Party System." Common Cause reprint from *Newsday* (1979).

Common Cause, *How Money Talks in Congress*. Washington, D.C.: Common Cause, 1979.

———. *Government Subsidy Squeeze*. Washington, D.C.: Common Cause, 1980.

Commoner, Barry. *The Closing Circle*. New York: Knopf, 1971.

———. "The Environmental Cost of Economic Growth." In R. G. Ridken, ed., *Population, Resources, and the Environment*. Vol. 3 Washington, D.C.: Government Printing Office, 1972.

———. *The Politics of Energy*. New York: Knopf, 1979.

Council for Public Interest Law. *Balancing the Scales of Justice: Financing Public Interest Law in America*. Washington, D.C.: Council for Public Interest Law, 1976.

Cox, Edward F., Robert C. Fellmeth, and John E. Schulz. *The Nader Report on the Federal Trade Commission*. New York: Baron, 1969.

Cunningham, Lynn, Florence Roisman, Polly Rich, Patricia Beatley, and Steven Barry. *Strengthening Citizen Access and Government Accountability*. Washington, D.C.: Exploratory Project for Economic Alternatives, 1977.

Daley, Herman, ed. *Toward a Steady-State Economy*. San Francisco: Freeman, 1973.

Bibliography

De Bell, Garrett, ed. *The Environmental Handbook*. New York: Ballantine, 1970.

Ehrlich, Paul, and Dennis Pirages. *Ark II: Social Responses to Environmental Imperatives*. San Francisco: Freeman, 1974.

Esposito, John C., and Larry J. Silverman. *Vanishing Air: The Ralph Nader Study Group on Air Pollution*. New York: Grossman, 1970.

Fanning, Odom. *Man and His Environment: Citizen Action*. New York: Harper and Row, 1975.

Frank, Richard, A., Joseph N. Onek, and James B. Steinberg. *Public Participation in the Policy Formulation Process*. Washington, D.C.: Center for Law and Social Policy, 1977.

Friends of the Earth. *Ronald Reagan and the American Environment*. San Francisco: Friends of the Earth, 1982.

Gardner, John. *Excellence*. New York: Perennial Library, 1961.

————. *In Common Cause*. New York: Norton, 1973.

————. *The Other Government: The Unseen Power of Washington Lawyers*. New York: Grossman, 1975.

————. "Why The Consumer Bill Went Down." *The Nation*, February 25, 1978. pp. 198–201.

————. *Winning Back America*. New York: Bantam, 1982.

Green, Mark, ed. *The Monopoly Makers: Ralph Nader's Study Group Report on Regulation and Competition*. New York: Grossman, 1973.

Green, Mark, and Andrew Buchsbaum. *The Corporate Lobbies: Political Profiles of the Business Roundtable and the Chamber of Commerce*. Washington, D.C.: A Public Citizen Report, 1980.

Green, Mark, James Fallows, and David Zwick. *Who Runs Congress?* New York: Bantam/Grossman, 1972.

Green, Mark, and Robert Massie, Jr., eds. *Big Business Reader: Essays on Corporate America*. New York: Pilgrim Press, 1980.

Green, Mark, with Beverly C. Moore and Bruce Wasserstein. *The Closed Enterprise System: Ralph Nader's Study Group Report on Anti-Trust Enforcement*. New York: Grossman, 1972.

Green, Mark, and Ralph Nader. "Economic Regulation vs. Competition: Uncle Sam the Monopoly Man" and "Winter's Discontent: Market Failure and Consumer Welfare." *Yale Law Journal* 82 (1973), pp. 871–889, 903–919.

Green, Mark, and Norman Waitzman. *Business War on Law: An Analysis of the Benefits of Federal Health/Safety Enforcement*. Washington , D.C.: Corporate Accountability Research Group, 1981.

Grossman, Richard L., and Gail Banekes. *Energy, Jobs, and the Economy*. Boston: Alyson Publications, 1979.

Halpern, Charles, and John Cunningham. "Reflections on the New Public Interest Law: Theory and Practice at the New Center for Law and Social Policy." *Georgetown Law Journal* 59 (1971), pp. 1095–1126.

Hardin, Garrett. "The Tragedy of the Commons." In Garrett Hardin and John Baden, eds. *Managing the Commons*. San Francisco: Freeman, 1977.

Harrison, Gordon, and Sanford Jaffe. *The Public Interest Law Firm: New Voices for New Constituencies*. New York: Ford Foundation, 1973.

Hayden, Tom. *The American Future: New Visions beyond Old Frontiers*. Boston: South End Press, 1980.

Henderson, Hazel. *Creating Alternative Futures*. New York: Berkeley Publishing Co., 1978.

Bibliography

Jaffe, Sanford. *Public Interest Law: Five Years Later.* New York: Ford Foundation/ American Bar Association, 1976.

Kazis, Richard, and Richard L. Grossman. *Fear at Work: Job Blackmail, Labor and the Environment.* New York: Pilgrim Press, 1983.

Lash, Jonathon, Katherine Gillman, and David Sheridan. *Season of Spoils: The Reagan Administration Attack on the Environment.* New York: Pantheon, 1984.

Lazarus, Simon. *The Genteel Populists.* New York: McGraw–Hill, 1974.

Meadows, Donella H., Dennis L. Meadows, Jørgen Randers, and William H. Behrens III. *The Limits to Growth.* New York: Universe Books, 1972.

Mitchell, John G., and Constance Stallings, eds., *Ecotactics.* New York: Pocket Books, 1970.

Nader, Ralph. *Unsafe at Any Speed: The Designed-In Dangers of the American Automobile.* New York: Grossman, 1965.

———. "Freedom from Information: The Act and the Agencies." *Harvard Civil Rights–Civil Liberties Law Review* 5 (1970), pp. 1–15.

———. "We Need a New Kind of Patriotism." *Life,* July 9, 1971.

———. "Consumerism and Legal Services: The Merging of Movements." *Law and Society Review* 11 (1976), pp. 247–256.

———. *Public Interest Perspectives: The Next Four Years.* Washington, D.C.: Public Citizen, 1977.

———. "The Consumer Movement Looks Ahead." In Alan Gartner et al., eds., *Beyond Reagan: Alternatives for the '80s.* New York: Harper and Row, 1984.

Nader, Ralph, ed. *The Consumer and Corporate Accountability.* New York: Harcourt Brace Jovanovich, 1973.

Nader, Ralph, and John Abbotts. *The Menace of Atomic Energy.* New York: Norton, 1977.

Nader, Ralph, and Mark Green. "Crime in the Suites." *The New Republic,* April 29, 1972.

Nader, Ralph, and Mark Green. *Ralph Nader's Conference on Corporate Accountability.* New York: Grossman, 1973.

Nader, Ralph, and Mark Green, eds. *Verdicts on Lawyers.* New York: Crowell, 1976.

Nader, Ralph, Mark Green, and Joel Seligman. *Taming the Giant Corporation.* New York: Norton, 1976.

Nader, Ralph, Peter J. Petkas, and Kate Blackwell, eds. *Whistle Blowing: The Report of the Conference on Professional Responsibility.* New York: Grossman, 1972.

Nader, Ralph, and Donald Ross. *Action for Change: A Student Manual for Public Interest Organizing.* New York: Grossman, 1971.

Nader, Ralph, and Cirardeau Spann. "The Justices Slam the Door." *The Nation,* November 12, 1972, pp. 495–498.

Onek, Joseph, and Simon Lazarus. "The Regulators and the People." *Virginia Law Review* 57 (1971), pp. 1069–1108.

Pertschuk, Michael. *Revolt against Regulation: The Rise and Pause of the Consumer Movement.* Berkeley: University of California Press, 1982.

Peters, Charles, and Taylor Branch. *Blowing the Whistle.* New York: Praeger, 1972.

Reich, Charles. "The New Property." *Yale Law Journal* 73 (1964), pp. 733–787.

———. *The Greening of America.* New York: Random House, 1970.

Bibliography

Rienow, Leona Train, and Robert Rienow. *Moment in the Sun.* New York: Ballantine, 1967.

Ross, Donald. *A Public Citizen's Action Manual.* New York: Grossman, 1973.

Sax, Joseph L. *Defending the Environment: A Handbook for Citizen Action.* New York: Vintage, 1970.

————. "The Public Trust Doctrine in Natural Resource Law." *Michigan Law Review* 68 (1970), pp. 471–566.

Schumacher, E. F. *Small Is Beautiful: Economics as if People Mattered.* New York: Harper and Row, 1973.

Schwartz, Donald E. "Toward New Corporate Goals: Co-Existence with Society." *Georgetown Law Journal* 60 (1971), pp. 57–104.

————. "Symposium—Federal Chartering of Corporations: An Introduction." *Georgetown Law Journal* 61 (1972), pp. 71–88.

Sharpless, Andrew, and Sarah Gallup. *Banding Together: How Check-offs Will Revolutionize the Consumer Movement.* Washington, D.C.: Center for the Study of Responsive Law, 1981.

Sierra Club. *Poisons on the Job: The Reagan Administration and American Workers.* San Francisco: Sierra Club, 1982.

Stone, Christopher. *Should Trees Have Standing? Toward Legal Rights for Natural Objects.* Los Altos: William Kaufman, 1972.

Wasserstein, Bruce, and Mark Green, eds. *With Justice for Some: An Indictment of the Law by Young Advocates.* Boston: Beacon Press, 1972.

Secondary Sources and Works of Related Interest

Ackerman, Bruce A., and William T. Hassler. *Clean Coal/Dirty Air.* New Haven: Yale University Press, 1981.

Ackerman, Bruce A., and James Sawyer. "The Uncertain Search for Environmental Policy: Scientific Factfinding and Rational Decisionmaking along the Delaware River." *University of Pennsylvania Law Review* 120 (1972), pp. 421–503.

Amott, Teresa, and Joel Krieger. "Thatcher and Reagan: State Theory and the 'Hyper-Capitalist' Regime." *New Political Science* 8 (Spring 1972), pp. 9–37.

Anderson, Frederick R. *NEPA and the Courts.* Baltimore: The Johns Hopkins University Press, 1973.

Arendt, Hannah. *The Human Condition.* New York: Anchor, 1958.

Auerbach, Jerold S. *Unequal Justice: Lawyers and Social Change in Modern America.* New York: Oxford University Press, 1976.

Bardach, Eugene, and Robert Kagan. *Going by the Book: The Problem of Regulatory Unreasonableness.* Philadelphia: Temple University Press, 1982.

Bardach, Eugene, and Lucian Pugliaresi. "The Environmental Impact Statement versus the Real World." *The Public Interest* 49 (Fall 1977), pp. 22–38.

Barnett, Richard. *The Lean Years: Politics in the Age of Scarcity.* New York: Simon and Schuster, 1980.

Barry, Brian. *Sociologist, Economists, and Democracy.* Chicago: University of Chicago Press, 1978.

Bennett, W. Lance. *The Political Mind and the Political Environment.* Lexington, Mass.: Lexington Books, 1975.

Berle, Adolph A., and Gardiner C. Means. *The Modern Corporation and Private Property.* New York: Macmillan, 1955.

Bibliography

Berman, Marshall. "Buildings Are Judgement or 'What Man Can Build.'" *Ramparts,* March 1975, pp. 33–39, 50–58.

————. *All That Is Solid Melts into Air: The Experience of Modernity.* New York: Simon and Schuster, 1982.

Bernstein, Marver. *Regulation by Independent Commission.* Princeton: Princeton University Press, 1975.

Berry, Jeffrey M. *Lobbying for the People.* Princeton: Princeton University Press, 1977.

Berry, Wendell. *The Unsettling of America: Culture and Agriculture.* New York: Avon, 1977.

Bickel, Alexander M. *The Least Dangerous Branch.* Indianapolis: Bobbs-Merrill, 1962.

Black, Donald. "The Mobilization of Law." *Journal of Legal Studies* 2 (1973), pp. 125–150.

Bluestone, Barry, and Bennett Harrison. *The Deindustrialization of America: Plant Closings, Community Abandonment, and the Dismantling of Basic Industry.* New York: Basic Books, 1982.

Blumberg, Paul. *Inequality in an Age of Decline.* Oxford: Oxford University Press, 1978.

Bosselman, Fred. "Ecology vs. Equality: The Sierra Club Meets the NAACP." *Yale Review of Law and Social Action* 2 (1971), pp. 93–94.

Bowles, Samuel, David M. Gordon, and Thomas E. Weisskopf. *Beyond the Wasteland: A Democratic Alternative to Economic Decline.* New York: Doubleday, 1983.

Boyd, Marjorie. "The Protection Consumers Don't Want." *Washington Monthly,* September 1977, pp. 29–34.

Boyer, Barry. "Alternatives to Administrative Trial-Type Hearings for Resolving Complex Scientific, Economic, and Social Issues." *Michigan Law Review* 71 (1972), pp. 111–170.

Boyer, Barry, and Errol Meidinger. "Privatizing Regulatory Enforcement: A Preliminary Assessment of Citizen Suits under Federal Environmental Laws." Unpublished paper presented at the annual meetings of the Law and Society Association, San Diego, March 1985.

Boyte, Harry C. *The Backyard Revolution: Understanding the New Citizen Movement.* Philadelphia: Temple University Press, 1980.

Braverman, Harry. *Labor and Monopoly Capital: The Degradation of Work in the Twentieth Century.* New York: Monthly Review Press, 1974.

Breyer, Stephen. "Analyzing Regulatory Failure: Mismatches, Less Restrictive Alternatives, and Reform." *Harvard Law Review* 92 (1979), pp. 547–609.

Broder, David. *Changing of the Guard: Power and Leadership in America.* New York: Simon and Schuster, 1980.

Buckhorn, Robert. *Nader: The People's Lawyer.* Englewood Cliffs, N.J.: Prentice-Hall, 1972.

Burlingham, Bo. "Popular Politics: The Arrival of Ralph Nader." *Working Papers for a New Society,* Summer 1974, pp. 5–14.

Buttel, Frederick, and William Flinn. "Economic Growth versus the Environment: Survey Evidence." *Social Science Quarterly* 57 (1976), pp. 410–420.

Cameron, Juan. "Nader's Raiders Are inside the Gates." *Fortune,* October 1977.

Carnoy, Martin, and Derek Shearer. *Economic Democracy.* White Plains, N.Y.: Sharpe, 1980.

Bibliography

Casper, Jonathan. "The Supreme Court and National Policy Making." *American Political Science Review* 70 (1976), pp. 50–63.

Chayes, Abram. "The Role of the Judge in Public Law Litigation." *Harvard Law Review* 89 (1976), pp. 1281–1316.

Cigler, Allen J., and Burdett A. Loomis, eds. *Interest Group Politics.* Washington, D.C.: Congressional Quarterly Press, 1983.

Clark, Peter B., and James Q. Wilson. "Incentive Systems: A Theory of Organizations." *Administrative Science Quarterly* 6 (September 1961), pp. 129–166.

Clark, Timothy. "After a Decade of Doing Battle, Public Interest Groups Show Their Age." *National Journal*, July 12, 1980.

Cobb, Roger W., and Charles D. Elder. *Participation in American Politics: The Dynamics of Agenda Building.* Boston: Allyn and Bacon, 1972.

Cohen, Joshua, and Joel Rogers. *On Democracy.* New York: Penguin, 1983.

Cohen, Richard E. "Public Interest Lawyers Start Looking Out for Their Own Interests." *National Journal*, April 19, 1975.

Comment. "The New Public Interest Lawyers." *Yale Law Journal* 79 (1970), pp. 1069–1152.

Comment. "Public Participation in Federal Administrative Proceedings." *University of Pennsylvania Law Review* 120 (1972), pp. 702–845.

Conkin, Paul K. *The New Deal.* New York: Crowell, 1967.

Connelly, William E., ed. *The Bias of Pluralism.* New York: Atherton, 1969.

Cook, Constance E. *Nuclear Power and Legal Advocacy.* Lexington, Mass.: Lexington Books, 1980.

———. "Membership Involvement in Public Interest Groups." Paper delivered at the American Political Science Association annual meetings, Chicago, 1983.

Corrigan, Richard. "Public Interest Law Firms Win Battle with IRS over Exemptions, Deductions." *National Journal*, November 21, 1970, pp. 2541–2549.

Cramton, Roger C. "The Why, Where, and How of Broadened Public Participation in the Administrative Process." *Georgetown Law Journal* 60 (1972), pp. 525–550.

Crawford, Alan. *Thunder on the Right: The "New Right" and the Politics of Resentment.* New York: Pantheon, 1980.

Creighton, Lucy. *Pretenders to the Throne: The Consumer Movement in the United States.* Lexington, Mass.: Lexington Books, 1976.

Crozier, Michael J., Samuel P. Huntington, and Joji Watanuki. *The Crisis of Democracy.* New York: New York University Press, 1975.

Culhane, Paul. "Natural Resources Policy: Procedural Change and Substantive Environmentalism." In Theodore Lowi and Alan Stone, eds., *Natonalizing Government: Public Policies in America.* Beverly Hills: Sage, 1978.

Currie, Elliot, Robert Dunn, and David Fogarty. "The New Immiseration: Stagflation, Inequality, and the Working Class." *Socialist Review*, No. 54 (November/December 1980), pp. 7–32.

Cutler, Lloyd, and David Johnson. "Regulation and the Political Process." *Yale Law Journal* 84 (1975), pp. 1395–1418.

Dahrendorf, Ralf. *Class and Class Conflict in Industrial Society.* Stanford, Calif.: Stanford University Press, 1959.

Davis, Kenneth C. *Discretionary Justice: A Preliminary Inquiry.* Urbana, Ill.: University of Illinois Press, 1979.

Demkovich, Linda. "Consumer Leaders Hope That Carter Will Go to Bat for Them." *National Journal*, December 11, 1976.

Bibliography

Denvir, John. "Towards a Political Theory of Public Interest Law Litigation." *University of North Carolina Law Review* 54 (1976), pp. 1133–1160.

De Toledano, Ralph. *Hit and Run: The Rise and Fall?—of Ralph Nader.* New Rochelle, N.Y.: Arlington House, 1975.

Devall, William. "The Governing of a Voluntary Organization: Oligarchy and Democracy in the Sierra Club." Ph.D diss. University of Oregon, 1970.

—. "The Deep Ecology Movement." *Natural Resources Journal* 20 (April 1980), pp. 299–322.

Dickson, David. *The Politics of Alternative Technology.* New York: Universe Books, 1975.

Dolbeare, Kenneth, and Patricia Dolbeare. *American Ideologies.* Chicago: Markham, 1971.

Douglas, Mary, and Aaron Wildavsky. *Risk and Culture: An Essay in the Selection of Technological and Governmental Dangers.* Berkeley: University of California Press, 1982.

Downs, Anthony. "Up and Down with Ecology: The 'Issue Attention Cycle.'" *The Public Interest* 28 (1972), pp. 38–50.

Dreyfus, D. A., and Helen M. Ingram. "The National Environmental Policy Act: A View of Intent and Practice." *Natural Resources Journal* 16 (1976), pp. 243–248.

Dworkin, Ronald. *Taking Rights Seriously.* Cambridge: Harvard University Press, 1977.

Edelman, Murray. *The Symbolic Uses of Politics.* Urbana, Ill.: University of Illinois Press, 1967.

Ellul, Jacques. *The Technological Society.* New York: Knopf, 1967.

Enzensberger, Hans M. "Critique of Political Ecology." *New Left Review*, March/April 1974, pp. 3–32.

Erskine, Hazel. "The Polls: Pollution and Its Costs." *Public Opinion Quarterly* 36 (Spring 1972), pp. 120–135.

Ewen, Stuart. *Captains of Consciousness: Advertising and the Social Roots of the Consumer Culture.* New York: McGraw-Hill, 1976.

Fiss, Owen. "The Supreme Court 1978 Term—Foreword: The Forms of Justice." *Harvard Law Review* 93 (1979), pp. 1–58.

Flacks, Richard. "Making History and Making Life: Dilemmas of the American Left." *Sociological Inquiry* 46 (1975), pp. 263–280.

—. "Populism in Search of the People." *Working Papers for a New Society*, January/February 1981, pp. 26–35.

Fleischman, Joel L., and Carol S. Greenwald. "Public Interest Litigation and Political Finance Reform." *Annals of the American Association of Political and Social Scientists*, May 1974, pp. 114–123.

Frazer, Andrew. "The Legal Theory We Need Now." *Socialist Review*, Nos. 40–41 (1978), pp. 147–188.

Freeman, Jo. *The Politics of Women's Liberation.* New York: David McKay, 1975.

Frieden, Bernard. *The Environmental Protection Hustle.* Cambridge, Mass,: MIT Press, 1979.

Friedrich, Carl, ed. *NOMOS I: Authority.* Cambridge, Mass.: Harvard University Press, 1958.

Friedrich, Carl, ed. *NOMOS V: The Public Interest.* New York: Atherton, 1962.

Fuller, Lon. *The Morality of Law.* New Haven, Conn.: Yale University Press, 1964.

Bibliography

Funston, Richard. "The Judicialization of the Administrative Process." *American Politics Quarterly* 2 (1974), pp. 38–60.

Galbraith, John Kenneth. *The New Industrial State*. Boston: Houghton Mifflin, 1967.

————. *The Affluent Society*. Boston: Houghton Mifflin, 1969.

Gardner, Roberta Ash. *Social Movements in America*. 2d ed. Chicago: Rand McNally, 1977.

Gartner, Alan, Colin Greer, and Frank Riessman, eds. *Beyond Reagan: Alternatives for the '80s*. New York: Harper and Row, 1984.

Gellhorn, Ernest. "Public Participation in Administrative Proceedings." *Yale Law Journal* 81 (1972), pp. 359–404.

Gitlin, Todd. *The Whole World Is Watching: Mass Media in the Making and Unmaking of the New Left*. Berkeley: University of California Press, 1980.

Glazer, Nathan. "Toward an Imperial Judiciary?" *The Public Interest*, Fall 1975, pp. 104–123.

Goetz, Charles, and Gordon Brady. "Environmental Policy Foundations and the Tax Treatment of Citizen Interest Groups." *Law and Contemporary Problems* 39 (1975), pp. 211–231.

Goodwyn, Lawrence. *The Populist Moment*. Oxford: Oxford University Press, 1978.

Gordon, Al. "Public Interest Lobbies: Nader and Common Cause Become Permanent Features." *Congressional Quarterly* 34 (May 15, 1970), pp. 1197–1205.

Gorey, Hays. *Nader and the Power of Everyman*. New York: Grosset and Dunlop, 1975.

Gorz, Andre. *Ecology as Politics*. Boston: South End Press, 1980.

Green, James R. *Grass Roots Socialism: Radical Movements in the Southwest, 1895–1943*. Baton Rouge: Louisiana State University Press, 1978.

Greenstone, J. David. *Labor in American Politics*. New York: Vintage, 1969.

Gusfield, Joseph. *Symbolic Crusade: Status Politics and the American Temperence Movement*. Urbana, Ill.: University of Illinois Press, 1963.

Hacker, Andrew. *The End of the American Era*. New York: Atheneum, 1974.

Halebsky, Sandor. *Mass Society and Political Conflict: Toward a Reconstruction of Theory*. Cambridge: Cambridge University Press, 1976.

Handler, Joel F. *Social Movements and the Legal System: A Theory of Law Reform and Social Change*. New York: Academic Press, 1978.

Handler, Joel, Ellen J. Hollingsworth, and Howard S. Erlanger. *Lawyers and the Pursuit of Legal Rights*. New York: Academic Press, 1978.

Hartz, Louis. *The Liberal Tradition in America*. New York: Harvest, 1955.

Hayes, Michael T. "Interest Groups: Pluralism or Mass Society?" In Allen J. Cigler and Burdett Loomis, eds., *Interest Group Politics*. Washington, D.C.: Congressional Quarterly Press, 1983.

Hays, Samuel P. "Political Parties and the Community/Society Continuum." In William Chambers and Walter Dean Burnham, eds., *The American Party Systems*. New York: Oxford University Press, 1967.

————. *Conservation and the Gospel of Efficiency*. New York: Atheneum 1974.

Hill, Stuart, and David Orr. "Leviathan, the Open Society and the Crisis of Ecology." *The Western Political Quarterly*, December 1978, pp. 457–469.

Hirsch, Fred. *Social Limits to Growth*. Cambridge, Mass.: Harvard University Press, 1976.

Bibliography

Hofstadter, Richard. *The American Political Tradition.* New York: Vintage, 1948.
———. *The Age of Reform.* New York: Vintage, 1955.
Holsworth, Robert D. *Public Interest Liberalism and the Crisis of Affluence.* Boston: G. K. Hall/Cambridge, Mass.: Schenkman, 1980.
Horowitz, Donald L. *The Courts and Social Policy.* Washington, D.C.: The Brookings Institute, 1977.
———. "The Courts as Guardians of the Public Interest." *Public Administration Review,* March/April 1977, pp. 148–154.
Houck, Oliver A. "With Charity for All." *Yale Law Journal* 93 (1984), pp. 1415–1563.
Inglehart, Ronald. *The Silent Revolution: Changing Values and Political Styles among Western Publics.* Princeton: Princeton University Press, 1977.
Jacqueney, Theodore. "Nader Network Switches Focus to Legal Action, Congressional Lobbying." *National Journal,* June 9, 1973.
———. "Common Cause Lobbyists Focus on the Structure and Process of Government." *National Journal,* September 1, 1973.
James, Marlisle. *The People's Lawyers.* New York: Holt, Rinehart, and Winston, 1973.
Jones, Mary Gardiner, and David M. Gardiner, eds. *Consumerism: A New Force in Society.* Lexington, Mass.: Lexington Books, 1976.
Kaku, Michio, and Jennifer Trainer, eds. *Nuclear Power: Both Sides.* New York: Norton, 1982.
Keisling, Phillip. "The Reagan Chainsaw Massacre" *New Republic,* October 1, 1984, pp. 25–31.
Keller, Bill. "Environmental Movement Checks Its Pulse and Finds Its Obituaries Are Premature." *Congressional Quarterly,* January 31, 1981, pp. 211–216.
Kelman, Steven. "Cost/Benefit Analysis: An Ethical Critique." *Regulation,* January/February 1981, pp. 33–40.
———. *Regulatory America, Regulatory Sweden: A Comparative Study of Occupational Safety and Health Regulation.* Cambridge, Mass.: MIT Press, 1981.
———. *What Price Incentives? Economists and the Environment.* Boston: Auburn House, 1981.
Kennedy, Duncan. "Legal Formality." *Journal of Legal Studies* 2 (1973), pp. 351–398.
King, Anthony, ed. *The New American Political System.* Washington, D.C.: American Enterprise Institute, 1979.
Kolko, Gabriel. *The Triumph of Conservatism.* Chicago: Quadrangle Books, 1963.
Kornhauser, William. *The Politics of Mass Society.* New York: The Free Press, 1959.
Kristol, Irving. *Two Cheers for Capitalism.* New York: New American Library, 1978.
Ladd, Everett Carl. "Clearing the Air: Public Opinion and Public Policy on the Environment." *Public Opinion* 5 (February/March 1982), pp. 16–20.
Lasch, Christopher. *The New Radicalism, 1889–1963.* New York: Vintage, 1965.
———. *The Agony of the American Left.* New York: Vintage, 1969.
———. *The Culture of Narcissism.* New York: Warner Books, 1979.
Lauber, Volkmar. "Ecology Politics and Liberal Democracy." *Government and Opposition,* Spring 1978, pp. 199–217.

Bibliography

Lears, Jackson. *No Place of Grace: Antimodernism and the Transformation of American Culture, 1880–1920.* New York: Pantheon Books, 1981.

Lefcourt, Robert, ed. *Law against the People: Essays to Demystify Law, Order and the Courts.* New York: Vintage, 1971.

Leflar, Robert, and Martin H. Rogol. "Consumer Participation in the Regulation of Utilities: A Model Act." *Harvard Journal of Legislation* 13 (February 1976), pp. 235–297.

Leighton, Richard. "Consumer Protection Agency Propositions: The Origins of the Species." *Administrative Law Review* 25 (Summer 1973), pp. 269–311.

Leuchtenberg, William E. *Franklin D. Roosevelt and the New Deal, 1932–1940.* New York: Harper and Row, 1963.

Lindblom, Charles. *Politics and Markets.* New York: Basic Books, 1977.

Lippmann, Walter. *Drift and Mastery.* Englewood Cliffs, N.J.: Prentice-Hall, 1961.

Liroff, Richard A. *A National Policy for the Environment: NEPA and Its Aftermath.* Bloomington, Ind.: Indiana University Press, 1976.

Lowi, Theodore J. *The Politics of Disorder.* New York: Basic Books, 1971.

———. *The End of Liberalism.* 2d ed. New York: Norton, 1979.

Luke, Timothy. "Informationalism and Ecology." *Telos* 16 (Summer 1983), pp. 59–73.

Lustig, R. Jeffrey. *Corporate Liberalism: The Origins of Modern American Political Theory, 1890–1920.* Berkeley: University of California Press, 1982.

Lynd, Staughton. *The Intellectual Origins of American Radicalism.* New York: Pantheon, 1968.

McCann, Michael W. "Resurrection and Reform: The Changing Status of Property in the American Constitutional Tradition." *Politics and Society* 13 (1984), pp. 143–176.

McCarry, Charles. *Citizen Nader.* New York: Saturday Review Press, 1972.

McCarthy, John D., and Mayer N. Zald. "Resource Mobilization and Social Movements: A Partial Theory." *American Journal of Sociology* 82 (1977), pp. 1212–1241.

McCloskey, Robert. *The Modern Supreme Court.* Cambridge, Mass.: Harvard University Press, 1972.

McConnell, Grant. *Private Power and American Democracy.* New York: Vintage, 1966.

McFarland, Andrew S. "Common Cause." Unpublished manuscript later published as *Common Cause: Lobbying in the Public Interest.* 1980.

———. *Common Cause: Lobbying in the Public Interest.* Chatham, N.J.: Chatham House Publishers, 1984.

———. "The Complexity of Democratic Practice within Common Cause." Paper delivered at the American Political Science Association annual meeting, Chicago, 1976.

———. *Public Interest Lobbies: Decision Making On Energy.* Washington, D.C.: American Enterprise Institute, 1976.

McPhee, John. *Encounters with the Archdruid.* New York: Farrar, Straus, and Giroux, 1971.

Marks, F. Raymond, with Kirk Leswing and Barbara A. Fortinsky. *The Lawyer, the Public, and Professional Responsibility.* Chicago: American Bar Association, 1972.

Marx, Leo. *The Machine in the Garden.* London: Oxford University Press, 1964.

Bibliography

Melnick, R. Shep. *Regulation and the Courts: The Case of the Clean Air Act.* Washington, D.C.: Brookings, 1983.

Miller, Arthur S. *The Supreme Court and American Capitalism.* New York: The Free Press, 1967.

Milliband, Ralph. *The State in Capitalist Society.* New York: Bantam Books, 1977.

Mitchell, Robert C. "National Environmental Lobbies and the Apparent Illogic of Collective Action." In Clifford S. Russell, ed., *Collective Decision Making.* Baltimore: Johns Hopkins University Press, 1979.

——. "Silent Spring/Silent Majorities." *Public Opinion* 2 (August/September 1979), pp. 16–20.

——. "How 'Soft,' 'Deep,' or 'Left'? Present Constituencies in the Environmental Movement for Certain World Views." *Natural Resources Journal* 20 (April, 1980), pp. 345–358.

Moe, Terry M. *The Organization of Interests: Incentives and the Internal Dynamics of Political Interest Groups.* Chicago: Chicago University Press, 1980.

——. "Toward a Broader View of Interest Groups." *Journal of Politics* 43 (May 1981), pp. 531–543.

Morrison, Denton. "The Environmental Movement: Conflict Dynamics." *Journal of Voluntary Action Research* 2 (1973), pp. 74–85.

Mosher, Lawrence. "Move Over, Jim Watt, Anne Gorsuch Is the Latest Target of Environmentalists." *National Journal,* November 24, 1981.

——. "Environmentalists Sue to Put an End to 'Regulatory Massive Resistance.'" *National Journal,* December 19, 1981.

——. "More Cuts in EPA Research Threaten Its Regulatory Goals, Critics Warn." *National Journal,* April 10, 1982.

Nadel, Mark V. *The Politics of Consumer Protection.* Indianapolis, Ind.: Bobbs-Merrill, 1971.

Nadel, Mark V., and David Vogel. "Who Is a Consumer? An Analysis of the Politics of Consumer Conflict." *American Politics Quarterly* 5 (January 1977), pp. 27–56.

Nash, Roderick. *Wilderness and the American Mind.* New Haven: Yale University Press, 1982.

Neuhaus, Richard. *In Defense of People.* New York: Macmillan, 1971.

Newfield, Jack. "Nader's Raiders: The Lone Ranger Gets a Posse." *Life,* October 3, 1969.

Nonet, Philippe, and Philip Selznick. *Law and Society in Transition: Toward Responsive Law.* New York: Harper and Row, 1977.

Nordlinger, Eric A. *On the Autonomy of the Democratic State.* Cambridge, Mass.: Harvard University Press, 1981.

Oberschall, Anthony. *Social Conflict and Social Movements.* Englewood Cliffs, N.J.: Prentice-Hall, 1973.

O'Connor, James. *The Fiscal Crisis of the State.* New York: St. Martin's Press, 1973.

O'Conner, Karen, and Lee Epstein. "Bridging the Gap Between Congress and the Supreme Court: Interest Groups and the Erosion of the American Rule Governing Awards of Attorneys' Fees." *Western Political Quarterly* 38 (May 1985), pp. 238–249.

O'Conner, Karen, and Lee Epstein. "Rebalancing the Scales of Justice: Assessment of Public Interest Law." Paper presented at the Law and Society Association annual meeting, Denver, 1983.

Olson, Mancur, Jr. *The Logic of Collective Action.* New York: Schocken, 1968.

———. *The Rise and Decline of Nations: Economic Growth, Stagflation, and Social Regulation.* New Haven, Conn.: Yale University Press, 1982.

Orren, Karen. "Standing to Sue." *American Political Science Review* 70 (1976), pp. 723–741.

Paglin, Max D., and Edgar Shor. "Regulatory Agency Responses to the Development of Public Participation." *Public Administration Review,* March/April 1977, pp. 140–148.

Paul, Arnold M. *Conservative Crisis and the Rule of Law.* New York: Harper and Row, 1969.

Pells, Richard. *Radical Visions and American Dreams.* New York: Harper and Row, 1973.

Piven, Francis F., and Richard A. Cloward. *Poor People's Movements: Why They Succeed, How They Fail.* New York: Pantheon, 1977.

———. *The New Class War.* New York: Pantheon, 1982.

Pollack, Norman. *The Populist Response to Industrial America.* New York: Norton, 1962.

Polsby, Nelson W. *The Consequences of Party Reform.* New York: Oxford University Press, 1983.

Polsby, Nelson W., and Aaron Wildavsky. *Presidential Elections: Strategies of American Electoral Politics.* 6th ed. New York: Scribner, 1984.

Pomper, Gerald, with colleagues. *The Election of 1984: Reports and Interpretations.* Chatham, N.J.: Chatham House, 1985.

Rabin, Robert. "Lawyers for Social Change: Perspectives on Public Interest Law." *Stanford Law Review* 28 (1976), pp. 207–261.

Ridgeway, James. *The Politics of Ecology.* New York: Dutton, 1970.

Rogin, Michael P. *The Intellectuals and McCarthy: The Radical Specter.* Cambridge, Mass.: MIT Press, 1967.

———. "Non-Partisanship and the Group Interest." In Sanford Levinson and Philip Green, eds. *Power and Community.* New York: Vintage, 1970.

Rosen, Gerald R. "The Growing Clout of 'Do Good' Lobbies." *Dun's Review,* April 1977, pp. 44–51.

Rosenbaum, Walter A. *The Politics of Environmental Concern.* New York: Praeger, 1973.

Russell, Clifford, ed. *Collective Decision-Making: Applications from Public Choice Theory.* Baltimore: Johns Hopkins University Press, 1979.

St. George, Arthur. "The Sierra Club, Organizational Commitment, and the Environmental Movement in the United States." Ph.D. diss. University of California, Davis, 1974.

Salisbury, Robert H. "An Exchange Theory of Interest Groups." *Midwest Journal of Political Science* 13 (1969), pp. 1–32.

———. "Why No Corporatism in America?" In Philippe C. Schmitter and Gerhard Lehmbruch, eds. *Trends toward Corporatist Intermediation.* London: Sage, 1979.

Saloma, John S. III, and Frederick S. Sontag. *Parties: The Real Opportunity for Effective Citizen Politics.* New York: Knopf, 1972.

Sandbach, Francis. *Environment, Ideology, and Policy.* Montclair, N.J.: Allanheld, Osmun, 1980.

Bibliography

Sanford, David. *Me and Ralph: Is Nader Unsafe for America?* Washington, D.C.: New Republic Books, 1976.

Sarat, Austin, and Richard Grossman. "Courts and Conflict Resolution: Problems in the Mobilization of Adjudication." *American Political Science Review* 69 (1975), pp. 1200–1217.

Scharr, John. "Legitimacy in the Modern State." In Philip Green and Sanford Levinson, eds. *Power and Community: Dissenting Essays in Political Science.* New York: Vintage, 1970.

———. "Power and Purity." *American Review: No. 19.* Toronto: Bantam Books, 1974.

Schattschneider, E. E. *The Semi-Sovereign People.* New York: Holt, Rinehart and Winston, 1960.

Scheingold, Stuart A. *The Politics of Rights: Lawyers, Public Policy, and Political Change.* New Haven, Conn.: Yale University Press, 1974.

Schmitter, Philippe C. "Still the Century of Corporatism?" *Review of Politics* 36 (January 1974), pp. 85–131.

Schnaiberg, Allan. *The Environment: From Surplus to Scarcity.* New York: Oxford University Press, 1980.

Scholzman, Kay Lehman. "What Accent the Heavenly Chorus? Political Equality and the American Pressure System." *Journal of Politics* 46 (1984), pp. 1006–1031.

Schrag, Philip, and Michael Meltsner. "Class Action: A Way to Beat the Bureaucracies without Increasing Them." *Washington Monthly* 4 (November 1972), pp. 55–61.

Schuman, David. *The Ideology of Form: The Influence of Organizations in America.* Lexington, Mass.: Lexington Books, 1978.

Shabecoff, Philip. "Bill to Create a Consumer Agency Alive Again, with Good Prospects." *New York Times,* February 2, 1978.

Shi, David. *The Simple Life: Plain Living and High Thinking in American Culture.* New York: Oxford University Press, 1985.

Shor, Edgar, Symposium Editor. "A Symposium: Public Interest Representation and the Federal Agencies—Introductory Comments." *Public Administration Review,* March/April 1977, pp. 131–132.

Sills, David. "The Environmental Movement and Its Critics." *Human Ecology Magazine* 3 (1975), pp. 1–41.

Singer, James W. "Liberal Public Interest Law Firms Face Budgetary, Ideological Challenge." *National Journal,* December 8, 1979.

Skocpol, Theda. "Bringing the State Back In: Strategies of Analysis in Current Research." In Peter B. Evans, Dietrich Rueschemeyer, and Theda Skocpol, eds. *Bringing the State Back In.* Cambridge: Cambridge University Press, 1985.

Skowronek, Stephen. *Building a New American State: The Expansion of National Administrative Capacities.* Cambridge: Cambridge University Press, 1982.

Stanfield, Rochelle. " 'Defunding' the Left." *National Journal,* August 1, 1981.

———. "Ruckleshaus Casts EPA as 'Gorilla' in State's Enforcement Closet." *National Journal,* May 26, 1984.

Steinfels, Peter. *The Neoconservatives.* New York: Touchstone Books, 1979.

Stewart, Richard B. "The Reformation of American Administrative Law." *Harvard Law Review* 88 (1975), pp. 1667–1714.

Stone, Christopher. *Where the Law Ends: The Social Control of Corporate Behavior.* New York: Harper and Row, 1975.

Bibliography

Stretton, Hugh. *Capitalism, Socialism and the Environment.* Cambridge, England: Cambridge University Press, 1976.

Sundquist, James. *The Decline and Resurgence of Congress.* Washington, D.C.: The Brookings Institute, 1981.

Teodori, Massimo, ed. *The New Left: A Documentary History.* New York: Bobbs-Merrill, 1969.

Thurow, Lester. *The Zero-Sum Society.* New York: Penguin, 1981.

Tocqueville, Alexis de. *Democracy in America.* Ed. J. P. Mayer. 2 vols. New York: Anchor, 1969.

Tolchin, Susan J., and Martin Tolchin. *Dismantling America.* Boston: Houghton Mifflin, 1983.

Topolsky, Mary. "Common Cause?" *Worldview* 17 (April 1974), pp. 35–39.

Trachtenberg, Alan. *The Incorporation of America: Culture and Society in the Guilded Age.* New York: Hill and Wang, 1982.

Trubeck, David M. "Allocating the Burden of Environmental Uncertainty: The NRC Interprets NEPA's Substantive Mandate." *Wisconsin Law Review* 77 (1977), pp. 747–776.

————. "Complexity and Contradiction in the Legal Order." *Law and Society Review* 11 (1977), pp. 529–570.

Truman, David. *The Governmental Process.* 2d ed. New York: Alfred A. Knopf, 1971.

Tucker, William. "Environmentalism and the Leisure Class." *Harper's,* December 1977.

————. *Progress and Privilege: America in the Age of Environmentalism.* New York: Anchor, 1982.

Unger, Roberto. *Law in Modern Society.* New York: The Free Press, 1978.

Vig, Norman J., and Michael E. Kraft. *Environmental Policy in the 1980s: Reagan's New Agenda.* Washington, D.C.: Congressional Quarterly, Inc., 1984.

Vogel, David. *Lobbying the Corporation.* New York: Basic Books, 1978.

————. "The Inadequacies of Contemporary Opposition to Business." *Daedalus* 109 (Summer 1980), pp. 47–48.

————. "Promoting Pluralism: The Politics of the Public Interest Movement." *Political Science Quarterly* 95 (Winter 1981), pp. 609–628.

Walker, Jack L. "The Origins and Maintenance of Interest Groups in America." *American Political Science Review* 77 (June 1983), pp. 390–406.

Walzer, Michael. "The Pastoral Retreat of the New Left." *Dissent,* Winter 1979, pp. 406–411.

Weaver, Paul. "Regulation, Social Policy, and Class Conflict." *The Public Interest,* Winter 1978, pp. 45–63.

Weidenbaum, Murray C. *The Future of Business Regulation.* New York: Amocom, 1980.

Weidenbaum, Murray C., and Robert De Fina. *The Cost of Federal Regulation of Economic Activity.* Washington, D.C.: American Enterprise Institute, 1978.

Weinstein, James. *The Corporate Ideal in the Liberal State, 1900–1918.* Boston: Beacon Press, 1968.

Weisbrod, Burton A., with Joel F. Handler and Neil K. Komesar. *Public Interest Law: An Economic and Institutional Analysis.* Berkeley: University of California Press, 1978.

Wenner, Lettie. *The Environmental Decade In Court.* Bloomington: Indiana University Press, 1982.

Bibliography

Wiebe, Robert. *The Search for Order, 1877–1920*. New York: Hill and Wang, 1967.

Williams, William Appleman. *The Contours of American History*. Chicago: Quadrangle Books, 1966.

Wilson, James Q. *The Amateur Democrat*. Chicago: University of Chicago Press, 1962.

———. *Political Organizations*. New York: Basic Books, 1973.

Wilson, James. Q., ed. *The Politics of Regulation*. New York: Basic Books, 1980.

Winner, Langdon. *Autonomous Technology: Technics Out-of-Control as a Theme in Political Thought*. Cambridge, Mass.: MIT Press, 1977.

Winter, Ralph. *The Consumer Advocate versus the Consumer*. Washington, D.C.: American Enterprise Institute Public Policy Research, 1972.

———. "Economic Regulation vs. Competition: Ralph Nader and Creeping Capitalism." *Yale Law Journal* 82 (April 1973), pp. 890–902.

Wolfe, Alan. *The Limits of Legitimacy: Political Contradictions of Contemporary Capitalism*. New York: The Free Press, 1977.

Wolin, Sheldon. *Politics and Vision: Continuity and Innovation in Western Political Thought*. Boston: Little, Brown, 1960.

Yeazell, Stephen C. "From Group Litigation to Class Action." *U.C.L.A. Law Review* 27 (1980), pp. 516–564.

Index

337

Index

Index

Library of Congress Cataloging-in-Publication Data

McCann, Michael W., 1952-
  Taking reform seriously.

  Bibliography: p.
  Includes index.
  1. Pressure groups—United States. 2. Public Interest—United States. 3. Political
participation—United States. 4. Liberalism—United States. I. Title. JK1118.M37
1986   322.4'3'0973   86-47647 ISBN 0-8014-1952-2